CYTRINGANIAN FAREWELL

Published by the Old Cytringanians 1995

We are indebted to J. Freestone, F. Lawson, J. Marshall, D. Palmer, G. Perry, H. Speight, P. Taylor, individuals unknown and The Evening Telegraph, *for permission to reproduce their original photographs.*

Any profits from the sale of this book will be donated to the Kettering Old Grammar School Foundation, whose admirable work is described in Chapter 33.

ISBN 0 9526782 0 9

Typeset by Gilcott Graphics, Rushden, Northants
Printed and Bound by Woolnough Bookbinding, Irthlingborough, Northants.

Contents

Foreword

John Newing, QPM, BA

Chief Constable of Derbyshire

It was early September 1951, when I jumped from the bus at Speight's corner, ran down Bowling Green Road and walked for the first time through the gates of Kettering Grammar School. Small, fair-haired, round-faced and ready for anything.

I had no notion at the time what lay in store. Captain of rugby, county player and England trialist, three years a member of an unbeaten cricket First XI and member of the basketball team that won the Kettering and District Men's League: these were achievements beyond my wildest dreams. Sport then was not the all-consuming passion it was to become.

The first three years seemed to pass in a flash, much of it in a haze. Within an academic environment in which I was no longer first among equals, sport became my focus for achievement – and rugby football my shield. As time passed I grew – quickly – and by the fourth year few in the School were taller.

Somehow I made the grade into 4M – languages and classics. It was surely as much to do with my dislike of the sciences as with any facility for languages. Sport continued to dominate my interests, both in and out of School. I always seemed to do well in exams, but the daily grind of term work was something else. Thank goodness nobody had thought of continuous assessment and projects which counted toward GCE 'O' levels in those days.

Those years were a kaleidoscope of personalities – staff and pupils. There was Mr Joline the American exchange teacher, who taught English and threw a cricket ball as though he was pitching at baseball. 'Archie' Bishop went over to the United States in exchange. I think we got the best of the deal. Joline got me into trouble by describing me to my parents as "the ring leader whenever there was trouble in class." They were not best pleased and I was not too happy either. I thought I always behaved in his lessons. Others might have had cause for complaint.

There was Pete Royle, who never seemed to last longer than ten minutes in John Cowell's History lessons before being given the heave-ho. It was no wonder he never passed his History 'O' level. Mind you, it did me a good turn; we used to sit together and it was always easier to concentrate when Pete was out of the room rather than in it.

'Mighty Joe' Young was both Form master and French teacher during my fourth and fifth years. I can clearly recall him telling me in the second year that under no circumstances would he have me in his form when, or indeed if, I reached the fourth year. I passed 'O' level French. Amazing really! Well I know I was quite surprised; I think 'Joe' Young was flabbergasted.

There were others. John Larcombe, 'Joe' Ashworth, Gordon Brown, 'Chippie' Mandale, 'Pecker' Hopkins – he had eyes in the back of his head and an uncanny accuracy with a wooden board rubber – Ted Ward, Geoff Perry, John 'Weaky' Wood, Deputy Head and John Dudley the Head: I have not named them all.

Some became friends, others I admired, some I respected, others I did not. I can look back now and see them over the distance of time in a clearer light. In truth they were all good men, working hard to prepare us for the life ahead and develop the potential they saw in us. Some were merely better than others. Not all of them got the cooperation and attention they deserved from me. All made an impression on me in some way or another. For good or ill, all played a part in shaping the man I am now.

They also played their part in shaping the person I was then. It wasn't all failure. I sat ten 'O' levels and passed nine. In the Sixth Form I studied Geography, History and English Literature, passed all three at 'A' level and was awarded a County Major Scholarship. But it was to be twelve years before I went on to university and then it was as a serving police officer, on a police scholarship, to study Social and Public Administration at Leeds University.

The reason for that 'slip twixt cup and lip' is an interesting tale, bound up in an end of school escapade and my subsequent, albeit temporary suspension, with two others from attending what should have been my final day at School. It all concerned a dummy on the School roof, attendant publicity in the Kettering *Evening Telegraph,* the consequential cancellation by the Head of the annual Staff versus School cricket match and subsequent action taken by myself and two others, who intended to chain the hall doors from the inside, so that the final Assembly could not take place.

Unfortunately, things did not go exactly according to plan and the three of us were caught red-handed by Inspector Martin Sykes of the Northamptonshire Constabulary, who just happened to take his dog for a late night walk through the School yard. As an aside five years later it was Martin Sykes who advised me to join the Metropolitan Police. Fate certainly played a hand that night. John Dudley, the Head, was called. He had a difficult decision. He saw what we intended as a deliberate attack on his authority; he saw it as a reprisal for his cancellation of the Staff versus School cricket match and in truth it was. Inspector Sykes pleaded on our behalf, but suspension was the inevitable outcome. The question thereafter was whether the suspension would be temporary or permanent. I know that Geoff

Perry and John Wood spoke up on our behalf and were successful in having us reinstated.

I was given the offer of staying on for a third year in the Sixth Form, so that I could attain a university place. Unlike most of my contemporaries, I had not acquired a provisional place; the common view was that it would be better for me to apply for a place at Loughborough or St Luke's, Exeter, which in those days were teacher training establishments specialising in sports and physical education. In true sporting tradition I took my bat and ball home and went to work in Barclays Bank. Had I not have done so, my life would have taken an entirely different direction. I do not believe in fate, but sometimes you have to wonder.

School is not just a place for cramming knowledge. It is a place of learning, in the widest sense. It is of learning about life and people. It is of learning about right and wrong; it is of learning about values. These are the things that lifetimes are built on. It is of learning how to cope with pressure and stress and the idiosyncrasies of others. It is of learning tolerance for things different. It is about developing intellectual curiosity, of wanting to know why or how. It is of learning about sportsmanship and a sense of fair play. It is about developing a sense of justice and the courage to fight for justice and the rights of others. It is also about having fun and enjoying life to the full.

Kettering Grammar School was such a place. My time there was eventful and rewarding. It did not complete my education: it began it. I do not owe it everything, but I owe it a great deal. It gave me friendships which have lasted a lifetime. I look back with pride, not on my endeavours, but on the endeavours of the School. Above all, the School gave me a foundation for life built on a rock of rich traditions and values. As is the way with these things, I appreciate them more now than I did then.

I have watched the demise of Kettering Grammar School with great sadness and not a little anger. It is the economics of the madhouse that insists on cutting costs by destroying institutions that have contributed so much, not just within the county but nationally and internationally as well. The loss in terms of social benefit is immeasurably greater than any cost savings which have accrued as a result of the closure. Value for money has to be the watchword of the public service. It is a pity it was not applied in the decision to close Kettering Grammar School.

Introduction

Duke: And what's her history?
Viola: A blank, my lord.
(Twelfth Night.)

Whatever begins, also ends. In the case of Kettering Grammar School, it began in 1577 and ended four hundred years later. Kettering Boys School, which emerged from it, faced a comparatively brief life before the dust of oblivion in July 1993. The motivation that informed this book sought to colour in the "blank", if only in part, as witness of the times through the memories of those who attended the School this century.

Memories can be frail and vague, "of half-forgotten things, not true nor false," but sweet or bitter to think upon. In that truth no restrictions were placed on who contributed, or what they wrote. If some pieces are affectionate, or sentimental ("the twin-sister to cant" in Carlyle's words) others have moments of harsh frankness. Whilst we commissioned (without payment!) certain writers, many were forthcoming as a result of an article in the *Evening Telegraph*, a speech at the Old Cyts dinner, or simply by way of social chat. Submissions have appeared from America, Ireland, South Africa and Sweden, not to mention Cranford, Geddington and Barton Seagrave. The outcome has been a fortunate, if fortuitous, blend of contributors in terms of age, background, career, renown, and viewpoint. Perhaps chance is the nickname of Providence after all.

We opted for a thematic rather than a chronological approach, believing this offered more flexibility. An obvious example concerns the internationally acclaimed Satellite Research team. Clearly their enterprise needed a substantial and discrete section; no other school can claim such remarkable achievements. Similarly, but in a different context, is the significant role played by Old Cytringanians in the world of local politics. Essentially, the structure allowed sufficient freedom for anyone to write about what interested them, in whatever format they chose.

Inevitably, therefore, there are omissions and probably errors – of fact and judgement – for which we apologise in the spirit of a certain distinguished bishop: "Better a little well kept than a great deal forgotten." In any case, it soon became apparent that the available material could not be confined to the size of book envisaged, determined by questions of time and cost. The content of *The Cytringanian* magazines alone provides a rich source of social (and educational) history and relatively little use has been made of them. (Volumes 2 and 3 perhaps?)

A glimpse of that history is in this book and is worth recording before it disappears for ever, like two of the buildings on the dust jacket. Vandalism takes many forms. John Wood would doubtless have quoted Cicero, so we must do it for him, sadly without his mellow tones. ''To be ignorant of what happened before you were born is to be ever a child. For what is man's lifetime unless the memory of past events is woven with those of earlier times?'' Our School can never escape us, no matter how hard we try. It is ours for always, touched for better or worse by our individual and collective experience. That touch is benevolent, or otherwise, but it is forever: remembered and unremembered. To quote *Twelfth Night* again: ''For such as we are made of, such we be.''

Our thanks to all contributors (included or not) and the many supporters of the project, especially the Kettering Old Grammar School Foundation, who made it possible.

Tony Hadden
Rex Moore
Sellick Norsworthy
Brian Slough

June 1995

CHAPTER 1

In the Beginning – The Gold Street Days

Sellick Norsworthy

When F. W. Bull wrote his *History of Kettering* in 1891 he suggested that although the date of the foundation of Kettering Grammar School was unknown, it was, most probably, 1626. Others, referring to a deed one hundred years earlier, have inferred that the School was founded by the trustees of Henry VIII in 1526. On balance, however, the evidence suggests that the true foundation date was 1577. On December 10th 1571, Elizabeth I had granted to William James and John Grey:

> "All the lands and tenements lying and being in Kettering then or lately in the occupation of the Church wardens of the Church there or of other inhabitants of Kettering and theretofore to the perpetual maintenance of the orbit priest or other like purposes in the Church of Kettering, given, assigned and appointed."

It would seem that this grant included the endowment, or part of the endowment, of the Grammar School. A petition was sent to the Crown by James and Grey outlining a proposed scheme for the education of boys in Kettering and, on June 15th 1577, the Crown decreed that a Free Grammar School should be founded:

> "In consideration that Kettering was a large town and great in the number of boys and replete in youths and that the said town might be adorned with a learned suitable and lettered man and schoolmaster by whom the boys and youths there might be instructed and educated in good learning and the fear of God."

Elizabeth I endowed land, seven houses and other properties worth £1. 2s. 4d. for 21 years for the use of the Free Grammar School. With the profits from sub-letting these properties, nine trustees were to maintain the School and pay a master who had to be approved by the Bishop of Peterborough. More land and houses were granted to the trustees in February 1597. Mentioning the previous grant of 1577, the new grant stated that the lease was for the maintenance of the schoolmaster and that it should benefit him only so long as he educated boys from Kettering.

Evidence for the definite existence of the Free Grammar School comes from the State Papers of Charles I in 1632, which record that the total rents from the grant amounted to £67. 12s. 2½d. Three years later the Schoolmaster, Mr Seaton, was accused by Sir John Lambe of being a non-conformist. However, Seaton protested his innocence and, following an inquiry by a representative of the Bishop of Peterborough, was exonerated.

A Commonwealth survey of the lands and houses owned by the late Charles I gives details of the schoolhouse occupied by the Schoolmaster, Mr Howett, at the junction of Gold Street and Lower Street, "containing a hall, a parlour and two chambers over them, and a garden measuring one rood and ten perches more or less bounded on the east by Samuel Houldman's house and on the west by William Anstie's."

By 1674 the Schoolmaster was the Rev. William Fowler, but no other information about the School is available until October 8th 1681, when the Rev. Joseph Knight, once Rector of Kettering, conducted an inquiry into the management of the School and its properties. He reported that most of the trustees were dead and no new appointments had been made. The new Schoolmaster, Samuel Sherwin, had been appointed even though there had not been sufficient trustees to make the appointment. As a result of the inquiry, under the Great Seal, the Commissioners appointed the following as trustees:

Edward, Lord Rockingham,
Sir Roger Norwich,
Sir John Egerton,
Francis Morgan,
Joseph Baker,
Abraham Sparrow,
Edward Sparrow,
John Ives, Jnr.,
Henry Bullock,
Thomas Webb,
and Ralph Soame.

Samuel Sherwin was also Rector of Kettering between 1680-84. His remit was to teach the boys of Kettering, English and Latin. He lived in the schoolhouse and held daily classes there. The inquiry stated that Sherwin was to remain as Schoolmaster and could only be removed by a majority decision of the trustees.

The trustees were given the power to grant new leases for the rented land and buildings belonging to the School, for a period of twenty one years. Should six or more of the trustees die, the survivors were to appoint new trustees in their places, so maintaining the number of trustees at eleven.

Sherwin was succeeded by Francis Sawyer, who exercised three-fold powers: he was Rector, Schoolmaster and his family were lords of the manor. A document dated 18th November 1705, promised that on the death of Francis Sawyer, the Rev. Richard Jones of Clare College, Cambridge would become the new Schoolmaster. This promise seems to have been kept when Jones took over as Schoolmaster only in 1709. His ambitions for the School are reflected in his rather amusing advertisement for boarders in the *Lincoln, Rutland and Stamford Mercury* on Thursday, October 31st 1717:

> ''At the Free School in Kettering in Northamptonshire, as the most rational and easie Method of teaching Latin Tongue, the Rules of the Common Grammar concerning Nouns and Verbs, and some useful Rules of Syntax being translated, are taught in English. Also plain Definitions of the Figures both of Grammar and Rhetorick, by R. Jones, M.A.
> *Note:* For the Accommodation of a young Nobleman and some Gentlemen's Sons, the School is made convenient with ceiling and chimney etc.''

Despite Jones' ambition to put Kettering Grammar School on the map, his personal ambitions resulted in his leaving Kettering in 1722 to become Headmaster of Oundle Grammar School, where he was in continual dispute with the trustees.

The history of the School was rather chequered for the rest of the eighteenth

The Free Grammar School
''. . . The School is made convenient with ceiling and chimney etc.''

century, with one indifferent Head following another. Thomas Allen was Rector and Schoolmaster between 1722 and 1755 and John Warner, simply described as ''of Kettering'', was Schoolmaster from 1755 to 1799. Warner's son, who had been an Army sergeant, carried the School on for another year. However, his regimented approach to education did not prove popular. One old pupil of the Grammar School commented:

> ''In allowing such an appointment the School Trustees must have been remiss indeed, but loose administration was not infrequent in those days and occasionally there were no responsible trustees left to manage at all.''

The Rev. James Hogg from Holbeck, near Leeds, was appointed Headmaster in 1801, a post he held until 1845. Not only was he the Headmaster, but he was Curate of Geddington from 1803 and Vicar from 1815.

Hogg was noted for his eccentric punishments. He had three old wigs of varying shabbiness, which he made the boys wear throughout the school day, according to the seriousness of their misdemeanours. Serious offenders were treated more harshly, several boys being sent home without their trousers! Another favourite punishment was to make a boy sit on a bench with a stone between his teeth.

The early years of the nineteenth century were neither successful nor happy for the Grammar School. In 1830 the Charity Commissioners, who conducted an Inquiry into the management of the School, found that the leases of the School's property were accurately recorded and that they provided an income of £147. 8s. 8d. They reported that the Rev. Hogg admitted as free scholars ''such boys, being sons of inhabitants of Kettering, as are sent to him, and instructs them in English, and as many of them as require it, in Latin.''

Hogg's assistant, who was paid the princely sum of £38. 1s. 6d., annually, taught the boys Writing and Arithmetic. He was evidently unhappy with his position, alleging that Hogg employed him ''in the performance of menial and servile offices.''

It was not uncommon at this time for Free Grammar Schools to charge for extra lessons, such as Writing and Arithmetic. However, it was agreed by the Rev. Hogg, and the trustees, that these subjects be taught free of charge.

Hogg found himself faced with objections from dissenting parents about the School teaching their sons the Church Catechism. He finally overcame this problem by omitting to question the sons of Dissenters on those parts of the Catechism to which they objected.

Despite the Rev. Hogg's reputation for great intelligence, undertstanding and fairness, the number of pupils at the Free Grammar School fell from 60 in 1801 to well below 30 in 1845. Hogg attributed this decline to the building of the National, or Elementary School, in School Lane in 1831. However, an article published in the *Northamptonshire Mercury* in 1876 attributed the decline to Hogg himself.

Following Hogg's death in 1845, the Rev. Richard Morton, Curate at Geddington, became Headmaster. It was during his time that the fortunes of the Grammar School reached their nadir. The number of boys in attendance had dwindled to the alarming number of two or three. To make matters worse, if these boys were to receive any education at all, they had to walk to Burton Latimer, where Morton had become the Curate.

The School building was in a dreadful state of disrepair, as was the School house. The thatched roof and crumbling walls were in such a state of dilapidation, that the School had to be pulled down and replaced by another building. Not only the School house was falling apart, but also the houses and cottages leased to tenants. Clearly the trustees were guilty of dereliction of duty and it was not until 1853 that they put a case to the Attorney General for a new School.

The trustees invited the people of Kettering to take part in a discussion about the future of the Grammar School. It took almost a year before any real decisions were taken. Following a committee meeting in April 1853, a public meeting was held at the Royal Hotel in December, at which time fifteen new trustees were appointed:

Sir Arthur de Capell Brooke,
Rev. George Stopford,
Rev. John Wetherall,
William Somerset Rose, Esq.,
Thomas Maunsell M.P.,
J. T. Roughton (surgeon),
W. Gibbon (surgeon),
Rev. Madge,
Robert Chettle (grocer),
Joseph Wells (grocer),
Thomas Waddington (stationer),
T. Davis Gotch (banker),
John Wallis (mustard manufacturer),
J. T. Stockburn (draper),
and William Toller (draper).

All of the new trustees were young, energetic men who wanted to revive the fortunes of the Grammar School, and from a third public meeting that they organised, the 'Kettering Grammar School Scheme' evolved in 1854. Under the Scheme the School was to have fifteen trustees who were to meet at least twice a year and have their minutes carefully recorded. The trustees were to appoint a man to survey the Estate's and Charity's property to ensure that tenants kept their houses in a state of good repair, and another to be the official Receiver of Rents. The curriculum was to include instruction in the principles of the Christian religion, Greek and Latin, English Literature and Composition, History, Geography, Mathematics, Arithmetic, Book-keeping, Reading and Writing.

The Headmaster had to live in the School house attached to the School and not elsewhere. He could have no other occupation and had to keep the premises in good order at his own expense. The number of boarders could not exceed 12, a safeguard against local boys being neglected. All boys between the ages of 7 and 18 could attend the School, but fees were introduced for the first time. Sons of journeymen, labourers and servants were charged 5 shillings per quarter, others 10 shillings per quarter. Boys who received education beyond Latin and English were charged 20 shillings per quarter. Parents had to provide their own books and stationery. An annual examination of boys was to be conducted by a graduate of an English university, duly appointed by the trustees.

Soon after the introduction of the Scheme, Richard Morton resigned to become the Vicar of Rothwell. In his place, the trustees appointed the Rev. Frederick Tearle of Trinity Hall, Cambridge. He proved to be a popular choice and under his guidance the School became highly respected, attracting the sons of all the worthies of Kettering. In recognition of his work, the trustees, in June 1856, made a public appeal for funds to build a new School and School house. The appeal met with great success with prompt responses from many leading townspeople:

G. L. Watson Esq.	£100,
T. P. Maunsell Esq.	£10,
Rev. Sir Geo. Robinson	£10,
A. A. Young	£10,
Viscountess Hood	£50,
Earl Fitzwilliam	£25,
Sir Arthur de Capell Brooke	£25,
and the Bishop of Peterborough	£10.

Mr Law, a County architect, was asked by the trustees to draw up plans for the new School to be built on the same site as the old one in Gold Street. Tenders were advertised and the builders, Messrs Bayes and Fisher, were successful with a bid of just under £1,800.

The appeal had raised almost £1,000 and with another £500 raised on the School estates, total subscriptions stood at £1,413. In March 1857, a Bazaar was announced to the people of Kettering for the sole purpose of raising the remaining £305. 17s. 2d. It was fortunate that this second appeal was successful, because a dinner at the Three Cocks had already been held in December 1856 to celebrate the completion of the School.

The distinguished Old Boy and author, Tony Ireson, describes the Old Grammar School in his book *Old Kettering – a View from the 1930s:*

"The Old Grammar School reflected the mood of confidence which gave it birth. The trustees commissioned a dominant yet whimsical building with a decidedly scholastic look – a sort of Greyfriars in miniature from which at any moment Billy Bunter might emerge, hotly pursued by the cads of the Remove. It was flamboyantly attractive, suggesting that the architect and builder thoroughly enjoyed putting it together. Its walls were of warm brown ironstone, with multifarious dressings, quoins, parapets, relieving arches, mullions and transoms in contrasting grey Weldon stone.

At each end two high gables faced Gold Street, one surmounted by the school bell turret and weather vane, and there was nothing dull about the rest of the frontage with its steeply pitched roofs, minor gables, windows in church and manor house styles, generous entrance porches, and a final touch of 10 rectangular chimneys set on the skew."

Kettering Old Grammar School and Master's House 1856-1913
"A sort of Greyfriars in miniature from which at any moment Billy Bunter might emerge, hotly pursued by the cads of the Remove."

As significant as the rebuilding of the Grammar School was, it soon became evident that the trustees had been short-sighted in rebuilding the new School on the site of the old. Kettering was a vibrant, expanding town, with its industries developing as the railway linked it to the rest of the country. Soon, the School would be far too small to accommodate the boys of Kettering.

Nevertheless, 1856 was a milestone in the history of the Grammar School, as the popular and respected Frederick Tearle dramatically increased the number of pupils. So great was the demand for places, that the trustees decided, in early 1857, that the boys from the parishes outside of Kettering should pay double the quarterly sum, that is, £1 or £2, and none would be allowed to pay less than £1. In 1857 two additional teachers were appointed: Mr A. Bailey as Second Master and Mr E. B. Tweed, who taught Writing. It was also decided that boys between 7 and 10 could be admitted as boarders at a cost of £35 per annum and those between 11 and 18 at £40 per annum.

In 1858 the first annual examination was conducted by the Rev. E. T. Vaughan M.A., Vicar of St. Martin's in Leicester. In his report he spoke very highly of the discipline and educational standards of the School. A similar commendation came in 1854, the year in which Tearle left to become Headmaster of Leicester Grammar School. After the Prizegiving, in June 1864, the Rev. Tearle was presented with a silver ink stand in recognition of his outstanding contribution to the Grammar School.

Curiously, it was the Second Master of Leicester Grammar School, the Rev. Thomas Widdowson, who was appointed as Head of Kettering Grammar School in September 1864. In that year, T. H. Green, the Government's representative on the Schools' Enquiry Commission, visited the Grammar School. He reported that the School had 38 boys and 9 boarders, but that the lessons were being taught in a rented room at the end of the garden, because the schoolroom proper could not accommodate the number of boys in attendance. By the time that Green's report had been published in 1868, the number of boys had increased to 52, 4 of whom were boarders. As Miss Anthea Curchin wrote in her thesis, *Kettering Grammar School:*

> "Although not known to the people of Kettering in 1864, Kettering Grammar School was only at the beginning of its seemingly endless expansion. As the caterpillar sheds its skin four times, so too would Kettering Grammar School shed its buildings."

Thomas Widdowson was, at first, almost as popular as his predecessor. One of his most popular initiatives was to introduce dramatic productions. In 1865 *Turn Him Out* and *Ticklish Times*, produced by the boys, received warm appreciation in the local press:

> "The performances were good enough to surprise the audiences, and were received with great applause."

After such promising beginnings, the School began to experience severe difficulties. Tony Ireson tells us:

> "From St. John's College, Cambridge, (Widdowson) was an undisputed scholar, but proved hopelessly out of touch with changing times and lacking in almost all qualities that made a good headmaster."

Within ten years, the number of boys had dwindled to 25, all of them local. Although another scheme in 1888 improved the curriculum and numbers went up to 61, by 1896 numbers were down again to 21. Although Widdowson faced public criticism, he let it be known that his resignation would not be forthcoming. His shortcomings meant that the School slowly declined into little more than a Prep School, instead of an establishment capable of preparing boys for university entrance. This was at a time when the population of Kettering had risen from 7,000 to 19,000 and the endowment income had risen sharply.

Eventually the Charity Commissioners were forced to investigate, as the people of Kettering began to blame the trustees, as much as Widdowson, for the failure of the School. It was pointed out that all the trustees were over 70 and very conservative in their educational thinking.

The Inquiry held Widdowson responsible for the School's demise, pointing out that parents demanded a commercial education for their sons rather than a classical education. The curriculum revision in 1888 had excluded Greek in favour of Modern Languages, Science and Music, but Widdowson remained the only teacher and could not possibly deliver the new curriculum. The Commissioners judged Widdowson a poor teacher, who was disliked as a man, unable to appoint masters to widen the curriculum, inept at handling human relationships, unwilling to take boarders and lacking the expertise to popularise the School. Ironically, Widdowson benefited from a ten-fold increase in the endowment income, which gave him automatic salary increases, so obviating the need to attract more pupils.

It was, therefore, somewhat of a surprise when, in 1896, Widdowson accepted a pension of £100 per annum, plus an undisclosed lump sum. Unfortunately, the damage had been done. Kettering Grammar School had fallen well behind other endowed schools and the next Headmaster, James Herbert Gill, also from St. John's College, Cambridge, would face a constant uphill battle.

Under the revised Educational Scheme of 1888, several amendments to the administration and organisation of the School were introduced. The School was to be administered by 13 governors; eight Representative Governors holding office for five years and five Co-opted Governors holding office for eight years. Boys between the ages of 9 and 18 were eligible for admission on the payment of a fee of not less than £4 and not more than £8. As mentioned earlier, the curriculum was modernised to include Reading, Writing, Arithmetic, Geography, History, English Grammar, Composition, Literature, Mathematics, Latin, two Modern Languages, Natural Science, Book-keeping, Land Surveying, Mechanical Drawing, Mensuration, Drill and Vocal Music.

With this Scheme came the modern method of paying a Headmaster a fixed stipend of £150 per annum. He was also to receive a capitation allowance of not less than £2 and not more than £4 per annum, for each boy in the School. The idea behind this provision was to encourage an increase in the number of pupils in the School, for any Headmaster would need a high capitation allowance to supplement his meagre stipend.

For the first time, boys were to take an entrance exam to ensure a high calibre of pupil. On the other hand, the Governors were keen to introduce

Kettering Grammar School Cricket Team 1904
Back Row (L. to R.): W. G. Fairey, M. Mackay, B. E. Pledger (Captain), T. H. Palmer, V. Mobbs.
Middle Row (L. to R.): E. B. Butlin, C. W. Bird, P. Childs, T. G. Mansbridge.
Front Row (L. to R.): G. H. Everard, G. Blackmore (See "The Great War")
The captain, B. E. Pledger, taught at the School from 1941 to 1952.

a free place system for ten per cent of the pupils, tenable for at least three years, but longer if the Governors deemed it appropriate.

It became very obvious in the first decade of the twentieth century that the condition of the School was in need of great improvement. It was just not big enough to educate more than 50 boys. A new School building was the only way in which educational standards could be improved. In 1907 F. W. Bull, in his short *History of Kettering Grammar School,* wrote:

> "It is felt that with such a history and such an endowment better scholastic facilities ought to be afforded, and for many years efforts, so far uncrowned with success, have been made to erect suitable buildings and to provide an adequate staff for a first class town Grammar School."

Unfortunately, the Endowment Fund was neither in a position to build a new School, nor even extend the old one. Outside help was necessary if the Grammar School was to provide a sound education for the boys of Kettering. The Governors saw their salvation in the Education Act of 1902, which made County Councils responsible for rate-aided secondary education. The Counties were given powers to acquire or assist the endowed grammar schools. The Governors, therefore, approached the County Council, but were soon exasperated by hold-ups at County Hall, where Conservative Councillors were anxious to keep the rates down and firmly believed that education was the responsibility of parents and not local government.

In their frustration the Governors introduced a scheme of their own, only to have it rejected by the Board of Education because it was underfunded. Dissatisfaction mounted, as more and more boys had to be sent out of Kettering to be educated. Although Henry Gotch and his supporters applied continual pressure, the County Council refused to maintain any school until 1907. In 1909 it finally approved a new scheme, but caused a major delay when it tried to appropriate the School's endowments for general running costs instead of scholarships. The County Council tried to get its way by breaking off negotiations for the purchase of land for the new School. Finally, matters were resolved when the Board of Education agreed that no more than 12 scholarships should be held at any one time and the rest of the endowment income should be used to maintain the School. More hold-ups came as details of the organisation of the two single sex schools, to be housed on the same site, were hammered out. Although the County Council continued to quibble about the minutiae, the scheme was eventually approved by the Crown on May 4th, 1911.

It was a distinguished former pupil and Mayor of Kettering, J. A. Gotch, who was commissioned to draw up plans of the new School building in Bowling Green Road. There was provision for over 200 boys and a similar number of girls in the new High School. Unfortunately, the Headmaster, Mr Gill, did not live long enough to see the plans come to fruition and it was a new Head, Mr J. I. Scott, who supervised the move for the first five forms. The Teacher Training Centre in School Lane housed the Sixth Form with its Head, Mr Eldridge, as Assistant Headmaster to Mr Scott. The opening ceremony was attended by 120 boys and 120 girls under their Headmistress Miss E. A. Bristol B.A. and, although classes began immediately, the internal work was not completed until March 1914. In the Magazine for 1914 Mr Scott wrote:

> "... For years the project of having a fine new Secondary School has been one of Kettering's most cherished aspirations. That ideal is now realised in the bricks and mortar of our School. Long may it prosper."

Prosper it did, until the caterpillar shed its skin once more, with the opening of the new building in Windmill Avenue in February 1963.

Aerial view of the Windmill Avenue School and Playing Field. ''The caterpillar sheds its skin for the last time.''

Rev. Thomas Toller

Sir Alfred East

Mr J. A. Gotch, J.P.

Rev. William Knibb

CHAPTER 2

Some Famous Kettering Names

Sellick Norsworthy

THOMAS TOLLER

Born on April 1st 1796, Thomas was the son of Thomas Northcote Toller, the Baptist minister who gave his name to the Toller Church in Kettering. Thomas was educated at the Grammar School and by the age of 19 had preached his first sermon.

In 1820 he was summoned from Shropshire to assist his ailing father in Kettering and, on the latter's death in 1821, was chosen as successor. For nearly 55 years he served the Baptist Church in Kettering.

The Jubilee of his Ministry was celebrated in July 1871 in a huge marquee erected in the Mission House Paddock. Here Thomas was presented with a cheque for £700 by Mr Joseph Stockburn, in recognition of his great service to the Baptist Church in Kettering.

Thomas preached his last sermon in 1875. His last public appearance came on September 26th 1883, when he laid the foundation stone of the Toller Sunday School in Meeting Lane.

WILLIAM KNIBB

Son of Thomas and Mary Knibb, William was born in Kettering on September 7th, 1803 and lived in Market Street. He was educated at Kettering Grammar School, where the Rev. James Hogg was Headmaster. On leaving School he went to work for J. G. Fuller, a printer, who moved his business from Kettering to Bristol.

In 1824 he offered his services to the Baptist Missionary Society and was sent to Jamaica to replace his brother, who had just died. William arrived in Kingston with his new wife and took charge of Mr Coulthard's Free School. After five successful years he moved to Ridgeland in the north west of the island. Eventually, he became Pastor of the Church at Falmouth, only to be faced with an attempted revolt by negro slaves. Despite his efforts to preserve the peace, the government of Jamaica persecuted Knibb and his fellow missionaries as if they had been responsible for the unrest.

In 1832 William returned to England to spend much of his time informing the British public of the state of affairs in the West Indies and the need to overthrow slavery. Up to this time the Baptist Mission had abstained from getting involved in politics. William changed its course at the annual meeting of the Baptist Missionary Society at Spa Field Chapel on 21st June, 1832, when he made an impassioned plea for the abolition of slavery.

Having described the atrocities against the slaves in Jamaica, the Secretary of the Mission pulled the tail of Knibb's coat as a friendly warning. Knibb reacted by continuing:

> "Whatever may be the consequence, I *will* speak. At the risk of my connection with the Society, and all I hold dear, I will avow this; and if the friends of missions will not hear me, I will turn and tell it to my God; I will not desist till the greatest of crimes, slavery, is abolished."

He carried the meeting with him, and ultimately the country, when Lord Stanley's Bill for the abolition of slavery was introduced into the House of Commons in May 1833.

In August 1834 Knibb returned to a rapturous welcome from the negroes. Four years later, slavery was finally abolished. Knibb drew his congregation together at Falmouth the night before and on the stroke of midnight he declared, "The monster is dead! The negro is free! Three cheers for the Queen."

Knibb returned to England in 1840 to attend the Anti-Slavery Convention and, although he went back to Jamaica the same year, 1842 saw him back in London. During that visit Knibb celebrated the Jubilee of the Baptist Missionary Society in Kettering. Following one final visit to England to raise money for his mission, Knibb finally died in Kettering, a village near Falmouth, Jamaica, which he had founded and named after his birthplace.

JOHN ALFRED GOTCH

When John Alfred Gotch attended the Anniversary Dinner on November 19th, 1938, Mr J. L. Holland, County Secretary for Education, described him as the School's most distinguished Old Boy. Born in 1852, his connection with the Grammar School went back to the 1860s, when he won a prize at an examination conducted by Mr E. N. Toller. His Headmaster throughout his time at Kettering Grammar School had been Mr Widdowson, of whom he had pleasant recollections.

After studying at the University of Zurich, Gotch was articled to R. W. Johnson, an architect in Melton Mowbray. On returning to Kettering he worked from a little office just above the Old Grammar School as Kettering's first resident practising architect. Together with Charles Saunders, he designed many important buildings in Kettering. These included the Art Gallery, St. Mary's Church, the schools in Stamford Road, Park Road and

Hawthorn Road, blocks at the General Hospital, the Midland Bank, the Newland-Montagu Street corner, Sunnylands, now St. Peter's School in the Headlands, not to mention the Old Post Office block in Gold Street.

Mr Gotch gained a national reputation as an architect, achieving the highest honour of becoming the first provincial President of the Royal Institute of British Architects. His books on architecture, which are standard works, include: *The Buildings of Sir Thomas Tresham, Architecture of the Renaissance in England* and *Early Renaissance Architecture in England.*

Locally, Mr Gotch held many important offices: he was Justice of the Peace for the County of Northamptonshire, County Councillor for the Southern Ward of Kettering and Commissioner of Income Tax. In 1938 he became Mayor of Kettering.

Perhaps his greatest claim to fame, in the context of the Grammar School, is the fact that he designed the Bowling Green Road building. In his speech at the Anniversary Dinner in 1938 he said that he was proud to regard himself as an old scholar of Kettering Grammar School and was sure that Mr J. I. Scott was to be congratulated on the present success of the School.

SIR ALFRED EAST (1844-1913)

Sir Alfred East was born in a little cottage in Lower Street in 1844. From such humble origins he was to become, arguably, one of England's greatest landscape painters.

As a child, he was forced to attend Fuller Baptist Chapel twice each Sunday. His father was so strict, that Alfred was not allowed to draw or paint on the Sabbath. However, his passion for drawing could not be extinguished as he himself admitted: "During the long sermons I passed the time decorating the book rest in the high pew with drawings of rural scenes with the point of a pin."

Alfred was educated at Kettering British School and Kettering Grammar School. Although a gifted scholar, it was widely reported that he hated school except, of course, for the drawing classes. Unfortunately, his parents opposed an artistic career and Alfred found himself working in a shoe factory owned by his brother Charles.

Shortly after his marriage to Ann Heath, in 1874, he was sent to Glasgow as the firm's representative. Having attended Art classes in the evenings, Alfred decided to leave the shoe trade to study at the Glasgow School of Art. From here he graduated to the École des Beaux Arts in Paris, where he fell under the influence of the great landscape painter Jean Corot.

Returning to England in about 1883, he established studios in London and Cornwall. For the next thirty years he travelled extensively in England and Europe, producing a succession of etchings and paintings that greatly enhanced his reputation as a landscape painter. Perhaps one of his best paintings was *Autumn in the Ouse Valley.*

His work rate was phenomenal. Edwin Bale wrote of East: ''Most men who went out with him painting were oppressed with a sense of his incessant, untiring energy. He must have accomplished as much in his lifetime as almost two other men, but he never seemed too busy to take on all sorts of engagements.''

Alfred also wrote a well respected book on landscape painting. He gave aspiring artists the following good advice: ''Don't be ashamed to do the constant drudgery of drawing and sketching. If you have no enthusiasm and lack courage, stay at home and do other work that befits your temperament . . . Take every means in your power of learning more about nature. For instance, in taking the trouble to paint the sky every morning for a few weeks, no matter what the weather, you will learn something more of the sky than you can read in any scientific book.''

On October 3rd 1899, a Complimentary Banquet was given by the town at the Royal Hotel, to Alfred, to celebrate his election to the Associateship of the Royal Academy of Arts. Also attending were Kettering's two other great painters of the day, J. T. Nettleship and T. C. Gotch, brother of John Alfred Gotch, and another ex-pupil of Kettering Grammar School.

In recognition of his service to Art, Alfred was knighted by George V in 1910. The next year Alfred offered a collection of his works to Kettering, on condition that they should be accessible to the public. The collection consisted of 36 etchings, 16 water colours and 11 oil paintings. The Alfred East Gallery, built to house the collection, was designed by J. A. Gotch and officially opened on July 31st, 1913 by Earl Spencer, Lord Lieutenant of Northamptonshire. Unfortunately, Sir Alfred was too ill to attend. Three months later, just before he died, he said to a friend: ''My life has been one long holiday.''

To commemorate his life, a bust of Sir Alfred East, by Sir George Frampton, was erected in the secluded quadrangle between the Gallery and the Library.

CHAPTER 3

J. I. Scott

Headmaster 1913-1942

J. M. I. Scott

> "His devoted work as Headmaster and his never failing interest and guidance as President and Friend during the years 1913-1938 will never be forgotten."
>
> (Illuminated address presented to J. I. Scott on the 19th November 1938, to mark his completion of twenty five years as Headmaster of Kettering Grammar School and President of the Old Cytringanians.)

John Irwin Scott was a schoolmaster by inheritance and inclination. He came to Kettering at the age of 35, having been on the staff at Trent College and Headmaster of Deacon's School, Peterborough for three years. His entire working life was devoted to three schools, by far the greater part to Kettering Grammar School, a new County Grammar School combined with an Elizabethan foundation. He was the son of Thomas Scott of Tweedmouth and Sarah Wallas of Wigton. Both parents were teachers and his only sister became Headmistress of Dover High School.

Thomas Scott died young and his son secured a place at Merchant Taylors', Crosby, whence he took a First in Natural Sciences at Merton College, Oxford, in 1901 and was admitted to a Master's degree in 1905. He came to Kettering Grammar School, then not formally opened, in April 1913, having married Maud Dunlop in December, 1911.

The infant School survived the hazards of the Great War. Many of the boys came from outlying towns and villages by train. Reduced services meant that daily journeys were no longer possible and the Headmaster's house, not in any sense part of the School, became a boarding house for the duration. Many years later, letters from Old Boys spoke of their fond recollections of their stay in Queensberry Road.

The Kettering Grammar School Old Boys Association, later to be known as The Old Cytringanians, was founded soon after the School opened and sprouted various subsidiary societies, including rugger and cricket clubs and, jointly with Old Girls of Kettering High School, a dramatic society, the

Old Cytringanians R.F.C. 1936-37, with J. I. Scott

From the back left to right: *M. J. Miller, H. Cooke, L. Newman, A. O. Mason*
L. S. Axe (Secretary), R. H. Potter, D. Abbott, J. G. Ireton,
R. A. Barlow, A. Humphrey, B. G. Bennett, P. Buckby, V. Fourt, B. Smith (Treasurer),
S. N. Allen, C. W. Elliott, (Captain), J. I. Scott, Esq. (President), N. F. Bryant (Vice-Captain), W. H. Cox
J. Robinson, J. Ward, R. Sindall, G. F. Moule, R. Woolston, C. Curtis. Trophies: *The Bryant Cup, The Nicholson Trophy (Runners-Up)*

Hygram Players and a tennis club. J. I. Scott was the first President of the Old Cytringanians and retained this office until his death in 1943. He greatly encouraged the Association and its offshoots and made the School premises available to them on a basis of trust, as the caretakers could not be expected to provide supervision. That trust was rarely betrayed and in it may reflect the interest and guidance given as a friend to nearly 3,000 boys, who passed through the School between 1913 and 1943.

As the Headmaster of a small rural Grammar School, J. I. Scott was not only an active teacher but, in the words of a tribute paid on his enforced retirement in 1942, ". . . he showed a complete mastery of every aspect of his office. He worked hard and unceasingly for the good of pupils and that of the School." Another tribute referred to his educational creed which was, "The necessity for hard nose-to-the-grindstone work and without it education is built on sand." A third tribute from a senior prefect said, "Whilst we feared him in the junior forms, in later years when in authority ourselves, we found the Head a constant support."

J. I. Scott was a disciplinarian, which gave rise to the fears of younger boys. School rules were for the good of the community as a whole and were there to be enforced. Boys who did not comply were simply being disruptive and a nuisance. The late H. E. Bates, not necessarily the most distinguished of boys or Old Boys, received the standard punishment for contravention of a well-established rule which, for some reason, he felt did not apply to him. He later used his undoubted skills as a writer, largely taught to him at Kettering Grammar School, to attack J. I. Scott publicly. The grudge, still harboured after 30 years and long after J. I. Scott's death, surfaced again in his autobiography. Bates well knew that J. I. Scott could not reply. Both have long since gone to their graves. May they both rest in peace.

The extract which begins this tribute expressed the feelings of an earlier generation of Old Boys of Kettering Grammar School. Over half a century later it has been a great privilege to write of one who was an outstanding Headmaster and teacher, who gave guidance based on sound principles to his former pupils, and was above all a good father to his family. He was one who gave his friendship and encouragement to all he felt deserved it.

E. B. Wright

Both my brother, T. J. B. Wright, and I, followed the same educational route – except he was three years ahead of me, having been born in 1920. We both attended The Bungalow (Montefiore) School in Spinney Lane, Kettering and then, at the age of eight, entered the Junior School in "temporary classroom accommodation" in the Grammar School playground. Miss Platt was the First Form mistress; she was a daughter of the

Wellingborough School master, who founded Platt's House for boarders.

My brother and I sat the Kettering Grammar School entrance examinations and were offered "Free Places". Since our parents' income was above the threshhold applicable, however, our fees were paid by them. Nevertheless, we both felt it an honour to be given the chance of a free education, if we had needed it. I have no knowledge of who endowed the "Free Places"; the Old Grammar School Foundation perhaps?

My brother was a contemporary of the then Headmaster's (J. I. Scott) son Jamie, who remains a lifelong friend. My parents were friendly with John Irwin Scott and his wife, Maud. My brother tells the tale of how John Irwin broke the ice when he first visited Jamie at his home. J. I. asked him to read some "Latin" before tea, and it proved to be:

See, Willie! See 'Er Go!
Civile, si ergo
Fortibuses in ero
Gnoses mare, Thebe trux
Vatis inem?
Causan dux! *Anon.*

My most vivid memory of John Irwin was during a Latin lesson with my junior form; I never enjoyed the subject, probably because I was never any good at it. My attention was wandering, when J. I. suddenly asked,

"Are you listening, Wright?"

Without pause for thought, I replied,

"Unfortunately yes, sir."

The consequences were painful.

The Junior School was a particularly happy place within Kettering Grammar School. K.G.S. itself was fortunate to have John Irwin Scott as Headmaster at that time; he was held in awe and respected fondly.

CHAPTER 4

The Great War

Sellick Norsworthy

At first glance, it might seem incredible that the editor of the Grammar School Magazine for 1914 did not even mention the outbreak of the Great War. However, it must be remembered that 1914 was momentous for quite another reason: it was the year that the new Grammar School building in Bowling Green Road was completed.

There is, nevertheless, an extraordinary article in that magazine entitled, *A Holiday in France during the War,* written by a certain WNT. Looking through the records it seems almost certain that the author was Mr W. N. Thomas, the Senior Languages Master, who joined the Staff in 1913. In retrospect, it now seems ludicrous that anyone would plan such an adventure, let alone carry it through.

Thomas arrived in Paris on July 31st 1914 and by the time he had reached his final destination – Grenoble – a general mobilisation had been ordered by the French Government. Even as he travelled, extra coaches for soldiers and munitions were added to the train. His retreat to Paris was now completely cut off.

On arriving in Grenoble the hotel manager, "seemed to think that coming at such a time for an ordinary holiday was an eccentricity truly English. . . . His gestures were truly Gallic!"

When Thomas visited the University, he was advised by Professor Rosset to leave France immediately. Easier said than done! On trying to catch a train to Marseilles, Thomas found that all trains had been commandeered by the Army and that civilians were not allowed to travel for at least the next seven days. To add to his misery, Thomas learned that he could not even leave the city limits without a "laissez-passer" and so had to be content playing tennis for two weeks, instead of taking the Alpine walks he had planned.

Eventually, all British citizens were requested to make their way home in groups of three or four, but not before obtaining special military permits. Thomas's journey home was tedious in the extreme, taking 28 hours in stifling heat to reach Paris. However, all his discomforts were quickly forgotten when he finally reached Boulogne, where excited French crowds were cheering British soldiers as they were disembarking.

By 1915 it had become obvious that the War had begun to inconvenience the School, as two members of Staff, Messrs Jones and Grimes, were drafted into the forces.

In that year Mr Eldridge formed the Cadet Corps, affiliated to the 4th Battalion of the Northants Territorials, and within a short time sixty boys had joined. The editor of the Magazine was at pains to stress the reason for its creation:

> ''It is no part of our aim to imbue the boys with the spirit of militarism, but we do hope by this training so to prepare them that if necessity arises, they may worthily take their places in the defence of their country.''

By the end of 1915 two Old Boys, Harry Lilley and Harry Buckby, had made the ultimate sacrifice in that defence. The report of Harry Buckby's death is particularly moving:

> ''Brave and self-reliant, a character not always easy to understand, but yet manly to the core, Harry Buckby, Cameron Highlanders, met his death in the charge at Festubert in May. Fighting side by side with his brother Charles, he fell mortally wounded, but yet desiring victory for his cause, rather than comfort for himself, he died urging his brother to leave him and fight on with the rest.''

Pte. Harry Buckby, 4th Cameron Highlanders. Killed at Pestubert, May 1915.

''Fighting side by side with his brother Charles, he fell mortally wounded . . . urging his brother to leave him and fight on with the rest''.

Lieutenant R. N. Jones, killed July 1917.

For another Old Boy, H. W. Asbrey, the year 1915 had another significance. It was his first year at Oxford University. He had been advised that it was not a good time to enter college because of all the disruption caused by the War. To his surprise, however, he found, "Life pursuing almost its normal course." He reported that though the number of men, particularly in their second year, were few in number, there was the usual enthusiasm for "sport, sing-songs, debates, ping-pong tournaments and general meetings." Writing about the twice-weekly training in the Officers' Training Corps, Asbrey reflected the same spirit as shown at the Grammar School:

> ". . . men are willingly cutting short their college careers and taking up commissions today; it is this same spirit, not the desire for conquest, but for honour, not for broad lands, but for true liberties, that will make us ready, if and when the call comes to take our part in the great struggle."

Ironically Asbrey did receive "the Call" and was killed in action in July 1917.

Another Old Boy, Glanville Blackmore, had a very narrow escape when, as one of the party of the Royal Naval Division, he was sent to Antwerp. Unfortunately, he was present during the last days of the siege and was interned in a camp at Groningen in October 1914. In February 1915 he made his escape from the camp disguised as a girl. He made his way safely to Rotterdam and boarded a ship. No sooner had it left harbour than it was pursued by a German submarine, which had chased another British vessel into port. The submarine, however, failed to overhaul Blackmore's ship, which finally made its way safely to Harwich.

Meanwhile, the Cadet Corps underwent ten days of military training at Boughton Park. Their exploits read like a script from *Dad's Army*!

> "The training caused several amusing episodes, to wit, the occasion when the entire Company was lost in the dark in the marshy fields off Burton Road."

Further disruption to the life of the School came in 1916 when three other members of Staff, Messrs Whitney, Sutton and Williams, were called up. Mr Peel, a Science master, went to work in an explosives factory. In July 1917 came the sad news of the death of Mr R. N. Jones, killed by a German sniper. In all, 109 Old Boys and 6 members of Staff were on active service in 1917.

Back in Kettering, the Cadet Corps went from strength to strength. Its general drill improved and a miniature shooting range was opened in the School basement:

> "One of our members has by his expert shooting already contrived to put the range in darkness on one occasion."

Earl Spencer, at the opening of a Red Cross sale, inspected the Corps and informed its Commander that it was "as smart as possible." In 1917 the Corps was commanded by Mr Rupert Scott, ably assisted by Mr Parker, who had already served at the Front. Unfortunately, it was impossible to maintain stability of command; Mr Parker was recalled to the service and Mr A. J. Ensor took over as Second in Command. When Mr Scott himself was called up in 1918 and Mr Ensor retired, Mr Parker, back once more from the Front, took over command.

The Corps was assisted, both practically and financially, by leading figures of Kettering. Donations to the Cadet Corps Equipment Fund came from Mr H. G. Gotch (£3. 3s. 0d.), Mr C. Lamb (£2. 2s. 0d.) and Mr C. Wicksteed (10s. 6d.). Mr Wicksteed also gave permission for the Park to be used for parades and field manoeuvres, while the Duke of Buccleuch continued to put Boughton Park at the Corps' disposal for training.

In actual fact, the Cadet Corps continued to function after the War, Mr Scott taking command once more in 1919. However, it was not long before he left Kettering, leaving Mr Parker once more in command. He was ably assisted by none other than Mr E. E. Kirby, who took particular interest in developing the shooting prowess of the Cadets.

Altogether, over 120 Old Boys served during the War and 29 lost their lives. Among those who were decorated were G. B. Spence, who was awarded the Military Cross, and B. C. Hales, who won the DCM. Mentioned in Sir Douglas Haigh's despatch of November 3rd, 1918, were Captain V. P. Mobbs of the 6th Battalion, Northants Regiment and Lieutenant A. H. Webb of the 7th Battalion, Northants Regiment.

The School's final loss came as late as October 27th, 1918, when Mr W. H. Sutton, Senior French Master, died of his wounds:

> "He was killed while gallantly leading his company in an attack. Although killed in the moment of victory, we all felt it was the death he would have chosen. A few days before his death his name had been put forward for the Military Cross for magnificent work in a previous action. He had served with us a long time and was universally admired by officers and men."

Amazingly, a letter written in November 1918 by Mr Sutton's sister to J. I. Scott has survived. It was found inside the official Register of Staff, which was unearthed after the closure of the School in 1993.

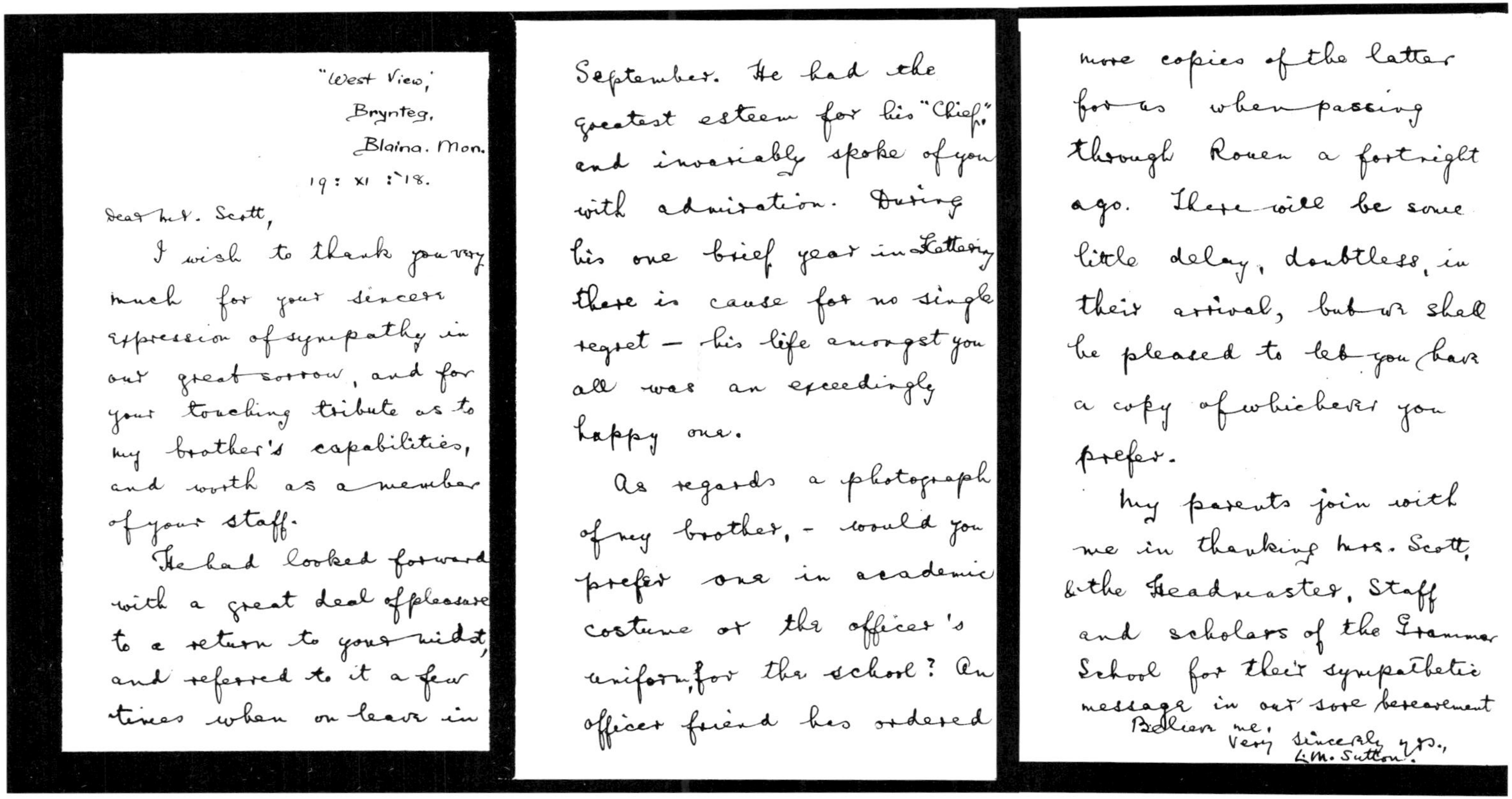

"West View,"
Brynteg,
Blaina. Mon.
19 : XI : '18.

Dear Mr. Scott,

I wish to thank you very much for your sincere expression of sympathy in our great sorrow, and for your touching tribute as to my brother's capabilities, and worth as a member of your staff.

He had looked forward with a great deal of pleasure to a return to your midst, and referred to it a few times when on leave in September. He had the greatest esteem for his "Chief," and invariably spoke of you with admiration. During his one brief year in Kettering there is cause for no single regret — his life amongst you all was an exceedingly happy one.

As regards a photograph of my brother, — would you prefer one in academic costume or the officer's uniform, for the school? An officer friend has ordered more copies of the latter for us when passing through Rouen a fortnight ago. There will be some little delay, doubtless, in their arrival, but we shall be pleased to let you have a copy of whichever you prefer.

My parents join with me in thanking Mrs. Scott, & the Headmaster, Staff and scholars of the Grammar School for their sympathetic message in our sore bereavement.

Believe me,
Very sincerely yrs.,
L.M. Sutton.

Miss Sutton's Letter

CHAPTER 5

The Best of Times, The Worst of Times, 1915-1932

Harold Tailby (told to Rex Moore)

This is an account of schooldays at the Kettering Grammar School between 1915 and 1920. It is made up from notes taken from Mr Harold Tailby of Desborough on 23rd December, 1994, when he was a spritely 90.

As a scholarship boy Harold was able to obtain tuition, books and train fare from Desborough, all free. School dinners, in the dining room at the top of the School, were subsidised.

These dinners were the only legitimate time that contact was allowed with the High School, then under the strictly enforced ''no fraternisation policy'' of the Headmistress, Miss Bristol. At lunch times the girls sat on tables at one end of the room, the boys the other. It was a favourable enough situation for him to make eyes at one girl, however, who was sufficiently impressed to provide his first romance.

The School in Bowling Green Road had only just opened and initially the Head, J. I. Scott, was without a secretary and was often seen carrying piles of paperwork about with him. One day the inevitable happened. A boy, ignoring the school rules, rushed along one of the corridors and cannoned into J. I. Scott. Papers and books went everywhere and the reader can imagine the consequences for the pupil.

The war had brought about an influx of lady teachers and one in particular was remembered for making English stimulating and interesting. To this day he remembers the lady well, a Miss Chalmers, and was able to identify her as Lady Macbeth in the photograph of the School Play of 1916.

Throughout the interview he was able to quote not only pieces of English literature he remembered, but also a considerable amount of Latin. He and a friend, Underwood, were chosen to play an adaptation of Edward German's *Merrymakers' Dance* as a piano duet, for a speech day. They were initially reluctant to become involved, because a successful recital would possibly mean playing the hymns in Assembly. ''Thankfully,'' he said, ''this didn't come about.''

Like most teachers, even J. I. Scott failed to see the ambiguity of certain statements he made, which pupils make the most of. Harold recalled the

The Cast of Macbeth *1916, with Harold Tailby's Miss Chalmers as Lady Macbeth.*

occasion when the boys had dug up the grass on the site where the tin huts later stood. This was for the purposes of planting potatoes for the war effort. Their efforts had not been very successful and admonishment came in Assembly, "When you turn the turf over, you must bury the sods."

It would seem that corporal punishment was prevalent, although only administered by the Head. More than an aggregated two hours' detention brought upon the unfortunate pupil "six of the best". This usually took place on Thursdays, nicknamed by the boys "Cosh Day."

Mr Tailby collected three canings. Two he accepted, both for breaking school rules. The third occasion had a flavour somewhat reminiscent of the H. E. Bates incident reported in his autobiography. As mentioned earlier, Mr Tailby travelled from Desborough to Kettering by train. There were no reliable buses then, so it was necessary to catch the 7.15 train in the morning and the 4.15 back in the afternoon. It was on the return journey, when the young Harold was in the Fourth Year, that the following incident occurred. Several junior boys were playfully fighting, using satchels as weapons. As things got somewhat boisterous, one satchel knocked a paper out of the hands of a reading traveller. The gentleman took exception to this and duly wrote to the Headmaster. There was no problem recognising the boy's school, as he was in school uniform.

The incident was investigated and, eventually, Mr Tailby stood in the Head's office to be asked why, as a senior boy, he hadn't put a stop to the proceedings. Young Tailby protested it wasn't really his job, as he was neither a prefect nor monitor. A lecture on responsibility eventually evoked a perhaps petulant comment from our "hero", that if he was to have responsibility

KETTERING
GRAMMAR SCHOOL.

A PERFORMANCE

Of SHAKESPEARE'S

MACBETH

in the

SCHOOL HALL, KETTERING.

ON

FRIDAY & SATURDAY, Dec. 15 & 16.

The Proceeds will be divided between the Kettering V.A.D. Hospital and the School Cadet Corps.

— DRAMATIS PERSONÆ. —

DUNCAN,	King of Scotland.	Reginald W. Tompkins
MALCOLM,	Sons to Duncan,	Frederick A. Neale
DONALBAIN		Frederick G. Yorke
MACBETH,	Generals in Duncan's Army,	Harold L. Cheney
BANQUO,		Ernest G. Brewer
MACDUFF,	Noblemen of Scotland.	Ernest E. White
LENNOX,		Charles S. Hoyles
ROSS,		Richard Williamson
MENTEITH,		Frederick G. Yorke
ANGUS,		Harold Abbott
CAITHNESS,		George C. N. Fountain
A Lord,	... ...	Wallace E. Panter
FLEANCE, Son to Banquo,	...	Thomas R. Hodson
SIWARD, General of English Forces,		Sydney E. Smith
Young SIWARD, his son,	... ...	Ernest A. Timson
SEYTON, officer attending Macbeth,		Joseph G. Avery
Doctor,	... ...	Arthur W. Thompson
Sergeant,	... ...	George C. N. Fountain
Porter,	... ...	Sydney E. Smith
Old man,	... ...	Arthur W. Thompson
Messenger,	... ...	John E. Percival
Boy, Son to Macduff,	... ...	Sidney Ferguson
LADY MACBETH,	... ...	Miss M. Chalmers
LADY MACDUFF,	... ...	Thomas R. Hodson
Gentlewoman attending Lady Macbeth,		S. Ralph Warren
1st Witch,	... ...	Cecil L. Burton
2nd Witch,	... ...	Harry L. Fifield
3rd Witch,	... ...	Samuel J. Curtis
HECATE,	... ...	Ernest A. Timson
1st Apparition,	... ...	Kenneth T. Garner
2nd Apparition,	... ...	... Ernest Parker
3rd Apparition,	... ...	Ernest C. Smith
1st Murderer,	... ...	Leslie F. Hales
2nd Murderer,	... ...	Reginald G. Lenton
3rd Murderer,	... ...	Frank N. Charles

Kings. Soldiers. Attendants.

CONDUCTORS OF ORCHESTRA { MR. A. H. ESSAM, A.R.C.O.
MR. H. CURTIS.

The Programme for Macbeth *1916*

in the future, he'd better be made a prefect. At that, J. I.'s patience gave out and Harold received the cane. To this day, he feels it was unjustified.

The final part of the story probably mitigated any possible bitterness. On the return train that night he, and his friend Bernard Esden, seized the guilty junior boy, stretched him across the carriage and gave him a good hiding with the leather strap used in those days to open and close the carriage door windows.

An interesting fact came out when he was asked about the Sixth Form. He said that it existed, but many of the boys were pupil teachers then. They would go into local Elementary and Junior schools on Tuesdays and Thursdays to teach and the other three days would be given over to teacher training. He remembered several senior pupils who eventually became masters in local schools.

When shown photographs of soccer teams of his time (soccer being the

Frederick Wallis: Entrant to the School in 1917. A contemporary of Harold Tailby.

School winter game then) he was able to put names to most of the faces. Edgar Towell and Peter Wilson were among them. He knew H. E. Bates reasonably well, as he used to come to Desborough and stay with his friend Esden. This was when H. E. Bates was courting Connie Ginns.

When he left in 1920, Harold somewhat reluctantly went into the family building firm. He carried this on successfully until his seventies. His son Ian, who also went to the School, is a teacher and indeed was on the staff of the Boys School for a time. Mr Tailby himself was a Governor of the Grammar School for several years in the 1970s.

He looks back on his time at the Kettering Grammar School with some fondness and was a member of the Old Boys' Association for many years, until age somewhat curtailed his activities.

F. G. Holland

I entered Kettering Grammar School as something of a shrinking violet in the September term 1922; my education pedigree was undistinguished. Prior to my entry, I had attended a nearby Council School which, while being only remotely reminiscent of Dotheboys Hall, had absorbed one of its characteristics. My memories of that establishment – the Council School that is – were painful. One of its principles seemed to be inculcating knowledge either through the buttocks or via the palms of the hands.

My entry into my new School was quite different. It was one of freshness and surprise, triggered by the prophylactic aroma of floorpolish, and the shine on the linoleum in the entrance hall. On its walls hung two framed mottos: "Non Sibi" and "Manners maketh man". Having as yet no Latin, I did not understand the former, but wondered vaguely if there was not something wrong with the spelling of the latter.

The implementation of the Education Act of 1901 was in its comparative infancy. Under its terms, Elementary and Secondary Education were vested in Local Authorities, i.e. County Councils and Urban Authorities. Thus came the emergence of the terms, "Council", "Central", and "Grammar" Schools. The latter were fee paying schools, but with 25% of the available places set aside for the budding scholars who had passed the appropriate examination, which I had not. I was supported by my parents, and having thus proved that I had no claim to intellectual eminence, felt no great slur upon my character to be placed in the lowly air of Form 2B. Form master W. R. Rees. From that point on, I was to realise that the teaching, the attitude of masters, and the general atmosphere of the classroom was very different and much more agreeable than in my previous school. The feeling of constant fear had gone; at times there was laughter in the house, and lessons became fun. As I look back, it was thus that the fundamentals of real education were in evidence, and the seeds sown (at least for me) to absorb what was taught, and at times voluntarily to go beyond that in private research.

My first report showed, to my surprise, that I had taken 2B by storm and had earned a promotion for my third term to the dizzy heights of 2A. This almost reckless force of "lift-off" continued, as for the next year I was catapulted into 3A. From thence, by steady, if unspectacular, progress the sparks of my endeavours flew ever upwards and (except for one painful hitch, which I shall deal with later in the confessional), I managed to keep a place somewhere in the top quartile of the form.

I hope readers will bear with me if I resort to anecdotes which emerge from the shades of memory, but which may nevertheless help to paint a polka-dot picture of the School community as I recall it. Certainly they feed the devotion I still feel for it.

Here is Mr Whitmore (French 2B) explaining a principle of French grammar, namely the use of "de" with the negative verb. "For instance," he said, "Let us take our own current National Anthem." (1922 please recall) "Oui, nous n'avon pas de banane." 2B saw the joke and I have remembered it as an illustration of the power of anecdote to defy the ravages of time.

On the same subject, Mr Tynan, all hard crust outside, and all marshmallow within. He of the tattered gown and fearsome, black book of non-permitted "howlers" was taking us through the Aesop Fables, English into French, in a round-the-form, boy-to-boy translation. It was Georgie N. who drew the short straw. The rest of us had placed the crow at the top of the tree with the cheese in its mouth and the fox below. Georgie, I recall, launched into what he imagined to be a cinch and sailed in confidently to disaster. "Le fromage," he confided in us, "était dans the corbeau's bouche." Tynan's howl of anguish must have been heard in the Cattle Market across the way. But in Georgie's favour, it must be recorded that he had the sweetest of cover-drives.

Now to the Sciences (not my strong suit) and the good-natured Mr Roland Whitney. He did his gentle best to guide us through its mysteries, with only limited success in my case. But I had, and still have, a feeling of sympathy for him. I am sure he was hot stuff on theory, but had not quite the same gift in practical demonstrations. So often they didn't work and he would offer the inevitable apology: "What should have happened is this . . ." There were sniggers, of course, as boys will be boys and sometimes not particularly attractive at that. But Mr Whitney did have one telling success, amounting almost to a schoolmaster's revenge. He lined us up in front of the demonstration bench, asked us to join hands, (in itself an act of dubious taste), and set a curious machine to work. It was the Whimshurst Machine, the engendering of static electricity its forte. Touch one brass knob against another, and bingo! The charge was no longer static, but tore out our stomachs on its mad rush to earth. There were the inevitable cries of relief from the victims, but there was one other result indelibly lined upon the tablet of my mind. The angelic smile on Roland's face, as he had, perhaps, a thought of having wiped the slate clean.

Also mixed up in this porridge of scientific terms were ''moments'' and ''inertia'', ''ergs'' and ''ohms''! Our tutor certainly had his moments, and his charges more than enough of the latter. In depressed moments, I sometimes have the vague feeling that the ''ergs'' and ''ohms'' may still be swanning around in my bloodstream, with heaven knows what effect upon my fragile frame.

In the interest of strict historical record, I must now enter my confessional. The Upper Fourth was to be the nadir of my career to date; the time when a local Icarus came down to earth with a bump, with wings clipped if not singed.

Whether it was the bewilderment of adolescence generally, or the distraction of the short-skirted, blackstockinged nymphs buzzing in the beehives of the premises next door, or my concentration on sport, I do not know. Perhaps a measure of all three. But I fell from grace, as my obvious lassitude did not escape the notice of G. Hopkins Esq, my Form master and Maths teacher. He recorded his displeasure in my term's report as follows: ''This term's work has been unsatisfactory; he has been lethargic and inattentive in class, and his written work has been untidy and inaccurate.'' No one could have spoken more plainly, and it did not escape the eagle eye of J. I. Scott M.A. I was accordingly invited to his inner sanctum on the ground floor to be told bluntly that, if I showed no improvement in the following term, there would be no rugger for me, and no cricket either. I already had a cricket ''cap'', but the prospect of a receding rugger ''colour'' (of which I harboured only a faint hope) was a turn of events I had not imagined. This, with the pain I saw in my parents' eyes, was enough to compel me into remedial action. In that Summer's vac, I got down to it in a hectic attempt to make amends. That time I had at most only a rudimentary acquaintance with Milton, and it was some time before I learned what it was that caused us to scorn delight and live laborious days.

The ''fame'' in my case was the possibility of a rugger ''cap'', and the rehabilitation of myself in the eyes of my masters to some measure of intellectual respectability. That is what, in effect, it did. As I look back to the severe strictures of Mr Hopkins, I see that he did me a signal service; had he not done so I might have been fated to see myself as the great Bernard Shaw saw himself. Self-proclaimed idiot, he was twenty-two before he realised that the symbols A+B were not shorthand for eggs and bacon. Mr Hopkins, however, had turned me out numerate enough to enable me to retire as Treasurer to a large group of hospitals in the North of England, following 23 years in the National Health Service, which I joined at its inception.

I do not expect many of my readers will be sitting on the edge of their seats in an attitude of expectant excitement as to whether or not I did get

''The situation of the School helped. It had the fine Perpendicular Church on one side and the cattle market on the other.'' (S. P. House).

a rugger ''colour''. The answer, simply, is ''Yes I did'', thanks to the watchful eye and concern of W. R. Rees the Games Master. I write this as a tribute to his skill as a teacher and his eye for the lad who, while having some promise, was nevertheless in need of concentrated conditioning. I was such a one. I had been blessed with some fleetness of foot; I could run, and score, but I could not tackle. And my nose has taken an upward shift from the blows I suffered from the succession of perfectly delivered ''hand-offs'', because I did not sink low enough to impede. W. R. Rees took me out of ordinary games on to a practice field, and with the aid of Ewart Flood (who was to become my inside centre) taught me the technique. I suppose that is one of the most important events of my life. The sinking violet began to win through, and that ''cap'' was just about the most treasured possession I ever had.

That shy boy who came into the School to the scent of floorpolish, vividly recalls the manner of his departure. A cold chill about his shoulders and sadness in his heart; a sense of loss; a newer nakedness, with forebodings of the challenges of life that were to come.

The economic depression of the late 1920s and the early 30s was looming.

As I began to write these memories in 1994, the Normandy Landings were in full rehearsal and I am tempted to write about those of my years who did not return. But I must have regard to the constraints of space, and will mention only the two friends most close to me in the latter years. Bill Burchell, who went down in the Atlantic as Captain of one of the first Liberty ships crossing at that time. Also Colin (Beefy) Panter, who survived the war in the Intelligence Corps only to die an untimely death as Librarian to the Borough of Kettering. Finally, the most important name of all – Edmund Kirby – lifelong friend, encourager and adviser, who instilled into me a love of literature in its many forms. The wonderful solace of my old age.

Stephen P. House

K.G.S. on your cap badge.

''Kettering Gutter Snipe,'' jeered the mockers.

Rumoured to be a school of Elizabethan foundation; it was neat, new red brick when I entered with a free place in 1924. One side for girls, 250 strong, the other for boys, all 11+, a wall between the sexes, but a large central hall used by both for Assembly, gym and theatre.

My parents, both teachers, had begged me off school for ill health until age 10. They sent me out to read by myself in the fresh air of the hedges. At 11 I was to have four years of work in class. At 15 most of my mates went off to work. Only three or four remained, to prepare for teacher-training, or other form of college. For me, it was henceforth independent study with teacher/counsellors to 18. Then another year to teach myself German. No teacher knew it.

Apart from five years classroom, I was at 19 a self-educated youth and ready to teach myself – with tutors once a week – at Oxford. Ready to teach myself other languages, other disciplines, in 25 years Foreign Service, 27 years as life insurance agent and 6 years as poet and essayist.

The quondam Head Boy of Eton, Sir David Scott, lived at Boughton House, five miles from K.G.S. When I joined the Foreign Service in 1936, he interviewed me – he was Head of Personnel. The Head Boy of K.G.S. felt at ease with the Head Boy of Eton. We both had self-respect and respect for others. I learned this from my family and also at K.G.S.

I respected Flood, the dashing three-quarter, Barritt, who tackled always at the knee, Morris the full back, who went berserk and ran the length of the field to score.

I respected the masters. Scott, the Head, prematurely old, who looked a bald fuddy-duddy, yet could be so wise and affectionate. The great E. E. Kirby, whose annotated *Chanson de Roland* I still treasure. He did much to foster the County's self-respect. Tynan, his French phonetics a help in other tongues. Wood, who made Latin gracious. Hopkins – all his students shone at Maths; he made it so easy.

1st XV – 1931-1932

Back Row (L. to R.): Mr J. Ashworth, R. L. Lyne, R. Snary, B. Kirby, F. C. Elliot, G. A. Sisman, A. L. Avery, H. A. Kilborn
Middle Row (L. to R.): W. J. Barber, G. S. Morris, S. P. House (Captain), H. W. Clement, E. J. Rice.
Front Row (L. to R.): G. W. B. Wager, R. O. Barritt, R. W. Hill, A. W. Hodges.
"The best of times" for the Captain, Stephen House.

I respected our institutions. The annual Shakespeare play, put on by Godfrey, later Mayor of Kettering . The Debating Society, where you learned not to fear to speak out loud. Our playing fields, two miles away, where everyone did something.

We were all brought up in right prejudice and sound taboo. There was character. We were poor and down to basics. The situation of the School helped. It had the fine Perpendicular church on one side and the cattle market on the other.

There was affection. Kirby had tears in his eyes when I left. There was conscience. My most arresting moment was when a boy – whose name I forget – refused to fetch the detention book for Tynan in an irritable moment. ''Sir, I have done nothing wrong,'' he said and did not budge. Tynan thought better of it.

Conscience applied to girls. Also we wondered from the other side of a wall. If they were too daring, the Headmistress took away their hatband. We boys had no money, no car. It was Depression. We were two-shirt boys, our bikes were second-hand and cost five pounds. No room for swagger. If we did not apply ourselves to books, there was no future for us.

I remember fondly three or four old flames on the other side of the wall. Luckily my enslaver lived three hundred miles away and was engaged to a heavyweight boxer. She was five years older than her mooncalf admirer – me.

''Youth should be educated to endure hardship and to pursue excellence,'' says Aristotle. K.G.S., 1924-32, gave me that training. Was it a good School? No, for me it was the best.

G. P. Dickins

My first day at K.G.S. in 1924 is powerfully impressed on my mind. Curiosity, apprehension and wonderment are natural in an 11 year old, when his school world is suddenly changed and he is launched into a new and unknown adventure.

There were 30 or so new boys marshalled in the entrance area, slightly bewildered and assailed by the faint odour of sweaty plimsolls coming from the adjacent locker-room. Boys were everywhere; all was chaos, until it suddenly went quiet. The boys had gained their destinations and the doors were closed. It was then that I saw the words ''Non sibi'' in a frame on the wall. Clutching my new shoe-bag to my chest, I mustered enough courage to ask the prefect in charge of us what it meant. A hint of perplexity shadowed his pudgy face, but then he brightened and replied with a superior smirk, ''Don't spit.'' Odd! How could anyone sink so low as to spit in these hallowed corridors. I was a slow learner. It took a year of Latin to tell me I had had my leg pulled; was it by schoolboy humour or schoolboy ignorance? I shall never know.

Old Cytringanians – 1931-32
A young George Dickins in the back row.
Back Row (L. to R.): S. N. Allen, C. W. Elliott, G. F. Marlow, G. P. Dickins, R. J. Robinson, R. A. Cooke, N. F. Bryant, L. Axe,
Front Row: (L. to R.): L. J. Newman, B. A. Brown, e. g. Groat, M. J. Miller, A. O. Mason (Capt.), W. H. Cox, A. Ball, A. J. Clarke

I cannot claim to have met many famous people in my life – two at the most. The first was on that same day.

We were allocated lockers that morning and I found that my neighbour was a senior boy who was helpful and approachable. During the next few weeks our infrequent meetings sponsored a friendly rapport between us, though my memories of him are very cloudy. After all, at that time I did not know he was to become a famous author, and neither, I suppose, did he. It was, of course, H. E. Bates. Sadly for me, he left shortly afterwards. That was my first brush with fame. The second was with Field Marshal Viscount B. L. Montgomery, but that is another story which has no place in this book. In any case, I would prefer to forget it.

Mr J. I. Scott M.A. was the Headmaster during my years at K.G.S. He was a small man with a powerful right arm. He was deadly with the cane, as I found to my cost – twice.

There was one equation which the most limited intellect understood: three detentions in one week equalled one caning of six strokes. The bonus from this knowledge was that the caning cancelled the detentions, with the result that he who had collected two detentions desperately tried for a third.

My third was collected through Mr Tynan, for disrupting the class. We were reading Molière's *Le Bourgeois Gentilhomme* when, being something of a musician myself, I commented that Molière's music master was more interested in money notes than musical notes. I did not, and still do not, think it was funny, and anyway it was the truth, but the class thought it hilarious. I was marched off to the Head and received my punishment, surprisingly tempered by a whispered apology that he had to do it because it was "the rule." That showed the compassion of the man, and for me the Dow Jones Index never rose as sharply as did his on that day. He knew that Mr Tynan and I were not the best of friends.

My second caning arose through a misunderstanding in the playground. The last boy who threw or kicked a ball out of bounds must retrieve it, even when, as in my case, it lodged in the guttering of the rain shelter. I shinned up a support pole and inched my way, hanging on the guttering, to the ball, and had just reached it when down came the ball, the guttering and myself. Damaging School property was an offence which required instant attention, and I got it, without an apology this time.

Nevertheless my respect for the "Old Man" never waivered. If anyone other than my parents had a beneficial effect on my character, it was he. He only once did something for which I could not forgive him, but that was much later, in 1944. I returned home from the Western Desert and paid him a courtesy call which resulted in being asked – or was it ordered? – to talk to some boys about the campaign. He assured me it would be to the Fifth or Sixth Form. I pictured myself sitting on a desk in a form room chatting to a small group. The reality was that he had assembled all 360 boys and the masters in the Assembly hall, and I had not prepared any notes. I think I made a fool of myself that day. I never saw the "Old Man" again.

Going back to 1930, when I left the school, he pressed me into becoming the Secretary of the Old Boys Association, which I was for five years. He was the President, and my mandate was to get something going of a sporting or sociable nature. Consequently, I had a hand in designing the colours of the tie which have survived to this day, the Rugby Club, Tennis Club, a Debating Society and the Hygram Players. I was therefore in close contact with 'J.I.' for a further five years and wished it could have gone on for ever.

CHAPTER 6

H. E. Bates

Form 5B, 1920

Back Row (L. to R.): Harris, Bell, Peggs, Esden, Bates, Pearson, Smith
Front Row (L. to R.): Payne, Cooke, Collins, Hoskings, Knight, Reid, Rimmington.

In Chapter Eight of his autobiography, *The Vanished World,* H. E. Bates described his acute sense of injustice and disillusionment after being punished by J. I. Scott. In the previous paragraph he had referred to his fondness of, and skill at, football: he played for the 1st XI at the age of 14. He also mentioned his love of cricket and tennis and how at one time he collected prizes in both the Open and Under-15 100 yards in one afternoon. In Chapter Ten he remembers, with affection and gratitude, the impact of being taught by Edmund Kirby. To commemorate his time at K.G.S., we include examples of Bates's early writing, previously published in rare editions of the *School Magazine,* and thus probably unknown to most readers.

JOHN CLARE: THE PEASANT POET (1793-1864)

In the little village of Helpston, between Stamford and Peterborough, John Clare was born in July 1793. His home was a mere hut, wretched almost beyond description – "more like a prison than a human dwelling." When quite a child he was sent to work in the fields and for some years he rarely left his occupation as a labourer.

It was when he was thirteen years of age that he showed signs of being a poet. He read Thomson's *Seasons,* and almost immediately after began to write verse. This consisted mainly of poems jotted down on odd pieces of paper. Shortly after this he ran away from home and for some time led an errant life, living occasionally with gypsies, and picking up a living as best he could. In 1820 he married Martha Turner, the "Patty" of his poems.

Just after his marriage Clare became almost a beggar. His few remaining guineas had gone in printing a prospectus for some of his poems and he was forced to claim parish relief. By good luck his poems fell into the hands of Keats' publishers, who issued them almost directly. The success was immediate; Clare was taken to London and for a few weeks he had a wild, gay time. Lords entertained him and he found many admirers, but few friends. He returned to Helpston, finding himself with an income of £45 per year.

On that income he thought he could live without working. He bought books and did little except read or wander in the open fields. But people had forgotten John Clare. He no longer found success and those to whom he appealed for help turned a deaf ear and he found himself poor and miserable. He again went to London but he was still as ill and wretched as ever. He still wrote verses, now more copiously than ever in the vain hope of selling them for money to support himself and his family. Debts, however, accumulated, and his life was misery itself. Then, acting on the advice of a friend, he once more took to farming, and for a time seemed fairly prosperous. But again he fell sick and was given a little cottage three miles away from Helpston by one of his well-meaning patrons. Leaving his native place, however, was more than he could bear. He used to roam about, muttering incoherently and showing signs of madness.

A few years later he published a new book of poems called *The Rural Muse.* That, like others, had a brief fame and then fell quietly away. Clare had now become more eccentric than ever and it was at last decided to send him to a private asylum in Epping Forest. There he received the kindest treatment and was allowed to act with as much freedom as possible. It was while in the asylum that Clare wrote many of his finest poems. There seems to be a touch in these later poems that his earlier work lacks, – "a new joy as if he is at last at rest."

Although Clare was a simple peasant, his poetry was not wholly peasant poetry. He had a natural gift for writing verse and as he saw the things of nature he put them down. His work is full of everyday happenings, expressed in everyday language. He rarely realizes when he is "original or obvious" in his poetry. He is full of the simple things and he loves them as he loves little else. He writes, not ony as a clear observer of nature, but as a dear, close friend who knows her every way or whim. With this in mind, it is curious how the verse written in the madhouse is of finer quality than that written in his own native haunts.

Clare was probably one of the most destitute of all poets. The surroundings in which he was born were wretched, while in after life, if the surroundings improved, his own faculties deteriorated and his mind was gone. His life – the latter years especially, – is touched with pathos. *The lines written in Northampton County Asylum* are particularly pathetic and echo Clare's great distress. Evidently the time spent in this Asylum (the last twenty-two years of his life) was one of great loneliness. He laments this in these lines:

"I am! yet what I am none cares or knows,
My friends forsake me like a memory lost;
I am the self-consumer of my woes,
They rise and vanish in oblivious host,
Like shades in love and death's oblivion lost;
And yet I am! and live with shadows tost.

Into the nothingness of scorn and noise,
Into the living sea of waking dreams,
Where there is neither sense of life or joys,
But the vast shipwreck of my life's esteems;
And e'en the dearest – that I loved the best –
Are strange – nay, rather stranger than the rest.

I long for scenes where man has never trod;
A place where woman never smil'd or wept;
There to abide with my creator, GOD,
And sleep as I in childhood sweetly slept:
Untroubling and untroubled where I lie;
The grass below – above the vaulted sky."

That his poems should have got so far in English Literature is astonishing, written as they were, on odd pieces of paper. But they at least are free from insanity; we see no mark of madness in them. They are simple as the author. On May 20, 1864, his unhappy life came to an end and he lies buried at Helpston, under a sycamore tree; as he wished to be:

"The grass below – above the vaulted sky."

SUNDAY

I love the Sunday cool of trees;
My mother's fine blue dress
That is a loveliness

I love the old sweet hymn that's sung;
The lovely tale of Him
Who breathed in Bethlehem . . .

A wonder now if Christ my Lord
In all His holiness
Loved once my mother's dress.

1924.

EVENING

Let the sun set, the summer sun
Let the pines grow dark
Against the crimson sky;
Let the moon shine against the white birch bark,
Let the day die.

Let the purple of even fade away,
White grows the road
Beneath the moonlit sky;
Home goes the wanderer to his own abode,
Dear day, goodbye.

1921.

ARMISTICE DAY, NOVEMBER 11th, 1920

I lingered in that last resting-place,
I lingered and I then did dream awhile.
Methought I saw a lustrous wingéd host,
Come down from Heav'n, drest all in purest white.
They hovered gently o'er that dark and lonely grave
And from it took, in shrouded linen wrapt,
The body of a man. And then forthwith
With loving arms they bore it up, as though
Of precious gold it were. So up and up
They bore it, through a dreary pall of dark
Then through a blaze of light, and up and up
So seeméd they to go. The abbey then did fade
And melt away, but in its place there came
A ring of light, and in that ring there stood
A Warrior, clad in white, and Known to God.

CHAPTER 7

The Late 'Thirties

H. Keith Traynar

Some new entrants in 1936 may well have queried the advantages of transferring to the Kettering Grammar School. Walking to School wearing a new blazer and cap displaying the distinctive red and white emblems of K.G.S., they sometimes risked being ambushed by hostile groups from other schools to be verbally abused as a ''Kettering Gutter Scraper'', or having to recover their cap from its assisted flight into someone's garden. And what was so special about a classroom in a wooden hut, in which you breathed coke fumes in Winter and baked in Summer?

Those of us who lived more than a mile from School were allowed to cycle. Returning home for dinner meant four journeys a day in all weathers, with no major traffic hazards other than avoiding the trails left by cart-horses. Policemen, wearing spotless white gloves, efficiently controlled the flow of traffic at the Gold Street cross roads and, when necessary, at the top of Bowling Green Road.

There was an underlying code of trust and honesty amongst the boys. Bicycles could be left unlocked under the cycle sheds and outer clothing and PE gear in black slipper bags could be safely stored in the banks of open black-rodded lockers in the cloakroom.

The playground was common ground for all ranks. During the Winter, those of us who arrived early on a frosty morning would get slides going, ''uppers and downers'', to be lengthened and polished by growing numbers of leather soled shoes. When these ''pistes'' were perfected, various members of staff would happily join the fun and assess the assorted runs. In the Summer, a game of cricket on the School yard with wickets chalked on a wall, was open to all. Anyone who owned a tennis ball could take his chance to bowl out a member of staff, or the stars of the 1st XI cricket team.

Another great leveller was the annual rugger concert, presented in the School with appropriate staging and lights. This was the occasion for talented song writers, sketch writers, actors and singers to entertain, with bold, yet good natured items featuring various members of staff and some of the more notorious characters amongst the boys. There was never any malice and the

"The playground was common ground for all ranks" (H. K. Traynar). This photograph, taken by Mr F. Lawson from the Chemistry laboratory in December 1950, also includes the infamous classroom huts.

staff joined in the fun, just as they would participate in various out-of-school activities. For example, 'Joey' Ashworth would enthusiastically demonstrate tactics and skills at rugger practices; 'Pecker' Hopkins never feared taking on several boards at once at the Chess Club; Mr Coakes, a fine university boxer, who ran the boxing club, was quite happy and competent to take on all comers – good practice towards eventually becoming an Army Area Champion.

Two notable spectacles come to mind. One was freely available to all from the upper classroom windows every Friday morning – the weekly Cattle Market – very much an audio-visual (and olfactory) spectacle. The other was strictly limited and could be extremely costly: taking a short cut and trespassing "out of bounds" along the balcony during a High School PE lesson always guaranteed a visual treat. Perhaps some would nominate a third spectacle – the issue of stock by EEK during the lunch break. With good aim he could flight a new exercise book to the recipient from the occasional background of an open staff-room door, revealing ghostly shapes groping amongst piles of exercise books in a fog of blue tobacco smoke. The dangers of passive smoking were unknown in those far off days!

Although gas masks, Identity Cards and Ration Books had been issued and corrugated air-raid shelters were available from the Local Authority and were being assembled in back gardens, fears of an imminent outbreak of war never seemed to trouble boys intent on studies and games. However, during the school holidays in August 1939, under the leadership of 'Joey' Ashworth, various members of the cricket and rugby teams were asked to round up volunteers to assist with making sand-bags. Dressed in old working clothes, we would assemble each morning in the School yard where, near to the old wooden huts, mini mountains of sand had been tipped. Working in pairs, one holding the mouth of a sack open whilst the other filled it and then tied it, we must have filled thousands. We would all assist to load the bags on to a waiting carter's lorry, which then, with a small team of boys on board, would drive off to build protective shields around the doors and windows of the police station, hospitals and other important buildings. By the time that this task was being completed, trainloads of children with their teachers evacuated from London, began to arrive at Kettering Station. These parties needed to be met and escorted to reception areas, of which K.G.S. was one. Long crocodiles of bewildered children carrying their gas-masks and cases were led into the School hall, where they rested and were refreshed with chocolate digestive biscuits and warm drinks, before being led off in smaller crocodiles to be found accommodation in welcoming homes around the town.

I vividly remember sitting amid such a crowded hall on Sunday, the 3rd of September, 1939. Someone had fixed up a radio on the platform. At 11.00 a.m., whilst a nation held its breath, Big Ben, in unhurried measured blows, struck the hour. There was a pause and then, in unforgettable words, we heard Neville Chamberlain announce that we were at war with Germany. When the School re-opened for the Autumn Term a few days later, we were informed that as the building was to be shared with Walthamstow Grammar School, our lessons would be held during the morning session and theirs during the afternoon. The High School shared their building with the Dame Alice Owen School, and whilst we had little contact with the visiting boys from Walthamstow, some of the girls from North London made a lasting impression on a number of K.G.S. boys!

Fortunately, our afternoon games lessons continued as before and inter-school fixtures for both cricket and rugby teams were maintained. But there were other activities, not only on George Barrett's playing fields, but on Mr Bennie's farm fields. With accompanying members of staff we would walk up to Barton Hill to the same fields through which we would run in the annual Cross Country Race – which always seemed to have been won by Phil Clarke, the only contest being for 2nd, 3rd and 4th places. Through the Autumn we would pick potatoes, in the Spring, weed and hoe, and later assist with the harvest in various farms around Kettering.

I look back with deep gratitude for all that K.G.S. has meant to me – not just for the rich shared experience with good friends and great characters in the classrooms and on playing fields, adventures at weekends and during holidays, but for the stimulation of imagination and for a broader education for life which charismatic figures like Messrs Kirby, Hopkins, Tynan, Wood and Woodward transmitted beyond their specialist subjects. Nor must the less ostentatious 'Joey' Ashworth be forgotten, nor the inscrutable J. I. Scott, who drew this talented team around him. Although JI kept his distance, he knew more than we ever realised about our conduct and progress, He, it was, who imprinted on all our minds the rule that "Manners maketh man" and whose last words to every boy at the final Assembly were contained in Romans, chapter 12.

Latin

Allan E. Baker

When I sat the Scholarship exam on that long-dreaded Spring morning in 1935, I hadn't the slightest expectation of shining in it. My handwriting was poor and, although I knew my tables (one never got the chance to forget them), my arithmetical reasoning powers were shaky.

I remember two questions only.

The first was about a dealer in shirts and socks. He had bought some shirts at 19s. 11d. each and had sold them for £1. 3s. 9d. He had then bought some socks at 4s. 5d. a pair and had sold them at the same percentage profit. How much had he sold them for? I took the 19s. 11d. from the £1. 3s. 9d. and added the answer to 4s. 5d. I recall thinking the profit excessive but never questioned its accuracy.

The second was: "Write a composition on one of the following subjects."

The first of the following subjects was "My Favourite Christmas Present". I read no further. I was a fully paid up member of The Hornby Railway Company and a committed train-spotter. Trains were my life and I'd had the Hornby No. 2 Special clockwork tank engine for Christmas.

The handwriting was barely legible but the words of love tumbled off the end of my pen as fast as I could dip it in the ink-well.

I won a Special Place to The Grammar School.

The transition from Park Road Junior to the Grammar School was largely a painful one. From Five Stones, Conkers and Follow-On Marbles in the gutters between Wood Street and my home in Wellington Street to rugger scrums on those muddy, freezing pitches so tantalisingly near to Wicksteed Park and its Lakeside Railway. From amiable unsupervised Hop-Scotch to terrifying vaulting horses and 'Joey' Ashworth. From happy home-times with Hornby Trains to homework.

But it was the Latin that kept me going.

Form 2A was in one of the huts at the back of the playground and it was there that I had my first Latin lesson. It was conducted, oddly enough, by the Headmaster himself. His twitching, tooth-brush moustache and bitter bark had me trembling with fear, but this new lingo he was on about was pure enchantment. "Regina. Queen. Regina. O Queen. Reginam: Queen Accusative. Reginae: Of a Queen. Reginae: To or for a Queen. Reginā: By, with or from a Queen." It was like The Bobby Bear Club Secret Code in *The Daily Herald.* Only better.

'Weaky' Wood took over from Mr Scott, when I was promoted to 3A on the ground floor of the main School building.

All went well for a time. I was lapping up the syntax: the mumbo-jumbo of passives and deponents, ablatives and gerunds. The Thursday games afternoons were borne and when 'Joey' Ashworth gave me forty-five minutes detention for doing my Latin homework in the dry and warmth of the pavilion where I got to be as often as I could persuade my mother to write me "excuse" notes (or, if she wouldn't, wrote them myself), I merely grinned. I was happy.

Until A. .L. Smith passed me that note.

It was the last period on a Friday and pent-up weekend spirits were running high. 'Weaky' Wood had just introduced us to the fifth declension which, because it involved new words ending in ū, I was enjoying immensely.

The note, which had reached me, via Nym Ballard and Peter Rudkin, read as follows:—

Caesar adsum jam forte
Pompey aderat.
Veni aditi vos verri
Sic ova amat.

I wasn't amused. I took my Latin seriously and I wrote BALLS in big red crayon on the back of the note and passed it back. But 'Weaky' saw me pass it and intercepted it. There was a two-minute silence as he read it through (both sides) and then he went on with the fifth declension.

When the bell went I grabbed up my satchel but, before I could escape, an icy hand fell upon my shoulder.

''Did you write this, Baker?''

''Only the red bit, sir.''

'Weaky' studied the red bit.

It must be remembered that this was 1937. Only a year or two later the film version of *Pygmalion* had had us all gripping our seat arms in the Odeon breathlessly awaiting the unbelievable first-time appearance of a real swearword on a cinema soundtrack.

'Weaky' was shocked. He told me he understood that K.G.S. was reputed to stand for ''Kettering Gutter Scrapers'' in the uncouth mouths of certain local louts, but that he had never imagined that I would be the one to lend any sort of credibility to such a despicable slander. He was deeply disappointed in me. That was all he felt able to say. I could go.

I went and a sense of utter degradation went with me.

'Weaky', I expect, reading the note again after I had gone, grinned and forgot all about it.

I did neither. My delight in Latin had come to an end there and then.

It never returned.

Latin was relegated to the list of anathemas that included 'Pop' Godfrey's ''Warm Wet Winters,'' 'Reggie' Gladden's balances that, every time they squealed, were being hurt and 'Bennie' Woodward's ''Bourbongs''.

I managed a shaky pass in Latin in the Oxford School Certificate but failed it in the Higher.

When I was in the Sixth Form Mr Kirby introduced me to A. E. Housman. His terse pessimism was just my cup of tea and he became my hero.

Had Caesar not had that jam for tea I might well have become a Professor of Classics. Or a poet. Like Housman.

As it was I became a shift control engineer in a power station.

''There's one spoilt spring to scant our mortal lot.''

I didn't even get to be an engine driver.

CHAPTER 8

Drop An Aitch and All is Lost

Professor A. H. Halsey

We are grateful to Professor A. H. Halsey (K.G.S. 1933-39) for permission to include the following extract from his forthcoming autobiography (tentative title: *No Discouragement*) to be published by Macmillan in 1996.

England, like Scotland and Wales, occupies a space among countries in the spectrum of opportunity, at least in the first half of the twentieth century, where search for talent, especially male talent, has been absolutely poor but relatively good by comparison with Germany or France. And in England this talent search is impressive despite the reputation of the nation as the most class-ridden in the world. Priests and pedagogues have been the main agents of exploration, though some charitable noblesse oblige was also erratically to be found among the aristocracy and the gentry in some parts of the country. At any rate after the 1902 Education Act, it was possible for local authorities to award tuition-free scholarships to elementary schoolchildren at age 11 to transfer to secondary grammar schools. The scholarship possibly dominated life at the Corby Council (later to be called Rowlett) school because there was also a Rowlett Scholarship each year to pay for extras like the cap and satchel. I have to say "possibly" because I don't think I was at all aware of this until after the written exams. But one morning in the late spring of 1933 I was hauled out at assembly and invited to the platform to be told that I had come out top of the county. To be truthful, I don't remember the occasion. But my sister Violet, always a socially sensitive creature, remembers with acute embarrassment that my shirt was sticking out through a hole in the back of my trousers. A roll of honour was kept, framed, and hung in the school hall. The headmaster warned me that it could all be stopped if I didn't behave myself and gave me sixpence. There was in any case a second round of vivas held at the grammar school in Kettering, an imposing three storey revivalist classical building next to one of the most elegant spired churches in all England.

No adult ever explained the purpose of this further occasion, but I do remember it. There was a middle-aged lady with a moustache, upper-class

A Wartime Old Cytringanians XV. Prof. A. H. Halsey is on the back row.

Back Row (L. to R.): P. Baxter, A. Halsey, D. Joyce, M. Owen, M. Ireton, J. Chaplin, K. Collins. Middle Row (L. to R.): R. Dunkley, P. Ballard, D. Marlow, P. Rudkin, A. Bennett, P. Adams, A. Smith. Front Row (L. to R.): M. Godfrey, T. Holmes.

voice and face to match, as well as woollen stockings above flat-heeled shoes. She asked me what would happen if it started to rain and never stopped. I started my answer with the anticipation that our mother would be irritated because outside workmen could neither build houses nor till fields and I ended with our making boats and retreating to the hills and mountains. But I said I didn't believe in the question. Later I heard one of my father's Labour Party pals say to him, "What will you make of 'im, Bill? Leader of the Opposition?"

I thus began a double life, connected by the ever present railway, with eight miles between a home at one end and, a "seat of learning" at the other. They were in vital respects worlds apart. The School was seen by me as a sustained cultural assault on my family. You don't say "we was", and you modify your home dialect. You prefer Latin to Anglo-Saxon. "Manners Maketh Man" had been borrowed from William of Wykeham. There was some contemplative anticipation. Doctor Clapperton's house in a lane round the corner from our Avenue was a new but, as I thought then, imposing detached stone residence with gardens and a tennis court. I was employed casually to weed the flagstones at the back. As I worked with trowel and kitchen knife I tried to imagine what it would mean to "have an education." It was a weird and arbitrary game as I saw it, for there were plenty of able lads in the village and the sons of middle-class people were not different except that they spoke and dressed differently and were assumed to have elevated futures to follow from the present strength of the family purse which paid their grammar school fees, fares and for their clothes. Would I join them and, if so, what would I be? A teacher or a priest or a doctor or what? And how would my parents feel about it? It all became a bit clearer after I started the diurnal oscillation. The new things were the cap and blazer and satchel, rugby football, Latin, French and Maths in all its branches and all carried forward at a brisk pace in the fast scholarship form.

Class, I mean social class, suffused it all. It wasn't at all that I learned any new theory of genetic and environmental determinants of IQ. Cleverness or performance was the measure. But performance in what? As a soldier, a cricketer, in music hall or film, or making things for the family to use? These attributes were to be found in the village at least as much as in the narrower frame of the school.

Drop an Aitch and All is Lost.

It was a double life, rather like the old film in which Alec Guinness appears as a sea captain shuttling backwards and forwards between Gibraltar and Morocco and changing his personality and his wife and, of course, the photos on the cabin wall each crossing. Certainly the assault on my parental culture was there and was painfully felt. But photos are pictures and wives women wherever you go. And I knew that my parents were in the end superior to my grammar school masters.

One day, after the railway journey towards the end of my first year at the grammar school, I had a great shock. I was learning French and had assumed that this was one of the pictures on the cabin wall to be kept hidden so as not to appear to swank. My father suddenly appeared at the kitchen door to say to my mother, "il y a quelqu'un à la porte qui parle français". Mother laughed. I looked dumbfounded and my father walked round to the side of the house to carry on a rapid and voluble working-class conversation in French with a tramp from Normandy. I could hardly believe it, until it dawned on me that he had served for five years as a soldier in France. Most soldiers, as George Orwell pointed out, survived this long residential investment in their Continental education with nothing but contempt for all things European, except that they admired the courage of the Germans. But Bill was a clever lad and picked up the French language, in all its raciness and argot just by being there. My mother was never far behind. Apparently when she first visited her descendants in Canada, the grandchildren asked her if she knew any French. She promptly stood up and, with music hall aplomb, sang the *Marseillaise.*

My mother likewise could "reckon up". I noticed it on a visit to the village Public Hall where she went to the Whist Drive every Thursday evening, normally won, and always knew who held which card on the last round. "How do you know that, mum?" I asked. "If you don't know that, lad, you ain't paying no attention." She always assumed that cleverness was essentially a moral rather than a cognitive trait. If anyone said or did something stupid she was wont to say, "Well I reckon he's gorn out." Cleverness was always first cousin to cunning and if Chaucer is any guide has the same etymology.

The cut and thrust of debate and raconteuring in the house was superb. "When we was gels," my mother would begin with a great throng of children and grand-children around her, and then would follow some tale of fetching milk in a pail from Chalk Farm. But what interested me in the end was the structure and pronunciation of her first sentence, for it graphically captures the point that the ends of class combined against the middle. A great deal of her vocabulary was as if lifted straight from Nancy Mitford's lexicon of the U and the non-U. Looking glass, pudding, napkin, lavatory: all the words avoided by the middle classes. I once heard two actors from the Royal Shakespeare Company telling the story of how they had gone for a walk along the river at Stratford between rehearsals of *Julius Caesar*. They paused to pass the time of day with two apprenticed hedgers and asked them what they did. "Oh, we just rough hews 'em, the master shapes their ends," was the ready answer.

My mother followed her grammatical rules exactly. Every aitch was punctiliously dropped; every plural pronoun was inexorably followed by a singular verb if it was from the verb to be. "Gels" were pronounced in perfect conformity with aristocratic usage. There was no mechanical grammar school preference for Latinate expressions but instead, without ever having lessons in grammar or syntax, she would unerringly combine Anglo-Saxon with Latin for maximum effect. I learned the same linguistic style but had always to remember at which end of the ferry I was speaking: and they could collide.

A double life perhaps: but there were bridges as well as channels. Or perhaps here the ferry metaphor breaks down. You could say instead that School and home conspired to create confusion. Both ends urged us to ambition as workers by brain rather than hand. Yet though all my uncles were heroes, railway clerks were despised. Woodwork at School was essentially for duds just as Art and Domestic Science were for girls. Yet again the lower forms were for ''thickies'' and many of these were middle-class fee-payers. Brute strength was at a premium in the rugger teams. But cricket offered an escape into respected craft skills ruled by a gentlemanly code of conduct. And, again at the home end, *Newnes Pictorial Knowledge* (''the Volumes'') was revered along with John Bunyan and Charles Dickens and bought alongside the *Daily Herald* and the *People* on Sundays.

Hollywood cut across between the village and the School. Its films had a tremendous effect on the Christian and Classical education I was receiving. Most of the twice weekly offering was rubbish. But two features, later to be reinforced, deserve remark. The first was an atmosphere of perpetual populist optimism. We could make a bright future for everyone if only we had the resolve. I was late by at least half a century but a fervent believer in progress: and the goal was the new Jerusalem. The other was a sober recognition of the limits of popular culture. Most of it, as I have said, was American small town or western rubbish. Occasionally, however, something unusual arrived. For example, there was John Steinbeck's *Of Mice and Men* with Burgess Meredith as George and Lon Chaney as Lemmie and Betty Field as the farmer's daughter – all in sepia. I thought it was wonderful. But the village audience was restless and sniggered loudly at Lemmie's idiocy: they showed a coarse peasant insensitivity to unfamiliar frailty, which made me ashamed of my parochial identity. Once again I longed to escape.

Another heaven-sent influence was the English master at the Grammar School. E. E. Kirby was a most remarkable connecting teacher. In the first volume of his autobiography, H. E. Bates describes his own dreary and apathetic life at Kettering Grammar School during the First War. ''I longed most of all to leave the place and never see it again. But then,'' he goes on, ''in the autumn of 1919 the hand of Divinity moved again and something of a miracle occurred. Our instructress in English, a gaunt, carroty Scotswoman, under whom I had suffered in steadily mute retrogression of interest in that subject, had left us at the end of the summer term.'' I should interrupt Bates at this point to say that my father had come back to Kentish Town at the same time, having served as a private soldier in the Royal Berkshire regiment with Kirby. ''There eventually walked into the classroom a young ex-infantry officer who looked, facially at any rate, as if he had some difficulty in holding the chalk as he wrote on the blackboard, a fact not surprising since he had lost three of his fingers. Nevertheless the painful distortions of the face, already showing signs of healing from a disordered parchment map into something recognisably human again, couldn't conceal that here was a very English face, once good looking and still alert, kindly and unembittered by all the War had done to him. . . . If it is possible to change human vision, or at least to waken it by the stimulus or even shock of a single experience, then this is a perfect example of it. I do not think I am putting it too highly or too fancifully to say that in one morning in the autumn of 1919 I not only grew up; I grew up into what I was to be. Fanciful as indeed it may sound, I date my literary career from that moment."

I came as a scholarship boy to the School in the 1930s. Edmund Kirby was still there – the senior English master by that time among a stable staff (only one left in my five years) of provincial schoolmasters. He was a lean, austere but kindly figure in the Upper School. I was doing badly and had quarrelled already with the Headmaster, a small Liverpool and Oxford snob who taught some Latin and had caught me in the first term reading the *Magnet* in one of his mechanically soporific lessons. Then, when I was thirteen, Kirby came in one morning to teach my class and suddenly I knew the magic and majesty of the English tongue. He loved Sam Johnson. But he also loved a letter from the local cabinet maker which read, "Dear Sir, Your box is ready, Yours faithfully." There was nothing but contempt for the pretentiousness of "Thank you for your communication of the 30th ultimo . . ." Here for me was the perfect complement to my parents and the home kitchen. Nearly half a century later, with Kirby in his grave, I never write a sentence without being aware of his benevolently caustic interest. When I first talked to him after the War he told me candidly that he had had two pupils whom, he thought, were potential masters of the mother tongue. "One was H. E. Bates, and the other has been something of a disappointment to me".

There were, of course, other notable characters among the teaching staff. It is perhaps too little appreciated that grammar school masters and mistresses were pillars of society in provincial Britain. In Kettering the amateur Dramatic Society was strongly supported by them. The French master, Tynan, was an Irishman of outstanding talent. The Maths master, Hopkins, was a star of the county chess team. The History master, Woodward, was a well known local preacher. The Art master was a notorious communist. The School provided a way of life for them. They would take boys by coach to play rugby football or cricket as far afield as Bedford or Leicester. These sporting relations were largely confined to other state grammar schools, but very limited connections were allowed, for example, with Bedford Modern School (where I remember being asked in the shower, "Are you Stowe?", knowing that only nakedness and silence could have permitted such an error). Not until the war and then only for the Old Boys rugger team, was it possible for matches to be arranged with Uppingham or Oundle. It must have been frustrating and perhaps a little weird for youngish masters who had come

A section of the School photograph of May 1938. John Tynan, "an Irishman of outstanding talent," is fourth from the left.

to Kettering Grammar School with high honours from Oxford or Cambridge. Kirby was different. He had taken his degree externally at the University of London and saw himself as ineligible for the headmastership because of a social deficiency in his educational background and despite a war record of exemplary bravery. A rigid hierarchy of class was maintained both between the elementary and the grammar schools and between the grammar and the so-called "public-schools". The grammar school was, however, an indispensable social lever into mainly the lower-middle, but also for a minority into the middle-middle and even upper-middle professions.

All this is by no means to suggest that the sociologists are wrong in warning us against exaggerating the effects of education. The structure of learning gives the school a feeble and limited independence from the forces of class, race, status and gender which act upon it from outside. At the same time it also follows that the gifted teacher may also sometimes and dramatically illuminate an otherwise obscure world of learning for the fortunately responsive child. I do not doubt that an inspired teacher had contributed to a minority of those who have made their way into the intellectual professions from working-class origins.

How meritocratic was Kettering Grammar School? To answer, one must first place the School in the national system of secondary schooling which was developing between the wars and in which the transfer rate from elementary to secondary schools varied from less than one per cent in East Ham to more or less a quarter in a progressive Welsh county. I am leaving out here those who attended private schools of one kind or another – about 5 or 6 per cent and declining. In the 1930s Northamptonshire was transferring about 8 per cent of its eleven year olds. So obviously there was a vast waste of talent. Moreover and sadly, it was a further blight that refusals of offers of grammar school places would come to schools or education offices written in pencil on blue paper torn from a sugar bag. Poverty heavily loaded the dice.

There were the beginnings of a trend towards meritocracy: something was happening, but that something fell far short of a systematic genetic selection of the kind sought by some eugenicists. The system was eugenically faulty in every way. There was the inverse correlation between fertility and family income, a blindness to talent in the wrong ethnic clothes, wrong skin colour or wrong gender. Even today the class chances of children when expressed relatively, that is in terms of the gambler's odds of reaching an advantaged educational or occupational position from a particular social starting point, are what they were in my own youth. I don't mean that there have been no changes. Absolute educational chances have risen in all strata and sections. Women and ethnic minorities have improved their relative chances: and, most significant, the proportion of the population in working class jobs has been reduced dramatically in the last thirty years. Moreover some professions have always lain close to the curriculum of the examinations for entry to them (maths for mathematicians). But many advantaged jobs are controlled by other factors such as personality or family influence, so that privileged parents find ways of turning their privileges into opportunities for their own children even in a system which is nominally meritocratic. Class still counts.

CHAPTER 9

E.E.K.

John Wells

I sat the scholarship examination at Rothwell Gladstone Street School in 1938 and, to the surprise of my teachers, classmates and me, I obtained a free place at the Kettering Grammar School. I attended the School from September 1938 to June 1943 and I am very grateful for the education received during that period.

During my time at the School the high quality of education available to pupils was enhanced by the permanence of the teaching staff. Although the declaration of hostilities in September 1939 led to the sudden disappearance of Messrs Coakes and Gladden and, about two years later, that very gentle man Atkinson Blaxland, the remaining staff of Messrs Scott, Kirby, Whitney, Tynan, Hopkins, Wood, Woodward, Godfrey, Smith, Ashworth and Corke were in residence throughout my five years at the School.

The outbreak of war brought a drastic reduction in the facilities and accommodation available at the School, but my recollection is that the staff coped remarkably well and, while accepting that perhaps pupils are not the best judges of schoolmasters, I doubt if many schools had a more devoted or better balanced staff. None was regarded as a tyrant and most were well respected by the pupils.

After a few weeks at the School, we learned through the usual schoolboy channels that Mr Kirby had served as an officer in the Great War and had been badly wounded, and as my father had also served in France and Flanders, this helped develop my respect for him. In class, however, I do not remember Mr Kirby ever making direct reference to his wartime experiences.

One of our set books was *Poems of Today*, 2nd series, published in May 1922, and therefore not surprisingly containing a large section of poetry from the Great War. I remember well that during my years in the Fourth and Fifth Forms this part of the anthology received special attention from Mr Kirby and his boys. I am sure that I am not alone among his students of that era in still being able to recite all or parts of *Home Thoughts in Laventie*, *Before*

Edmund Kirby

Action, Into Battle, At the Wars, Back to Rest, The Volunteer, Fulfilment, Epitaph on an Army of Mercenaries, and others.

Mr Kirby was a fine example to his scholars; he was always smart of dress and appearance and carried his wounds with dignity. His lessons were interesting and informative and indicated that he had prepared his subjects with care. He never lost his temper, he was calm and chose his words carefully, and even young, unworldly schoolboys realised he was a man of great talent. I left the school before my sixteenth birthday and therefore missed the benefits of the Sixth Form and the opportunities of extending my education under Edmund Kirby's influence.

I saw very little of him for many years, but shortly before his death I met the late Jim Carr, at whose suggestion I visited Mr Kirby at his home and much enjoyed seeing him again. I asked him about his experiences on the Western Front during the Great War and, even at his then great age, he gave me a lucid and detailed account of the events leading up to his being wounded.

The Germans had established a machine gun post on the West Bank of the Canal du Nord and Lieutenant Kirby was ordered to take a patrol of the Royal Berkshires to investigate. He led his men along the system of trenches and suddenly came face to face with an enemy patrol. His last recollection of the event was of a German soldier preparing to throw a hand grenade.

On recovering consciousness, he found blood pumping from his face and seeping from numerous other wounds. His Sergeant lay dead at his side: his patrol and the enemy had disappeared. His thoughts were of his mother and her reaction on receiving the news of his death in action. He made himself as comfortable as possible and waited to die.

The surviving members of the patrol returned to their unit, where a brother officer enquired of Lieutenant Kirby's fate and was told that he had been killed by the enemy. The officer led the patrol back to the scene of the action to recover Kirby's body and discovered him close to death. He was carried on a ground sheet to the nearest casualty clearing station, where he was given immediate attention. In due course, he was well enough to be transferred to a base hospital and there suffered a serious setback. A conscientious night orderly on his rounds discovered him lying in a pool of blood following the haemorrhaging of his wounds. Happily, a first class surgeon was on call and saved his life. At this time, before blood transfusions became common, the further loss of blood was a serious threat to his life and it was necessary to raise the foot of his bed to ensure that an adequate supply of blood reached his brain. After long hospitalisation and convalescence, he was restored to something less than robust health and was eventually offered a post at Kettering Grammar School.

Some years after Mr Kirby's death, on a tour of the Western Front, I visited the Honourable Artillery Company British Cemetery at Ecoust St. Mein and, amongst several graves of men of the Royal Flying Corps, I found one bearing the name of Captain Auberon Thomas Herbert, who was killed on 3rd November, 1916. The years suddenly faded away and I was back in Form 5A with Mr Kirby and *Poems of Today*. Auberon Herbert was the airman whose death prompted his friend Maurice Baring to write the poem, *In Memoriam A H,* one much loved by Mr Kirby.

Auberon Herbert was privileged from birth. The son of Earl Carnarvon, he was educated at Bedford Grammar School and Balliol College, rowed in the Oxford Boat in 1898 and 1899, went through the South African War as *The Times* correspondent, was wounded and had a leg amputated. He took his seat in the House of Lords in 1905 and, by 1914, was a member of the Cabinet as President of the Board of Trade.

It would have been easy for him to have avoided taking any part in the Great War, but despite his disability he joined the Royal Flying Corps as a pilot, went to France during the Battle of the Somme and was subsequently shot down over enemy lines in November 1916.

We are all aware of some of the consequences of the Great War, the sowing of the seeds of the Second World War, the financial cost to our country, and the large numbers of maimed and killed. But surely the greatest price was the loss of so many men of outstanding qualities. How much poorer would Kettering Grammar School have been if Edmund Kirby had succumbed to his wounds in 1918.

The Dinner at the Overstone Country Club given by the Old Boys in honour of Mr Kirby.
From left: L: Smith, H. E. Bates, E. E. Kirby, P. A. Thornton, A. F. Scott, C. W. Godfrey.

CHAPTER 10

The Second World War

Sellick Norsworthy

The War Memorial designed by Mr Eric Loasby, F.R.I.B.A., *an Old Boy of the School.*

Inevitably the outbreak of the Second World War brought many changes to Bowling Green Road, not least the sharing of the building with two evacuee schools, the South West Essex Technical College from Walthamstow in the Grammar School "half" and the Dame Alice Owen School in the High School "half". The war years also saw feverish activity on the part of the senior boys who filled sandbags for the hospital, carried out fire watching duties, worked on the land, processed ration books and worked for the Post Office.

The evacuation of children to Kettering began on September 1st, 1939, with the first train arriving from London at 11.50 a.m. Some evacuees were put on buses for their journeys to outlying villages and schools, while boys from the Grammar School, acting as Reception Officers, escorted others, in groups of 50, to various destinations in and around Kettering. As two more trains arrived at 1.30 p.m. and 3 p.m. the boys repeated their escort duties, before wearily "knocking off" at 4 p.m. The evacuees continued to arrive the next day to be followed by two more trains on September 3rd. Although the boys on escort duty should have gone home at 4 p.m. many stayed on to meet the arrivals on the 6.30 p.m. train. All the Reception Officers were issued with special armbands, which were kept as souvenirs after it was all over. I wonder if any Old Boy still has one of those armbands today?

One pupil from Walthamstow, A. Gillingham, wrote in the School Magazine about his impressions of Kettering. He arrived utterly bewildered with all sorts of questions going through his head, the most important of which was how long he would be staying in Kettering. After settling in, he was surprised how big the town was, since he had been told that Kettering was a "small country town". He found Kettering very peaceful and very clean. To his joy he discovered a shop where nothing cost over sixpence! The School seemed small compared with his school in Walthamstow. He admitted to missing London, but wrote that he would never forget the kindheartedness and hospitality of the people of Kettering.

As soon as the school year began, the timetable had to be dramatically amended. Peter Hanger, quoted in Tony Ireson's book, *Old Kettering – A View from the 1930s, Book 3,* outlined the changes:

> "In September 1939 'Sergeant' Coakes and 'Reggie' Gladden went to the war, and we did not return to school until October because the air raid shelters were not completed. Then we attended only for an hour and a half on three mornings a week, virtually to be given homework. In November we began a regime of 8.30 am to 12.50 pm, Monday to Saturday, and the homework continued very heavy."

Games were played on two afternoons a week whilst the School was occupied by the pupils from London. It was not until after the Blitz, and the pupils from London had returned home, that afternoon school was reintroduced.

Inevitably many School activities had to be curtailed, whilst other duties took their place. For the first three years of the War the School Play had to be abandoned. Other casualties of the War were the Debating Society and the Rugger Concerts. Games also suffered badly in the early years. Several cricket matches had to be cancelled mainly because of the difficulties of raising a team. The First XI played ten matches but only managed to win one of them. The First XV also experienced setbacks, caused mainly by the severest winter that Kettering had seen in many years. No games were possible until early March 1940 and unfortunately the only two games played were both lost.

The War also brought to an end the annual camping holidays. However, during the summer of 1940, Messrs Ashworth, Godfrey and Phillips took a working party to a forestry camp in the Lake District. The boys assisted in the war effort by sawing pit props. Two Old Cytringanians, Brian Jackson and James Higgins vividly remember the camp.

Jimmy Higgins begins the story:

"It had long been the tradition for senior boys to go camping and climbing in the summer holidays, led by the popular games master 'Joe' Ashworth. The war put a stop to that. It was proposed that a work camp be arranged, and it was not surprising the camp was in the Lake District near Keswick, where we were engaged in cutting pit props for the princely sum of 6d. per hour. The location was ideal. We camped beside a stream on the Wilatter Pass, not a house in sight, and the village a mile away.

Accordingly some sixteen boys, complete with kit and the odd cycle and accompanied by 'Joe' Ashworth and 'Pop' Godfrey, entrained at Kettering Station. We had to change at Penrith for Cockermouth, where we were picked up by a lorry and deposited at the camp site."

Brian Jackson remembers many of the boys in that party. They included Roy Dunkley, John Stanley, Desmond Felce, John Peacock, Don Joyce and John Chaplin. Brian writes:

"The camping field was close to the work site and it sloped fairly gradually down to a stream at the bottom, to provide a cold morning wash."

Jimmy recalls that, "The tents were quickly erected, including the cook's tent in the charge of 'Pop' Godfrey, who was very popular. I won't say anything about his cooking!"

Brian also has something to say about the culinary skills of Mr Godfrey:

"Other fairly clear memories are of the food. 'Pop' Godfrey did the cooking and a particularly large boiled potato with of course its skin on, was given with the warning that the inside was probably not cooked. In the open air, after a long day, this did not seem particularly relevant."

A few days after the camp was established, a new member of Staff, Mr Phillips, arrived. Jimmy Higgins has a confession to make concerning this gentleman:

"Here I must plead guilty to giving him the nickname of 'Ghastly Gustave', later reduced to 'Gus'. I was reading P. C. Wrenn's books and this was the name of one of his characters. He quickly gained all our respect.

The work consisted of cutting trees into pit props, the length being determined by the diameter, e.g. 3ft×3″ and 5ft×5″. This was done with two-handed saws. The boys sat opposite each other with the tree between them and with a push-pull motion reduced it to pit props. They were then rolled to the road side and stacked ready for transport. (No one complained of repetitive strain injury). We worked from 7 a.m. until 2 p.m. with a 15 minute break about 10 a.m. or when the cook's assistants arrived with the cocoa."

It wasn't all work. Brian remembers the weekends:

"Saturdays and Sundays were all our own and Desmond, Jimmy and I set off by bicycle for Keswick. Freewheeling down the steep slopes into

Keswick, we failed to notice important uphill forks in the road so that, upon returning, we found ourselves on what seemed to be a mountain top, in the dark without lights. I have no recollection of how we got back to camp."

Sand bagging operations began with the arrival (in the school yard) of two lorries carrying soil. Boys from the Grammar School reluctantly "volunteered" and were joined by pupils from the South West Essex Technical College. Despite some grumbling, the boys were kept going with lemonade in the morning and tea in the afternoon, so that by the end of the day the pile of soil had disappeared. In its early stages the operation was chaotic, but gradually the process was rationalised, so that by the end of the day there was a sense of pride in what had been achieved. Masters set to just like the boys and acquired what was described as "a sweet disorder in the dress."

The arrival of soil and bags continued with monotonous regularity, but by dint of practice the boys got ahead of the deliveries to earn themselves longer and more frequent rests.

On the fourth day a mechanical digger arrived and on the following morning five lorry-loads of soil appeared. After that the boys steadily lost ground, as the pile "assumed massive proportions." However, it wasn't long before the pile grew less daunting and sand-bagging became "one of the natural functions of the body, like breathing."

At first, the sand bags were removed by lorries, which arrived now and again bringing with them new bales of sand bags. As the boys got into the swing of things, more vehicles had to be used and at one point a bus with its seats taken out was drafted into service.

A major contribution to the war effort made by the boys of the Grammar School, was their work on the land. One group who lifted potatoes reported that it used to eat lunch under a hedge in the traditional style and held pitched battles with crab apples before resuming work in the afternoon. Another group was involved in threshing, whilst a third cultivated the Technical School site in St. Mary's Road. Yet another group was involved in "beet banging" on a farm near Broughton. They picked up the ploughed beets, "banged" the soil from the roots and laid them side by side in rows down the field. The straightness of the rows seemed to have depended on how long the "banger" had been "banging"! Work stopped for lunch at 1 p.m. when the boys would plod wearily up the hill through the mud to their small black creosoted hut on wheels. They would then ride into Broughton to buy "pop and pork pies" and return to eat their lunch seated on sacks of chaff. Each day they awaited the arrival of a red faced farm worker, whom they nick-named the 'great High Lama'. Every day he would shout, "Shift aht o' my corner," and each day the boys would oblige, watching him eat huge chunks of bread and cheese with his rusty pocket knife and listening to his incredible tall stories.

Work ended at 4 p.m. after which time the boys were left to their own devices. Some ate sugar beet until it made their throats sore, others played ''conkers'' with two beets whilst others used beets to play ''skittles.'' For all of this the boys were paid the princely sum of 2s. 6d. a day!

One pupil describes three weeks of horse-hoeing during August 1940. He had two horses that only had two speeds – slow and very slow. One horse that kept treading on the boy's foot was referred to as ''the corn crusher.'' It also had a nasty temper and repeatedly tried to bite the boy's hand. He also rode a horse for two weeks during the harvest. When he was finally paid off, he reported being very sore in the ''region which is supposed to have a magnetic attraction for a headmaster's cane''!

Some senior boys were put to work in the Food Control Office, a depressing room with tasteless wallpaper and a circle of tables covered with Ration Books. The boys found themselves sitting beside piles of National Register forms and Ration Books, whilst the method of processing them was explained.

At first they experienced hesitant uncertainty in their work, but this was quickly overtaken by confident assurance. It was not long, however, before this changed to wearying boredom, relieved only in part by making fun of the names of the people with whose Ration Books they were dealing. Their other diversion from boredom were the visits of two ''guardian angels'', girls who were called in to help the boys with any difficulties they might have.

Another group of senior boys worked in the Post Office sorting office, during the holidays, alongside soldiers and ''centenarians''. The letters were brought round to them on wheeled trays, used by some including a certain D.L.J. (could this have been D. L. Joyce?) as personal transport. The sorting office was a most depressing large room, with an office at one end and a pay counter at the other. The floor in between was occupied by an elevated desk where the manager ''sat and glared'', several rows of letter racks and the noisy stamping machine. The most pleasant part of the day for the boys was the half hour tea breaks, when they could read their *Picture Posts.*

In 1943, forty senior boys helped at the Post Office during the Christmas period. They dealt with parcels of every description, including some mouldy parcels of lamb all the way from New Zealand! Between 2.30 p.m. and 6 or 7 p.m. the boys delivered between 50 and 100 parcels around Kettering. Other boys emptied letter boxes between 9 a.m. and 7 p.m. and then went on to sort letters until 9 p.m.

Fire watching duties were carried out by members of the Grammar and High School staffs, assisted by senior boys and girls. Some boys worked alongside their fathers, one night in every twelve, between the hours of 1 a.m. and 5 a.m. Many found it difficult to keep awake after the B.B.C. closed down at midnight and, not surprisingly, it was reported that the teapot was in constant use. One Grammar School pupil living in one of the villages described how he and his father took it in turns to patrol while the other took a nap. Often the quietness was frightening and they would freeze at the slightest sound, hoping that the ''Hun'' wouldn't spring out in front of them!

In September 1942, the Army Cadet Corps was re-formed under the command of Second Lieutenants Ashworth and Wood. Fortnightly parades were instituted and dummy rifles, used by cadets of the First World War, were again used for drill purposes. The basement of the main building was again fitted up as a rifle range and Second Lieutenant Kirby once more gave rifle instruction along with Lance Corporal Colvin. Training in aircraft recognition was given by ATC Sergeant Minney, map reading classes were taken by 'Joey' Ashworth and Cadet Cox, while signalling classes were given by Cadets Weeks and Brookes.

Throughout the war years, despite all the difficulties and disruption, there was a conscious effort to educate boys as normally as possible. In the School Magazine of 1941 a certain A.G.L. reminded everyone that, though wartime education was difficult, it was up to the individual pupil to maintain the high standards of the past. As if to underline A.G.L.'s point, in the same year D. L. Loake gained a State Scholarship and J. C. Ireson won an £80 Scholarship to Nottingham University. Both went on to gain high academic honours. In 1943 K. W. Mobbs won an Organ Scholarship to Clare College, Cambridge, whilst C. F. Griggs gained a well deserved Exhibition at Peterhouse just after the war. There were many other talented scholars who overcame wartime difficulties to go on to Higher Education: P. J. Blackmore and R. P. Dyson went to Birmingham, C. E. Newton and G. F. Howard went to London, W. L. Timmins and J. S. Cox studied at St. Batholomew's, J. E. Proctor went to Nottingham while G. R. Rawle studied at Bristol. There was success on the sports field too, as the First XV remained undefeated during the last two years of the war.

An unfamiliar aspect of the playground in 1939: digging the air raid shelter.

Allah Buksh

The question: ''Which was the most bustling, bizarre or unusual period in the history of the Grammar School in Bowling Green Road?'', would surely open a long debate, with protagonists pressing their claims, obviously relevant to their own experience.

But surely there cannot be a serious challenge to my own claim that the war years 1939-45 witnessed the greatest upheaval and the most radical inroads on the normal life of the Kettering Grammar School.

I arrived at K.G.S. in September 1941, a rather lost and alien soul, an evacuee from London.

It was a time of terrible and momentous happenings: British cities under nightly heavy bombing raids; the merchant fleet being slowly decimated by U-Boats; our armies suffering major defeats; the imposition of severe food rationing. Things could not have been much worse in the country.

My arrival was unique: as a scholarship boy from an evacuated school, I should have joined the appropriate school evacuated to Towcester. After consideration of my case by the education authorities, on a chilly autumn morning I recevied a TELEGRAM requesting my presence at Bowling Green Road. (A telegram was a means of supposedly fast communication in those pre-telephone days).

I have never ceased to believe it was some incredible mistake!

I joined the sons of local families, mainly middle classes. They were, I hasten to add, a wonderful bunch, with whom I soon felt at home.

And what a mixed group we were geographically. Several boys came from Corby, others from Rothwell and Desborough, Gretton, Cottingham, Stanion and Brigstock, Pytchley, Broughton and Burton Latimer. Others were from Pipewell, Walgrave and Geddington; one boy even came by train from Rushden. If nothing else, we soon learned the geography of the local district.

I think three of us were evacuees, but whereas I had come to Kettering with a London school group, the other two had come privately with their families and lived with relatives.

One peculiar wartime advantage, gained from being part of a mixed local group, was early news of happenings and incidents over a wide area. I remember hearing about a Doodlebug coming down at Creaton, near Northampton, which might otherwise have gone unnoticed, had it not been for a Walgrave boy bringing the information. Such incidents were much disguised and unreported in wartime newspapers.

The School's intake of 1941 became something of a highly sensitive intelligence unit that gathered information throughout WW2.

During this period there was another school using the building, The North London Polytechnic, who were best remembered for the violent snowball battles in which we became involved.

Their presence meant attendance and lesson times had to be adjusted and staggered. We attended for six mornings and two afternoons and presumably the Poly boys had two mornings and six afternoons. It seems to have coped with a very difficult situation, though I am sure studies suffered considerably from this fragmentation.

Our neighbours at the High School had to make provision for Dame Alice Owen Girls School, which had a large number of students. I remember my own particular favourite: a very attractive young lady with long flowing red hair, and how we broke school rules by sitting in the nearby Manor Gardens holding hands, swearing to comfort each other during those hard times. Our allegiance lasted just a few weeks, considerably shorter than the seventy four months duration of the war.

Surprisingly few people remember Dame Alice Owen's presence in wartime Kettering, perhaps because so much was going on all the time. The town was practically a seething mass of servicemen from all parts of the globe, including the regular sight of German and Italian prisoners-of-war at local cinemas. They were imprisoned in nearby camps, but amazingly allowed out to go to the cinema. I knew one who even helped to make ice-cream at a local cafe.

In the School playground there was an underground air raid shelter, to which we resorted whenever there was an air raid warning. A cold, damp, smelly concrete bunker, it was a highly unpleasant place. On any day with a P.E. Lesson, Mr Ashworth required us to bring a top coat in case of any emergency while we were wearing P.E. kit. Anyone failing to comply with this was punished across his thinly covered backside, receiving several strokes from the leather end of the ropes which hung from the ceiling in the Hall-cum-Gym. This was as unpleasant as being in the air raid shelter, thus a double punishment. The underground shelter is still there in what is now the car park at the Municipal Offices. At one time, during the "Cold War", it was designated as a Civil Defence Control Room.

Mr Bernard Pledger, our Latin Master, for some strange reason would take us out to the top of the air raid shelter to enact certain sequences from the Latin text book. We had to stand on the surround wall and expound speeches in Latin.

In the Spring term of 1946 a unit of pre-fabricated concrete classrooms was erected above the undergound shelter. Within days of its opening in September, some clever lad flattened the lead waste outlets from a line of washbasins, causing quite serious flooding.

Detention was awarded not only for the usual school transgressions but also for failure to bring your gas mask each day; wartime school life had its own tedious problems. This could cause extra hardship for any of the boys who came by bus, since wartime bus schedules were quite strained. A boy could be forced to miss a bus home, when the next bus might mean a two hour wait.

At one stage of school life I felt certain I was on the way to becoming a farmer, when I finished my five years residence. From 1942, the school year was regularly punctuated by farm work, when boys were called on to undertake many of the seasonal operations.

The most obvious was the task of harvesting the potato crop, vital to a nation desperately short of food. In those far off days, this was labour intensive, requiring large numbers of workers to hand pick the potatoes.

As the appropriate season arrived, off we went in groups of 30 or 40, usually transported by an ancient United Counties bus. Sometimes we had to make our own way, either on foot or bicycle, if one was available.

On one of these ''outings'', a cycling classmate met me walking from Kettering to Warkton, and gave me a lift on his cross-bar for about two miles. We were usually accompanied by a Master to supervise us, but more often we had a burly land-girl as our taskmaster, or should that be ''taskmistress''?

These new ladies of the land, strengthened by their heavy farm work, were not slow to administer a hefty wallop to any boy misbehaving (in their eyes). This was unfortunate, since it was not unusual for a teenage boy to find himself physically attracted to these young women. Even this could result in one of the aforementioned thumps.

We were taken on foggy, frosty autumn mornings to desolate and often remote fields, there to spend long, cold hours, with frozen fingers and aching backs, filling buckets with muddy potatoes. These were emptied into enormous sacks, earning the princely sum of about seven old pence an hour, less than three new pence today.

The machine spinning the ''spuds'' invariably dug faster than we could pick, frequently resulting in the landgirl tractor-driver leaping from her hard iron seat to administer a hearty blow to the tardy victim.

We learnt respect.

On one memorable occasion during potato picking at Rockingham, the wartime lady driver of the ancient bus climbing the infamous hill, missed a gear. The bus started to roll down backwards, but mercifully our fate was checked by the high kerb.

We went off in groups to carry out other tasks, the most dreaded being the singling of sugar beet. As a result of the severe sugar shortage, sugar beet was being grown on a vast scale. Fields that (to me) resembled endless Canadian prairies, had miles-long rows of inches-high beet plants about six inches apart. At an early stage, using a standard garden hoe, these had to be thinned to allow sufficient growing room. And we were the ones ''press-ganged'' into doing the thinning!

What an appalling job, hour after hour, row after row, stretching far off into the distant horizons. With backs bent, we hacked and chopped relentlessly, only stopping if the frequent rains became too heavy.

On one of these ''joyful'' days near Burton Latimer, a local monsoon brought matters to a complete halt for the day and I struggled through the rain and mud to my bike under a hedgerow, only to find punctures fore and aft. The misery of that cold, wet four mile trudge back to Kettering will forever remain an unhappy memory.

We stooked corn, singled beet, and potato picked our way across the local district: Barton, Burton, Gretton, Pytchley, Cranford, to name but a few. It became a Cook's tour of all the wretched muddy, thistly fields in the county, lightened only by mid day breaks round a blazing fire of twigs and branches, naturally, roasting fresh potatoes. We came into conflict with land girls, mean tight-fisted farmers and itinerant tramps, but learned almost enough to become farmers ourselves, instead of the eventual and ultimate National Servicemen.

I made further small contributions to alleviate the wartime labour problems by helping to load and transport pig iron from Kettering Furnaces, and helping to load and transport coal from Desborough Railway Station to Rothwell Gas Works, and the two flying units stationed nearby, American and R.A.F.

I helped unload more coal at Rushton Station, filling the lorries of A. & A. Darby of Avondale Road, Kettering. In between, I assisted in delivering and pumping out paraffin to farms, via a Pool lorry. Pool was a wartime substitute distributor for today's BP, Shell, etc.

There must have been some thoughts about our physical contribution to the war effort, as there was considerable correspndence between the School, the farmers, War Agricultural Committee, even individual Land Army girls, though I understand very little of this was complimentary.

Oh yes, it was a merry life for the boys of wartime K.G.S. At Christmas we did Postal work. For the lucky ones in those bitter, raw winters, there were inside jobs sorting letters in the office.

For a fortunate few more it could mean riding around in a lorry delivering parcels. For most of us, it was daily trudging around cold, foggy streets laden with a heavy bag of letters and Christmas cards. For all of us it brought the "luxury" (?) free dinners at the British Restaurant in Dalkeith Place, the only perk of the job, courtesy of the State-run refreshment rooms.

Did I say "luxury"?

If the Second Front had been opened using as ammunition the vegetables served up to us, our enemies would have surrendered immediately, while the sausages made of 90% bread defy comment. Our compensation was the cheerful company of friends, at a time when there wasn't a lot to smile about.

The British Restaurants were established by the Government, across the country, their intention being to provide a supposedly inexpensive, nourishing hot meal to workers, at a time when food was in short supply. They enjoyed a reputation that fortunately is now perhaps almost forgotten.

The School had its own Army Cadet Platoon where, amongst other military matters, we studied armed warfare, firstly using 18th century muskets of unknown origin. Perhaps it was thought our enemy was still Napoleon! Later, we progressed to Sten Guns.

Kettering Grammar School Army Cadet Platoon 1942. A. H. Buksh, third from right, middle row. Messrs Ashworth and Wood on the front row.

I further weakened the already strained relationship with our Second Lieutenant J. Wood when, failing to properly secure the steel endplate of a Sten gun, it shot into the air propelled by a powerful spring, landing heavily on Mr Wood's head. Unfortunately, he was my Latin Master and we did not get on at all well for a long time afterwards. I must have eventually gained his forgiveness, for it was Mr Wood who, in later years, proposed me as President of The Old Cytringanians. Could it be he thought I still had the Sten gun with which I could control meetings?

In the School Cadet Force we were instructed on how to immobilize German tanks, using bombs that had to be stuck to their sides, or somehow slipped in between the caterpillar tracks; I am forever grateful we were never required to do this in earnest.

There are still pleasant memories of summer afternoons cycling around the countryside on map reading exercises, or slithering through the grass in the Castle field at Barton Seagrave, in greater fear of the widespread cow manure than detection by the ''enemy''. We went to the Lawns Centre (now long gone) in George Street, where we were expected to study and learn aircraft identification, another weakness to add to my academic failings.

At Cadet meetings after school hours we studied Morse Code, which to me was as strange and incomprehensible as Algebra. I think it was at this stage I realised I had no future in the Army Cadets and transferred my affections to the School's dramatic arena.

This enabled me to find my name, not quite ''in lights'', but at least listed among the ''also rans'' in the programmes of Shakespeare's *Henry The Fifth* and *The Merchant of Venice.* I expect as a hungry wartime boy I had the constant ''carrot'' dangling in front of me, in the form of the parties held after the production finished.

Parties of any description were to be carefully cultivated and nurtured in those days of hard rationing and food shortage, and were as much hoarded and enjoyed as the one or two invitations to tea with Graham Mudditt in Spinney Lane and later with Dennis Finking in Poplars Farm Road.

Throughout my absence for farming work, Army Cadet exercises, or anything at all, Mr Woodward our History master, renowned for his endless hours of dictation, insisted these historical orations should be borrowed from another boy and written up in our own time, resulting in many hours of this wretched imposition.

Another delight of Kettering Grammar School during the war years was the opportunity to learn, and become proficient in, vegetable gardening. This was regularly ''studied'' at the School allotment in St Mary's Road.

The School had this seemingly vast acreage of potatoes, cabbages, brussels sprouts and similar mass-consumed vegetables, which the boys were expected to cultivate as more of our war efforts. Generally, we went to St Mary's Road to work, when it was considered impossible to play games on the playing field in Windmill Avenue.

But vegetables cannot wait for cultivation, so we also had to undertake gardening at many other times. We were marched to the allotment and carried out our tasks, still wearing School uniform. It must have been quite an odd sight, seeing all those boys wearing School caps while hoeing, raking and digging. Advantage was taken of the potatoes when they were high enough. Boys would lay down between the rows and enjoy a sneaky cigarette. Again, it must have been quite an odd sight, for any passer-by, to see smoke curling up from between rows of potatoes.

Our ''gallant'' war-work brought no special reward, apart from the seven pence hourly rate for farming. I think we should have received certificates in horticulture!

I suppose we learnt something valuable, though I can't think what, unless it was advance warning to find a job anywhere other than among the cold forbidding fields of rural England.

Looking back at those strange and difficult days of wartime schooling, one must certainly admire our masters. Many of them were beyond normal retiring age, but remained to teach while younger men went to war.

There were the not-uncommon, sad times when friends learned a relative was missing or killed in action; the constantly changing scene around us. For all our years at K.G.S., there was non-stop military activity. Each morning, American Flying Fortresses rendezvoused above the town, before setting off for occupied Europe on a bombing mission. The town was full of troops, and classrooms were filled every day with the engine roar, as long military convoys drove past the School buildings.

Perhaps the personal highlight of my school days was being called to the Head's study (not noted as a pleasant experience) and being informed that evacuee boys were to receive a tin of chocolate powder from the American Red Cross, presumably to soften the separation from our parents. I kept my tin under the bed where I was billeted with the Richards family in Oakley Street. Each night I moistened one finger, stuck it in the powder and licked it very slowly; a few moments of luxury. I made it last several weeks!

During those wartime years,a group of Old Boys produced a small link magazine entitled *Reveille,* a compilation of letters sent in by former students who were serving in the various theatres of war. We were encouraged to buy a copy and perhaps send it to someone we knew. They were a superb record of the great contribution to the Allied cause, made by former members of the School. A few of these letters even originated from German prisoner-of-war camps, and must now be considered unique.

Looking back, it now seems quite strange, if not bizarre, to have spent all of my years at the School under the shadow of a country at war, to have been a pupil for five years of evacuation, rationing, black-outs, air raids, carrying gas masks and school-time farming.

Which all serves to confirm my earlier claim that the period was the most tumultuous in the School's history, which would never have been repeated,

even had our splendid School not been assassinated by the politicians.
They achieved something that Adolf Hitler never managed: to close the doors forever.

Rabbi Michael Leigh

One morning, early in September 1939, somewhat scared, I approached the main entrance to the School in Bowling Green Road, only to be ordered by the Senior Master, Mr E. E. Kirby, who was looking through the window, to come in through the ''bicycle sheds'' entrance. I was aged eleven and had been evacuated a short while earlier to Ketterng from London with the Dame Alice Owen School, a girls' school, to look after my little sister who had just joined that school. As I had been to the boys' Owen's School, a grammar school, I was sent to K.G.S., presumably its nearest equivalent. There were only a few other evacuee boys at K.G.S., unlike the High School, which shared its building with Dame Alice Owen's.
Already there were signs of wartime. An underground air raid shelter was created in the playground. We had to report to School with our gas masks and the staff consisted of middle aged or elderly gentlemen, because presumably the younger teachers had gone off to the Services. This, in retrospect, turned out to be a bonus, because the staff were experienced and dedicated teachers who must have been at their height in the 1920s. I think it contributed to the quality of the teaching at the School (a theme to which I will return) and later I was to learn that K.G.S. had a reputation for being a renowned grammar school.

I warmed to the School immediately and soon made many friends. It was by present day standards relatively small, about 360 boys as I recollect. Work was the order of the day. In fact, there was little else to do, because apart from the cinemas (Kettering at that time had five!) the radio, and books from the local Library, there was little else to do of a recreational nature. Later a ''milk bar'' opened in the town, which somehow represented ''high'' life and a Youth Club started at the end of the War, though one teacher warned us not to go there, as it would interfere with our school work.

Life must have been very drab, but what you don't know, you don't miss. There were no school trips and certainly no overseas outings as in today's schools. However, I do remember going with the School to see Laurence Olivier in *Henry V* and the French film *Les Enfants du Paradis* at the Empire Cinema and once going to a Molière play at Wellingborough. We had got used to not having sweets or fruit and mercifully Kettering was relatively quiet during the War. The air raid sirens went off from time to time, but I think only one bomb fell on the town. There was, of course, heartache and we heard of relatives and Old Boys who had been killed overseas – the father of a K.G.S. friend of mine lost his life in the Merchant Navy. Soldiers came and went and, to my excitement, some Canadian and later Czech soldiers encamped in the Co-op field opposite my parents' flat near Wicksteed Park, and some were billeted on us. Later the Americans came and had a big base at Grafton Underwood with Flying Fortresses, which we saw and heard from time to time.

We boys were encouraged to "do our bit", as it was called. Some afternoons we were sent to local farmers to help the war effort for food. I remember pulling and "banging" beets used to make sugar, to get off the earth, planting potatoes and hoeing lettuces (sometimes accompanied by friendly Italian POWs). All this was compulsory and part of School activity. Then the School Army Cadet Force Company (attached to the Northamptonshire Regiment) was started by 2nd Lieutenant Ashworth. We paraded with wooden muskets preserved from the First World War and later had khaki uniforms and went to a highly disciplined camp near Northampton and engaged in "battle drill". The cadets marched in local rallies on behalf of National Savings and assisted in first aid practices locally. We were aware, of course, of the terrible military struggles at the time through the radio and press, the Western Desert campaign, the Russian Front which went back and forth and the Second Front after 1944. The revelations of Belsen and Auschwitz confirmed our worst suspicions of the Holocaust. There was an odd contrast between reading in class of Joseph Addison's graceful eighteenth-century character, Sir Roger de Coverley and the bloodshed, massacres and terror going on during the War, though I don't suppose this really impinged on our young minds.

Education, I think, is about stimulating interest, not necessarily imparting all the facts. K.G.S. during this time, the 'forties, was a good example of how, for me at any rate, in spite of the fact that facilities and teaching aids were spartan (perhaps non-existent compared with today) inspiration, and the personality of skilled and inspired teachers, won through. To this day, fifty or so years on, I am still inspired to read (even more so in my retirement) English and French Literature and European History (I was on the Arts side) as a result of seeds planted by teachers at the School. We never undertook "projects" as my children did at their comprehensive, nor did we move far from the schoolroom itself. I suppose there was a lot of chalk, talk and text work. But it was solid stuff, perhaps unimaginative in presentation at times, with an accent on facts, especially in History. But at the end of my schooldays, in 1947, I had a broad basis of knowledge, including Biblical and literary texts by heart. But, through inspired teaching, I acquired a thirst to read and explore more in the following years and decades. This, I think, is the gift which K.G.S. gave me and for which I am eternally grateful.

Some outstanding teachers come to mind. The Headmaster, A. F. Scott, came about 1941 and brought an air of freshness and innovation. He was a Cambridge man and taught English in the Sixth Form – those were the days when Headmasters taught! He opened our eyes to the "greats" of the day who warned of contemporary attacks on culture – Clive Bell in the field of Art, F. R. Leavis in literature, and Lewis Mumford in architecture. He had empathy for these themes and encouraged us to go on to university, Oxford, Cambridge or "redbrick".

Edmund Kirby was a veteran infantry officer of the First World War who taught English in the senior classes with quiet sagacity, love and immense knowledge – he told me once that he read about four novels a week. John Tynan, who cycled in every day from Isham, was a genius of a teacher. Possessed of a certain gruff manner, he taught French Literature, especially drama, with passion and enthusiasm. Alec Woodward, a Methodist lay preacher and a very fine person, taught History which I, after National Service, read at university. I remember having solo lessons with him in the Sick Room, the only space going, in seventeenth-century history, as he thought I needed another century other than the nineteenth, which we were doing in class, for the university entrance exam. Then there was C. W. Godfrey, an enthusiastic character, who later became May or Kettering. He taught me English and Geography and produced many amateur Shakespearean plays at the School, which were great fun and gave me a love of drama. Interestingly enough, in those days the female parts were played by the High School teachers, never the girls themselves!

Education at secondary school can ideally be a preparation for life. In fact, we were being prepared for life in the midst of death and destruction, the horrors of the Second World War – though on the surface, at any rate Kettering seemed at the time a haven of peace. Wartime conditions and the pressures on our families must have formed the backdrop to our schooling, though in an odd way we became accustomed to the situation. Yet I remember a certain idealism in the air, that the War was being fought to rid the world of tyranny, everything which was the opposite to what Britain stood for. I remember the class being asked by Mr Kirby to write an essay on what sort of society we hoped for when hostilities ended – already an indication of the mood of the time. I wrote an essay in a super optimistic, even revolutionary, vein and Kirby told me to be more realistic. In spite of the many disappointments since the War's end, I still retain that optimistic view of society, which the issues of the War engendered. They were nurtured for me, and I hope for others, amidst the relative quiet and security of K.G.S.

Trevor Holmes

My schooldays at Kettering Grammar School were from 1938 until 1942 and my first form was situated in "the hut" under the guidance of Mr Smith. We needed to leave the class many times during the day, because of the antiquated heating system: a coke stove.

Most of the local boys cycled to school and a policeman was always on duty at the junction of Gold Streeet and Newland Street directing the traffic – principally bicycles.

Friday – cattle market day – was difficult, as we were mixed in with the farmers and herds of sheep and cattle on their way to the old market opposite Kettering Cemetery, and the animals were the dominating influence.

The first year passed uneventfully, but by the beginning of September 1939 tremendous changes were taking place: air raid shelters were being built and gas masks had to be carried. Perhaps the most important event of all, however, was the arrival of the evacuees who were, in the first instance, from three girls' schools and one boys' school. The over-crowding of schoolchildren was coped with successfully by staggering hours at the various schools and halls and this was even enjoyed by many of us! New friendships developed very quickly and, as the months went by, sport, particularly cricket, football and hockey, was the common denominator which helped to link us all in this new community.

Perhaps the most popular meeting place to find ''new friends'' was the Kettering Public Library, where it was, in fact, difficult to park your bicycle. Because there was a complete ''blackout'' of all lights from houses, shops, street lamps, etc., and for other reasons, the evacuated schools imposed quite severe curfews at 6 p.m. in winter and 9 p.m. in summer. Even so, liaisons could be made without risk of punishment, if one were extremely cautious. Because of the absolute darkness, pedestrians were asked to walk on different sides of the pavement, dependent on which direction they were heading, in order to avoid collisions.

During this initial period of the war, many other changes were taking place and already several senior boys were joining the Armed Services. Many visited the School when they were on leave but, sadly, some were never to return.

We continued with our schooling, but gradually our way of life began to change; little extra duties appeared and we were encouraged on to these by the oft used phrase ''war effort''. Instead of our Woodwork lessons, these two periods were spent digging an allotment and producing vegetables on a plot at the top of St Mary's Road. Farming during the holidays was very popular and the going rate was about five pennies per hour. I like to think that we were valuable to the farmers, as labour was so short, and we certainly enjoyed the extra spending power we had.

Perhaps our greatest adventure at this stage was to go to the Lake District – about 25 of us – volunteers of course. We left by train complete with camping kit and spent three weeks cutting pit props in a most beautiful spot close to Keswick. Other popular activities included joining the A.T.C., which was taken very seriously, but still gave great pleasure, companionship and preparation for the future years. Our sporting activities never really suffered and besides the normal school games, into our fixture list came the Home Guard, a fixture that we always expected to win.

I left the Grammar School with the Oxford School Certificate,as it was then called, and a short time later joined the Royal Marines, with whom I was eventually sent to the Far East. Three years later I was demobilised, complete with bright blue suit and trilby hat. Many celebrations and reunions followed – maybe that should be another story.

I might add a little personal rider. Following the outbreak of peace, I married one of Kettering's evacuees and even after 47 years we are able to reminisce both happily and sadly on those impressionable and important years of our lives: the companionship, the deprivations, joys and sorrows, "the one for all and all for one" era.

J. Stanley

What were the possibilities for a newly matriculated fifteen year old in 1940? The "Civil Service" Sixth Form was cancelled; masters who were reservists were departing to the war. Strange boys from Walthamstow schools occupied the Bowling Green Road premises for parts of each day. As a prefect, I had certain "privileges": to fit the Headmaster with his gas mask; to fill sand bags; to teach Mathematics to the First Form; and to help keep order.

One remembers many dedicated and talented teachers. Among them was John Tynan, with remarkable eyebrows, his phrase "miserable worms" and the deduction of marks for "dragged in" phrases in French essays. E. E. Kirby, with his wonderful restraint, missing fingers lost in an earlier war, and always treating us like gentlemen. C. W. Godfrey, not only for his consistent successes with dramatic productions, but for incorporating girls into them. Fond memories also, of course, of friends and contemporaries: Don Joyce, Jack Eady, Brian Jackson, Keith Traynar, and Raymond Dainty.

Fifty years on and school days seemed full of halcyon experiences and harmless pranks, such as placing kippers on the High School heating pipes. Gone from memory are the stresses: homework every night and weekend, reinforced by weekly performance tables.

Supposedly, Queen Elizabeth I made the following observation on the founding of grammar schools: "We have too many philosophers and not enought Mathematicians". The Kettering Grammar School did well for both disciplines. We left School well educated and imbued with "Team spirit", a fitting preparation for the service demanded of us during the subsequent five, terrible years.

Gordon Moore

In the summer of 1940, J. I. Scott announced in Hall that boys of 14 and over would be encouraged to assist local farmers as and when required. The rate to be a whole sixpence (2½p) per hour, payable in arrears at the end of term. Duties were to include sugar beet thinning and "banging" (a back breaking task), pea, potato and fruit picking and help with the corn harvests. (In those days we called it corn, although it would have been wheat, barley or oats).

Three of us, Tom Harding, Jimmy Proctor and myself were allocated to the large farm in the Loddington and Cransley area owned by Mr Willis. It so happened that Mr Willis had a very pretty daughter, unattached, slender of figure and with a halo of golden hair. Unfortunately, the young lady was several unattainable years our senior, but this in no way prevented many visits being paid to the farm buildings, on some idiotic pretext or other, to catch a glimpse of the fair creature.

Work entailed ''stooking'' sheaves of corn that had been dropped by the combined cutter/binder. A ''stook'' consisted of 6 or 8 sheaves which were arranged in such a way as to enable the entire drying of the stock before carting and stacking in the yard prior to threshing.

We had ''stooked'' several fields – one as large as 20 acres – and to give us a break, the farm manager devised a day's relief from the rather monotonous process. A flock of between 60 and 70 sheep had to be herded from one pasture to another, a distance of no more than 2 miles. The three of us were duly entrusted with this task.

Have any of you attempted to lead, cajole or reason with a flock of sheep? Our journey, no doubt through our lack of experience and the utter stupidity of our charges, took, not a morning, but a whole day. Given half a chance any one of the 70 would have disappeared into a cottager's garden through a gap in a hedge – anywhere save where they should have been.

Extremely embarrassing it was when our route took us through a small village, most probably Thorpe Malsor. News of our arrival had somehow preceded us, because the whole populace had turned out to witness the event. Much gratuitous advice was banded about by the inhabitants, most of whom were retired farm hands.

Eventually, after pulling some of our charges from ditches, or thickets, for the umpteenth time, we arrived at our destination to find the farm manager, his patience exhausted. Solicitously, he enquired after our welfare, wondering whether our Odyssey had included a grand tour of both Desborough and Rothwell. Under normal circumstances we would have wished him in the latter's crypt but, so great was our relief that the head count revealed no deserters, and so exhausted was our vocabulary, that no suitable rejoinder was made.

This was a journey that could not possibly have taken place a year or so later, when all roads in the area were more than busy with the heavy construction traffic for the new U.S. Army Air Force Base at Harrington.

Richard Portwood

When we look back on our school days our most vivid memories are not about academic work, but about the extra-curricular activities. I suppose this is because they were voluntary and therefore of greater interest than the work in the classroom. My two interests during the 5th and 6th Forms were laboratory technician to Mr Lawson and Mr Whitney; the other interest was lighting assistant to Bill Ashby for School Plays. In both cases our activities were highly dangerous and would have been banned by the present day H&S Regulations.

During World War Two availability and cost were the two factors that drove us to construct very simple, but very effective, stage lighting equipment. The late Bill Ashby was the brains behind it all, because he was an electrician with the Electricity Board on Rockingham Road and he was a member of the Hygrams; he therefore made lighting equipment for their plays and had the artistic flair for creative lighting on stage.

Some equipment, such as the big spots, Bill had acquired from somewhere, but the foot lights, back drop and overhead batten floods we made ourselves, from timber offcuts and old biscuit tins. I don't remember where he managed to get the coloured gelatin film to make the filters, but we had a wide range of filters which were always known by their number, not their colour!

The most extraordinary devices, though, were the consoles used to dim the lights. I remember them well, since I spent many hours in the basement at the School helping Bill to construct them. They consisted of a wooden frame 2′6″ high, 2′6″ wide and 9″ deep. It was boxed in at the bottom, front, sides and top. Mounted inside were 4 asbestos concrete pipes, 6″ diameter and 18″ long, which we had sawn up to size and sealed at one end by a disc of bakelite. We then melted old lead pipe in a mould to form a contact 4″ diameter and 1″ thick with a stout insulated cable welded into it. A similar lead contact with cast in hook was suspended by string and counter balanced by another lead weight over a 4″ pulley, which protruded through the top plate on the frame, just like a thumb wheel dimmer, but 10 times bigger. One could therefore adjust the distance between the two lead contacts by using the thumb wheel and, by filling the pipes with salt and water of varying strengths, one could cater for all power needs. The rest of the frame accommodated the switches, sockets and mains breakers etc. It weighed about 100 lbs when operational and Bill and I used to take all this equipment, including a couple of these consoles, to village halls in the district for pantomimes, plays, variety shows all put on by local churches and chapels.

But the greatest challenge was the annual Shakespearean production in the hall produced by Mr Godfrey and Mr Tynan. The standard of production was superb, especially considering the lack of resources. The splendid scenery was all made by Mr Corke and his pupils, but what I believe gives any performance that touch of magic is the effective lighting. I can see even now the brilliance of the street scenes in Rome in *Julius Caesar,* the eerie dungeon in *Macbeth* and the ethereal woods in *A Midsummer Night's Dream.* The atmosphere in each case was created by the lighting.

But we never thought of the risks of asbestos, lead or chlorine poisoning, or of electrocution. We learned how to work as a team, were given a lot of freedom, trust and responsibility that was just as important as the academic work. I look with admiration at the solid state lighting consoles of today and think back nostalgically to the days at the K.G.S., when things were much more basic but the results equally good.

CHAPTER 11

Reveille

Sellick Norsworthy

In March 1940 a monthly newsletter, *Reveille,* appeared for the first time. It was the brainchild of Reg Tailby, then Hon. Secretary of the Old Cytringanians. His vision was to keep Old Boys serving in the Forces in touch with others and with the School, which would act as a sort of clearing house. In the early stages there were many, including E.E.K., who doubted that there would be sufficient material once the Censor had had his way. However, *Reveille* proved to be a great success from the very beginning, due in great part to L. J. Bartley, its first editor. Several hundred *Reveilles* were circulated monthly to Old Boys, who received their copies free of charge in exchange for their letters which made up most of the "copy". An Old Boy who served in the First World War, J. L. C. Loake, assisted by Guy Wilkes, was responsible for dispatching the copies. Another Old Boy who worked extremely hard was Bernard ('Dump') Smith, who collected 2s. 6d. from "home front" subscribers, a sum which secured a year's supply of *Reveilles,* post free. When Bartley joined the Royal Engineers, the post of editor was taken over by Mr C. W. Godfrey, that popular master who had the happy knack of getting the best out of *Reveille's* contributors.

The pages of *Reveille* make fascinating reading, with Old Boys serving in every theatre of war, bearing witness to history in the making. As early as April 1940 about 100 Old Boys had joined the ranks, including two sons of the Headmaster, J. B. I. and R. D. I. Scott. By the time of *Reveille's* first birthday the number on active service was 200 and a third son of J. I., 'Jimmy', had received a commission. Within less than another year the number was over 300.

At least a dozen Old Boys took part in the evacuation from France. Lance Corporal G. P. Dickins popped into School to announce his safe return. Lt. W. J. Allen crossed safely from Dunkirk as did Lt. R. C. Cawdell who, initially, had been reported missing. Two sets of brothers – A. R. and R. Larratt and D. A. and G. N. Marlow – were also among the evacuees. Others who crossed the Channel to safety were N. H. Parker and R. W. Cox, who took advantage of his short time at home to get married. Sapper Olney was another Old Boy who made it home, but not from Dunkirk:

''We were definitely more fortunate than the lads who came back from Dunkirk. We were the last convoy to leave St. Nazaire, and believe me I was glad to leave.''

Victor Fourt also returned from St. Nazaire in June 1940 and was present during the sinking of the Lancastria. Seemingly, the only Old Boy to be wounded during the evacuation was Richard Sumner.

A. H. Ryan, an AB on the destroyer *Bedouin* took part in the ill-fated Norwegian Campaign. At the second battle of Narvik, *Bedouin,* along with two other destroyers, *Hero* and *Icarus,* sank two German destroyers. Ryan's description of the first engagement is quite atmospheric:

''When we did get within range, our forward guns opened up, and we kept up a continuous fire for about twelve minutes during which time the other destroyers were also firing at the enemy vessel.

You might not think that this is a very long time but it certainly seemed like hours, for every minute we expected a shell to hit us, though luckily none did. During the short action we fired more than 240 shells and also registered a hit with one of our torpedoes.

When the German ship was sinking, her one gun that had not been put out of action – the aft one – was still firing, but it was very erratic. The joy of our ship's company when she eventually disappeared beneath the icy waters (temperature about 36°F) knew no bounds.''

Another Old Boy whose name appears regularly in *Reveille* is C. N. (Nelly) Marlow. In May 1941 he was serving on a destroyer on convoy escort duty. He described vividly the battle against the German submarines:

''They slide up in the darkness, fire their torpedoes, and slash away with their superior speed. The last trip a tin-fish missed our stern by yards. Bombers also worry the convoy, but have sufficient respect for our armament to sheer off when we open up.''

Among others who served at sea was J. P. Creasey, who worked in the shell room on board H.M.S. *Revenge* that took part in the hunt for the *Bismarck* but, unfortunately, was not in at the kill. Sub-Lt. E. C. Denton had a hectic time in the Mediterranean. He reported: ''I have been kept quite busy with invasions, having taken part at Algiers, Sicily and Anzio.'' N. J. Robinson, who served in the Merchant Marine, was senior Third Officer on board the *Queen Elizabeth* when it made its secret crossing of the Atlantic in 1940. Later we hear of him as First Officer on a ship carrying troops to Aden.

Many Old Boys found themselves serving in various parts of Africa. Flight-Lt. L. T. Bird served in that ''delightful hole'' Aden and was glad to get away once in a while to places like Addis Ababa where he shot a gazelle and saw plenty of toucans that reminded him of ''the Guinness adverts of the old days.'' C. A. Walker, a pilot in the R.A.F., served in South Africa, the Rhodesias, West Africa, the Congo, the Sudan, Egypt and Palestine.

Denis Panter was stationed in West Africa in early 1941. He wrote:

"There's not a lot to do out here, no dancing, Europeans all married, so, with all the apparent bright spots, it's dull in places." He spent Christmas 1941 on the Volta River in the Gold Coast canoeing, sunbathing and swimming. Denis then moved to the Belgian Congo, where he found himself the only Briton among soldiers from Belgium, France and Portugal. Although he missed playing rugby he did have a few games of soccer, most of which produced either a fight, a penalty or a sending off. His most amusing story tells of a Portuguese player who was sent off, and two others who walked off in sympathy. After half time one of the protesters returned and, when the referee ordered him off the field, he refused to go. After arguing for about five minutes, with accompanying boos and cheers, the referee handed his watch and whistle to Denis's captain and walked off the field himself!

Lt. G. M. Tompkins claimed to be the first Old Cyt with the West African forces in S.E.A.C. and his account of his time in Africa makes amusing reading:

"We are learning Hausa, which I'm glad to say is much easier than the languages I learnt (?) at school. The trouble is that a man from S. Nigeria, Gold Coast, Sierra Leone or Gambia does not normally speak Hausa, which rather cramps our style! I still don't know why the War Office sent me here when I was under the impression that I was going to East Africa."

In June 1940 Sapper B. A. Gibson was stationed in Malta. He reported that, "Life out here tends to be very lazy." By December the tone of his letter was slightly different: "Events tend to be on the dull side, except for the occasional air raid." By September 1941, he is writing about the German dive bombers in action and an occasional visit from the "ice cream vendors." By March 1942, the tone of his letter has a much greater urgency:

"Since I last wrote to you things have certainly brightened up, a bit too much though. We have raids lasting practically all day and all night. . . . What usually happens is that we are bombed for about 20 minutes and then peace for about half an hour and then it might break out again."

C.Q.M.S. Newman served under Wavell in North Africa before being transferred to Greece in March 1941. Unfortunately, his detachment was forced to evacuate in April and he was one of only 39 men who escaped alive. Sid Stephenson, who was in the same detachment, was taken prisoner: he was among the unfortunate prisoners of war whom the Nazis handcuffed for a whole year. Newman managed to reach Egypt, whence he was transferred yet again, this time to Iraq. For two years he lived midway in the 600 miles of desert between Jordan and Baghdad as his unit built 200 miles of the Haifa to Baghdad road. Newman reported: "Food, particularly in the intense heat of July, was terrible, bully was just poured out of the tin."

Many Old Cyts served in North Africa and the Middle East. Ken Mayes was with the Australian Forces who helped push the Italians back 800 miles and took 100,000 prisoners. Unfortunately, Mayes was killed shortly after in April 1941. Sadly, British and Commonwealth forces could not sustain the advance. As Rommel turned the tide and took Tobruk, Corporal J. H. C. Burditt was captured in November 1941 and spent the rest of the war in camps at Ancona, Vienna and Dresden, before returning to Desborough in 1945. In late 1942 Ivan Barlow followed the victorious 8th Army from El Alamein to Tunisia. Another who shared in that exhilarating campaign was Bdr. G. M. Tompkins, who reported that "the final attack was very exciting while it lasted." His letter continues:

"I think the thing which will stick in my memory was how the civilians of Hammam-Lif welcomed us when we broke through the defile there. They came flocking back from the hills where they'd been sheltering, and gave a royal welcome. It was the first and only time I've had roses thrown at me."

Among those who served in Palestine during the latter part of the war was Flight-Sergeant R. A. Pollard. His account of a visit to a colony of Germans, all exiles from Nazi persecution, is a testimony to the strength of the human spirit and an insight into the forces which would eventually mould the state of Israel:

"They have suffered much and feel they can never return to Germany, so bitter are their memories. I left the colony feeling that I had met some remarkable people, counting it a privilege that I had done so. They had suffered as we, I think, will never have to suffer, but they had worked hard, to forget and to create, in nine years, out of desert; and a beautiful green little village."

Once the Germans had been driven from North Africa, the Allies turned their attentions to Sicily and Italy. L.-Cpl. F. Barker took part in the invasion of Sicily in July 1943. In his letter to *Reveille* he wrote:

"Syracuse seemed very peaceful and quiet when we sailed into the harbour but we were soon disillusioned when three enemy planes dived out of the sun. . . . A few hectic days and nights followed; the barrages at Augusta and Syracuse were terrific, but after the fall of Catania things became reasonably quiet and the real job of getting stores and spare parts to the units began in earnest."

Corporal Sindall and L.-Cpl. W. Mole served together in the 2nd Battalion Northamptonshire Regiment under Montgomery as he moved through Sicily. In a joint letter they "followed a kaleidoscope of grapes, American-speaking locals, dust Marsala, surrendering Italians, tomatoes and not so amenable Panzer Grenadiers of the Herman Goering species, finally coming to rest in a pleasant village between Mount Etna and Catania." Unfortunately, shortly after this letter arrived, Wilfred Mole was killed.

Another Old Boy who could be found in Sicily in the summer of 1943 was none other than J. B. I. Scott. He was restoring the water supply of some of the devastated towns and paying tribute to German thoroughness!

As the Allied advance moved on to mainland Italy, Sgt. D. H. Pollard of the R.A.F. was languishing in Sicily. Despite having climbed Mt. Etna twice he, "began to chafe at the static life." Eventually, after ten months, he crossed to the mainland, but was disappointed not to have had longer than a day in both Naples and Rome. During the summer of 1944 Pollard moved about frequently, this being a period of continual progress during which the Gothic Line was broken and many other obstacles overcome. However, as Autumn approached, the weather changed and North Italy experienced one of its wettest periods ever. Consequently, progress was slowed up by, "mud, water, water, and yet more water!" By Christmas the rain had turned to snow.

Another subscriber to *Reveille*, but who was not an Old Boy, was Lt.-Col. J. Profumo, M.P. for Kettering. He had taken part in the North African landings and also served in Italy. He wrote:

"Just about the time that our Armies were marching through Rome, amid cheering crowds and scenes of wild excitement, I received a copy of the publication *Reveille*. It seemed to me such a splendid and constructive effort on behalf of the amateur editorial staff, and such an appropriate title at this moment when so many souls long enslaved are hearing the sound of the liberators' reveille – a call to a new and free life. I am therefore very pleased to be permitted to send through the medium of your own paper a message of good cheer to all its readers wherever they may be, and I would like to invite you to write me a line personally at the House of Commons setting out your own views on the post-war problems which may interest YOU. I cannot promise to answer all your letters at present, but I do feel your views will be of inestimable value to me, and they may form a basis for discussion which we may be able to have in the near future, perhaps in the quiet and peaceful precincts of your old school when we all get home again."

A number of Old Cyts took part in the Invasion of France. The first group to write to *Reveille* were T. S. S. Goode, Victor Fourt and Private F. Dix. Characteristically, Goode has a word to say about the weather, as well as the din of the artillery; Fourt makes a comparison with the days of 1940 when he experienced at first hand the evacuation of France. Dix was involved in a truly historic venture:

"I am now allowed to tell you that I was stationed at Arromanches les Bains, better known as 'port of Mulberry'. I am proud to say that my unit helped to play a great part in getting the port working."

Corporal Bob Messinger was in hospital when the 2nd Northants Yeomanry went to France, but eventually he caught them up and stayed with them until they were disbanded after helping to close the Falaise Gap. Trevor Goode was exhilarated by the rapid advance through France after Falaise. No sooner had he reached Paris than he was on his way to Brussels:

". . . my! what a reception we got! It even put the Tunis Victory Parade into the dim limelight.

The advance of our tanks was so swift that we R.A.S.C. drivers were the first British troops to pass through several towns and villages, and we had some quite heartbreaking and also dangerous escapades. . . .

Since then I have moved up of course, and been into Holland several times, and within one mile of the 'Fatherland.' Who knows? Next time I write we may be in Berlin and this ghastly war finished once and forever.''

In the Spring of 1945 Trevor's predictions had been fulfilled.

The ''Forgotten War'' in the Far East provides us with some of the most heroic stories involving Old Cytringanians. As the Japanese invaded Malaya, Squadron Leader Robin Scott took possession of a train at Butterworth and loaded it with 150 men and the station's records. He climbed into the cab and drove it to safety, even though it had a leaking regulator gland which, from 11 a.m. to 6.30 p.m. turned the cab into a steam bath.

In 1942, a Chinese woman, Bing Ooon, wrote to the wife of W/O R. P. Cox about how he saved the lives of her and her family. He visited her house in Butterworth after travelling eight days from South Patani without sleep or food. His open car was strafed by a Japanese fighter, as he drove to Bing Ooon's house to warn her of the Japanese advance.

Private G. Taffs escaped the Japanese only seven hours after they took Singapore. He was at sea in an open boat for six days, lost in the swamps of Sumatra for three days and took another five weeks to reach the safety of Ceylon. In a letter to Reg Tailby, Taffs wrote: ''I wish to lay claim to being the first (to my knowledge anyway) Old Cyt to become an escaped prisoner of war.''

It was Taffs who later reported that G. W. Ipgrave, previously reported missing, was taken prisoner by the Japanese in Singapore. He was to spend the rest of the war working for the Japanese. He spent six months in Singapore before being moved to Siam in October 1942 to build a railway from Bangkok to Moulmein. On his return to England, Ipgrave recalled those painful days:

> ''When I meet the morning beam,
> Or lay me down at night to dream,
> I hear my bones within me say,
> 'Another night, another day'.''

'Come and get it.'

I slip from under the sacking which serves me for a blanket, pick off some of the more adventurous lice, and massage the tender areas where bamboo notches have been pressing into my skin as I grope for my battered mess-tin. I go and get it. With visions of egg and bacon in my mind I draw my level pint of soggy, gritty rice and my teaspoonful of sugar. I have just forced down the last unpalatable mouthful and it is time to collect the tools for the day's work. I grab a buckled shovel in preference to a broken pick and we set off for the railway track, squelching and slithering through the mud in bare feet, with occasional gasps as one of us strikes a sharp stone. A cockney half-heartedly remarks that it is 'Just like Sarfend, chum'. I force a grin.

> ''Try I will; no harm in trying,
> Wonder 'tis how little mirth
> Keeps the bones of man from lying
> On the bed of earth''.

We work in the cutting until dusk with a short break for tiffin – more rice and a 'stink-fish', our 'haversack rations'. The sun beats down relentlessly on sweating, half-naked bodies, draining our last reserves of strength. Some are grotesquely inflated with beri-beri, while others are bent double with dysentery. Many are dragging their emaciated bodies on horribly ulcerated legs.

It is five o'clock and we begin to ease up, but the dreaded cry of 'Speedo' and a heavily-wielded length of bamboo keeps us at it. Then comes the rain and I begin to shiver with malaria as we trudge back to camp. On the way I notice there are two or three more rough, wooden crosses in the cemetery plot.

"Lovely lads and dead and rotten;
None that go return again".

He was returned to Singapore in September 1944, where he spent the next six months stevedoring at the docks. In February 1945 he was taken to Saigon where he worked on the completion of two airfields. He was in Pnom-Penh when the war came to an end. Having arrived home he wrote:

"I cannot attempt here to express just what it feels like to be home again. It's just GREAT! Apart from a slight deafness I am feeling pretty fit; though I doubt if I could stand up to anything very strenuous yet. Malaria, dysentery, dermatitis and beri-beri feature pretty prominently on my medical card but it is really amazing how quickly one recovers on better food and in more familiar surroundings."

While Ipgrave and Ronald Brown (who was shipped to Osaka to work) were prisoners of the Japanese, the 14th Army were more than matching the enemy in Burma. W. H. Jacques served in Burma from 1943. He arrived at Chittagong thinking that he was going to North Burma. Instead he was sent to Arakan:

"I thought it would be a bit more peaceful down there – but it proved to be very lively indeed.

The climate was an enemy more formidable than the Jap, believe me; a thousand foot climb up the side of a jungle-covered hill, with a wireless set on one's back is no picnic, especially when it's about 125°F in the sun, and the Japs at the top are doing their best to keep us at the bottom.

One of our toughest jobs was taking and holding Hill 170. The Japs tried hard for that hill, and a few other hills around it. In one of their attacks I passed an order over my set to the guns to keep firing until I told them to stop. They were firing from 8 p.m. till 4 a.m. with only an occasional break to pour water down the barrels."

No matter where the Allies faced the Axis forces, Old Boys from Kettering Grammar School seemed to bump into each other. Flight-Lt. Bird's journey to Aden was made very enjoyable when he met N. J. Robinson, who was the ship's First Officer:

"As you can imagine, his cabin was a Godsend on a crowded troopship, to say nothing of the contents of his locker."

Norman Lamford recounts a meeting in a remote part of the Midlands:

"Here I came across what I thought was a very old man sitting on a plank supported at either end upon a box, which plank bridged a seemingly bottomless pit. Something seemed familiar about this old man's face. Was it? Could it possibly be? It was none other than C. R. Linnett."

Norman hadn't seen his old pal since he left the School some ten years before.

Ricky Bates ran into an old School mate, Dick Hill from Wellingborough:

"As you probably are aware he (Hill) is a warrant officer in the Education Corps and I hardly knew whether to call him 'Sir' or 'old man'. However, he produced two copies of *Reveille* just like Mr Whitney used to lead us out of the fog on a mountain top, and for a moment I was back at school again."

In June 1941, G. P. Ipgrave wrote: "I relax in a deck chair on the balcony to play table tennis in the Recreation Room with private Geoffrey Tapps, whom I bumped into the day I first arrived. We have so far managed to stick close together, through . . . foreign draft and postings to other Companies." They were still together when the Japanese invaded Malaya. Unfortunately, Ipgrave was taken prisoner of war while Taffs managed to escape (more on this later).

R. D. I. (Robin) Scott wrote that two members of 2A in 1923 were also at his camp – Dick Cox and Lewin from Desborough. R. D. Stebbings, who spent much of the war as a flying instructor in Canada and U.S.A., met up with Douglas Jackson Turner in Alabama. John Barlow spent most of his time in Khartoum, where he met Ray Stebbings' brother Neil just before he was taken prisoner of war by the Italians. Barlow also met L. A. C. Brace when he visited Cairo. H. E. Bates, otherwise known as Flying Officer X, found himself sharing quarters with none other than L. T. Bird of Aden fame. But perhaps the most curious meeting of all took place in the depths of the Belgian Congo:

"When D. A. Panter met another Old Boy, Essam of Thrapston, in the Belgian Congo, he did not say, 'Mr Livingstone, I presume,' but promptly began to discuss the 440 relay race of 1932." Curiously, when Denis moved on to Gibraltar he met up with another schoolmate, Colin Whitney. L.-Cpl. A.H.S. Green served in Egypt where he met George Barratt shortly before he was taken prisoner of war. He also bumped into Ivan Barlow, Eddie Lyles and Geoff Watson. Tony Ireson and G. N. W. Kay met on a village station platform somewhere in India. Finally, Neil Stebbings and John Ireton experienced the most dramatic reunion of the war, as they came face to face in a German prison camp.

Looking back through the pages of *Reveille*, one of the most striking aspects of the letters is the great respect that the Old Boys had for the School and many of its masters. Time and time again there are references to, and messages for, particular teachers. Pilot Walker had messages for both Mr Kirby and 'Tommy' Corke:

"Mr Kirby, if he remembers me, will be glad to know that, through my wanderings, and meeting people all over the world, a small part of that discipline and steadiness which he tried so hard to instil in me during our constant encounters in the classroom, is being slowly drummed into my head.

Mr Corke will, I think, be sorry to learn that I have given up working with my hands, being a fighter pilot, or at least that is what I am supposed to be."

L.A.C. Peter Hague wrote from North Africa:

"Luckily I happen to be near the sea and my main recreation has been swimming. I shall never regret those difficult hours in the belt under the expert tuition of Mr Woodward."

Sub-Lt. E. C. Denton was also indebted to a French master:

"I must also pass my thanks to Mr Tynan for his unremitting efforts to teach me French, without any great sign of appreciation on my part. For eight years I did not use French, or speak it, and one November day, to my surprise as much as anyone else's, I found myself flung down in French territory – the ony person on the ship who had ever learnt or even attempted to learn any French. It became very necessary that the ship should have an interpreter and there was not much choice as to who it should be."

Wilfred Mole writing from North Africa commented:

"One thing is certain, my knowledge of Geography, so painfully drummed into me by the long-suffering Mr Godfrey, has been greatly supplemented by personal, sometimes painful, experience."

A. Denton acknowledged his debt to Kettering Grammar School when he wrote:

"I am glad that Mr Hopkins and Mr Whitney instilled into me the love of Maths and Physics, for I am feeling the value of it now, more than ever."

One further tribute came from L. T. Bird stationed in Aden: "I show *Reveille* to others out here with pride and so far I've not come across anyone whose old school had produced anything like it. I've found, too, that I've been able to hold my own at most things – another proof of the excellent training we had."

One has only to read the "Visitors" section of each magazine to realise just how much the School meant to all those Old Boys serving in the forces. Many of those mentioned above were frequent visitors: 'Nelly' Marlow was always popping in and even brought a gift of ship's tobacco for certain masters. On Speech Day 1943, Mr Kirby, doubtless one of the recipients, said that the gift, "enables us to understand why Nelson did not see the signal!" On one occasion Linnett visited the School only to find everyone on holiday. Not to be beaten, he called round to Mr Scott's house for a chat and to catch up with "school gossip". Other Old Boys gave talks on their wartime experiences: Major George Dickins, returning from North Africa, gave a clear account to the school of the organisation of the Army in the field while N. G. Trehearn, who had emigrated to New Zealand and was a pilot in the R.N.Z.A.F., gave the boys a talk on his adopted country. S. House, who was a diplomat in Panama, made time to look up his "alma mater" during his visit to England.

In all, 54 Old Cytringanians gave their lives during the Second World War. Their deeds and those of all the others who survived are recorded for posterity in *Reveille*. Acts of bravery abound and many received decorations for their gallantry. One of the earliest was Sergeant Ray Lewin who was awarded the George Cross for rescuing his co-pilot from a blazing bomber. Although wounded himself, he carried his companion to safety. Sadly Ray was killed on active service in late 1941. F/O K. V. Panter who was injured on landing when his Mosquito caught fire, still managed to rescue his navigator from the burning plane. For his gallantry he was awarded the D.S.O. Major F. S. Rimmington was also awarded the George Cross. Among those who received the D.F.C. were R. T. Goucher, A. J. W. Hills and D. J. Turner. Flight.-Lt. G. B. Sharman was awarded the D.F.C and Bar while G. W. Allen received the D.F.M. Four Old Boys were mentioned in Despatches – C. N. Marlow, D. A. Marlow, J. B. I. and R. D. I. Scott.

How can one assess the importance of *Reveille*? At the end of the war L. J. Bartley returned to edit the last few issues. His evaluation of its importance cannot be bettered and is here reproduced in full:

"Before another magazine is published *Reveille* may have taken its honoured place among the historical records of the School; and if the hopes of the nations are fulfilled we may not look upon its like again.

Now, therefore, on the eve of its sixth birthday, it behoves us to pay a tribute to our own Forces magazine, unique in Service literature even among the many publications of the last few years: and there is no qualification to 'unique'.

Since that February night, six years ago, when *Reveille* was born by an English fireside, the 47 numbers have maintained a constant link between Old Boys in the Services and the School itself. Its circulation of nearly five hundred copies – although a remarkable total – cannot do justice to the bonds that it has forged; to the pleasure it has given its readers; the goodwill of its contributors; nor to the long and conscientious work of the Editor and his assistants.

If a returned trooper might voice his grateful appreciation, that would include all who brought *Reveille* into the world, and have kept it in being, among them the young gentleman from the School who pushed a copy of the latest number through our letter box. A very great friend of the School has borne the considerable financial burden: if in rendering thanks we honour that anonymity, those thanks are none the less sincere.

The pages of *Reveille* provide a history of the war, for we have fought on every sea, in every land, and over most of them. Copies have been posted to cryptic addresses, disguising every clime as only the Services know how.

TopLeft
Major W. J. ALLEN, M.B.E. (R.E.),
1924–9

Top Right
C.P.O. JONES, H.C., M.B.E. (R.N.),
1918–23

Centre
Squadron-Leader R. T. Goucher,
D.F.C. (R.A.F.), 1930-8

Bottom Left
Major B. SMITH, M.B.E. (R.A.O.C.),
1916–22,
Joint Secretary of the Old Cytringanians

Bottom Right
Flight-Lieutenant H. C. BIRD, M.B.E.
(R.A.F.), 1919–25

Top Left
Captain J. B. I. SCOTT (R.E.),
Mentioned in Despatches. 1923–8.

Top Right
Flight-Lieutenant K. V. PANTER,
D.S.O. (R.A.F.), 1933–8

Centre
Squadron-Leader R. D. I. SCOTT,
Mentioned in Despatches (R.A.F.),
1920–4.

Bottom Left
Captain R. SNEDDON, M.B.E.
(Intelligence Corps.), 1935–8

Bottom Right
Flying Officer A. J. W. HILLS, D.F.C.
(R.A.F.), 1929-32

Some of those who received decorations for their gallantry.

It has recorded triumphs with pride and sacrifices with sorrow. To it Kipling, who drew both his schoolboy and his soldier (there was no Air Force then) in the rare hand of a master, and with Ian Hay discovered that the boy is father to the man, would undoubtedly have given his august blessing. To say that the growth of the Old Cytringanians is in some measure due to the spirit *Reveille* has engendered and fostered, would not, one feels, be an exaggeration.

Can we account for its success, apart from the natural links of former days? Yes, it is a forum with very little barred. An early commentator observed that 'on the whole *Reveille* tends towards liveliness'. It still does. Its style, if not salty, at least smacks of the camp and the open air. Five hundred letters from nearly as many writers proves the success of a policy which has never changed.

Born in the gloom of war, *Reveille* lives in the hard-won peace and, like its homecoming readers, finds that things are not quite the same. To everything its day and place, and we honour *Reveille* and all it has meant to us wherever we may have been, to our wives at home, and to the School, by observance of that dictum.

Time will inevitably dim the now vivid memories, but never so much that we shall not occasionally stretch out a hand to the book-shelf whereon rests our bound volume of *Reveille*; and one of the gallant company of ghosts from those memorable years will hand it to us. Let it not be too infrequent, or he may, as an old friend, even blow the dust from the edges of the leaves (since such things are not of woman's care) as a silent rebuke that we have neglected it too long.''

A. F. Scott and prefects – 1944-45

G. C. Hulett, C. E. Newton, G. N. Ashman, J. S. Dodge, J. R. Kirkup, E. J. Colville, R. Moffatt, W. R. Arnold,
C. F. Griggs, C. Tite, G. A. Lawrence, A. F. Scott, R. P. Dyson, R. Stonehouse, M. A. Williamson

CHAPTER 12

A. F. Scott

Headmaster 1943-1951

By a colleague

When A. F. Scott joined us in 1943, speculation was rife as to the kind of Headmaster we were getting. We knew he came from Taunton School and that he had to his credit certain English text-books. We soon found that he combined a love of scholarship with wide cultural interests and a charming personality.

Other hands have written of his work in the classroom; it will be sufficient for me to emphasise that never in the School's history have so many boys proceeded to universities as during his eight years.

He found the Old Cytringanians a vigorous and flourishing society; he took an immediate interest in its work and joined in its activities with enthusiasm. He quickly established a reputation as a witty and fluent speaker, and the reply to the toast of ''The School'' at the Annual Dinner was always eagerly awaited. The dignified Honours Board commemorating the dead of two World Wars owes much to his wise advice and unfailing good taste.

It was not long before he changed the appearance of the corridors and classrooms by hanging first-rate reproductions of famous paintings. Later his enthusiasm for the visual arts proved infectious, and on a memorable afternoon, with Eric Newton on his right, and H. E. Bates, the donor, on his left, the admirable collection of original water-colours was formally declared open.

His cultural interests found a wider field in the Three Arts Club and the Film Society. Of both he was the Founder-President. Both owe a great deal to his keen interest and unfailing support. He was also a member of Kettering Rotary Club, where his speeches were much appreciated.

The wise guidance which he bestowed on the Sixth Form later helped future teachers at Borough Road Training College.

Contributed by an Old Boy whose span at K.G.S. coincided with that of the Headmaster

Looking back on the eight years' headmastership of Mr A. F. Scott, one realizes rather strikingly the effect of his modernizing influence. More than at any other time during the School's history, the atmosphere of the building must have seemed to returning Old Boys, one imagines, very changed under a fresh young hand. New schemes of decoration, building and organization followed each other, one by one; some – like the prefabricated classrooms – were demanded by force of circumstances. Others were introduced by design, to mention just a few: the greatly increased number and range of paintings in rooms and corridors, the fostering of new School societies, and the institution of valuable annual events like the Oratory Competition, the Photographic Exhibition and the Boxing Tournament.

In such "extra-mural" activities as these (if one may use the term), Mr Scott was peculiarly adroit; but the academic achievement of the School, too, especially in the three examination years at the top, more than kept pace with the unprecedented expansion of the School in scope and numbers. Mounting figures of successes year by year in the School Certificate and Higher School Certificate examinations were themselves overshadowed by the Cytringanian entry into the universities. It cannot too strongly be stressed how tireless were Mr Scott's efforts on behalf of his leavers to fit them into a suitable milieu for their further education. One quails to think what headaches one was spared by his own belligerence in that battle of forms and trunk calls, interviews and personal pressure which proved to be the result of the new educational opportunity. In outposts like Edinburgh, Reading and Bristol, in nearer centres like Nottingham, Birmingham and London, and particularly at Cambridge, there were many Old Boys who owed a great debt to A. F. Scott.

His own most successful style of teaching Sixth-Form English was based on university method and carried with it a vivid awareness of the many facets of the world outside the classroom. A life begun in the Orange Free State with close Irish ties, and lived in the most interesting circles, early in Northern Ireland, then at Cambridge, and later in the public-school atmosphere of Oakham and Taunton, provided him with ample resources for illustration and digression – those "hangers-on" to the teacher's stock-in-trade, which are so necessary for a wide and balanced view of any Modern subject.

One who grew up under the Headship of A. F. Scott very willingly acknowledges the success and the solid achievement of that period and the happiness which new methods, as they settled down, produced in the running of an all-too unwieldy building – full of boys.

CHAPTER 13

Those Golden Times

CIVILISED EXPECTATIONS

Jim Dodge

My brother John and I were at the Grammar School during the 'forties. The School had, at that time, admitted from the Naseby Road estate only five pupils. Twenty years later 'Joe' Ashworth was to tell me that John and I were the two rudest boys the School had ever come across. Looking back, I dare say we were – but not intentionally, I think. The School was the making of us both and despite our rudeness, we received endless help and kindness from a surprising number of the masters who taught there.

This is really the whole point of what I want to say. My regard and affection for the School (and distress at its demise) are entirely a response to a group of what I now know were rather remarkable men. Tributes to Edmund Kirby have been paid, justifiably, from H.E. Bates onwards and I add my own for what it's worth. I still scan whatever I write to try and make sure it won't make him raise his eyebrows, tap my shoulder and call me his "dear old chump." I return increasingly to the poetry of Clare and his other favourites, all now in fashion again. A. F. Scott approved of both *ITMA* and *Paradise Lost* and from him I learned a different but still invigorating approach to literature and received hours of painstaking personal attention, for which I never thanked him properly. (A few years earlier I had experienced a minor act of kindness from the seemingly cold J. I. Scott and only recognised it long after he was dead.) When I left after School Certificate in 1944, A. F. Scott summoned my mother, persuaded her to send me back and arranged discreet financial support. I owe debts of a similar kind to 'Joe' Ashworth and John Wood, the latter of whom I only came really to appreciate after I finally left School. I could multiply examples although, funnily enough, I was introduced to music not by a master but by David Barlow, a fellow pupil. That was another stroke of luck.

I remember being very rude to John Tynan when I was really old enough to know better. He wasn't everybody's taste but he influenced me more profoundly than almost anyone else I have ever met. I am still ashamed of my rudeness to him and so I should be.

Like most of the others, he had served in the Great War. He said the main

A Birthday Message.

from the President, A. F. Scott, Esq.

The Hygram Players are to be heartily congratulated on attaining their twenty-first birthday. At this time of celebration we would remember their long list of previous successes, their notably ambitious choice of play and their signal distinction in the British Drama League Festival earlier this year. The vitality of the Society was seen in the way it continued its activities throughout the difficult war period; since then, with fresh impetus it has achieved a new and wider reputation. I am sure all who know the Hygram Players will join me in this message of congratulation today and in offering every good wish for continued success in the future.

Previous Productions include :—

1927—Mice and Men
1928—The School for Scandal
1929—The Admirable Crichton
1930—Lady Windermere's Fan
1931—You Never Can Tell
1933 The Skin Game
1934—The Farmer's Wife
1935—The Late Christopher Bean
1936—Family Affairs
Pygmalion
1937 Distinguished Gathering
1938—Noah
1941—Fresh Fields
1942—Ladies in Waiting
1942—Ladies in Retirement
1943—At Mrs. Beam's
1944—Arms and the Man
1945—Quality Street
1946—They came to a City
1947—Our Town
1948—The School for Scandal

The Hygram Players express their gratitude to :-

A. F. Scott, Esq. and Miss Woodrow for the use of the School during rehearsals.

Palmers' Music Stores for the booking of seats.

The Editor and Staff of the "Evening Telegraph".

The Programme Sellers, Stewards and others who have freely given their help.

THE DARK LADY OF THE SONNETS

AND

ANDROCLES AND THE LION

HYGRAM'S TWENTY-FIRST BIRTHDAY CELEBRATION

John Tynan, who produced Androcles and the Lion *in November 1948, also provided the drawings for the Programme.*

demand the conflict had made on him was learning to ride and his backside had never recovered. In the years I knew him he rode in to School from Isham on his wife's old tall bicycle with the skirts of his mustard-coloured overcoat held back with safety pins. He looked like a Napoleonic artilleryman. He taught French with the kind of resignation that acknowledged defeat as inevitable. He taught German in the same spirit and told us of a former pupil who, serving in France in the first year of the Second War, used a copy of *Die Zeitung* to line the seat of a doubtful French lavatory and left with German mirror-writing on his buttocks. He never explained how the gendarmes found this evidence, but his former pupil was held in custody by them as a suspected German spy – until the print faded, I supposed.

John was an Irishman and an artist sooner than a French master. His curly, greying dark hair and his spiky eyebrows made him a figure of foreboding in his depressive moods. In his manic periods he would scribble frantic but fluent drawings on the blackboards and wipe them off with the sleeves of his ragged gown. (I still have a copy of his sketch of me, then a first year undergraduate, patronising him as he buys pints at the Royal Hotel in 1949.) He got me to look at Paul Nash's paintings and at Duncan Grant and Graham Sutherland and John Piper – all in the Penguin *Painters* series. He and Godfrey (who warned my future wife against me after I was rude to *him*) produced the School Plays and he struggled for weeks to cure my Kettering pronunciation of the diphthong *ow* –

"Now, by this hand . . . ."

I still can't do it and I was a very awkward Gratiano. More to the point, he got me to read Eugene O'Neill and J. M. Synge and Sean O'Casey and didn't think they were unsuitable for one of my age.

He and Mrs Tynan lived in a lovely, compact Georgian house near the church in Isham. They asked me to tea from time to time and I biked over. Mrs Tynan petrified me, whilst their sophisticated children, Oliver and Alathea, scared me almost to death. Tea was taken in the drawing room, perched upon wing chairs and settee, a technique I've never mastered. Their ponderous old bulldog slept on the hearthrug, snoring and breaking wind with disconcerting frequency. I think John and his wife must have been amused by my attempts to ignore the animal.

I don't know why they bothered with me, but they did. They took me to the ballet and to the cinema to see *Fantasia* and *The Wizard of Oz.* At the time there didn't seem anything exceptional about it. They taught me the meaning and value of cultivation.

But it wasn't only them. Kirby was prominent in founding the Kettering Three Arts Club and Sammy Hulls, a shell-shocked Guardsman whom we tormented unpardonably, sang Schubert *lieders* that we were encouraged to hear. Kirby got H. E. Bates to present a collection of English water colours to the School and A. F. Scott augmented it. It was the sort of school that expected you to be interested in civilised things even in the depths of a war. It also expected you to play cricket and rugby, to run deadly cross-countries and to enter slow bicycle races. I don't think we were ever told that all this was what ''Maners makyth man'' really meant – the gnomic frame looked down on us daily, as did ''Non sibi'' (Don't spit).

If we cared to, we received an education. I suppose there must have been narrowness of a sort as well – it was a school of its time and not everybody appreciated it or had reason to. Quite straightforwardly, it made *me*, if that's anything of a recommendation. I try not to be sentimental about it and I know how nostalgia warps and tints. Until the Old Cyts dinner, two years ago, I had been convinced for forty years that there was broken glass set into the top of the wall dividing the Grammar School yard from the High School's. There wasn't, of course, but there's a kind of truth about it and perhaps there ought to have been.

THE VISUAL ARTS IN SCHOOL AND AFTER SCHOOL

The Revd. Canon D. H. Palmer

Towards the end of the Second World War, energised by the young Head, A. F. Scott, School activity beyond the classroom took on a freshness which had perhaps been lacking for a long time, School drama apart.

Schoolchildren were catered for, at a rather elementary level, by the tumultuous Saturday morning clubs at the town's cinemas. They were also probably taken by staid parents to suitable shows as a treat on occasional weekday evenings. Ordinary commercial cinema – none the worse for that, maybe.

The new element of ''art films'' arrived with the Kettering Film Society screenings in the School hall in Bowling Green Road. A. F. Scott was a leading influence in hiring classics which could be shown on a portable projector, and senior boys were allowed to participate. If any upcoming film promised to contain ''adult'' material (innocent as much of it now seems with late-20th century hindsight) boys wishing to attend had to line up after morning assembly to obtain the Head's nod. I don't remember any refusals.

Thus it was, in the mid-40s, that an eager generation of later teenagers sat on those very slippery folding chairs, in what would now seem almost intolerable discomfort, to see acclaimed or innovative ''shorts'' and main features of enduring cinematic importance.

Before we could ever travel to France, and before television had returned, we imbibed the flavour of a wider world in films like *La Bête Humaine* and *La Règle du Jeu,* directed by Jean Renoir; *Le Jour se Lève* and *Les Enfants du Paradis* (Marcel Carné), while there were other masterpieces like D. W. Griffiths' *Intolerance,* Fritz Lang's *Metropolis,* Eisenstein's *Battleship Potemkin* and great early Chaplin like *Modern Times.* Maybe some of these titles seem quite unremarkable to readers who are film aficionados thanks to BBC 2 or Channel 4. But I count it really noteworthy that so many black-and-white classics were booked and screened for a Kettering clientele when life was still far from normal. Along with the estimable Three Arts Club, which must not be overlooked, these were formative influences in School and town.

The first thirty years of the Gotch building found the walls of that dignified pile distinctly under-used for hanging pictures. Yes, I do remember the framed motto "MANERS MAKYTH MAN", and (opposite the Head's study) a large coloured reproduction of the Doge of Venice in odd headgear which we loved because he looked like Mr Whitney, Head of Physics. I recall few others – and they from an educational catalogue, I suspect, of the 1930s.

A. F. Scott (again) persuaded H. E. Bates to allow a munificent gift to buy in various original works both old and recent. Among the latter, I remember an abstract in black and white by John Minton which was found to have been hung upside down! Among many other works, I specially appreciated watercolours by Edward Lear, with his zany notes in sepia ink, here and there, reminding him of the colour he should later paint on top of the words. I have followed in his footsteps in various places, specially while working in Italy, and marvel at the scale of his output. Perhaps he could offer so many works to clients and buyers precisely by that method of fast production, perfected later. At all events, there was a lot more at work in that ungainly body and sometimes depressed mind than the public guess from his nonsense drawings and verses. I would like to think that a lifetime's interest in Lear had its beginnings as I came and went on the balcony and its adjacent corridor. Art brought to boys in a way it never was in the Art Room.

After-school activities in the War had, for obvious reasons, been minimal – except for valiant fire-watching and other public-spirited duties. There was, of course, the venerable Debating Society under the stern control of A. W. H. Woodward. I was one of a long line of boy secretaries who produced minutes of such unnecessary fullness that all subsequent committee work has seemed a relief.

But for real creative enjoyment I would pay tribute to the Camera Club set up by Frederick Lawson, Chemistry master and smoker in excelsis, who benignly gave much time to teaching and encouraging amateur photography in the Upper School.

His knowledge of solutions and papers and processes (there was virtually no amateur colour then) can be taken for granted. But he personally constructed an enlarger in *wood,* using old lenses and other components;

and he gave countless hours in the fug of the blacked-out Sick Room (imagine that under today's hygiene regulations!) to supervise keen, and increasingly able, boy photographers.

Exhibitions became a feature, with modest prizes. The School magazine blossomed with half-tone illustrations. (When I was editor, I fear that these sent it way over cost, but there was no reprimand from on high). The exercise, and the friendly rivalry, of learning to compose and produce good pictures made us more observant and helped us to branch out in various fields, not least the treasuring of Northamptonshire landscape and the county's wealth of fine building.

My own love of the camera (as of the cinema and of the framed picture) continues unabated fifty years on, and I bless the men who enlarged our small-town horizons in those rather spartan days, introducing us to new skills and to wider interests which would endure.

AN ENTRANT BOY

Rex Moore

For many years there were two ways of entering the Kettering Grammar School. One could win a scholarship and get a free place, or take an entrance exam and pay fees.

It was in 1943 that I sat the entrance exam, for a place at the School, aged eight. Of the exam, I remember nothing, but the preliminary interview stands out quite clearly. It took place in Room 1. I was impressed by the kindness of the interviewer and his courtesy to my mother, who accompanied me. For the first time in my life I had met Mr Kirby.

It had all started with lengthy discussions at home, in the evenings of the spring of 1943. I had little say in those proceedings, but unbeknown to my parents, I was sitting at the top of the stairs listening in! The main topic of discussion was the fees. Could they afford them? At £4. 5s. 0d. per term it represented a sizeable commitment to my father's modest salary. Eventually I was told, to my great relief, I was going. Throughout my eavesdropping I had been willing them to say yes.

To a youngster of nine, the ivy clad building in Bowling Green Road was more than impressive. It was then, and probably still is, by far the most impressive building in Kettering, except for the Parish Church. It seemed to have been there for ever and would remain so, although the fact was that it was over halfway through its "shelf-life" as a school.

I cannot remember my first day at the School. I had left all my friends at the Henry Gotch Junior School. Some envious, some hostile, when they saw me kitted out with blazer, short trousers, cap and long grey socks. These items were suitably chosen by Mr Poyner, the manager of A. Webbs in Market Street. This was complemented by leather satchel from Stanleys, the smell of which remains with me to this day. Oddly enough, that satchel and subsequent ones never lasted as long as those of my fellow pupils!

That first smart satchel, worn regulation position over both shoulders, was a far cry from my latter years at School, where its many times replacement was my father's army small pack.

It is almost certain this smart new boy's first trip to School was with Bob Barnard, an older boy, who lived opposite us in Hazel Road. Bob had regaled me, as a member of his little gang, with various tales of the School and its teachers. None of these was daunting; in fact, just the opposite. I went willingly to School.

This attitude was not betrayed or dashed. Into IB I went, with about thirty others, to meet our first teacher. This lady was a Miss Hutchinson, whom we subsequently found to be the epitome of kindness and understanding towards children.

We were in the classroom just before the balcony and I had what was probably the best time of my school life. I was not to know, in September 1943, that it was only to be two terms long.

Oddly enough, some weeks into that term Miss Hutchinson upset me. We were taking various tests to decide as to whether we were to go into the Upper or Lower division of 1B. Half way through the Maths section, the book from which I was working was taken away, despite my protests that I could do the work, and I was in 1B Lower.

The rest of life, however, was wonderful. We kept silkworms, some of us taking them home. There are two Mulberry trees in Kettering: one in the Manor House gardens, the other along the Headlands. All 1B pupils learned that those silkworms had more than voracious appetites.

We learned about the life cycle of frogs, the species of newts, flowers, trees and the whole world of nature. Sent to seek out Scarlet Pimpernel, I remember finding some in the stubble of a field off Gipsy Lane.

Friday afternoon was story time. Wonderful adventure tales covering the whole world about a man, whose name I've forgotten, and his boy assistant. These were purely part of Miss Hutchinson's wonderful imagination. We also met Richmal Crompton's William. Interwoven with this "story afternoon" was a magic handout to pupils who had achieved well in the week. A treasure trove of various items was brought out and some lucky lad was the proud owner of some unusual item. I remember getting a picture, in oils, of a sailing boat, painted, according to Miss Hutchinson, by a Mexican.

So this idyllic experience went on. We would look at the rest of the School in wonderment. The heroes of cricket and rugby in the upper years. The masters whom we should meet one day. But we were firmly and safely in the hands of our Miss Hutchinson. Then, in the Spring term of 1944, the bottom dropped out of our world. Miss Hutchinson quietly told us one day that she was leaving. As is the nature of all safe, secure school children, we were upset. We all begged and pleaded, ''Stay!'' All to no avail. We collected and bought her a leaving present. I cannot remember what, but I'm sure it was 'Podge' Laing, one of her favourites, who presented her with our farewell gift.

Our devastation was completed when, in the Summer Term of 1944, we met our new form mistress. Gone was the happy atmosphere. Gone were the smiles. Gone were the stories. No matter how many times we asked, Miss Cotterell refused point blank to countenance such a waste of time. Life at School took a considerable downturn. At this distance in time, when memories usually become mellowed, I still cannot remember a kind word to anyone from that lady. Discipline with a capital 'D' was the order of every day, to the exclusion of all else. I do not know what satisfaction Miss Cotterell derived from her job, it certainly did not appear to be the liking of children.

Other memories of the Summer Term of 1944 were connected with the war. Tanks were parked in the Cattle Market, their guns sticking over the wall into Bowling Green Road. They were probably connected with D-Day. The memory of that event is still very firmly fixed in my mind. A fellow classmate and friend, Brian Blake, told me about it as we stood under the guard-railed tree, which stood in the middle of Bowling Green Road at the junction with London Road. We were just going home for dinner. How he knew I've no idea, but I recall it vividly.

Some time passed. Fortnightly orders were introduced, a fact I kept from my mother, and on return from the army, my father, as long as possible. Why? I was always at the bottom of the list! A fact that A. F. Scott, the Head, reminded me of one day, when I was called to his office to be told I was bottom of the School!

Fellow pupils come to mind. Norman Smith, Fraser Gold, Geoff Harris, Ian Bird, Mick Miller, to name but a few.

Then we heard in one assembly that Mr Morgan, the fiery Welshman who had terrified me in Music lessons, little more than two terms ago, had been killed in Italy, flying a Spitfire.

September 1944 saw us go into 1B Upper. My goodness, didn't we get airs and graces as far as the new lot were concerned: Mick Cotton, Philip Brading and company. However, we were still to suffer under the redoubtable Miss Cotterell. It was about this time that this lady decided that some of us needed to improve our handwriting. We were given books of beautiful scroll writing, the subject of which I well remember. The mountains and lakes of South America. Beneath the scroll were horizontal lines corresponding with those above to enable us to make a fair copy. I'm afraid the copy in my case was far from fair and certainly failed to improve my handwriting. The geographical information met the same fate, forgotten the next day.

Frighteningly, someone introduced the same books into the school at which I was teaching in the '80s.

Life was a little easier, as we also had Miss Jagger occasionally. A cheerful, if somewhat fiery lady, who could laugh. I have to admit I was an increasing nuisance for this poor lady, but nevertheless she did not bear grudges and I remember her quite fondly, as I am sure others do.

The year passed with interminable games of tick in the playground, with some of us finding our feet and joining in the everlasting game of football with completely indistinct sides, which surged between the goalmouths of the girls' typing room at one end and the tin hut at the other. One of the senior boys involved was Eddie Hapgood's son.

Memories of walking to School with the aforementioned Bob Barnard, sometimes also in company with Bob Scotney, much senior to me, and Alan Godson. Occasionally, we would see the B17 Flying Fortress returning to Grafton Underwood, some damaged or on fire. Red and green flares would be fired out of these aircraft, indicating states of damage and casualties.

Boys would obtain bits of perspex from an aeroplane crash dump at Burton Latimer to make various items of jewellery. Shelter drill was also an aspect of the wartime period. Norman Goudie was pushed down the shelter entrance, by a pupil who shall remain nameless, and cut his chin badly. The same shelter eventually became the Kettering Council nuclear funk hole!

Somewhere around that time a boy in the Third or Fourth Year died. It was a shock: terrible to all, certainly to me at the age of 10. Although I cannot remember his name, I can still picture him now as he lined up in the small playground by the detention room.

The year 1945 came and with it the end of the war. Now, perhaps, the Tuck Shop would open again. Mrs Old's opposite the School had been the pre-war regulatory institution that all schools of note had at that time. Sadly, the apocryphal buns, cakes, and sweets never reappeared in my time at School.

A boost in our fortunes came in September of that year. We became 1A under Miss Jagger. A year, I suppose, that became my apprenticeship for wasting the academic opportunities offered by the Kettering Grammar School. Acting the fool became the order of the day for me and one or two others. In case I sound too regretful, we certainly enjoyed it at the time.

Imitations of Harry Hemsley's Horace, complete with my own puppet, which I still have, and an incident I will mention later, were all part of the fun. By now, we were in the Woodwork room, soon to be the Biology lab. We were still playing soccer on the rugby pitches – a bit unfair when you consider the height of the crossbar for the poor ten year old goalie. A few were promoted on games day to play rugby (Mick Miller comes to mind) with the School proper. Miss Cotterell sometimes refereed. I suppose she had something about her to do that in those days.

One day A. F. Scott came into the classroom and told us about the 11+.

We all had to take it. We all passed, officially that is, except one, but he was not forced to go.

Under Miss Jagger the year passed pleasantly enough as far as I was concerned, mainly because of the much relaxed attitude of this good natured, if sometimes short tempered lady.

I suppose the climax (no pun intended) of my clowning came as a result of a find I made when walking back to School after lunch one day. I discovered some mysterious small packets in St. Mary's Road. They were at the entrance to the then American Red Cross Club, later to be the School canteen and today, completely changed, Tresham College. What was inside these silver attractions? In the middle of the first lesson I blew one up. I'll leave the reader to guess what they were and the reaction of poor Miss Jagger.

Over forty years later, whilst Deputy Head of Thrapston Middle School, I had a boy brought to me by an irate dinner lady. His offence? Using a condom as a balloon. Who says the Grammar School did not prepare pupils for life? Promising the good lady that I would assuage her outraged feeling, the boy got away with an earwigging, after she had left the scene. Hypocrisy has no place in the life of a schoolteacher.

In July 1946, the ''prep school'' era for me was over. The 1944 Education Act had negated the need for fees. In September 1946 Dick Thorpe, Fraser Gold, Andrew McKay and myself found ourselves in 2P, under the patronage of 'Joe' Ashworth, with nearly thirty new boys, all of whom had passed the 11+. Entrant boys no longer, Butler boys all.

As has already been mentioned, I did not become one of the School's high flyers. However, I enjoyed most of the next five years at the School. I was involved with such diverse activities as rugby, boxing, the Debating Society and Photographic Club. A regret was that I did not go into the 6th Form, but that's another story.

Twenty years after leaving School, after a varied career, I took a three year mature student training course to become a teacher. In that occupation, memories of the vagaries, good and bad, of the masters of my time at the Kettering Grammar School stood me in very good stead in dealing with the variety of pupils I met in my twenty years on the other side of the classroom.

DIVERSE AND IDIOSYNCRATIC

Fraser Gold

As a pupil from 1943 to 1954, I recall a School which was served with distinction by an array of staff, many of whom had unorthodox teaching styles or characteristics which leave an impression long after most of the content of lessons has been forgotten.

When I transferred into the Junior section of the School, the Acting

Headmaster was E. E. Kirby, whose quiet authority, love of the English countryside and the skills and traditions of those who worked to create it, and delight in the power of language must have influenced many. He needs a section of his own in this volume, but how about remembering his preference for the eighteenth century writers as models of style, and his passion for the expressiveness of the old vernacular speech? The Northamptonshire expression ''pudge'' for puddle, and derivatives such as ''pudgy'' stick in my mind. He also saved up his most penetrating questions to the end of a lesson, rewarding correct answers with ''a small silver coin'' (6d.).

The class teacher for the Junior class in those days was Miss Hutchinson. She must have travelled widely, and knew other countries and their ''geography'' so well that she held us spellbound as she made up adventure stories about Old Harry in various settings. They were told as serials, each episode ending on a ''cliffhanger''. When one story was completed, she would even invite us to request where Old Harry would go next. What a way to teach Geography, multi-cultural education etc. Old Harry and Young Jim – never published. When she left to take up a post in Liverpool College we wept.

Moving up into the Senior School, the Form master was the kindly, twinkling 'Joe' Ashworth, one of a group of teachers with north country connections and a love of the Lake District. There were various expeditions over many Easter Holidays.

It was potentially embarrassing to me to know that a number of the teachers had been in the Home Guard with my father. Was this why 'Weeky' (vici) Wood always turned to me when one of the Corby boys, thick Lanarkshire accent still untouched, would attempt to ask or answer a question? ''What's he saying, Gold?'' He loved his Classics and the precision of the Latin Language. Sadly, I doubt if many of us ever read our Virgil of a winter's night with our feet on the mantelpiece, as he dreamed for us. Not in the original, anyway. Yet I still hear in my mind the declamation of Virgil's *Aeneid Book II.* Whole successions of lines, and those telling phrases that rang a bell with the fortunes of teenage romance. . . . ''oscula summa''. Did he ever realise that his beloved Latin could sometimes speak to a generation of ''Milk bar Romeos''?

'Pecker' Hopkins, the lean and sharp featured Mathematician was another of the Home Guard contacts. Totally unorthodox in his teaching style, speaking almost inaudibly, writing almost illegibly, leaving out steps in the working of formulae, with his back to the class for minutes on end, he quietly kept control. For this writer, he was also effective in rescuing a lost cause to a first time pass in 'O' Level Maths. How? Enthusiasm for his subject, linked to his running of the Chess Club and his habit of watching as you made a mess of your written work, then quietly he would interrupt. ''Very interesting, how did you get that?'' And he *listened* as you fumbled an

John Wood encourages the "Milk bar Romeos", 1950.

explanation. I've been in teacher education myself for years, and would never wish to turn out a stereotype teacher, but his strong points I would always want to see.

Habits in staff? 'Cuthbert' Godfrey, who taught Geography, had a number of mannerisms in speech and gesture which appeared with sufficient regularity for a number of us to keep cricket scorebooks in his lessons, England v Australia. Their comparative frequency led to their use for "dot balls", singles, boundaries etc. Over lunchtime the various books were compared. Did he think we were writing up notes? He knew every boy in the School, and when he acted as Headmaster for a term following a difficult spell for the School, the general running of the establishment from day to day, all round behaviour in classrooms, playground and corridor, were a tribute to his attention to detail.

So many of the staff gave their time out-of-school for clubs and activities, and in our Sixth Form days even invited us home or accepted social invitations, sharing their interests. 'Basher' Coakes, an Arnhem veteran with his boxing club, 'Joe' Young, David Bishop, all the staff who came to the Music and Debating Societies. Who would ever forget that good sport George Laywood, grappling with the motion drawn in the Hat Debate: ''He who laughs last laughs longest''?

They loved their subjects, took an interest in their pupils, shared their interests and ideals. They were diverse and idiosyncratic, but as a group they held together an institution which we remember with affection and gratitude.

BRAVERY, BRAVADO AND BREAKS

Roger Long

There was a tradition that the lessons in the daily Assembly read by Sixth Formers from Mondays to Thursdays should be chosen by a member of staff. On Fridays, however, Sixth Formers were granted the privilege of choosing their own readings.

I remember one Friday. Briggs was a Sixth Former only weeks away from the end of his last term at School. He was two or three years older than me and an object of my admiration. We had played together on the rugby field and had acted in the same School Play. He was a tall, slender, fair skinned lad with a shock of blond curls. He had a light voice and a very distinctive delivery. He chose *The Soldier* by Rupert Brooke.

''If I should die, think only this of me:
That there's some corner of a foreign field
That is forever England''

Briggs was a very able pupil. Was he one of 'Benny' Woodward's star pupils? He had won a place at Cambridge to read History. He chose to do his National Service first and joined the Royal Air Force. He was sent to Canada to train as a flyer. His plane crashed and he was killed.

''There's some corner of a foreign field . . .''

★ ★ ★

In 1947, Mr Godfrey produced *A Midsummer Night's Dream* for the annual School Play. His co-producer was Mr Tynan. It was a joint production with the High School.

Of course, that is the play which has parts for a number of small people, and members of the first and second years were invited to audition for the parts of fairies. A crew was assembled and, when the members were all greased up, no-one but their mothers would have recognised Mick Cotton, 'Bert' Brading, Keith Foreman, Alec Tite and Roger Long. They might have recognised the girl fairies who did not have to be adorned with the green greasepaint. They would not have recognised Roy Church who played a green faced Puck.

For a young pupil who had been a member of the School for only three terms, the Play was a chance to break into the community which was wider than that of his class. We hovered around the big Fifth and Sixth formers. We observed them from a distance. We watched them talk casually and confidently to the older girls from the High School, while we boy fairies looked longingly yet silently at the pretty girl fairies who shared our rehearsals but not our conversations.

Rehearsals went well. We knew our lines, our songs and our moves. The first night was a triumph. For the rest of the week the performances were even more triumphant. That is – until the last night. No one in the audience knew how close we were to disaster. But the fairies knew. Bottom had brought beer into the dressing room and had consumed it all by himself. From his demeanour in the dressing room and particularly in the wings it was clear to us that Bottom would not be able to get through his big scene with us.

But he did. In fact, he put in the performance of a lifetime. The fears of the fairies were unfounded.

Looking back now, I realise that there must have been a lot of bravado in the incident. But it kept the fairies on their toes and gave at least one fairy an interesting insight into life at the top.

★ ★ ★

The proximity of the High School and the fact that the two schools boxed and coxed with some of the classrooms made life very interesting for pubescent boys and girls. The official messages from the two schools was that social intercourse between the pupils was not encouraged. The joint Play productions, the Chemistry classes in the Sixth Form and the Sixth Form dances were carefully supervised privileges.

Many liaisons started under those difficult circumstances – I remember our fear of Miss Woodrow's anger.

Couples used to coincide at various places and times during the school day. This was in spite of the fact that prefects were on duty to stop us peeping into the hall when the girls were doing P.E. and that they used to usher us away from the gate between the two playgrounds in case we saw the girls at netball. The prefects even paraded the top corridor, near the Prefects' Room, but that did not prevent assignations near the statuette of Laocoon and his sons.

I knew that the girl who is now my wife walked along the first floor corridor overlooking the Biology lab on Thursday mornings at break time and I would always manage to recline elegantly on the milk crates drinking my morning milk as she did so. She was also in one of the classrooms, used by the High School, which overlooked ours and she would wave to me as I sat in my seat during Maths on Friday mornings – that is until there was a room change and one day she saw Jimmy Smith where I should have been. I was a little annoyed that he responded to her that day and many others. Jimmy Smith – aka Jim Dale – was like that.

How many couples can boast their very first tryst was outside a men's toilet? The one at the top of Bowling Green Road was the closest place to the School where we felt confident enough to put our caps in our pockets or meet our girlfriends.

FORTNIGHTLY MARKS

Tony Hadden

One cloud hung over my life at the Kettering Grammar School from 1946 to 1951: the pinning up of the "fortnightly marks". Failure, an acknowledged educational concept in those days, doomed you automatically to a Saturday morning detention. The legality of such detentions was never questioned; parent power did not exist in 1946. The threat of a curtailed week-end, as Roy Church and I cycled through the town's only traffic lights, remains a haunting recollection. On one such occasion, sod's law intensified the gloom, as we received a detention, anyway, for not wearing our regulation caps.

The system of fortnightly lists imposed its own peculiar burdens on the masters, as well as ourselves, though at the time we were unaware of such ironies. We did realise, however, that during the final stages of every fortnight, lessons were often geared (in assorted styles of panic) to mustering sufficient marks to establish a Form "order". The curriculum seemed exhaustive; we were taught around fourteen subjects, by different masters, each needing to fill the columns in his mark book. Methods varied – some meticulous, others haphazard – but they were never questioned: not openly, at least. A few illustrations must suffice. If nothing else, they taught us that apparent success, in the eyes of the world, often stems from exploiting the system and those within it.

In the case of the usually benign and scholarly Mr Woodward the looming lists meant that questions were about to attack us like flak. His military gait and hairstyle seemed to bristle during quick-fire "turns round the class" or "questions on paper." My fate during the former was partly determined by the seating arrangements. Immediately before me was the erudite Fraser Gold, who invariably knew the correct answer. Hence, the fresh question was mine, with no time to blink before, "Next, next," rattled forth. It is ironic how often our fate depends on alphabetical order.

John Wood adopted a similar method to his near-namesake: 100 questions requiring one-word answers, generally focused on our recent coverage of grammar. We wrote our answers in so called "rough books" and marked them ourselves. This meant that the form order in Latin was only occasionally determined by ability and industry; more often it depended on levels of dishonesty and bravado. Moreover, once again alphabetical order played its significant part: "as flies to wanton boys, are we to the gods, they kill us for their sport." Those whose surnames began with A or B faced the tricky moral dilemma of where to pitch their submitted score. Mr Wood's conviction that I had "bats in the belfry" was further substantiated when he once asked to check my arbitrary marks, not only inflated but hidden amongst drawings of aeroplanes and the initials of numerous amours.

It was equally difficult to assess the validity of our marks in Art. Mr Corke ("with an e") was not only a gifted artist, but a captivating story teller, whose views about topics as varied as the Titanic, or his brother's role in the invention of the wireless, left little time in which the artistic talents of the "rats" might emerge.

As an aspiring architect, I was also fascinated by John Tynan's superb chalk drawings on the blackboard, as he illustrated the likes of Renoir or Courbet. Unfortunately, I was a weak linguist, symbolised by my marked exercise book winging its way back to me, while the successful received their accolades in more genteel fashion. Even Mr Kirby seemed to be no friend of mine. Indeed, he once gave me a Saturday detention for notching two successive noughts for failing to learn poetry "by heart." Strangely, I still remember chunks of *Julius Caesar* and several poems.

I certainly bear no grudges. Perhaps one reason for this is that we learnt to understand and accept our responsibilities. More important, no matter their idiosyncrasies, we were taught by men who possessed a generosity of spirit, with few exceptions. A simple, but informative illustration confirms this point. One evening, a friend of mine severely damaged his eye while messing about with carbide. In a letter from Northampton hospital he wrote, "I expect Beaky says what a fool I am." The reality was that one of the first visitors to the hospital was a concerned George (Beaky) Laywood, complete with sweets and comics – rare commodities in 1947.

That kind of magnanimity matters far more in education than any league table of grades. Maybe, now the School is laid to rest, I might stop trembling on entering the Council offices for fear of phantom lists. But I doubt it.

ANOTHER STEPPING STONE

Keith R. Mitchell

After a few months of nervous deliberation in the summer of 1947, I received a long awaited letter informing me that I had been successful in my

Scholarship examination and was to report for Secondary education that September at Kettering Grammar School.

On that particular morning around 90 of us assembled in brand new uniforms (the best that money and coupons could buy – not forgetting that the Second World War had only finished two years previously) and, as new boys, no doubt looking as green as each new intake did. We were all ushered into the main hall by 'Reggie' Gladden, whose tinted glasses gave him an air of authority in the Mafia mould. We were split into three classes, 1P, 1Q and 1R, having been told that we would be assessed in dur course as to our academic prowess.

There were then four School Houses, North, South, West and Country, and dependent on where you lived in the town, this was your House for the duration of your stay. The only exception to this general rule was Country House, in that the School served Corby and surrounding villages, who came in this category. The School also served Rothwell and Desborough areas, but for some reason these were categorised as West House. There was, of course, "friendly" rivalry between all Houses and one budding poet, who was not too enamoured with the likes of Desborough pupils, penned the following masterpiece.

"If you come from distant Desborough
The place that you may know,
If your name's not Panter or Marlow
The blighter's sure to be Coe."

Certain words have been replaced, but the message remains true to this day.

The School was situated in Bowling Green Road, right next to the Girls High School, which brought many escapades, often involving the balcony every time the High School held P.T. Lessons in the main hall.

Fee paying pupils were still being admitted, but this decreased considerably and finally stopped after a few years. Unfortunately, only a small percentage of pupils went to university: those with a very good academic brain who were able to win one of the few grants available, or those with parental financial support. It was considered more popular then to earn a living after 'O' Levels rather than further one's education, which is the action I took.

Schooldays were, I suppose, another stepping stone in life, whether or not one appreciated the fact at the time. Holidays were eagerly anticipated, whilst examinations and homework were not. I think everyone, generally, looked forward to the end of School life so that an honest (or otherwise) living could be earned. But looking back at one's School career, I am sure everyone was glad that it had been done, but would not want to do it again. These thoughts also applied to most National Servicemen, of whom I was one.

Although scraping in for a few South House rugby and cricket matches, I wasn't good enough for School representation. To make matters worse, living opposite me was a fellow pupil called Phil Oram, who on the athletics side won Junior, Middle and Senior Victor Ludorum titles. I often wondered that if I was as talented, and I must stress that at this time I had only just been introduced to Latin, could I aspire to these dizzy heights and win the title of Victor Ludmitchell. Everyone seemed to be in possession of a nickname and 'Mitch' was the obvious choice for me, until one unforgettable day. Suffering from a gigantic boil, causing a very inflamed and painful nose, No. 1 in the Hit Parade was announced as *Rudolph the Red Nosed Reindeer.*

What makes a school? It could be described in order of preference as staff, pupils and buildings. The latter normally remain for all to see; whilst some pupils keep in contact, others disappear for ever. The staff are the ones that are remembered best, particularly those with extreme idiosyncrasies.

We travelled the world with 'Pop' Godfrey, our overweight Geography teacher, whose formulae of HAS W3 (hot, arid summers and warm, wet winters) to keep us reminded of the Mediterranean type of climate and BASMOQ (Canadian provinces from west to east) are still imprinted in one's memory. Our physique was kept in trim by 'Joey' Ashworth, whose punishment by a sliced severe clip on your backside, whilst only wearing shorts, prevented further misdoings. History teacher, 'Bennie' Woodward, a master in the pronunciation of the letter 'S' and the spray that went with it. The front desks always unoccupied. 'Isaiah' Watson, with one eye definitely higher than the other. 'Sammy' Hulls, sadly affected by war nerves 'Pop' Whitney, one of those persons who can never be considered as ever being young. Northern Science teachers, Maurice Crabtree with a bent nose, and 'Fanny' Lawson, who used to speak out of the side of his mouth.'Basher' Coakes, a small ebullient English teacher and 'Gus' Phillips who taught French. Mr R. Smith kept us musical and Mr B. E. Pledger tried to teach us Science, without much success. A certain youngster, 'Tarzan' Cowell, was also on the staff during this period.

Perhaps the two most remembered staff by past pupils were Tommy Cork(e) and George Edwin 'Beaky' Laywood. Tommy's lessons were usually double periods, about one and a half hours. He used to talk continually and leave about ten minutes at the end for work. The milk monitors of the day were not afforded this luxury. A short man of just over five feet, he kept on reminding us of his average height and telling us nautical stories. He was proud of the fact that his brother designed half of one of the funnels of the Queen Mary. 'Beaky', who used to walk at an angle, was a Science master, prone unfortunately to gaffes, although innocently made. As his nickname implies, he owned a nose that would make Jimmy Durante envious. When writing at the blackboard, he would turn round and shout, "Every time I open my mouth, some silly fool speaks." We once made up a full bottle of milk (⅓ pint) from the dregs of the other thirty in the crate and watched him secretly drink it.

All in all, we had a good set of teachers and I feel proud to have attended the School for five years. Unfortunately, I must end by voicing my extreme opposition to the closure of the School, whilst an all-Girls' School is allowed to continue. I often wonder what the outcome would have been if the shoe had been on the other foot. I feel sure that the Sex Discrimination Act would have been more strictly adhered to, irrespective of financial and other issues.

OPPORTUNITIES

Keith Foreman, O.B.E.

Kettering Grammar School was a revelation to one very impressionable eleven year old in 1947. Black blazer, tie and cap were worn with pride – at least until the third year when other priorities took over. The Bowling Green Road site seemed huge – far bigger and more daunting than Hawthorn Road Primary. It was all so competitive. No girls, of course – though they weren't far away and eminently watchable – so it was a masculine place where scholarship and sporting prowess were lauded.

I owed my place to the 1944 Education Act coming, as I did, from a working class family. No previous member had attended a grammar school, so my success in the 11+ examination was greeted with great joy. My parents gave me all the support any youngster could wish. Money was short but never so short that essentials could not be funded. We never ran to white trousers for cricket, but they were luxuries and could be done without.

Sadly, my success took me away from my old primary school friends, most of whom failed the 11+ and went elsewhere. Our paths rarely crossed. I felt superior to them. Only in later life as a teacher did I realise how divisive the selective system really was. It explains why I became a staunch advocate of the comprehensive school serving its local community. In the meantime, the priority was to do well in weekly fortnightly class lists. There was time for piano lessons and sport, especially rugby, but not much else – though a part as a fairy in a school production of *A Midsummer Night's Dream* was a welcome, if occasionally embarrassing episode. But by the third year things began to change.

Up till then I suspect I was an ideal pupil. Having been border-line in the entrance exam, I thrived in the atmosphere of 2P. We all seemed to want to do well. We were after all among the educational élite. But the third year spelt change. Other, more masculine and "social" interests began to intrude – and marks began to slide. Stern warnings about friendships and being "led astray" – and eventually the cane – helped to stem the tide, but only partially so. 'O' level was reasonably successful and then it was the Sixth Form.

It has been said on countless occasions that the Sixth was the highlight of a school career. That was most certainly so in my case. It was then that more equal relationships were made with staff who, previously, had seemed remote, whether admired, feared or despised. You might describe it as a period of rapid maturation. Even the Head, J. K. Dudley, was suddenly easy to talk to! It was in those two critical years that priorities were somehow decided. I do not imply that rationality played the largest part – but choices were made, and I found myself en route to Durham University to read History and another culture shock.

Somewhere back in the third year I chanced to set eyes on a lovely High School girl called Ruth Sail who, from time to time, sat opposite our English class. If my attention wandered (one of the reasons for declining academic performance!) it led to the happiest of marriages which is currently in its 38th year. I can have no regrets about a School which presented so many opportunities for personal growth and fulfilment.

I look back on Kettering Grammar School with great pleasure and few regrets. It opened the door to scholarship, set me on the educational ladder, gave me some understanding of teamwork and the importance of personal commitment and provided role models of teachers who have remained my mentors during a long career in education. Of course, I could have taken more advantage of all the chances it offered, but that is to strain credibility. It was a very good School for me.

PLACES

Don Breckon

For Corby boys, in their first year in 1947, the chance to get out of School and go "downtown" at lunchtime was too good to miss. When the dinner parade got back to School, we had about half an hour before the bell for the afternoon session. So we were away, tumbling down Bowling Green Road to the delights of Woolworths.

Two or three of us kept going downhill, however, to the railway station. There were platforms linked by a subway, a bookstall and a buffet, but most of all, trains. To schoolboys with Latin and Maths on the afternoon timetable, the whole atmosphere of travel was very appealing.

Two expresses were timetabled to pass through, before it was time for us to leave. But if we were late, we would be looking at the clock and giving it "just one more minute," until either the train arrived or we ran out of nerve. After a prolonged sprint up the hill, we would come in sight of the church clock and know that time was running out. A hundred yards from the gate the School bell would ring and it was lucky if we were in before the unsmiling prefect with the detention book was in place.

The coke cellar is an unlikely place to remember from one's school days – not a hide-out for games or cards or smoking, but the location for three of us to do our 'A' level Art.

We – Peter Tiney, Charles Lumby and myself – had opted for Art as one of our Sixth Form subjects, only to discover that there was nowhere for us to work. Wandering about with our drawing boards, we were getting concerned about being drafted into Applied Maths, or some other unattractive subject, when we came upon the coke cellar.

It was a small room, which led off from the underground cycle racks and was furnished with a large boiler and several mounds of coke. Consoling ourselves with the fact that it would at least be warm in winter, we collected some chairs and moved in. Our only human contact during the sessions of Art on our timetable was with the caretaker, who threw a few shovelfuls of coke into the boiler and chatted with us about the state of the world.

The slight feeling of rejection was quickly assuaged by the realisation that no-one knew where we were – an ideal situation when "volunteers" for monitorial duties were chosen.

We did a fair amount of drawing and painting in a relaxed fashion, which left little time or inclination to decorate or furnish our spartan surroundings.

When the examination came round we all passed 'A' level Art (in my case only just). We had been right about the coke cellar – it *was* a good place to be in the winter.

Rugby was a mystery to me. My lasting memory of the game was standing about on the field in an icy wind. As one of the carefully chosen "left-overs" teams, we were generally left to potter about on the far pitch. A few of the more adventurous went through the motions of how they thought the game should be played.

From time to time one of the games staff would come running over to stir us up. There then ensued a bizarre ritual where we all ran around miming "playing Rugby," but avoiding the ball at all times. Luckily, a rugby ball when it bounced was liable to go in any direction. So we did the same, calling out "pass" or "catch it" enthusiastically.

On one occasion the ball unexpectedly came to me and I caught it, which was also unexpected. I called out "Mark!" thinking that this entitled me to a free kick or something similar. A dozen lads, including some who were supposed to be on my side, leapt on me. As I picked myself up, the games master gave a look of disbelief and departed to a proper game, leaving the "left-overs" to their own devices once more.

THINGS FELT

Roy Chapman

Of all the myriad things that happen to an individual in a lifetime, it is said that the only events which claim a lasting place in the memory are those whose impact at the time was emotional. You remember only what you *felt.*

The School Bus
". . . there were occasions when the passengers hailed Tom."

The "left overs", 11th May 1949.

It is 40 years since I left Kettering Grammar School and it is indeed true that the things remembered best are the things felt; some important, some trivial; some long-lasting, some ephemeral; some happy, some not so happy and only later, often much later, put in perspective.

Four centuries ago the first Queen Elizabeth, in 1577, made possible the foundation of the School for, and I quote, ''Boys to be instructed and educated in good learning and the fear of God'': these are noble ends indeed. Then in 1856 the School moved to the Gold Street site and in 1913 to the Manor House site. I suppose the next major event, before Mr Perry's world-famous Satellite Tracking Group was established, before the move to Windmill Avenue and the development of the comprehensive system, was the Butler Education Act of 1944.

It was this great leap forward which permitted many of us, myself included, to be educated as we were, though it goes without saying that this was not known to us at the time. We did not appreciate it and, in the way of the young, took everything for granted. The system of free education for all might well have been with us for a thousand years, for all we knew. Like most young people, we were unaware of the often superhuman efforts of those who had gone before us, by which the benefits we enjoyed were created. Education and all the other civilising influences upon us did not come about by accident, but were created by the energy and sacrifice of previous generations. But reflections such as these are the reflections of later years. This is not how it seemed at the time. We had our own problems, our own preoccupations and our own pleasures.

Getting that coveted first school uniform, at Webb's the outfitters in Market Street, was a source of secret excitement matched only later on by that first pair of long trousers. At twelve, this was really living. I remember the sensation of riding my bike to School under a yellow cycling cape to keep out the pelting rain; and of wheeling it daily through the gates just in time for morning Assembly, that now unfashionable occasion where you could not only see everybody, get to know what they looked like, who they were, size them up and so on, but also sing rousing hymns if you felt like it. It helped to draw the School community together.

I can still feel the weight of my satchel, home-made by my father, as it was crammed nightly with books for homework. Unrelenting, ever-present homework. We didn't think or worry about it; it was just *there,* part of life. I recall clearly the permanent schoolboy smell in the lockers; the ringing of the school bell, the end of freedom; the pleasures of exploration in the library; the School Plays; the High School, ah! the High School! Rare glimpses of forbidden fruit to fill the furtive schoolboy imagination. The boys; the changing and developing pattern of friends; the masters, Mr Ashworth, Mr Lindley, Mr Cowell, Mr Hopkins, Mr Wood and many others; gentle, understanding men, their acts of kindness long-remembered.

The ''Houses'' were North, South, West and Country. Country equalled

Corby; providing us with our first exposure to the determination and fierce pride of the Scots. And games! The trek to the games field . . . the School jersey . . . the coach to away games . . . the winning . . . the losing . . . the singing. The pain of growing up . . . the joy of achievement . . . the shame of failure . . . starting again to do it right. We were taught resilience, staying power, fortitude.

The pall of examinations would overhang each summer. I recollect that glorious sense of release after the last exam each year; then off to the cricket field for House matches, lying in the sun, then end of term. ''Lord dismiss us with thy blessing.''

Like many others I grew up and was transformed in those years. I owe much to that period of my life, but three things in paticular do I owe. First, it drew out whatever was inside and it taught us all how to think for ourselves; second, it instilled a capacity for hard work, which has been a lifelong advantage. I worked hard because I was made to work hard – to my everlasting benefit. One was stretched almost to breaking point, only to discover that a lot more was possible; and third, it engendered a deep and lasting respect for education itself and a love of learning. Education is not simply a meal ticket – though it is that, and must be – but it is also the conduit to a lifetime of pleasure. The pleasure of reading and thinking and conversing and exploring the intricate byways of the human condition. My debt is great and I take pleasure in this opportunity to acknowledge it publicly.

My deepest regret is that the institution from which I benefited so much is now no more. Everything changes: not all change is for the better.

THE NOMADIC FIFTH

Anonymous

The 11+ examination, an interview with an imposing inquisitor and then attendance at what was undoubtedly the cream of the state school system. How proud our parents, and how embarrassing that first day in the unaccustomed sartorial splendour of a brand new school uniform and unable to tell the prefects from the masters. Our intake was of a year when we could still spend our sweet ration coupons in the tuck shop across Bowling Green Road.

Doomed never to belong to the main School house proper, our first two years were spent in the precast concrete classrooms in the playground; our second two years in the wooden huts across the end of the playground and for what was to be the final year for most of us, as the pariahs of the Fifth, wandering itinerants with no classroom of our own. Intelligence espied the empty classrooms of students engaged in gymnastics, science laboratory activities, or sports afternoons and compiled a master plan whereby we took our study books from the personal lockers on the first floor and scuttled furtively to use the absent party's classroom. Anything amiss, in any classroom, anywhere, at any time, invariably involved an inquisition for we, much maligned, vagrants. Free time was shortened for us, while other students closed their desks and ran for the playground, we trudged to the first floor to return our books to the lockers and collect the next topic text and exercise books.

A minor recompense for these impositions was that we were always on the spot when 'Pop' opened his stationery cupboard for trading. Even if not making use of his service we could always be entertained by his tirades on those with missing pages from exercise books to be renewed, or scrap books with doodles and noughts and crosses.

One majestic occurrence made it all worth while. It was a winter Monday, the day the main hall Assembly always looked to the balcony gathering for signs of bruises and bandages on the First Fifteen members after the weekend game. We had returned to our lockers and were sorting through the contents when one of our group called us to the window. Below in the playground a master, (no names), with three or four text books under his arm and leaning as though to counterbalance their weight, was walking across the snow covered playground leading a single line of junior pupils, all of whom were in perfect step with the master and all leaning at the same angle.

When there was no snow in the winter, the playground would be full of a fifty odd a side soccer match using a tennis ball; in the summer there would be six or seven sets of cricket stumps drawn on the playground wall. The main purpose of this wall was to keep the High School from getting at us. In both seasons the singular game of "cockit" could be watched in wonderment. In play, this game looked as though the rugby scrum had made a mistake and arranged themselves in a single line, not noticing that the opposing team was behind them. The opposition then proceeded to leap on the back of the weakest link in the misaligned scrum and either the scrum was crushed to the ground or, if it held the load, the chant "one, two, three, cockit" would signal that the teams should change over. Only in Kettering!

The masters, on the whole, were a tolerable lot: each with his own form of admonishment. 'Fanny' would insist, " 'Ave a sniff at that lad," proffering a bottle of concentrated ammonia. 'Mighty Joe', if catching someone chewing gum, would agreeably ask for the gum to be stuck behind the ear and then promptly press the ear hard back into the hair. 'Beaky' would insist constantly that "you don't shine."

I was there at the christening of a new master. During a lesson in the wooden huts in summer it had become stuffy. The window latch pole was missing; the newcomer summoned the smallest boy to the front, gripped him by the knees, raised him to within reach of the transom window and asked for the window to be opened. 'Tarzan' was established. Yes, I know a school of thought preferred 'Aubrey', though for what reason I know not.

'Izaiah' did have one eye higher.

All who used 'Tommy's' Art Room must remember illicitly stoking the coke burner until it glowed in the midst of winter but what was that stuff, that when put on the burner, would reward us with a plume of white smoke that descended as a blanket of snow?

The Mafia of the Sixth: the prefects and their soldiers, the monitors; now, they were a class apart. Without imparting education in exchange for the right to punish, forgetful of their recent origins and franchised to hand out "lines" and detention, their sole purpose was to quash any signs of "joie de vivre" in the playground.

I know there were some prefects who were a pleasure to provoke to the point of receiving "lines", followed by the game of completing them but avoiding the castigator for days until, when caught, insisting and complaining that they had been looked for everywhere. These few knew it was a game and played without malice.

However, my opinions were influenced by experiences such as the prefect and monitor in control of a dinner table. This was the time when school dinners were served in the top floor Art Room and adjoining corridor. The plan was to position oneself in the dinner queue such that one ended up on the table in the corridor with one's favourite prefect adversary. The chat would sparkle and the general idea was not to try for punishment. The problem was that if you miscounted the queue, you could end up on a table regulated by one of the "master of the universe" versions of prefect. Here conversation was subdued; our table superior tolerated no banter. When the steamed pudding arrived for the prefect to divide into portions, belief was suspended as he cut it in two, split one half into eight for we minors and the other half into two for prefect and monitor. Power corrupts?

The advent of the St Mary's Road dinner hall brought an end to prefect control at dinner tables. All tables were full of one's peers, except for the Sixth Form who were required to entertain the duty master. Impartial dinner ladies provided the portions. The revenge of the prefects involved this new canteen nevertheless. When we had returned to the School, a small gathering of us, one hundred or so, would honour the march past of the High School on their way to the same dinner hall. Eventually the Mafia would have none of this; theirs was a two foot three above the ground world.

Similarly, the members of the smoking circle would meet in the playground toilets most breaks, each adopting his particular Humphrey Bogart pose. All innocent fun ending up with prefects, face to face, with hands on each other's shoulders, blocking the entrance to the toilet and subjecting would-be users to inquiry and allocation of times. These same prefects could be seen enjoying a "fag" in town of an evening. Absolute power?

It is entirely possible that there must be some ex-pupils who never incurred any punishment; for them I will outline the various retributions available for inflicting on the misunderstood.

The lowest form of chastisement was "lines"; this was the commodity used for games with masters and prefects. Next came detention at lunch time and after School; the inconvenience suffered with these two punishments depended on whether you lived in town, or belonged to Country House. Lunch time was reasonably acceptable to the out of town group, they would be at school anyway; those living in town would have to explain away their rushed meal at home and early return to School. After School was acceptable to those in town – just a bit late getting home; out of towners, having missed the bus, were subjected to harassment by conductors insisting that the bus pass was only acceptable on the School bus. Then there was Saturday morning detention; no great infringement for those in town, but to those out of town, bus journeys there and back for normally one hour's detainment. Two hours detention from independent sources in the one week was the stuff of heroes. The normal hour on a Saturday could be quite pleasant if you were selected for cleaning the Chemistry laboratory and setting up Monday morning's first experiment. Industry here could be rewarded by " 'ave a Woodbine lad." Bear in mind, the cigarettes of those days were void of the modern terrors. Next in the ladder of seriousness was a caning from the Headmaster. Here the fine line between heroism and stupidity becomes blurred. Last of all was expulsion: never admired, although I admit to a sneaky regard for the super-hero expelled for exiting a top floor classroom and scrambling round the high outside ledge to come back in on the opposite side of the building.

As well as school holidays, we enjoyed the annual inter-House cricket contest. A splendid conception, a week free of studies supporting the best cricketers of our School House. As I got older, it amazed me how I could constantly lose my way to the playing fields and have to resign myself to going home.

One escapade almost curtailed my enforced nomadic skills. This was the event of the annual boxing tournament, held in the Drill Hall at the bottom of Northampton Road hill. We were all formed into double columns and marched down to the Drill Hall, one afternoon each year. On this unfortunate occasion, fate decreed that our form was at the rear of the group who, at that particular time, were marching down the hill. The attendant masters moved ahead and into the hall to confer about arrangements. Arriving at the gateway, with no masters around, two of us continued down the hill, quickly, and turned left onto Northfield Avenue towards the railway station. Running now seemed to suit the occasion. However, with the benefit of a superior education we quickly realised it would not do to return up Station Road, too soon, possibly to meet other classes making their way down Northampton Road to the hall. We entered a builder's yard to while away half an hour. After fifteen minutes I stood on the shoulders of my accomplice to peer over the wall to check the area. As my head was raised above the wall, I came face to face with the Headmaster against the wall of the newsagents, looking directly at me. I fell to the ground in the scramble to get out of sight. "The Head is across the road," I hissed in anguish to my friend, "he saw me." Self preservation compelled me to analyse the situation at speed. "He will come in the gate in Northfield Avenue, or the gate in Station Road, which do we leave by?" Seeing my friend was already halfway to the Station Road gate I decided it was better, if we were caught, that we should die together and ran to follow him. It seemed we had chosen correctly and our escape was completed in an uneventful panic. "He may not have recognised me," I assured my accomplice forlornly; I had already experienced the Head's phenomenal knowledge of all pupils.

In the event nothing ever came from this momentous confrontation. I came to the conclusion the Head was playing hookey too. . . .

Someone told me that the memory does not retain bad experiences, only the pleasant. Dammit, I must have enjoyed my five years at Kettering Grammar School.

BLACK BLAZERED FIGMENTS

Ian Addis

My recurring dream portrays Kettering in the 'fifties as a "land of lost content," reminiscent of an updated Hovis commercial. Men swarm from shoe factories at the sound of a hooter, cycling in comradely ranks, bound for allotments and pigeon lofts. Women smile over kitchen sinks, packets of *Oxydol* clasped to pinafored bosoms, while saucepans of jam bubble aromatically on blackened stoves. Children squat on linoed floors before flickering images of *Muffin the Mule* on twelve inch television screens. And at night families retire, poor yet happy, to sleep virtuously behind unlocked doors.

Order and a sense of permanence prevail.

A blue-remembered make believe?

Not for one who spent most of his waking hours during 1953 being Wilf Mannion. Or Bob Cherry. For Friday afternoon pilgrimages to the Public Library yielded volumes of those stories in which japes abound, dormitories resound to midnight revels and good-natured House-captains conjure unlikely victories in the breathless hush of the close. By September I was writ, magically, into that very world. Crossing the playground on my first morning bound for prefabricated Formroom, black blazered, satchelled, cap tugged severely over Brylcreemed quiff, I had not entered Kettering Grammar but some fictional public school. Each successive day became part of a continuing saga, an unknown writer's grand design.

The script did not disappoint, nor the characters.

From registration – Addis, Anderson, Bell, Berridge, Breakspeare, Currie

. . . to four o' clock detention, painstakingly copying pages from the *Essays of Elia,* everyone performed their roles with relish. Clown, sage, philosopher, wit. Bunter, Nugent, Wharton, Cherry.

Here was archetypal Quelch, bent and crotchety, leading wavering voices in *Men of Harlech*. The eccentric Science master, gown smouldering, singlemindedly attempting to pass a heated iron ball through a metal ring. The Art teacher raconteur, punctuating some highly animated, oft repeated story about a watch, an airbubble and a stricken ocean liner with a staccato command to ''rub it out!''

Such sayings entered apocrypha, etched in the memory long after principles of Archimedes, theorems of Pythagoras, or chemical formulae for hydrochloric acid were neglected and forgotten.

Only a short time ago, travelling to London, the coach passed through Isham. A voice at my shoulder announced in unmistakable tones,

''No singing through towns, villages or hamlets!''

Forty years were shed in an instant. We were the under-14 cricketers bound for Deacon's School, Peterborough. I answered my old team-mate with the immortal line uttered by that self-same teacher and witnessed one faraway summer afternoon.

''Where's the six boundary?''

There was drama too. Midway through my second year the School Flashman, that armtwisting, ear thumping extortionist, terror of the toilets, bully of the bogs, received his comeuppance in true *Boys Own Paper* style.

We'd crowded into the hall for the Fourth Year boxing final, hoping to see him beaten, though in truth we'd probably have settled for a draw.

He was thrashed, humiliated, by the present Chief Constable for Derbyshire. Unforgettable, especially the enduring image of our tormentor looking up from the ropes, bruised and battered, desperately seeking respite through glazed eyes, only to find referee 'Joe' Ashworth's fixed grin of indifference and the rasping words,

''Fight on!''

By the time the final scene was played out in July 1958, Albert Quixall had supplanted Wilf Mannion, and thanks to David Bishop I'd discovered Dylan Thomas. I left to seek fame and fortune, ingloriously, in the Orient. (Leyton not Cathay).

Today the tin roofed Horsa huts at the bottom of the yard are long since demolished. Yet incredibly the prefabricated building that housed our First-Form classroom remains, a monument to another day, another age.

Pieces of that past spin relentlessly like fragments of coloured glass, a surreal kaleidoscope bursting with unlikely patterns.

The car-park behind the Council offices is transformed into a playground once more. Groups, huddling noisily round reluctant combatants, chant the familiar litany,

''Fight, fight, fight . . .'' Until, incredibly, a bewildered heifer, separated from its herd bound for the neighbouring Friday cattle market, cavorts around the yard in panic, scattering hordes of sweat stained soccer players vainly pursuing pieces of stone across the asphalt confines of the basketball court. Chaos. While on the other side of the wall, the other side of the world, occasional female shrieks provide meagre rival fare.

And throughout, faces float like Captain Cat's drowned sailors. As I recite their names they nod and smile as well they might, black blazered figments, confident of immortality.

THE SIXTH FORM

Prof. Richard York

When I was eleven, I was sick in class. This proved to be the first sign of appendicitis, which later that day took me into hospital and then into a very boring period of recuperation. But first it gave me an exciting new experience. I entered the Sick Room. It might be thought that being sick ideally fits one for the atmosphere of a Sick Room, but this was far from so. For the Sick Room was in fact used as a Common Room by Sixth Formers, who did their best to ignore the intrusion of this pallid and passive First Former, and carried on with their conversation. They were it seemed to me, huge men, members of the adult world since they didn't consistently wear school uniform and appeared to be free of the routine of attending lessons, their only task in life being to hold conversations. Of the conversation I recall only one line: "I can't stand reading dictionaries – there are too many characters." What wit, what sophistication! What a misfortune that the rest of the conversation is forgotten by me and perhaps lost to posterity! But even so, one small boy had learnt something, in those feverish and embarrassed minutes: that schools are not just about acquiring facts, that education is not just being instructed, that it can lead to an enjoyment of dialogue, of talk as intelligent conviviality.

Five years later, I entered the Sick Room again, this time with the rightful title of Sixth Former. And this was the beginning of a time of intellectual curiosity and discovery that could hardly be bettered as preparation for Higher Education. Discovery needs leisure, of course, and Sixth Formers were not entirely lacking in that. Especially the small number who continued into the third-year Sixth in order to take Oxbridge entrance examinations, and the even smaller number who stayed on after the Oxbridge exams to take an extra A level in Russian, found that there were few constraints on the way they used their time. Some of the activities of the Sixth Form were not directly academic, no doubt: there were such things as the daily musing over the *Times* crossword, the immersion in the *Spectator* book reviews and literary competitions, the occasional browsing in ancient and battered volumes of *A Treasury of World Literature,* the games of badminton in which copies of *Murder in the Cathedral* were used as bats, and later, when we had moved to the Prefects Room in a tiny corner of a top corridor, the games of table tennis played in a confined space on two tables of uneven size and with bevelled edges which could give the ball some very surprising angles. One attraction of the Sick Room was that it was furnished with large basket chairs (no doubt to aid convalescence). One summer we formed the habit of taking these chairs out on the flat roof immediately outside the window, where we could bask in the sun and enjoy the sight of the adjacent cattle market. This was first discouraged by Mr Horton, the German master, who entering the room and finding me well on the way through a first-floor window, cried in mock alarm, "Don't jump." It was then forbidden by discreet word from the Headmaster, no doubt anxious that passers-by might be confused by the sight of pupils reclining at great height in what might have appeared to be a spirit of *far niente* (and perhaps also anxious about the dangers of boys falling from the roof). We then had to transfer our basket chairs to the playground, where we were less visible and less endangered, though we had the inconvenience of having to take the chairs inside at playtime.

Conversations were various. I particularly recall our scepticism at Steve Yorston's claim that racing cyclists used six-inch (or possibly six-ounce) wheels. The Light Programme's coverage of rock and roll and of big-band music was the subject of much debate. The films of Pat Boone were the subject of some irony. The exact width of trouser that would be fashionably narrow without reaching Teddy-boy excess was given careful consideration, the sixteen-inch trouser being favoured by the progressive elements.

But as well as these normal teenage topics – used, I think, essentially in a spirit of self-mocking playfulness – there was a lot more talk that related to the official activities of the School. Those of us who were studying either English or foreign literature found rich material for discussion both of artistic questions and of the quality of behaviour depicted in the literature we read. And we owed a great deal to the teachers who had communicated to us their own enthusiasm and their own sense that literature poses questions which each individual reader has to answer for himself. If I mention here Ken Horton in German, Edgar Lindley in French, John Wood in Latin and Peter Wilson in Russian, that is only a reflection of my own curriculum and I have no doubt that my contemporaries will have equally warm and respectful memories of staff in other disciplines. Above all, I think one should recall that these were teachers who, like any good teachers, showed the pupils that their own opinions mattered and fostered an atmosphere of open exchange of ideas. In German, I particularly recall, the pupils themselves were invited to identify the topics for discussion in studying the set books. Having found the set question "*Wilhelm Tell* is a tragedy because it shows a good man forced to commit murder", we proposed – inter alia – the same topic for a discussion of any work of German literature, the more comic the better, with appropriate modification of the last word. We were immature and trivial perhaps, but we were creative. A further stimulus came from the

Headmaster's Period, a class in which all the Sixth Form was taught together without any set syllabus. There were moments of tedium, as various routine administrative procedures were dealt with in this class, and there were moments of incongruity, memorably the Headmaster, J. K. Dudley, continuing to address the class while simultaneously repairing a chair which had collapsed under him. But there was also an extraordinarily wide range of topics, transcending the limits of arts and science, with speakers allowing themselves to be questioned by the pupils. I recall with much respect the very strong human interest of Mr Dudley's own account of his experiences as a prisoner of war, and with a good deal less respect the remarks of a speaker from *The Times,* who very valuably indicated the importance of reading a good newspaper but had great difficulty in maintaining that there was no element of snobbery in a paper that was running the slogan "Top people read *The Times.*"

The atmosphere in the classes was reinforced by some extra-curricular activities, in which again staff played a positive and tactful role, obviously sacrificing a considerable amount of their own time. The Religious Discussion Group – reinforcing the compulsory RE lessons which themselves were, at Sixth-Form level, very much like discussion groups – were far from propagandist and allowed serious and wide-ranging discussion, which allowed full force to scepticism and questioning and were, for many pupils, a significant step to finding what, if anything, they really did believe (and here let me mention 'Joe' Young and T. F. Thompson amongst staff with their real conern for the roots of belief and their gift for communicating the bases of philosophical thinking to young people.) The Debating Society was perhaps the greatest centre of intellectual drama amongst us, and a true testimony to the ideological fissures of the 1950s, with my own juvenile leftism confronting the solidly traditional conservatism of such as Reg Abbott and Chris Groome or the liberal moderation of Brian Slough and Nick Sharman, the practical eclecticsm of Dick Coles or the ironic scepticism of Stephen Hawkins. Debates could grow heated; but they remained rational. We recognised that argument, evidence, judgement mattered, and we learnt in the tension of debate to present argument lucidly and pertinently.

We did well in university entrance, by the standards of those days when Higher Education was rarer. This, I am sure, was the result not only of the unremitting concentration on high standards of accuracy and pertinence in our academic work proper, but also because the School brought it home to us that, in Emerson's phrase, "the unexamined life is not worth living", that it was always worth thinking about the way we lived and the opportunities that were open to us. And the universities were not the only opportunity that was opened to the lively and critical mind that we were encouraged to develop: many pupils who decided that their vocation did not lie in academia must have felt equally that they could live more fully thanks to the spirit of inquiry they had acquired at the Grammar School.

THE DEBATING SOCIETY

Brian Slough

'Nothing speeds up the heart like speaking on your feet.'

(Clive James)

The Literary, Dramatic, and Debating Society is known to have existed in 1916. Its venerability, not to mention its assumed superiority, was inescapable, rather like the Royal Navy. *The Cytringanian,* for example, listed its titled officers (president, vice-president, chairman, vice-chairman et al) prior to the annual reports, as if to confer public accolades on these luminaries. Their duties were hazy, but they tended to wear waistcoats and carry umbrellas. The Society's reports appeared first, followed by others in alphabetical order. They were the lengthiest and most bombastic, often with an embryonic whiff of the Oxford Union, to which their authors were probably progressing, or so they hoped. Moreover, there was a committee, an Annual General Meeting, and recorded minutes of every gathering. When the 1953 A.G.M. was attended by a piffling seventeen members, the secretary sternly predicted that this was "a foretaste of things to come." He had recently played the part of the Soothsayer in *Julius Caesar* and had taken a liking for gloomy predictions. Doubtless his daily travel on the blue bus from Pytchley was another contributory factor.

The Society was usually referred to as just "the Debating Society," well before that became its dominating activity. For most of its life, however, that shortened title did scant justice to its range of interests. Indeed, the 1951 secretary thought it a pity, considering it was always known familiarly as the Debating Society, that this activity was often the least successful.

The "Literary" part of the Society's title most often involved reading aloud from literature, or the literary canon (as defined by recent government curriculum quangos). On other occasions, members would read their own original compositions – listed in one report as: "essays, straightforward and ingenious; poems, simple and in parody; and a revue." It is known for certain that the selection of literary readings included the likes of Horace Walpole, Stevenson, Chaucer, and Churchill, leavened (almost as a token gesture to the groundlings) by snippets from Thurber, Wodehouse, and Lewis Carroll "at his most mimsy." In that scenario lies a glimpse of a forgotten world that is far distant from arguments about personal "growth" – emotional, aesthetic, moral and social – that literature can stimulate. Now, at four o'clock (or three twenty) the rush home is driven by *Mega Drive* and *Super Nintendo,* featuring Mickey Mania and Super Bomberman 2. "Old man," said Orlando, "thou art not for the fashion of these times."

The adjective "dramatic" is open to many interpretations and the Society made best use of that freedom. It certainly involved improvised readings of plays, such as Obey's *Noah* or *The School for Scandal,* directed by David Bishop with "a large cast." There were regular theatre visits, not least to the Kettering Rep. (of blessed memory) in Russell Street. The ritualistic drama of the Mock Trial was enduringly popular, long before Perry Mason aroused our pity and fear on the small screen. Thus, in 1957, over two hundred participants found Oliver Twist guilty of obtaining school dinners under false pretences, a result that provides a sharp insight, not only into the School's cruelty, but the quality of the food at the Tech. The periodic, mock General Elections (nearly four hundred from the Grammar and High Schools attended the 1961 event) were equally well received. There was laughter, but the sub-text was a serious interest in politics, not yet mutilated by cynicism.

Evidence at the Mock Trial, 1950-51.
From left: D. Palmer, B. Short, R. T. Smith, S. Horrocks, G. Palmer.

The annual programme offered various debating formats: hat, balloon, "knock-out" competitions, and the temptingly titled "novelty evenings" among them. These variants were generally frivolous, often scurrilous, yet also effective in honing debating skills as an incidental by-product. In the Junior Debating Society (a separate body) it was not unusual to find exotic figures like Sabrina (remember her?) and Wilfrid Pickles (remember him?) fighting for survival in a balloon and hence the right to continue the human race. Now there's an idea for a mega video game.

Full-dress debates (the phrase itself is evocative of cigars) were the real thing: the "more serious functions of the Society" in the words of one secretary. They focused most often on the controversial, universal issues: blood sports; the educational system; nuclear disarmament; gender equality; the role of the media; the welfare state. Other motions concerned the hot topics of that particular moment, such as pirate radio or the traditional English Sunday. Some were more esoteric, or so it seemed, reminiscent of the *Brains Trust* and the *Home Service.* In this vein, a joint meeting with a discussion group from Corby debated whether paradise could ever be achieved on earth. The ironies in that are unforgivable. In 1951, of course, "Wonderworld" was no more than a comic strip myth, which only met reality at the annual fair on the Northampton Road recreation ground. Surprisingly few subjects, such as the role of the prefectorial system, were insular. This did not indicate an unthinking acceptance of the status quo, far from it, but rather that such matters were for other times, in other places. "Decorum is the grand masterpiece to observe."

Insularity was also avoided by regular, shared meetings with outside organisations, such as the one from Corby mentioned above. Among others were Wellingborough Grammar School, the Technical College (now Tresham), the High School, the Old Cyts, and numerous church groups. Versions of *Any Questions,* or *Question Time,* also brought in local dignitaries as members of the panels. These occasions were arranged by the Society's officers, with loyal support from the staff, particularly the longest serving "guardian angel", Mr A. W. H. Woodward, alongside Messrs. Laywood, Lindley, and Phillips.

A trawl through the Society's named protagonists produces the inescapable conclusions that it had some influence in their later successes as professors, politicians, clergymen, novelists, chief constables, solicitors, barristers, headteachers and television "personalities" (a certain D. Frost appeared in a joint debate with Wellingborough Grammar School). The Society also saw its fair share of spivs, shysters, and sharpers, not necessarily in separate bodies from the professions listed above. But that, as they say, is another novelty evening. One of the most intriguing references to the Society's distinguished personnel appeared in 1950: "Mr C. C. Hebron was loaned by the Army in order to participate as a guest speaker on over-education." Now that really is fame, even if the military's generosity is open to several interpretations.

The decline and fall of Debating Societies seemed to coincide with the disappearance of the grammar schools. To the educational angries they were identified with each other; they were derided as élitist, and irrelevant to the imagined demands of the modern world. Such nonsense ignores the many important skills that debating, in all its styles, helps to develop; not least, the enduring importance of arguing a point of view within a structured format, which remains at the heart of many of our democratic processes.

CHAPTER 14

Mr J. K. Dudley

Headmaster 1952-1964

By a colleague: A. J. Cowell

The period from 1946 to 1976 was probably one of the happiest in the history of Kettering Grammar School. The School had settled down after the Second World War, there was little interference from county, government or educationists. The staff in general were of a high standard, the boys in general, well-behaved and responsible. There was a good spirit in the School; we had morning Assembly, Saturday detention, Speech Days; rugby and cricket were popular, and teams from nearly all age groups played Saturday matches. Examination results were good, league tables had not been invented and for aspiring candidates we had rather a ''hot line'' to Cambridge.

John Dudley became Headmaster in 1952. He came trailing clouds of glory. He had been a fighter pilot in the Royal Air Force during the war. By autumn of 1940 the RAF had defeated the German Luftwaffe, and a projected invasion of Britain by the Germans was now not on the cards. John was not involved in the ''Battle of Britain'' but took part later in ''fighter sweeps'' against German aircraft and aerodromes. In one of these, his aircraft was damaged and he had to bale out. He was injured in landing, but well cared for by the Germans, and became a prisoner of war. He returned to England when the war ended.

He was in his thirties when he became Head. He was young for his age. John Wood said he thought ''he was a nice young man who would get on well with Miss Woodrow.'' Not getting on well with the Kettering High School hierarchy was regarded with apprehension.

John Dudley restored a measure of calm to the School after the resignation of Mr A. F. Scott, the previous Head. A Headmaster should always be something of a commanding figure in a school, and should hope that staff and boys support him. They will do this if the policy and personality are acceptable. John Dudley retained the respect, and in many cases, the affection of the staff. He was no egoist, but a naturally kind man, tentative at first, sometimes rather apprehensive, but determined and stubborn when necessary. He was honest, careful and thoughtful. As a prisoner of war in Germany he was given the task by his fellow prisoners of collecting and issuing fairly the Red Cross rations which came to the camp; surely the acme of trust.

John was a keen cricketer who played for Kettering Cricket Club. A slow right arm bowler, he ''opened'' for the staff in matches against the School First XI. A dropped catch off his bowling was rewarded with a sympathetic smile, far from the reaction, perhaps, of Mr F. S. Trueman.

There were minor crises during his period. In 1962 the Central School amalgamated with the Kettering Grammar School when the School moved to Windmill Avenue. This laborious undertaking was achieved with the minimum of fuss, though there are still murmurs about the ''missing pictures''!

John Dudley was a mathematician and taught the Sixth, whom he knew, and the younger boys, so that he could get to know them. He also entertained the Sixth on occasions with readings from the Father Brown stories.

He was a patient man, but had sharp edges when stirred. Some senior boys at the end of term raised a flag on the Grammar School roof extolling the delights of a ''visit to Dudley Zoo'', then a popular place. To the staff this was a humorous, not very serious prank. But the Headmaster took umbrage; he also took a County Grant from the main culprit, preventing a university place. Mr Dudley saw this incident as a diminution of his authority, but we must be glad that the main culprit recovered his spirits and has become a pillar of the British police force.

J. K. Dudley and Prefects, 1952

Standing (L. to R.): K. Brockway, D. Swingler, A. Pridmore, R. J. Toseland, A. Southwell, J. Moodie, J. Lord, J. R. Knibbs.
Seated (L. to R.): L. Panter, A. Bald, J. K. Dudley, P. Wilson, B. Short.

John Dudley had his private problems too. His wife unfortunately became handicapped and remained so. He felt deeply about this, but he was essentially a private man.

John left the Kettering Grammar School in 1964 to take over at Wakefield Grammar School, where he had a successful period as Headmaster until he retired. He died in Wakefield and members of the Old Cytringanians attended a memorial service in the Cathedral there.

John Dudley was a pleasant man, and a good Headmaster.

By an Old Boy

John Dudley epitomised the grammar school ethos, and his life was in large part devoted to promoting its cause. Born in 1915, he was educated at Bradford Grammar School and Queen's College, Oxford, where he read Mathematics. He began his teaching career at Radley, before moving to Bristol Grammar School in 1939. In both appointments he gained an enviable reputation, not only as a gifted teacher, but for his contributions to extra-curricular activities.

At the outbreak of the war he joined the R.A.F., becoming a pilot in 1942. He was shot down in 1943 and spent nearly two years as a prisoner of war. In 1945 he returned to Bristol and was appointed Head of the Mathematics Department soon afterwards. One pointer to his success was the significant number of Open Scholarship awards to Oxford and Cambridge gained by his students. He also continued to enjoy a major role in the provision of games and music, in addition to his work with the Air Training Corps.

He came to Kettering as Headmaster in January 1952, without fully realising, perhaps, that his period of office would involve effecting distinct changes in the School's history. One obvious example was the opening of the new Science building in Windmill Avenue in 1956, which meant the inescapable organisational difficulties of operating a split-site school. This was followed by the 1962 amalgamation of the Grammar and Central schools. The problem of split-sites and amalgamations – physical, administrative, of morale etc. – cannot be underestimated (as the School painfully discovered some twenty years later). Those who have experienced comparable upheavals, especially involving schools, will readily applaud J.K.'s leadership throughout those testing times.

Less obvious to outsiders were far-reaching, post 1962 changes to the curriculum; essentially, it became more flexible with the introduction of subject ''options'', allowing boys some freedom of choice to cater for their own tastes and aptitudes. There was no loss of academic rigour, nor diminution in the Headmaster's belief of offering a range of ''out-of-school'' activities. His active support and encouragement for them made this plain.

He was noted for his impeccable appearance, whilst also possessing that indefinable ''presence'' (which used to be associated with headmasters) whether sitting bolt upright in his study, or striding briskly to church, umbrella in hand. He was devoted to his family and the Christian faith, and fulfilled the requirements of the medieval knight's ''gentillesse.'' Not least, he was kind and generous when it mattered most.

He was a keen cricketer who, for several seasons, bowled offspin for the Kettering Club, as a Titmus clone. His passion for the game communicated itself to the School and doubtless had a positive impact in helping to create the successful sides of the 'fifties.

Like all cricketing Yorkshiremen, he wished a return home. His career ended, appropriately enough, at another distinguished grammar school – Queen Elizabeth's in Wakefield.

CHAPTER 15

A Grammar School Education

Brian Slough

The College of Mont Aigu at the Sorbonne was known in the fifteenth and sixteenth centuries as "the cleft between the buttocks of Mother Church." Of its alumni, Erasmus and Rabelais hated their experience there; Loyola and Calvin spoke of it with the warmest affection. Schools, it seems, have always provoked extreme responses, which rarely mellow with the passage of time. In a piece about Gresham's, W. H. Auden put it this way: "No account of school life ever appears disinterested to those who disagree with it; it will always appear the work of either a nest fouler or a nest whitewasher." Thus, to many who attended the Kettering Grammar School in the 'fifties, I shall be castigated as a "nest whitewasher" for thinking it a privilege to have been educated there from 1951 to 1959.

That period is often heralded as the "golden age" of grammar schools, for reasons stronger than sentimentality. They flourished, even in a climate of rumbling comprehensive hostility, spurred through the additional stimulus of reformed public examinations: the General Certificate of Education, at Ordinary and Advanced Levels, began in 1951. The academic culture of the 'fifties grammar school was still modelled on the non-vocational ideals of the ancient universities, with an acceptance of learning for its own sake. Its academic traditions invoked the classically oriented "liberal arts", pure science, and close association with the professions. In 1955, David Eccles argued that these grammar school traditions "are too good and too precious to be endangered." Eric James, a former High Master of Manchester Grammar School, saw such schools producing a "meritocracy" from an aspiring clientele: he praised "their astonishing success in tasks of immense social importance" and their capacity "to provide opportunities for the child of any class to compete successfully with his more fortunate contemporaries."

Such rhetoric was a partial truth: applicable to me, and my near neighbour (who gained an Open Scholarship to Cambridge) while our contemporary across the street was fated to experience what Edward Blishen called "a slave's education." Statistics suggest that, on average, one child in five attended a grammar school, though the provision of places throughout the United

Kingdom was uneven (40 per cent of Welsh children were selected, but under 10 per cent in Lincolnshire). Prior to the opening of a grammar school in Corby in 1955, competition for places in Kettering was particularly intense and it would be naive to pretend that this limited allocation did not deny many able children the kind of education from which they might ''compete successfully with more fortunate contemporaries.''

Public opinion labelled 11+ selection as ''the scholarship'', which a child passed or failed. This was nonsense, for many reasons. For example, research suggested that poor social background could distort test results for the working class. Indeed, in 1956, A. Halsey and J. Floud in *Social Class and Educational Opportunity* argued that the 11+ examination was too often a social divider rather than a just assessment of intellectual ability. Thirty years later, the Head of the National Foundation for Educational Research recognised the defects, but also the strengths of the 'fifties examination: ''It was the selective system that was at fault more than the tests – the tests were about as fair, reliable and accurate a means of prediction as you could have had at that time.''

So-called 11+ ''failures'' were nothing of the sort, of course, yet research and theoretical arguments carried little clout when opposed by long standing and fondly cherished prejudices. It is ever thus, especially in education. It is not my purpose to rehearse yet again the conflicting viewpoints about the structure of secondary schooling. Suffice to say, that in 1951, after expert tuition from Miss Wills, I left Park Road Junior School to undergo the grooming process which prepared the lucky few for entrance to university, or the professions, as recruits to the middle-classes. That process is worth recording, whitewashed or not.

One oft forgotten advantage of the Kettering Grammar School was the benefit of learning in the imposing building in Bowling Green Road, ''comfortably sensible in its neo-Georgian style, with nothing mean or cheap about it'', in Tony Ireson's words. Even now, in a reduced role, it retains its hauteur, a superior presence to mock other utilitarian school buildings in the town. ''For always I am Caesar''; ironically, both were assassinated, but their influences linger. In one of his letters Heine recounts how a friend once asked why we no longer build cathedrals like Amiens; he replied that, ''Men in those days had convictions, we moderns have opinions.'' The same might be said of the building in Bowling Green Road: substitute, or add, education for religion.

Grammar school pupils' life chances were further enhanced by generous resourcing: a favourable pupil-teacher ratio (if not smaller classes) and teaching from graduate subject specialists were immediate benefits. Text books were never shared (though ritually covered in brown paper, for reasons of durability rather than dubious content) and exercise books were of glitzy quality, far superior to anything available in the 'nineties. Likewise, the games equipment. The School enjoyed its own playing field and pavilion, maintained

J. A. Gotch's masterpiece – the Grammar and High Schools, Bowling Green Road.

by a loyal, long serving (and suffering) groundstaff. The library was well-stocked and a popular haunt for learners, poseurs and romantics (so I'm informed). In 1958, Professor John Vaizey maintained that the average grammar school pupil received 170 per cent more a year in terms of resources than the average secondary modern school pupil. Whatever that means, he was probably right.

In the process of providing a route to the qualifications and credentials required for university entrance and particular kinds of employment, a grammar school education was a means to transmit, and create, culture; it shaped attitudes and values, aesthetically and morally. Such schools had their own homogeneous national curriculum, a cultural capital accrued through time and experience, from evolution not revolution – political, or otherwise. Their aims were well-defined and understood, even by those who disagreed with them: there were no uncertainties about their role within local communities and society at large.

It is arguable that one of the main problems facing comprehensive schools in the 'nineties is to establish a common ''culture'' that makes sense to the whole range of their students. The difficulty is apparent in the breakdown of the original premise for the national curriculum through its universal entitlement and the continuing mish-mash of courses and qualifications for post-sixteen students. A grammar school curriculum had an academic breadth (most studied for 10 'O' levels) even if its balance suffered from too early specialisation. Ironically, current curriculum initiatives suggest the wheel is turning – to the detriment of balance – as so-called "vocational" courses become the universal panacea, or excuse.

I remain appreciative of being given the chance to study Latin with its hard intensity (and Greek in the Sixth Form) to start German in the Fourth Form alongside French, to continue with History, Geography, Scripture, and Art to sixteen. Education is imperilled if children look outwards and find little else but "basic skills" in various disguises. To train youngsters largely within a curriculum of job-specific, non-transferable skills is to do them few favours. Training is not education. The grim irony is that an obsession with vocational training will strengthen the social divisions supposedly responsible for our problems in commerce and the manufacturing industries: an oft-quoted reason for those who seek to abolish "selective" schools, whether state or independent.

The grammar school curriculum encouraged individual growth through effective learning and hence a feeling of self worth for valid reasons: pupil self-esteem was never divorced from worthwhile achievements. To do otherwise, however well-intentioned, can be not only patronising but misleading. It is true that there was no need to adapt the system to the child, the child was adapted to the system, but no ceiling was placed on enterprise and expectation. Inevitably, there were those who excused their sloth under the pretext of difficulty. That is not unknown in the comprehensive system.

The role of the teachers was an active one – as expert, leader and guide. They were also "enablers", "facilitators" and "advisers", in the current jargon, which they would shudder to use. There was no shortage of direct didacticism. They were never marginalised, as is often the case today; they were paid to teach, so they taught. Our teachers were important to us, "the cashiers in the new world of brain currency" (in Hoggart's phrase). Many were real scholars and we wanted to join the club. Whole-class teaching is open to criticism, like any other methodology, particularly with mixed ability groups. Ours were not: rather, some were more able than others, like the top batch in the First Class batting averages. We learnt through instruction, explanation, guidance and motivation, from books and people: our teachers and each other. There was also laughter and banter amidst the high seriousness. Good teachers vary their approaches; ours did, but they would never apologise where whole-class instruction was the dominant method.

There was tacit agreement that not every lesson or topic could be fun or "exciting" (lamented by Rattigan as an inane craving). Learning can be difficult, frustrating, sometimes repetitive and calling for intense application: rather like the world outside. Few underwent an emotional spasm in acknowledging that. Our application was helped because the furniture was organised to provide our own space. The desks were prehistoric, graffiti-free, and built to last; their honesty and style the very antithesis of the bakelite cheapness in many of today's classrooms. They were generally arranged in rows, but not exclusively so. In English, for example, one recalls a performance of Act 3 of *Julius Caesar,* of ''snuff flick'' proportions. Caesar was played by an engaging American exchange teacher; his assassins were played by the Corby bus boys, for reasons unknown. As far distant as 1952, we scripted and broadcast our own radio programmes, with the help of low-tech equipment. The School placed emphasis on articulacy, both spoken and written: we learnt to weigh up issues, to argue them. We were encouraged to be confident in handling words and expressing ideas which many of us rarely heard in casual family talk.

Indeed, there is plenty of evidence that the teaching staff unlocked potential and liberated many pupils from impoverished intellectual backgrounds. John Marks has argued that ''true creativity only flourishes in that tension between spontaneity and disciplined, rigorous study.'' It is likely our teachers would have agreed with that. Likewise, that the freedom to learn necessitates a systematic and coherent introduction to well-established skills and bodies of knowledge. This established process was vehemently attacked in Richard Hoggart's *Uses of Literacy* (1957) as requiring ''conscientious passivity'' for pupils to be successful, and he quoted Herbert Spencer's famous remark in his autobiography (1904) that established systems of education encouraged ''submissive receptivity'' instead of ''independent activity.'' It is difficult to accept that we were ''passive'' or ''submissive'' and a glance at the School magazines indicates there was no lack of independent activity, within and outside the classroom. Somewhat poignantly, in a telling 1990 interview, Hoggart expressed the dispiriting view that there now seemed less opportunity for today's bright, working-class children. These were his words: ''The atmosphere is anti-intellectual, anti-intelligence. Our society seems to have lost much of the sense of what education is about.'' Set that view against his famous chapter on the ''scholarship boy'' and make of it what you will.

The right wing press has never walked alone in its belief that children of the aspirant working class or the new ''underclass'' – those for whom grammar schools supposedly brought salvation – have lost most by their virtual disappearance. In July 1989 the liberal establishment, in the form of the Policy Studies Institute, questioned many of the notions that had surrounded comprehensive education since Tony Crosland published his famous 10/65 circular some twenty years earlier. Their report, *School Effect,* scotched the shibboleth that comprehensives can be instruments for engineering social equality. In 1993, Ken Roberts in *Youth and Inequality,* writing about the educational mirage of supposed improvements, was convinced that educational success for young people is still limited by social-class origins.

Meantime, the debate about educational ''standards'' goes round and round in ever increasing circles. Britain, probably more than any other country, seems obsessed with the topic, as with the Lottery, with which it has much in common. Obsessions are generally accompanied by the sound of emotive axes being ground, not least when the subject is a grammar school. The tone was set on one side of the political divide by Mr Crosland (whose school/college also had the motto ''manners maketh man'' – but that's another chapter). Allegedly, he swore to ''shut every f------ grammar school in the country'', thus forgetting his motto in the heat of passion, a lesson for us all. The opposing view is still regularly asserted. A *Daily Telegraph* (yes, I know) editorial of June 1995 referred to the remaining 160 grammar schools as ''jewels in a mountain of dross'', and urged Gillian Shephard, Education Secretary at the time, to preserve them at all costs. In that same month, Andrew Neil in *The Sunday Times* (yes, again) wrote about the genocide of the grammar schools; how earlier governments had destroyed excellence in the state system.

Yet standards are nearly always thought to be falling, as Caroline Gipps pointed out in *Judging Standards and Effectiveness in Education,* published in 1991. One of the many convincing (and amusing) pieces on this matter appeared in *The Guardian* (June 1994), written by Richard Wilkins, who illustrated the dissatisfaction of employers with the standards of school leavers over the past 120 years. In the decade 1900-10, for example, employers reported that they were having to import German workers because they could not recruit English clerks who were literate and numerate. Sounds familiar? Is it this persistent nagging of employers which is partly responsible for driving education into a neurotic, unending hunt for ''better methods'', which employers then decide are less successful than the ''old methods''? The music goes round and round, as Mr Gladden once wrote on my diagram of the inner ear.

There is also a whiff of neurosis about the piles of statistics, surveys, reports, green papers, and white papers concerned, and concerning, ''standards.'' At least they provide employment for inspectors and academics, if confusion and pointless unease for the rest of the population. There are those (and not just Professor Ted Wragg) who believe their lasting impact is nil. Consider, for example, the claims about ''rising standards.'' The extensive, and separate, research of Professors Andrew McPherson (Edinburgh) and John Gray (Sheffield) relating to school leavers (1976-92) concludes that their rising success rate has nothing to do with schools, Exam Boards, or Government policies. It is the impact of demography. Turn, then, to Stephen Bates in *Where the System is Failing* (*Guardian* 1990) who is far from a lone voice in thinking that comparisons between GCSE and the old 'O' Level and CSE systems are almost certainly flawed. Most recently, Harvey Goldstein, professor of statistics at London University's Institute of Education has said that league tables (i.e. educational), ''value added'' or not, are a ''statistical nonsense.'' One Saturday, in the pavilion at Lord's, I was told that Denis Compton was a better bat than Brian Lara. I bought my companion a gin and tonic and asked if he'd ever seen Dennis Brookes. Now he could really play.

What might be important is the striking shift from the 1950s to the test-led education in the 1990s and thence to what Brigid Davies has called the ''depressingly utilitarian philosophy which decrees that education is a matter of ensuring that the output fits the needs of the state.'' In the context of that remark we need to ask whether the whole concept of ''standards'' is questionable. Whose ''standards''? What constitutes ''standards''? Is there some aethereal level from which our schools have dropped, or risen, since the disappearance of most grammar schools? Or are the heaps of surveys simply identifying non-causes for non-effects? I don't know the answer. The conflicting conclusions of others suggests no one else can be too certain.

That won't stop the tin gods with their assumptions about the ''wasted talent'' of the grammar schools, determined by their own choice of ''performance indicators'' and what constitutes ''productivity.'' Only the omniscient God can judge whether talent is wasted. Recently I have read about the so-called ''wasted talents'' of David Gower, John Osborne, and Tim Rice. Sadly, none of them attended the Kettering Grammar School in the 1950s, but Jim Smith (Dale) did, and doubtless satisfied and enjoyed his own ''performance indicators.'' I wish I had appeared on Broadway or, come to think of it, in the *Carry Ons.*

John Skillman, a brilliant Iago, in the 1958 production of Othello.
''Relationships with the High School blossomed . . .''

Education is about being able to do what you've never done before, or to do it better, to fulfil your potential. The School sought to develop "wholeness", through all round achievements and sensitivities. Edmund Kirby wrote in one of his *Cytringanian* editorials that "the vitality of a grammar school . . . should stimulate and foster a diversity of cultural interests." His editorial successor, however, whilst supporting that belief, also confessed his disappointment that a mere nine societies were flourishing. One wonders how many of today's state-maintained day schools, of comparable size, still offer that number of cultural societies, meeting outside formal school hours with strong support. If few, it is not idle speculation to explore the reasons why.

A major cultural occasion, for the School and town, was the annual production of a Shakespeare play. Rehearsals, often lengthy, were held each day after school and on Saturday mornings throughout the Michaelmas Term, building to five nights of public performance, plus a Saturday matinée. The choice of play was often adventurous for student actors and included *Hamlet, Othello,* and *Henry VIII.* The production involved a high proportion (60 plus) of School personnel, on and off stage. Relationships with the High School blossomed; some continue to do so forty years on. The School regularly entered mini-productions in local festivals and organised theatre trips, to London and Stratford in particular.

Such cultural cultivation had met with contempt from certain infamous Headmasters in the nineteenth century. One was Coterill of Fettes, (Tony Blair's "alma mater") who reputedly fulminated against so-called "cleverness": ". . . it neither makes or keeps man or nation." In his time, sport was more important, initially as a means to a disciplinary end and then an end in itself. As the culture of athleticism began to play a dominant role in the system of élite education, its influence spread from the ancient public schools into grammar schools. When A. B. Haslam, formerly of Rugby School, told parents at Ripon Grammar School speech day in 1884 that he believed in the old phrase "mens sana in corpore sano", he was the forerunner of a breed of Headmasters (including John Dudley) with a similar philosophy and the readiness to say so.

This belief in the value of sport in education can be illustrated by personal anecdote, for which I apologise. In a match against Wyggeston I had shown dissent whilst returning to the pavilion, after being given run out by their umpire. The next morning, after Assembly, the Headmaster gave me a roasting, controlled in its ferocity, traditional in content, and fully justified. What followed was unexpected, but more significant. Instead of the cane, he delivered a cogent argument for playing games. It was essentially the credo of the Victorian gentleman amateur: respect for the written rules, but also the spirit of the game. It enshrined the ethic of fair competition, learning to understand and cope with a variety of outcomes, not least success and failure. These principles are now categorised in the national curriculum for

Physical Education, unsurprisingly, as the committee who devised them was chaired by Ian Beer.

That said, it was important to win and results were ritually announced in Assemblies, if only in the neutral tones of James Alexander Gordon. It became fashionable in many educational cabals (outside of independent schools) to deride this kind of competitiveness and the value of games, especially team games, as a focus for group loyalty. It is difficult to accept, however, that any boy suffered through the School's pursuit of the games-ethic, whereas it is certain a large number gained considerable and enduring benefits.

Belief in the concept of group loyalty was furthered in other ways. The uniform, a city-smart mix of blacks, greys and whites, was distinctive, compulsory and visible identification of a community. As with team games, uniforms fell from favour in the 'sixties, when they were mocked as additional instruments of repression. It is no surprise in the marketing-conscious 'nineties that they are back in favour, along with other ritualised features of school life, as ways of binding institutions together and symbolising an orderly body, both individually and communally. Interestingly, in 1994, the Grant Maintained Trust acknowledged that all the opted-out schools had some form of uniform and several admitted to becoming more intensely uniform-oriented after their switch from L.E.A. control.

The Butler Act of 1944 stated that "the school day . . . shall begin with collective worship on the part of all pupils." Our day did just that: a hymn

Prize Day, March 1954. The eminent historian, Prof. A. L. C. Bullock of St. Catherine's Society, Oxford, presents the prizes, watched by C. W. Godfrey (centre) and J. K. Dudley.

(sung to a recognisable tune) a reading from the Authorised Version of the Bible (by a prefect) and prayers. No gimmicks. We were exposed to our Christian heritage, not to mention some of the most beautiful language ever written. We stood in rows, youngest at the front, the Sixth Form on the balcony, begowned masters (there were no mistresses in the 'fifties) compulsorily alongside.

Prize Day was another important annual event, held at the Savoy Theatre in Russell Street to accommodate the pupils, staff, parents, and other assorted visitors. Speeches were delivered by the Headmaster, Chairman of the Governors, and visiting dignitaries (Alan Bullock was one such) who presented numerous prizes and certificates. This was a public occasion, whose efficacy was never questioned. It implied the significance of competition, prizes, rewards for endeavour and success (especially academic) and the good manners to sit still throughout the proceedings, tedious or otherwise. It was a celebratory showpiece of what mattered most to a grammar school, and why not.

Such occasions are now often denigrated and dismissed as embarrassing anachronisms, along with other ''traditional'' characteristics. Grammar schools were mostly single-sex, spartan and hierarchical. They held that manners made the man, and parents should not interfere. Above all, their autonomy meant accepting responsibilities with their undoubted privileges, whilst encouraging individuality and enjoying, even valuing, eccentricity. Most of those characteristics are still to be found at Eton, Harrow and Winchester, where the school chooses the parent rather than the other way round.

Each of those independent schools benefits from its strong sense of community, as did the Kettering Grammar School. It was a relatively small family, marked by a forceful leadership, with high expectations regarding learning and behaviour, and which encouraged self-reliance in their pursuit. Discipline was firm and generally fair, with a healthy balance between punishments and rewards; its injustices were no more frequent or serious than in any other civilised society. Which is not to say they were not fiercely felt at the time. There was a positive atmosphere about the place, of an orderly society that respected each other and each other's property. I recall little foul language and only one physical bully who – in the best traditions of Roy of the *Rover* – received his retribution in the boxing ring. You moved about the building without running, shouting or barging; you opened doors for others; put litter in bins: no, not trivial, significant. You were expected to raise your cap to a master's wife (sorry, Germaine). There was a consistency within the School's processes which stemmed, in part, from continuity and stability in its many guises. In those days staff served the community, body and soul, which this book makes abundantly clear. It was true of the teachers, but also Connie Phillips, Peggy Perkins, Mr and Mrs Eric Cook, Miss Richards, Harry Barrett and many more. The wisdom and charm of Peggy, in those

Prize Day 1951. ". . . the good manners to sit still throughout the proceedings, tedious or otherwise."

difficult days before closure, was even more welcome than it had been forty years earlier.

In the 'fifties the entropic, whizz-kid careerist was not then the fashion, in schools or the various Departments for Education. The so-called "management of change" occurred within a stable context, not the shifting sands of externally imposed directives. In recent years, "reforms" have blitzed the schools in an unco-ordinated, even unconnected pattern – though a five-year moratorium is promised. Forty years ago, present demands were mostly unknown: design and implementation of curriculum edicts; new forms of assessment and in-service training in the constant requirement to update "skills." Were teachers then expected to impart understanding of, and positive attitudes towards, the world of work and other nations; to master new technology and methodology, along with programmes for multi-culturism and mainstreaming children with "special needs"? Were they made increasingly accountable for the moral and social responsibilities of their students, or was that accountability still largely the province of parents, churches, and communities? O, brave new world. As Richie Benaud once said about comparisons via cricket statistics: not better, or worse, but certainly different.

One of the major differences between the 'fifties and now is the structure of post-16 education. If you locked a group of wise men and women in a room and told them they could not emerge until they had devised a coherent system for 16+ education, they would not invent the present tragi-comic arrangements. In an article in *The Times Educational Supplement* (May 1990), called *Advances on an Arid Ritual,* I wrote about the urgent need for curriculum change, with this conclusion: "It is questionable if this is feasible within constraints imposed by the present institutional organisation post-16 and it is likely this will need reconstructing in a radically different manner, before the curriculum can follow suit." Five years later and that is still true. It is also true that the best teachers can triumph in any system.

I count myself fortunate to be taught at Advanced Level by the likes of John Cowell and Ted Ward, two of the best, if ever I met them. Ted made me aware that "there are things that only literature can give us, by means specific to it." One of our set books was *Religio Medici,* in which Sir Thomas Browne wrote about the wonders in true affection: ". . . it is a body of enigmas, mysteries, and riddles." The School wove itself into the fabric of our lives, whether we liked it or not. I did. When I look back at my years there, I recognise that it was the teachers who encouraged me, helped me to search beyond my own immediate expectations, whom I respect, and whose presence remains with me. The enigmas, the riddles, the mysteries of honourable affection.

THE ENGLISH WAY

John F. Joline

(J. F. J. was an American exchange teacher at K.G.S., in the academic year 1954-55.

Taken, by kind permission, from the *St. Louis Country Day News* of October 21st, 1955.

Three or four busloads of boys arrived from the surrounding villages and town, 100 or more bicycles careered through the gates, numerous walkers poured in from the near end of town, the exchange teacher from America dodged in among the rest – and the Kettering Grammar School began another year. Sixth Form boys, in navy blue caps and blazers, with black ties and gray flannel trousers (the same uniform that all students wore), straightened up the double files of each class as it gathered in the school yard before marching into the school hall, or auditorium, for the chapel service that opens each school day all over England. If any of the younger boys caused trouble, the monitors took their names and gave them the opportunity to serve a 30- or 60-minute detention after school.

If the boys were guilty of repeated breaches of school regulations or if they committed really disrespectful or contemptible acts, masters saw to it that they became candidates for Saturday morning detentions or for a visit to the Headmaster's study where six resounding whacks of the "cane" awaited them. The "cane" itself is a yellowy length of cane or bamboo that serves its purpose with a master present as witness to the appropriateness of the action.

Boys must Stand during Chapel programs.

In the hall, which served as gymnasium, auditorium, and chapel, the masters stood along one wall, while the boys took their positions in lines facing the stage. First Forms (eleven-year-olds) standing in the front rows, Fifth and Sixth Forms (16 to 19-year-olds) lining the balcony above. At 8.45 the Headmaster in his academic gown strode in, mounted the stage, and surveyed the 600 pupils who stood silently facing him. The entire congregation remained standing through the 15-minute service and the announcements which followed. They remained standing because there was no room for 600 boys **and** rows of chairs or benches. Everyone accepted this situation as a matter of course, and on cold winter days when boys occasionally fainted during the service, a master would invariably catch the boy before he actually dropped and would haul him quickly and efficiently to the nearest exit.

Two 40-minute periods followed chapel; then came a 20-minute break. Monitors from each class distributed bottles of milk to all. After drinking their milk, the classes would be dismissed to relax in the school yard, an asphalt-surfaced playground, where there would immediately be ten or fifteen separate soccer games going on in the same place, with smooth pebbles or old tennis balls serving as the "football". All masters but the one on duty – he would stay discreetly inside behind a door or window, emerging only to administer necessary discipline – would retire to the staff common room for tea and biscuits, a smoke, and ten minutes' adult conversation before the pupils were again docilely filing into classrooms for the next two periods. Then came an hour and a half for lunch, when all who lived in Kettering walked or cycled home, while two masters shepherded 320 boys on the quarter-mile parade to the school cafeteria. After lunch came two classes, a ten-minute break, and a final class before school was over at four o'clock.

"Rugger" and Cricket are Major Sports.

Each class had one afternoon from 2.15 to 4.00 on the "games field" playing "rugger" from September to April, cricket from then until the end of school late in July. Boys on school teams (1st and 2nd XV, under 15 years, under 14, and under 13) would play scheduled games on Saturday or Wednesday afternoons, in addition to their usual afternoon of practice. School time was also taken during the year for an intramural program in all sports, from boxing to basketball. Those trying out for badminton, basketball, tennis, and track teams found time for practices occasionally during the lunch period or after school, and they played against other schools or amateur clubs in the evenings. The track, or "athletics" team had regularly scheduled dual meets and several larger meets against other local and district athletes.

Rehearsals for the school play, *Hamlet* last year, began the day school opened, and with five masters coaching daily after four o'clock, until December, received the kind of emphasis that football claims in most American schools (there were four pages of diagrams for the manoeuvres of Hamlet and Laertes during the duel, and these were practiced as we drill our off-tackle play). The Debating Society, the Music Club, the Photography Club, the Religious Instruction Group, the Railway Locomotive Spotters' Club all met once weekly at 4.15 in the afternoon, with pupils and masters participating.

Students take State Exams for Advancement. Boys from eleven to sixteen years old were taking nine or ten subjects every year, with two or three homework assignments weekly in each course. The normal weekly academic schedule for most of these boys would be composed of five periods of English, five of Mathematics, three of History, three of Geography, three of Latin, three of French or German, three of Physics, three of Chemistry or Biology, one or two of Art or Music, and two of Scripture. At 16 years of age the boys would take nationally-sponsored examinations and hope to gain a School Certificate passing grade in as many as ten subjects. Only the very able and conscientious would pass more than five or six of these examinations. A few would pass only one or two. The Sixth Form, a two or three-year period of specialization on two or three subjects in preparation for Advanced Level or university entrance and scholarship examinations, would be open to those who showed promise and who had the initiative to go on beyond the 16-year-olds' General Certificate examinations. Most of the Sixth Form boys would be appointed to positions of responsibility in governing the daily routine of the school and would carry out their duties conscientiously.

This is the training that England provides free of charge for the boys (and girls, in separate schools) who show the ability and aptitudes to profit from it. Approximately 20 per cent of the children of the country go to schools of this kind, and they are chosen entirely on the basis of ability to do superior academic work. Of the children who attend these Grammar Schools, perhaps one-third stay on for Sixth Form work, and perhaps half of these will go on to a university.

By comparison with the intellectual level of most American school programs, the English Grammar School system seems demanding. It is, but boys and girls are not withering away under it. Their innate abilities are no greater than those of our children, but the leaders in England recognize the necessity of a full development of those mental capacities if the younger generation is to be able to cope with the complex problems facing community, nation, and world in this age.

By comparison with the material benefits lavished on American boys and girls, the children of England may seem under-privileged. Before anyone makes such an assumption, however, he should try to visualize our children's way of life through others' eyes. To the English – children and adults alike – the American youth's life looks soft, pampered, sheltered, hardly suitable to form the kind of steadfast character needed to serve in a world where the individual must often deny himself much that he would like to have, if all are to survive.

My feeling is that the English could learn from us the value of the originality and daring experimentation that have led to much American progress; and at the same time, we could learn from the English the enduring truth of the idea that a human being can attain maturity only through a realization of the demands of a disciplined life.

CHAPTER 16

School Matron

Joan Cowell, MBE

In September 1949, I was appointed as School Matron to both the Grammar and High Schools. My duties were equally divided between the Schools but, because Miss Kathleen Richards, the Schools' Secretary was over in the High School, I was based in the Grammar School office.

My duties consisted of general health care of all the pupils, overseeing the cleaning staff and appointing them when necessary, liaising with the caretakers on behalf of the Heads of both Schools, sitting in on School Medical Examinations and organising tea and coffee for the staff of both Schools from the little kitchen at the end of the top corridor on the High School side.

I can assure you that this was no easy task, particularly in regard to the Grammar School staff, because they liked to make their own after-lunch tea and consistently lost or broke the china. On one occasion the masters complained that the tea "tasted funny." It transpired that Mr Laywood, who took it upon himself to be in charge of the tea pot, had filled it with Dettol and had failed to wash it out properly afterwards.

I was also responsible for collecting, counting, and banking all the dinner money on Friday mornings, recording all absence notes in both Schools, and for making arrangements to transport all sick pupils to their homes when necessary.

Miss Woodrow (Headmistress) felt I needed some assistance, so she arranged for a recent school leaver from Kettering High School to help in both offices for a small remuneration. The first girl was Dilys Hiscock, who stayed until she got married.

Not to be outdone by Miss Woodrow, Mr Scott gave me the assistance of a Sixth Form boy to help with the dinner money. Romance blossomed when Dilys' successor met my Sixth Form helper over the heaps of coins. They eventually got married and, to the best of my knowledge, are still happily together with their family.

Every Tuesday afternoon, Miss Woodrow held a little ceremony in her study, when all the office staff partook of ice cream. I think she must have told Mr Scott because, shortly after the ice cream feast started, he sometimes invited Dilys and me into his study after 4.00 o'clock on a Friday for a glass of sherry.

He was a man with a great sense of humour and a law unto himself. For instance, County Hall issued a statement that the last day of term must continue until 4.00 p.m. Mr Scott ignored this and School finished in the morning at the end of term.

I remember when Ted Ward came to be interviewed for the job of junior English Master. I cannot remember how many candidates were seen, but the interviews took place in the Library and after the last one had been in, Mr Scott came out at about 5.00 p.m. and asked Miss Richards, Dilys and me which one we liked the best. We all agreed on Mr Ward, who was duly appointed and we still keep in touch with him and his wife, Pauline.

Once, when the School photograph was being taken, one boy put a white mouse on his shoulder (in the days when all boys wore the regulation black school blazer). Mr Scott made him ink out the mouse on each and every one of the photographs. It took him a lot of days, from 4.00 to 5.00 p.m., to complete.

The detention book was kept in the office. Some reasons given for detaining a boy after school, or on a Saturday morning, were quite bizarre, i.e. "for dismantling a desk in class with intent to disturb" and "often wearing no School cap in a B.U.A." (built up area).

Owing to the increased numbers in both Schools, Speech Days were held in the Savoy Theatre in Russell Street, with rehearsals in the morning and prize giving in the afternoon.

I would like to digress on behalf of my own old school. In 1952, Kettering High School Speech Day was on 6th February, the day on which King George VI died. After much discussion between the Chairman of the Governors (Mr Clarke) and County Hall, it was decided to go ahead and thus Kettering High School were the first in Kettering to sing *God Save the Queen.*

The boys' Sick Room was where Sixth Formers used to spend their free periods. Sometimes when I was in and out in the course of my duties I would be asked for an opinion on the many varied topics under discussion – oddly enough, they always ended with violent political debates. Sixth Formers in those days were oddly mature in some ways, but also quite naive compared to their modern counterparts.

Some of you may remember the Rugger Concerts that took place before the 1939-1945 war, which were usually produced by Mr John Tynan and written by Mr A. Woodward and Mr John Wood. Mr Tynan was a very versatile man. I knew him well, as he lived with my parents in Isham for some time during the war, while his wife was working away. I have two of his etchings of Isham scenes, one of which I watched him do when I was 12 years old. He was very artistic and had many talents.

Mr A. F. Scott left at Easter 1951 and Mr Godfrey acted as Headmaster for the Summer and Christmas Terms. Mr Dudley was appointed in September and I left at Christmas at the same time as Mr Pledger, to whom we eventually lived next door in Ridgway Road.

Of all the members of Kettering Grammar School staff I have known over the years he was the one with the most impeccable manners. He was also an Old Boy of the School; his education took place in the Old School building in Gold Street, which was demolished to make way for the Newborough Centre.

Miss Richards regularly used to ask me to count the pictures in the H. E. Bates collection. There were some on the wall of the Gallery and others on the wall of the Library corridor. Most, if not all, classrooms had a few pictures hanging on their walls and there were others in various corridors throughout the School, to say nothing of the Head's study and the Staff Room. After 43 years I do not remember much about any of them, or from whence they came originally, although Miss Richards knew the origin of them all.

I enjoyed my time at the School and was succeeded by Connie Marlow, who eventually married Bill Ashby, whom many of you will remember, as he organised the lighting of the School plays and for the Old Boys' New Year's Eve dances. Sadly they both died some years ago.

CHAPTER 17

Bowling Green Road – Relations with the High School

Prof. John R. Knibbs

A key feature in the design of the new Grammar School in Bowling Green Road had been the siting of the High School for Girls alongside it. The middle section was shared, with the two wings dedicated to facilities for either the boys or the girls. The centre portion represented a major part of the total space: the most important of this was the hall, in which a daily Assembly was held, as well as various sports, P.T., and dancing activities. Other shared facilities included the library and a laboratory on the ground floor, two laboratories on the first floor, Domestic Science and Art studios on the second floor.

It is presumed that the primary reason for the decision to share facilities was economic, but the design and resourcing of the two schools give no impression of financial stringency. The middle section in particular was on the grand scale. The hall was splendidly designed, tall and well proportioned, lighted by huge windows; there were high quality wall bars, flooring and plaster work. Similarly the laboratories were well equipped for that era and the library had a certain grandeur. The Art studio, located at the top of the building, was blessed with pitched ceiling windows that maximised the quality of light. (This provision was of such a high standard that the Borough Council, who currently occupy this building, has allocated this room to the Architects Department).

The sharing of these central facilities must have provided the Headteachers with many time-tabling problems. Tony Ireson records that the first Headmaster at Bowling Green Road, Mr J. I. Scott, and the first Headmistress of the High School, Miss Edith Bristol ''were personal friends'' and because of this, ''harmony with the Grammar School was guaranteed'' (T. Ireson – *Old Kettering: Book 2*). This harmony, one can be certain, was strained on a number of occasions and there are hints that relationships between other Headteachers were not always harmonious.

An important strategy to facilitate the joint use of the buildings was the staggering of starting and finishing times. The High School started slightly later in the morning, 9.05 a.m. (9.00 a.m. for the Grammar School) and had a later lunch break, 12.30-2.00 p.m., as opposed to 12.00 noon-1.30 p.m. for the boys. This meant that the School Meals Services could cope with two seatings, which were held initially on the second floor at Bowling Green Road, and then in a building at the top of St Mary's Road (where Tresham Institute is presently situated). The time-tabling of classes was made particularly difficult during the 2nd World War, when both Schools were joined by others, evacuated from London. This called for drastic measures – half-time education for many, classes in the Tordoff Building in School Lane and the Labour Club in Newland Street.

Pupils streamed in and out of the middle section through a number of connecting arteries. The central staircase (not entirely central, for its only outside access was in the boys' playground) was a main thoroughfare. It could be reached through the hall and a corridor past the library on the ground floor, via the balcony on the first floor and by a connecting corridor on the second floor. Each of these routes provided opportunities for formal and informal contacts.

We do not know whether in designing the Schools it was envisaged that educational benefits would be gained from their juxtaposition, through joint classes and events, reciprocal staff provisions etc. In retrospect it is clear that over the 49 years there were only a limited number of such activities and some of these generated tension and difficulties.

It was not until 1957 that the High School appointed the first man to their staff to teach Science, Dr. Szele. For many years 'Pop' Whitney took the girls for Science subjects. At different times, throughout the shared occupancy, a few girls studied Science subjects at Sixth Form level. This meant joining in classes with the boys. These were rare occasions, but one former High School girl recalls how in 1944/5, she and two other girls took Physics (with Mr Whitney) and Chemistry (with Mr Lawson) in the company of Sixth Form boys. The girls, she reported, remained very detached from the rest of the class. Physics classes provided no embarrassments, for 'Pop' Whitney was well used to teaching girls and was a well loved figure. Chemistry, however, was quite different. Fred Lawson apparently resented their presence within his male-dominated class and on a number of occasions displayed this with biting sarcasm.

Less fraught, and perhaps more frequent, were the Sixth Form German classes, when a High School girl would join the boys under the tutelage of John Tynan. These were very small classes, only 5-6 students and a former male participant observed that the presence of a girl within the class made little or no difference in the atmosphere. He recorded that these were very serious and pressured learning events, although he did suggest that things might have been different if she had been "desperately glamorous."

These were examples of the limited sharing of classes for educational reasons. One Old Boy, Maurice Bayes, had quite a different story to relate. As a small boy, he contracted pneumonia and, having recovered, was diagnosed as having a ''weak heart.'' In consequence, when he arrived at the Grammar School in 1945, he was excused P.T. lessons. He records that, for a period of perhaps half a term, 'Joe' Ashworth, rather than have him sitting in on P.T. lessons, arranged for him to attend Cookery classes with the High School. Picture this 11/12 year old lad being obliged to join in what was then seen as a female pursuit, alone in the company of a class of girls. He remembers very vividly feeling ''degraded'' by the whole experience.

One joint activity that was undertaken at different times throughout the 49 years was the School Play. High School girls then filled the female parts: on other occasions, these parts were taken by High School staff members. Grace Thornton related how in 1924 the two schools came together for a performance of *A Midsummer Night's Dream.* She observed that ''the experiment of the joint venture was never repeated – why I do not know but can guess'' (her personal diary).

In this she was not correct. Further joint performances were given in the post 2nd World War period, and in the 1947-8 production of *A Midsummer Night's Dream,* boys were not required to play the parts of the fairies (much, I suspect, to their relief).

Another joint activity, not organised by the respective games teachers, but sanctioned by them, was the annual hockey match between the High School 1st XI and a selected number of the Grammar School 1st XV rugger team.

An unusual mating ritual. The High School girls feign indifference.

It was a rumbustuous event: the boys, I recall, for I played in such a match, borrowed hockey sticks from girl friends and careered around the pitch, frequently penalised for ''sticks'', a mysterious offence which involved illegally swinging the hockey stick and equally frequently being rapped about the ankles by the more skilled and nimble members of the opposing team/sex. I suspect, but can't actually remember, that the High School were the victors.

Former students of both schools recall with affection the interest they displayed in members of the opposite sex whilst at school. This was not a universal pastime. Grace Thornton, again writing in her diary, observed ''I do not think I knew one boy there, nor I think did I have any over-riding urge to change the situation''. A significant number of Grammar School boys, particularly from the '20s and '30s held a similar view about members of the High School. Individuals recall little or no contact or interest; they were too concerned with academic demands and were not prepared to challenge the strict rules of segregation. But for others, boy/girl watching, in all its various forms, consumed a great deal of time and energy, providing a challenge and spice to an otherwise boring routine. H. E. Bates belonged to this latter group. In his autobiography, *The Vanished World,* he writes about how he first caught sight of Con (Connie Ginns), a High School girl, whilst attending a performance of the School Play, – how he was ''hypnotised by this head and the small dark-eyed face which now and then turned sideways.''

The School Play was only one of a number of possible points of contact. The balcony provided a special viewing platform from which to watch the girls at P.T. Passage across the balcony was only permitted to most pupils when they needed to join a class on the first floor. Prefects and monitors were not so restricted, nor was the lab. boy who needed to be able to visit the laboratory to perform his various duties. Tony Ireson, a former lab. boy of the '20s, records in *Book 2* of his series on *Old Kettering,* how he ''crossed the frontier bearing communications from headmaster to headmistress, had the run of the Botany lab, as operator of the volcanic equipment that produced a supply of distilled water. Occasionally I went along the balcony when the young ladies were performing eurhythmics in the hall wearing their Grecian Tunics''. Delivering messages and undertaking errands across the frontiers were not sought-after tasks. It required a high level of self assurance to accomplish these without embarrassment. To find yourself, a lone self-conscious boy, engulfed by a tide of girls moving between classes whilst carrying a message, was not usually seen as an enriching experience. A particularly stressful task for two 11/12 year old girls, one former High School girl remembers, was to have to fetch the sole and shared skeleton from a classroom, full of boys studying some aspect of Biology. The skeleton, which had a long-forgotten nickname, had to be separated into two pieces under the watchful gaze of 30 plus pairs of eager male eyes and then carried away, bones dangling and clicking, encouraged by a somewhat aloof commentary by 'Reggie' Gladden.

But girl/boy watching could be undertaken under less difficult circumstances. It was possible to look out of the window of the laboratories within the middle section and while away the tedium of classes. 'Reggie' Gladden had a method of dealing with this. David Naylor reports that he would force the voyeur to stand outside the room for a closer view. Although David regarded this as the ultimate indignity, Ted Freestone recalls that it became for him a favourite location, a means of escaping classes and an opportunity for closer scrutiny of passing girls.

Careful timing made it possible to meet girls for a fleeting moment (and even pass a note to them) at lesson changes, whilst classes were en route up the central staircase, for example, to the Art studio or the laboratories.

H. E. Bates recalls these meetings between boys moving in one direction, and girls the other, as moments of "Much confusion, dropping of rulers and notebooks, giggling and a great rustling of paper." (*The Vanished World*). They were also opportunities for Con's love letters, carried up the leg of a friend's knickers, to be transferred to Bates.

This practice of note passing was a daring manifestation of the interest shown between the pupils of the other school. The playgrounds were separated by a high brick wall, but not too high to prevent signalling and note passing, especially at the Parish Church end where a large tree provided a platform. There was also an open slatted gate between the two playgrounds. This enabled limited girl watching and some note passing; limited, because it was frequently policed by staff. In addition, there was the boiler room situated in the basement and accessible from both sides of the central building. Over the years, it therefore attracted a flow of correspondence that rivalled the Royal Mail. Tony Ireson told me how David Warren, the arthritic caretaker of the '20s, occasionally found these and handed them directly to J. I. Scott. If the writer was identifiable, 6 strokes of the cane was the price of postage. Tony felt irritation with David Warren for this and believed some addition to the notes, in transit, would have produced more interesting results. A later assistant caretaker in the 1940s adopted a more supportive approach by not intercepting the flow; he went on to marry a former High School girl!

Notes were sometimes left in a more permanent form, as graffiti and carvings on the desks, particularly in the shared Art room. Here the desks were collapsible and guarded with less diligence than the benches in the laboratories, although even here messages incorporating a heart, pierced by an arrow were sometimes to be found. (The Art room's collapsible desks were not infrequently knocked over and this caused a tremendous clatter through to the hall, thus disturbing the girls' Assembly and resulting in irate messages being delivered to W. B. Gash, the Art master).

The second floor corridor, which linked the two Schools, was another means of viewing and contact. It was less often visited by academic staff and for a period of time, costumes for the School Plays were hung there in a type of open fronted wardrobe. Notes could be hidden there and even, according to one former High School girl, who became a headmistress of a primary school in Kettering, it could house two young persons, intent on more than contact by the written word.

The precise contents of the notes that passed between the pupils of the Schools are now lost. Writers and recipients of these recall that, in addition to affirmations of undying affection, they included details of suggested meeting places. There was a rich range of extra school opportunities. The Public Library attracted many young men, not, as Trevor Holmes remembers, because of the books on the shelves, but because the Public Library attracted many young women. The school buses, bringing pupils from outlying villages, including Corby, were segregated with girls upstairs and boys downstairs, but contact and viewing were still possible. No such restrictions were placed on the trains and a former Grammar School boy from Gretton remembered, with affection, the carriages without corridors on the trains that came to Kettering from Gretton via Corby. He spent many enjoyable journeys in the company of Central School girls (not High School!) locked away from the intervention of authority.

The school dinner service provided staggered meal times for the boys and the girls. When the boys processed to St Mary's Road, there were no voyeurs. The girls were still at classes. The girls made the same journey around 1.00 p.m. and by returning early to School after lunch, daring boys, aspiring

The Dinner Parade to St. Mary's Road Canteen (site of today's Tresham Institute).

peacocks, could cycle by the long procession. But this boy/girl watching had some unanticipated side-effects. For example, a former High School girl 1946/51, commented how, in those pre-contact lens' days, she would remove her spectacles and put them in her tunic pocket to avoid being seen in them by passing boys. The result was a significant number of broken pairs of spectacles when, having forgotten their whereabouts, she sat upon them.

The presence of the Girls School alongside the boys, had an impact upon the type of pranks, conducted by successive generations of pupils. For example, High School gym knickers provided a special fascination. Pupils recall these were made of black sateen, a shiny type of material, with elasticated bottoms, quite baggy in design and with the owner's name embroidered in red on the side. On a number of occasions, these were placed upon the tower at the top of the building by intrepid (if somewhat foolhardy) groups of boys. David Naylor recalls how, in 1951, he and two other boys at lunch time climbed out on the roof to fly such a pair on the tower. Two returned safely and undetected. The third, he remembers, came down by a different route, got lost and put his foot through the Art studio, occupied at the time by a girls' class. The full punishment is not remembered but it included a severe caning. On a later occasion, this escapade (not including the foot through the ceiling) was repeated on consecutive evenings. After the first climb, when none was caught, J. K. Dudley, the Headmaster, concerned not only about the adverse publicity, and the breach of discipline, but also about the possible danger of the exploit, gave a stern warning to all the pupils. For a number, as this was the end of their life at the School, the warning went unheeded. The rest of the story appears elsewhere in this book.

Another prank, far less dangerous to life or limb, but still quite risky, if the miscreants had been caught, involved displaying a rude word, spelt out by cards held by a number of boys. Apparently in 1946/47, eight Grammar School boys, standing at the bottom of their playground, each held up, towards the first floor laboratory, a card bearing a letter of the alphabet. The first letter was a 'B' and there were included two 'L's' and two 'O's'. In the first floor laboratory at the time of the transmission, the High School class, 1Q, were about to receive Science tuition. Unfortunately, the prank failed to achieve maximum impact because, with their 1940s naivety, none of the watching girls knew what it meant.

Notwithstanding these boy/girl activities, and many more unrecorded, the two Schools maintained a high level of segregation, operating essentially as two separate institutions, siamese twins, sharing facilities but living almost completely separate existences. Roy Tinsley (1933-40) summed up the experience of many, by describing the two Schools as "poles apart," regarding the High School as "another world", "closely guarded against contact". The Headteachers of these 49 years, J. I. Scott, A. F. Scott, and J. K. Dudley, were all remembered as stern disciplinarians, ready to punish severely any breaches in the code of discipline, governing relationships between these two Schools. Commentators on this period believe that this stern approach, to some degree, was urged upon them by the demands of their colleague Headmistresses, Misses Bristol, Whyte and Woodrow, each of whom guarded their School and pupils with a fierce determination.

In 1962 the Boys School moved to Windmill Avenue, eliminating the tension of this shared existence. Perhaps the timing was fortuitous for, in many respects, this period of 49 years, 1913-62, was for most pupils an ''age of innocence'' supported by the vigour of the Heads and teaching staff. If they had remained linked together in this fraught and, in later years, overcrowded manner during the swinging and permissive sixties, the pastimes and pranks might have been far more difficult to contain within reasonable bounds.

Jumbo

Jim Dale

Jim Dale, Sports Day, 1950. Can you spot him?

For someone who forgot his wife's name at their marriage ceremony, it is asking a lot to expect me to recall moments and incidents from as far back as 1947. However, certain details of my years at The Grammar are beginning to creep out of the cobwebs of what one master called, ''That hollow shell above that loud mouth of yours, Smith!'' God knows which master said that, but eventually they all voiced similar remarks over the next few years! Yes, the name was Smith then, Jim Smith, or 'Jumbo' to certain privileged friends of mine.

Looking back, I can place all lessons onto ''My Most Hated'' list, except for Nature Study, namely bird watching. This became a passion on my first day there, when I looked through a knot-hole in the wooden gate dividing our playground from the Girls High School! I couldn't believe the view. There were girls of every shape and size as far as the peeping eye could see! Walt Disney films of racing lemmings had nothing on this view! I had never gazed on so many pairs of naked feminine legs running nowhere in particular, and I knew at that moment that my Meccano set had been replaced forever by a much more invigorating hobby! Rothwell Primary School couldn't hold a candle to this lot. I fell in love that day with every long and short and fat and thin chickadee I copped me peepers on. I had never been moved this way by the sight of a girl in my life. At my age, SEX was a posh word for what the coal man brought the coal in!

I became a Peeping Jim at every opportunity I could find. If the girls were in the Main Hall doing P.T., I was on the balcony watching every sexy little figure. Bouncing breasts were not the order of the day for nine out of ten of them, but as there were more than thirty in every class, at least three girls stood out more firmly than the rest. Eventually, just looking at those little teasers wasn't satisfying enough for me, I had to touch one. I tried to do this at every sneaky opportunity that presented itself. I would brush past them slowly at the bus-stop, pretending to adjust my tie while trying to feel soft flesh with my elbow. Walking slowly along in front of them, I would kneel down suddenly to tie my shoelace in the hope they might trip over me and flash something – anything! In the sweet shop, I would hold out my hand for change hoping one would lean into it while reaching over to grab a piece of toffee! I didn't quite know what I wanted, but I knew whatever it was, they had it! Looking back, I never did quite get it, but I had fun trying!

Over the next few years, I had ''Close Encounters Of The First Kind'' with a total of five giggly girls, who did their homework on me every afterschool on the other side of the School wall. That place was Cattle Market Heaven for me. My dear Mum may have made sandwiches for my lunch, but she would never have guessed what I was having for tea!

Where are they now, those little Lolitas? I shall always remember the pet names they called me. 'Whippet', 'Ramrod', 'Gherkin', 'Squishy' and my favourite one of all, 'Nibbler!' Perhaps I shouldn't mention their names, you may be married to one of them. But if they ever read this book, I'm still thinking of you my beautiful 'Booby', my fabulous 'Fuzz', my little wonder 'Wabbit', my darling 'Squeaky', and the little nutter I called, 'The Nipper'!

These then are my fondest recollections of the old Grammar School days. No doubt there were a few teachers I must have bumped into occasionally, and other boys I must have known, who sat next to me for four years, but all that pales alongside the memories of those virgin views of adolescence the K.H.S. girls gave me.

Bless 'Em All! Bless 'Em All! The Long And The Short And The Tall!

CHAPTER 18

1949 And All That

Edgar Lindley (member of staff: 1949-1974)

The late 1940s, with all the excitement of being back from the war and amongst family and friends again – "Bliss was it in that dawn to be alive". Not that re-adjusting to civilian life was easy, nor resuming a teaching career after a gap of six years. And when in 1949 I found myself involved in the upheaval of moving to Northamptonshire with a young family, in order to take up a new appointment – that was a challenge indeed.

Kettering, of which I had previously known nothing, proved to be a pleasant market town, much smaller than the cities in the North of England where I'd lived and worked before, but we were made welcome and very soon settled in. My new colleagues at the Grammar School included some formidable characters, and as the newest Head of Department I could easily have felt somewhat daunted, particularly as it was made abundantly clear to me what a charismatic personality my predecessor, the late John Tynan, had been. I certainly didn't endear myself to either staff or pupils when, on my first day "on duty", I rang the bell for the end of morning break five minutes early – not through excess of zeal but due to a regrettable confusion over timing (the morning break was longer than the afternoon one then). Incidentally, that rather splendid handbell saw service on several occasions in the 1950s down at the Cricket Club, summoning umpires and players into action during Kettering's three-day county match, which used to be an annual fixture in the Northants calendar.

But back to my colleagues. I can't help thinking that if J. L. Carr had written a novel about a secondary school, as a companion volume to his entertaining *Harpole Report*, the staff-room at K.G.S. in 1949 would have provided the necessary assortment of characters: Tom Corke, 'Reggie' Gladden, the two Georges (Godfrey and Laywood), Fred Lawson, Bob Smith, to name but a few. It was, however, a happy staff-room, with the banter always good-natured, and it remained so throughout my time at the School. One colleague became a particularly close friend, sharing that quarter of a century with me until we retired together. Jack Young had found out quite a lot about the Northants countryside before I came, and introdued me to its many delights

Some of Edgar Lindley's colleagues, Sports Day Recorders, circa 1951. Messrs Woodward, Godfrey, Ashworth, Smith and Phillips.

on our occasional walks during holiday times, when our respective families could spare us. We had much in common, in addition to our northern roots, and Jack's death in 1993 has left a big gap in my life. He and his wife, Edna, who survives him, have been wonderfully kind to me ever since my own wife's death in 1970.

I was privileged to have Edmund Kirby as a colleague during his final year before retirement, and our association and friendship continued through the Kettering and District Three Arts Club, which he and many others had founded in 1946 and of which he was the last President when, due to declining membership, the Club folded in 1978. More of that later.

For the School, and for me, the 1950s was an exciting decade. Some first rate new additions to the staff of the Department were recruited: Ken Horton, and later Paul Sharpling, to re-start and develop German studies, Peter Wilson, followed by Cliff Brown, to introduce and build up Russian, and Brian Perrett, who became another good friend. Meanwhile trips abroad for senior boys became a feature of the Easter holiday. I've not forgotten my first experience of setting out at 4 o'clock on a cold morning in early April, with only the coach driver for company, to collect bleary-eyed members of the party from various pre-arranged pick-up points in Northamptonshire! Then it was breakfast in London – the Strand Corner House (three cheers for Joe Lyons!) – and the boat train at Victoria, with Paris our final destination. Among many happy memories of Paris I recall one occasion in particular, when Jack Young showed his versatility. We were crossing the city in a hired coach to pick up our French guide for a visit to Versailles, and Jack enlivened the twenty minute journey by taking the microphone and improvising an hilarious spoof commentary on various public buildings, cafes, statues, and the like: it was a tour de force.

Throughout the 'fifties and 'sixties K.G.S. contributed much to the status of the town, not only in its academic successes, but in sporting achievements, by individuals and teams (athletics, rugby, cricket, tennis, and later soccer and hockey), in drama, music and, of course, in science. The Debating Society provided a lively forum for both serious and light-hearted discussion, and with the move to Windmill Avenue, and the arrival of Maurice Till, the School choir, into which I found myself recruited, soon established a fine reputation for choral singing. We gave recitals in several churches in and around Kettering, and enjoyed two exceptional engagements to sing Evensong in Peterborough Cathedral and, also by special invitation, to provide the choir for a wedding at a church on the edge of Clapham Common! This latter "date" gave me the excuse for a whole day out, ending in an enjoyable evening at a London theatre, and a lively sing-song on the midnight coach home!

Other vivid memories? The excitement (and teething troubles!) of the School's first language laboratory, many Saturday afternoons spent umpiring First XI cricket matches, home and away, with my son Peter playing a prominent role in the mid-sixties, and (thanks to the High School's co-operation) some splendid productions of Shakespeare plays, in one of which my daughter Ruth took part. I remember, too, chairing a special *University Challenge* type quiz in which a team of Sixth Formers took on (though failed to defeat!) four members of staff.

Meanwhile, through the 32 years of its existence, the Three Arts Club continued to use the School for most of its monthly meetings; and an impressive list of individual artistes and speakers, musical ensembles, drama groups, etc. provided the entertainment, and there was no shortage of "home-grown" talent, with Edmund Kirby in particular giving us some delightful talks. One final memory is of a Friday afternoon, at the end of a busy week in the life of the Windmill Avenue School. It was just after four o'clock when members of the distinguished Lindsay String Quartet arrived to rehearse for their recital that evening. Some hasty sorting out of chairs, music stands, etc. and tuning of instruments, and they settled down to test acoustics by playing through the slow movement of Debussy's quartet. A sudden hush fell on the hall, which only minutes before had been a bustle of activity, and all who'd been involved in that activity – staff, boys, caretaker, cooks, cleaners – stood, silent, motionless, and, I believe, entranced by the beauty of the music: a magic moment indeed.

CHAPTER 19

TC

Brian Slough

It is important to match written form to subject matter and readership. Since my subject is Mr Thomas Corke, and a hefty percentage of readers will have been taught by him, it is appropriate that the form is anecdotal.

I wonder what the Chief Inspector of Schools and his OFSTED warriors would have made of TC. Not much, I expect. The feeling would have been mutual. To start with, Tom held to the philosophy that every teacher should be guru in his, or her, own castle. He was particularly protective of his Art Room, even one disguised as a tin hut and fuelled by a stove straight out of Laurie Lee's schoolroom in *Cider With Rosie.* As a likely OFSTED outcast, he would be in distinguished company. Former teachers such as Auden, Waugh and Betjeman would have been certainties for the black spot: Rhodes Boyson and the prime Jean Brodie distinct possibilities. Tom wasn't of that ilk, but he shared similarities with one of my Oxford tutors, a genius but not cross-curricular. The late Professor David Palmer, an Old Cytringanian, told me that my tutor was once flattened by his own car, while cranking it up with a starting handle. Tom would have liked that. It occurs to me that David probably heard it from Tom in the first place.

I think it was Ibsen who wrote that the first to be slain are the eccentrics, followed by the individuals. He might have added that the eccentrics are also remembered first, and longest: one of the few certainties in life. Thus, wherever two or three former pupils of the Kettering Grammar School are gathered together, then the words and deeds of Thomas Corke will enter the conversation. It was no surprise that, among the unsolicited contributions to this book, the name most mentioned was Tom's.

The simplest explanation is that he was at the School a long time. He came to Kettering in 1929, initially to take over the teaching of Art and Woodwork, previously fulfilled by visiting staff. After the War, the increase in pupil numbers, coupled with the introduction of Biology, resulted in the disappearance of Woodwork. The outcome was that TC assumed responsibility for Art alone, along with legendary status. I should add that this is the most straightforward version of events: needless to say, there are others more bizarre.

Several contributors point to the hallmark of his teaching as the ability to inculcate essential principles, artistic and otherwise. Decades later, they remain fixed in the mind: the importance of vanishing points in perspectives; the fundamental requirement of accurate observation (the number of windows in a bus, the length of an arm, the presence and length of shadows). Buses and height were important to Tom. He was right about two other key principles, recalled by all. First, upright lines are upright on all occasions. Second, the profligate use of gold and black paint is hideous. Heavy Metal T-shirts confirm this truth. Whilst we cannot be certain of his response to Heavy Metal rock bands, D. H. Isherwood (1958-62) remembers Tom having trouble with Adam (pronounced 'Aydam') Faith. Indeed, on more than one occasion he threatened to take him to Mr Dudley for writing his name on desks. I suppose he would have issued a similar warning to Led Zeppelin and he wasn't the only master to feel confronted by the *Living Dead*. ''If you lot are the cream of the cream, then God help the skimmed milk.''

''Narrative has been described as a primary act of mind; children construct the world through story. It is the teacher's role to recognise this, to encourage it. . . .'' I wrote that in the original National Curriculum. I can't pretend that I had Tom in mind, but it fits. His fame lives on as a teller of tales (and what better legacy?). His output was phenomenal, far beyond the range of a Chaucer, Cartland or Cookson. If only we'd written them down; a fortune waited. Carl Howard (1948-53) writes: ''I clocked him covering over thirty during one double period, but when Bryn Williams realised what I was doing, he did help along with cunning questioning.'' (Bryn denies that his success as a Headteacher rested on such machiavellian skills – ed).

The stories often featured recurring motifs, such as the sea, and were of the surrealistic genre, not dissimilar to Dali. Conrad mixed with *Monty Python*. Phil Bradshaw (1962-69) maintains that many arose from a ''fetish about punctuality.'' Apparently, on one occasion during the Second World War, Tom had to walk to School from his home in Geddington. As he approached the Ise Bridge, two frogmen emerged from a U-Boat. Tom ran to his house in Newton Road for his shotgun, disposed of the enemy, and still arrived punctually at K.G.S. in time for Assembly. This was a story with a purpose: ''If I got here on time, why can't you?'' Eminently reasonable. The story raises other questions, however, beyond its immediate message. Was Geddington the centre for British intelligence, which these Germans were sent to destroy? Was TC, M?

Punctuality was an essential part of his moral code. Two Old Boys mention his writing regularly to the local press, listing the lateness of buses on the Geddington to Kettering route. A crusader for uprightness in all its modes, he would hum quietly and contentedly in its presence. Miscreants' ears would also hum in its absence. Justice was straightforward and immediate: you knew where you stood with Tom, especially if you lived in Corby. There were mitigating circumstances for this political incorrectness. Daily, the Corby double-deckers sped past Tom, stationed at the top of West Street. One passenger, a bob and weave artist, sat next to me in Art classes. He is now a distinguished attorney, and television pundit: clearly a man to trust. He admits that there were occasions when the passengers hailed Tom through the open windows of the bus. This was confirmed by my late uncle, who was a bus driver. Is it not understandable, therefore, that Tom ''got his retaliation in first'' – in the best traditions of the British Lions. The lion versus the rats, perhaps?

Tom was a popular resident of Geddington. My aged aunt, long deceased, spoke highly of him in the 1940s as a gentleman. He invariably raised his hat as he greeted fellow villagers. He was a lively, iconoclastic politician at meetings of the Parish Council, evident from my scrapbook of newspaper cuttings. For example, in days gone by (contrary to the myth of the rural idyll) village streets were often troubled by cattle excreta, a far more testing problem than parking. At one meeting, Tom remained silent through the bullshit, then proposed the obvious solution: colostomy bags. Reports of the Council meetings vied with the *Goon Show* as the hot topics for conversation. Latecomers sometimes wondered where reality blurred into illusion.

I shudder to think of TC's reaction to the current demands of record keeping and assessment in schools. His own descriptions were ''Good'', ''Fair'', and ''Weak'', accompanied by a number and the famous initials. His system was clear-cut and easily understood by pupils, parents, and employers – if not always. Carl Howard tells how his end of term report had nearly always been ''31/33:.Fair''. Sometimes, however, it was 32/33: Weak.'' Tom knew a thing or two about rising standards.

His thirty six years at K.G.S. are remembered vividly and fondly by most, as editions of the War-time *Reveille* and reunions (formal and informal) testify. Given my time again, and knowing what I know now, I'd still opt for Tom as my Art teacher. Not because my pass in O-level Art was entirely thanks to him, for I have no artistic talent (as my wife will tell you). Not just because he encouraged us to look at pictures in the local Art Gallery. Most of all, he brought colour to our lives (minus the black and gold).

It is certain Tom is in heaven, having reminded St Peter on entry that ''it's Corke (of average height) with an 'e' ''. On the way in, he would have checked that the pearly gates were upright. Should I ever make it, he'll be waiting; a quick hitch of the socks, then a biff round the ear for writing this.

DOUBLE ART

John Hunt

Tom Corke, ''spelt with an 'Ee you fool'', or TC for short, a name and an initial guaranteed to bring a smile to the face of anyone who knew him. It's a Friday afternoon in June 1960. From the lofty, isolated wastes of the Art

Room, I look at the church clock, 1.36 p.m. Ten minutes ago I was speaking to my father in the cattle market, which was then held next to the School. He was by now swishing home to our 300 acre rented farm in his beloved 1950 Ford Pilot. I envisaged father sitting down to his ample lunch of cold mutton, new potatoes and salad from the garden, followed by treacle tart and cream.

A near-riot was occurring, as it usually did in the Art Room, as we sat down. Tom bawled, "Right, let's have a few names for detention. We'll start with er, err, erh . . ." He scanned his school list, "Baxter."

A boy volunteered, "Baxter does Woodwork, Sir."

"Thorne," bawled Tom.

"Thorne's in hospital, Sir, having a tight foreskin removed."

Huge amounts of laughter followed. Tom took a swing at the nearest pupil. Blam. The pupil and desk nearly fell over.

"Sit down you little rat and face the front," hollered Tom, almost enjoying his usual start to a lesson. A little voice announced from the middle of the class, "Please Sir, my desk is broken."

"O.K." yelled Tom. "Put it on the pile at the back of the room. Move back, I will do it for you."

He picked up the desk, whose lid had fallen off, heaved the desk above his head and threw it towards a pile of wreckage some ten feet away. Smash! What had been a reparable desk was now firewood, as a leg ricocheted off the wall, dislodging a lump of plaster. As an encore, the desk lid followed, hitting the wrecked desk like a Howitzer shell and falling in half. Tom dusted his hands and pulled up his left sock, a smile on his face. He started his usual tale, "This is my room. I do what I like in here."

I looked over at the church clock, thinking the lesson must be half over. 1.39 p.m. Despair hit me. Only three minutes had passed. We had got Tom until 2.45 – another hour or more. My lunch had been eaten by 12.30 in the school canteen. Hunger was never far away from a 15 year old lad. A quarter pound of jelly babies was in my blazer pocket. Tom had a nasty habit of catching you eating sweets in class and taking the goodies for himself. I would wait until break.

Tom was raving on, "They don't like me in the Common Room, so I ignore them. They are fools. If I have a lesson up here, I leave them ten minutes before the bell and run over the bloody bal-coney (balcony) and then it's my room. I do what I like in here." To emphasise this point, he jumped three feet high and came down, CRASH, onto the floor, the room shaking and reverberating. He did this four times, each time just as hard. Twenty seconds later, a young frightened-looking High School mistress opened the Art Room door. She must have been teaching in the room below.

"Are you all right, Mr Corke?"

Tom ran at her, "Get out you fool. This is my room. I do what I like in here!"

The poor lady slammed the door and ran, screaming. The boys roared with laughter. Tom really enjoyed that. He pulled up both socks, not taking his eyes off us, in case a missile was launched at him. During this diversion, a few of the genuine, talented artists in the class had lurked over to the sink to fill their water jars. Tom was affronted. He hadn't authorised this. "I say," he yelled, "get away from the tap will you." Near bedlam occurred. Tom pushed his specs back onto his nose with his middle finger and made haste from the front desk towards the sink. Someone shoved a handful of paint brushes down the plug hole, two large jamjars of water were dropped and smashed, the tap was turned on full bore, floating the paint brushes part way out of the plug hole. Tom had armed himself with a half-metre rule and intended using it. As boys strove to get away from the sink area, a desk was knocked over. Tom slipped on the spilt water and nearly ended up on the floor. A chant of "Tom, Tom, Tom, Tom" started. Meanwhile his desk was being attended to. A bright spark tore up Tom's bits of paper he had been writing notes and names on and threw them into the waste basket. Tom's HB11 pencil followed in four bits, as did the board rubber intact.

Glory be. The church clock struck 1.45 – eleven minutes of our double Art period had gone. The church bells seemed to quieten the class down. Everyone sat down and awaited developments. T.C. was shaken, but hardly showed it. He had somehow got a peppermint into his mouth without anyone noticing. He sat on the edge of his desk, "Put your pencils down, face the front." Story time was about to begin.

Everybody has heard the Titanic, so it won't be repeated, but – have you heard the one about the bloke who Tom's brother knew? Tom was a wonderful artist. He ought instead to have been a sort of Roald Dahl. He rabbited on about this bloke his brother knew could step exactly a yard without trying, every step not 36 1/32″ but bang on 36″ day in, day out. Soon the guy was snapped up by the Ministry of Works and became a human tape measure. The illustrious chap stepped out roads, bridges, buildings, etc. etc. according to Tom. His downfall came when his pet dog brought a golf ball home and left it in the hallway for the man to step on, spraining his ankle. For ages the man continued his marking out, then disaster. A building he had marked the footings out for was erected, but the internal girders were too short. It was found the man was no longer stepping a yard but 35 31/32″.

Tom waffled on until 2.20 p.m. – just 25 minutes left. He put the wooden stool from behind the desk on a chair, then the waste paper basket on top of that. Two or three rolled-up sheets of art paper adorned the artistic creation. "Oh, draw that."

At last our bell went at 2.45. "Hand in your books," yelled Tom, as he tried to dodge the mass exodus. Someone kicked the chair over; down came the stool and basket, which rolled over towards the door. The door was flung open and down the stairs went the basket. It continued down the stairs over the heads of two High School girls who got in its way, pencil shavings, used straws, milk bottle tops, chalk dust and the board rubber disgorging themselves on the way. At last the ground floor and the entrance to the caretaker's den. Hoof! down the basement went the wrecked basket. ''Oi!'' yelled a voice from the depths. We had got him as well.

Into the School yard, which was quickly filling up with boys out for their afternoon break. We stood around in high spirits, laughing and joking at the events of the last 15 minutes. Our classmates emerged from the Woodwork Room, glum-faced and not laughing; they looked pale and exhausted, poor things. So ended double Art.

There is a post script. We were in 4G and our Form room was over Jake's study. This cramped our style considerably. Just when a useful riot was brewing, Dudley would appear in the doorway and demand in his best English, ''Could someone inform me what the stampede was in aid of?'' The illustrious and highly thought-of Mr Aubrey John Cowell was our Form master. Sometime during 1960 he had to give evidence in court after some money was stolen from our Form room by a burglar. T.C. filled in for Mr Cowell first period Friday morning, which was usually a free period for Tom. Quickly Tom started one of his stories after the register was completed. He had never seen or taken our full class before (12 took Art, 13 Woodwork). Tom did very well, simply because we were performing under constraint. A tale started, ''The whole world was inhabited by fools. Mr Dudley was a fool. This is my room now, so I do what I like in here. If Mr Dudley comes in here without knocking, I'll knock his teeth down his throat.'' The door did open just as Tom said those words, and in walked Mr Dudley. Tom shook like a leaf, ''Errh hello, Mr Dudlee'', stammered Tom, and fished a piece of paper out of his top jacket pocket, ''w-w-would you like to see this?'' We never heard what Mr Dudley said to Mr Corke on that day over thirty years ago and we never will. All I and twenty four others can remember is trying not to laugh and be sent down to the Head's study for the twig. Tom must have been nearly as old as the century. I hope he and all the other masters who taught me, who have departed this life, rest in peace.

CHAPTER 20

Expeditions

Sellick Norsworthy

Legend has it that School expeditions began in 1927 when the Headmaster, Mr J. I. Scott, decided that a party of senior boys led by Mr Whitney should witness the total eclipse of the sun in Giggleswick, walking and camping part of the way there. Mr Scott provided a large bell tent and a trek-cart. The party went to Giggleswick passing over "Buttertubs", a high pass in the Yorkshire moors. Unfortunately, after all their efforts, clouds prevented them seeing the eclipse.

In the following years Mr Whitney led summer walking and climbing holidays, using the trek-cart and tents, in Wales and the Lake District. In 1932, Mr Ashworth joined Mr Whitney on a trip to the North Welsh Mountains and these trips continued yearly until 1939 under the same

One of the many Lake District trips, Easter 1951 at Borrowdale.

leadership. Their camping and climbing expeditions took them to North Wales, the Lake District, the Isle of Arran and the Isle of Skye.

After the War, Mr Ashworth began climbing holidays during the Easter holiday, staying in C.H.A. and H.F. hostels. These continued until the early 1950s, when it proved almost impossible to book accommodation in the School holiday period.

In 1962, the idea of School expeditions was resurrected by Gordon Brown, who, as a Scotsman, naturally looked towards his beloved country and especially the Cairngorms, for inspiration. John Dudley wrote from Wakefield in 1971, on the tenth anniversary of the Cairngorms Expeditions:

''The views of the peaks must have had a profound effect on the Midland Youth, possibly their first real experience of the splendours of nature. But more than this, there was that comradeship which arises from living together as a small community, preparing meals, facing the elements in all their variety, enjoying fun, and overcoming crises, all of which play their part in the building of character.''

Little did he realise, at the time of writing, that there would be another fourteen trips to the Cairngorms and dozens of letters of appreciation from parents whose boys had experienced just what John Dudley had written about in 1971. It was a great tragedy that Gordon's sudden death in 1985 prevented him from completing his 25th expedition. Not only did Gordon complete 24 trips to the Cairngorms: he was involved in Govilon during its early years, an expedition to the Isle of Rhum and perhaps his greatest triumph, an expedition to the Canadian Rocky Mountains in 1979.

An ex-pupil, Michael Bosworth, now a teacher heavily involved in Outdoor Pursuits, remembers the Cairngorms and Gordon with great affection, recognising the enormous influence this master had on him and many other pupils in the 1980s:

'' 'Jock', this stoic character, offered the example of commitment, energy and enthusiasm, traits that have made the transition to so many of his protégés who still fondly remember their education 'out of the classroom'.''

Phil Bradshaw has similar happy memories:

'' 'Jock' Brown was the instigator of many happy times when he organised the visits to Braemar at Easter each year. None of us will ever forget the blizzard on Bein A' Bhuird, in 1967, when the temperature dropped well below freezing in seconds and visibility was non-existent. How we managed to get off the mountain in one piece was a miracle and due entirely to 'Jock's' compass ability in avoiding a huge crag only metres away. 'Jock' himself did not emerge unscathed from all the trips. In 1968, after everyone in the group had been 'bum skiing' successfully, using old fertiliser bags, 'Jock' was persuaded it was his turn. Unfortunately, he hit a submerged rock at full pace and took off. He didn't walk properly for months afterwards and had to be carried a mile or so to the nearest ski lift, from where he went to hospital.''

The twenty-second Cairngorms Expedition, 1983. Michael Bosworth, extreme right, back row.

GOVILON

Govilon was the brainchild of two men with remarkable foresight – the Headmaster of the Grammar School, John Steane, and Col. Robert Jeffery, Clerk to the Governors of the Old Grammar School Foundation.

John Steane first visited the site in 1969 and quickly realised that it was an ideal place for a field centre, situated as it was in the middle of three entirely different economic and geographical areas. On the opening of the Field Centre in May 1971, John stated: ''We are here to learn by observation with our own eyes – not culling facts sitting in libraries – we are here to record, in notebooks, by data, drawings and diagrams, our findings; we are here to do research to establish, for instance, by plant counts, the relationship of species to altitude and temperature and soil.''

John went on to describe the contribution of Bob Jeffery, ''without whose tremendous enthusiasm, mastery of detail, drive and energy, the project would never have got off the ground. His tenacity of purpose, cheerful unwillingness ever to give up, and care in communication, so that at all times the parties were fully informed of the progress of the project.''

The Field Centre was, originally, the old village school which the Old Grammar School Foundation leased from the Church of Wales. In the initial stage £5,000 was spent on the conversion of the school into a study centre. It certainly needed it! Tony Simmons who, along with Les Berridge, was the first teacher to take a party of boys to Govilon in June 1970, describes the hardships endured:

''Of all the visits I made to Govilon with parties of boys from Kettering Grammar/Boys School, the first one has left most memories. Les Berridge and I boarded a Yorks coach one Wednesday morning in June 1970 with 26 Fourth Form boys and two Sixth Formers as prefects.

I had seen Govilon at the Whitsun break when a group of boys with John Steane decorated the old school. I don't think the boys or Les quite knew what to expect. I, too, was a little taken aback, since the situation was not quite what we had been led to expect – 27 broken windows, a hole in the roof through which a wheelbarrow could be passed. The only cooking facility was a kettle! The classroom was a concrete square. The beds were in kit form and the only furniture were six trestle tables with benches. There was no bedding, no pillows, no crockery, no cutlery and no cooking utensils. The Electricity Board had failed to deliver the cooker, stating that the canal bridge was too narrow to pass.

Mrs Drew and her ladies produced our evening meal of salad with cooked meats, followed by plums and evaporated milk. Just as we sat down to eat,

Opening of the Govilon Field Centre, May 1971

Left to right: Mr R. J. Soans, Chairman of the Management Committee; Alderman R. L. Denney, Alderman Mrs D. Oxenham, C.B.E., *Mr John Steane, Rev. D. A. Lewis, Rector of Govilon.*

Pink and Jones delivered all the crockery, cutlery, utensils and bedding. As a result, the first evening was spent washing the dining equipment and building the beds. Late to bed, Les and I had to sleep in the boys' dormitory, the first of many nights "persuading" the boys to go to sleep.

Both Les and I recall climbing Blorenge several times and getting very wet in chest-high bracken. Without the luxury of a drying room, we had to lay the boys' kit out in the playground. Neither did we have the luxury of minibuses. We walked everywhere, every day! Election Day sticks in our minds as a long hot walk, when in our desperation to save our legs and to cool down, we waded the River Usk.

Despite all the difficulties we were able to get a great deal of work out of the boys in the evenings, when they wrote up their experiments without complaint. I think that the boys, Les and I, obtained a great deal of pleasure out of that trip. We were picked up at about 1.00 p.m. the following Wednesday, when Gordon Brown and Barry Wright arrived with the second party. Teaching on Thursday was a real shock to the system."

John Steane's major project was to trace the old tramway on the side of the Blorenge from Llanfoist to Garndyrrys Iron Works. Within a short time, the group found some of the old stone sleepers to match the rails found earlier by the owner of the Llanfoist Wharf. This first essay in industrial archaeology later led to the major excavation of the Garndyrrys Iron Works.

Since those early days thousands of boys have experienced the joys and perils of a week in Govilon. Tony Simmons, who must have visited the Centre more times than any other teacher in Kettering, led countless Biological expeditions on Blorenge and in the My Ddu. Other teachers concentrated on teaching History through visits to medieval castles such as Goodrich, Raglan and Chepstow and to abbeys such as Tintern and Llanthony. Teachers with a Geographical bias visited the Brecon Beacons, Ystradfellte and the Wye Valley. In the late 1980s and early 1990s Outdoor Pursuits became very popular, with Ian Coleman passing on to the boys his expertise in caving, rock climbing and camping.

Some boys went to Govilon with some reluctance, but few returned without many happy memories. Who could forget the meals of Mrs Reynolds and her ladies, and who could forget the way in which she woke boys up in the morning with her water pistol! Some, however, came to grief; there weren't many teachers who did not experience a visit to Abergavenny Casualty Department. A boy called Kirle, on his first night at Govilon, fell down the steps which led from the classroom to the main school and broke his ankle. A master carried John Bisson for over a mile in Ystradfellte, after he gashed open his thigh on a rock. Ken Mandale recalls the time when a boy was kicked on the head by a pony and had to be rushed to Stoke Mandeville Hospital. Others came to grief because they refused to go to sleep. How many boys would admit to being hauled out of bed and made to sleep on the cold corridor floor or to stand out in the school yard in their pyjamas?

Govilon was a place where boys developed both personally and socially. They also gained a new perspective on the teaching staff, coming to appreciate what they were trying to achieve. Twenty five years on and many more thousands of pounds spent, the Robert Jeffery Centre, as it was later renamed, still provides pupils in Kettering and beyond with an invaluable educational experience.

CHAPTER 21

Sport

Brian Slough

"The dread of beatings! Dread of being late!
And, the greatest dread of all, the dread of games."
From *Summoned by Bells* by John Betjeman.

★ ★ ★

"The role played by sport is what appears most worthy of notice in English education." Baron de Coubertin, founder of the modern Olympic Games.

★ ★ ★

Far from the madding crowd of Sports Day in 1945, with its full quota of excitement and amusement, one rotter was discovered doing his homework behind the pavilion. He probably did not share the conclusions of Her Majesty's Inspectorate, expressed in a 1989 curriculum document, that Physical Education in schools should build on pupils' enjoyment of, and need for, activity and movement. Perhaps he was an embryonic poet, for the likes of Causley and Betjeman might well dismiss the Inspectors' comment as pompous nonsense. They would not be alone. Many notable Cytringanians have loathed "activity and movement", especially disguised as organised school sport.

In particular, those of like mind have always seen an Orwellian (another sport-hater) nightmare in the time and significance accorded to team games – even those endorsed by such varied luminaries as A. J. Ayer, Mick Jagger, or the Prince Consort. The undeniable importance of team games in the School's history, however, has not been at the expense of other forms of physical activity. Many on the menu may be less well-documented than the major sports, but granted considerations of time, facilities, staffing, and number of pupils, have helped to provide a remarkable balance of options. Sport, of some kind, for all.

As early as 1904 a shooting class was formed under the instruction of Colour-Sergeant Morris, but doubtless the unique circumstances of the First World War were responsible for its development. In 1916 a miniature rifle range was opened in the basement; the consequences were often frightening, to the building if not the enemy. The aptly named ''basement'', venue for notoriety, is a story all its own. But I digress. By 1920 a number of boys were expert rifle-shots: Furnell, Peggs, Esden, and Tutt, in particular. Considerable interest sprang from a match between boys and masters, which the former won. Parents were even encouraged to buy rifles for their sons (imagine that in 1996). Also in 1920 a School team fired in the shooting competition for the Imperial Challenge Shield, gaining a ''creditable position'' and an ammunition prize from the National Rifle Association. However, shooting practice came to an abrupt standstill at the end of the Spring Term in 1921, when the police descended and confiscated the bolts of all the rifles. They were never returned.

Clive Tutt, who represented the School at most sports, in addition to shooting, also achieved fame in a more unusual manner. In the 1929 Amateur Tourist Trophy, in the Isle of Man, he finished fifth. His machine was a 499cc overhead valve Rudge-Whitworth and he completed the full course of 228 miles at an average speed of 59.99 miles per hour. 'George' Godfrey came in first with the tutt-tutt jokes.

Another branch of shooting was introduced in 1964, when archery became an ''official'' sport. A number of bales of straw were given to the School by a local farmer and were set up on the old grass tennis courts as target-backs. They provided effective substitutes for proper woven straw targets. Such initiative was not unexpected, as Derek Slater and Stephen Harris were the staff involved, although the impetus for introducing the sport came from senior pupils.

Clive Tutt on his Rudge Whitworth, Isle of Man Tourist Trophy, 1930.

The year 1964 also saw the introduction of rowing; the local club loaned equipment and provided coaching through Mr Sproson and Dr Rowe. The next year a crew competed in two regattas, where the opposition comprised Bradford Rowing Club, the RAF, and certain independent schools with rowing traditions. The School had often produced oarsmen: in the 1920s, for example, four Old Boys (W. E. Searle, A.N. Patrick, F. W. Patrick, and L. C. Dengate) had won the Kettering Rowing Club's premier trophy.

Similarly, many Cytringanians played squash before its initial mention in 1958, when the Kettering Rackets Club allowed the Sixth Form to use its facilities in the Headlands. Before the squash boom of the 'seventies, this was the only court in the town. The School's first formally organised team appeared in 1980, captained by Richard Phelan, who later represented the British Universities.

Student drive was often important in establishing sports. In 1937 School swimmers proposed that races, "strangely absent in a school of so many and varied activities," would be enthusiastically supported. Swimmng classes had been in existence for a long time and in 1903 replaced "drilling". In 1937, Mr Woodward, assisted by Messrs Ashworth and Gladden, organised and coached swimming and life-saving on two evenings each week. This enterprise probably proved useful to those spartan pupils who apparently "disported themselves in the icy and shark-infested waters of the Firth of Clyde" during August 1937. What they were doing there remains a mystery, but these hazards were trivial set against those endured in the original Kettering pool. Was such cynicism misplaced in 1934? One authority was B. G. Bennett, the School's outstanding swimmer at that time, who had recently won a "splendid wristlet watch" at the local gala. Bennett maintained it was necessary to go as far as Leicester to find a finer indoor bath, yet he had reservations about the water quality in Kettering ("pea soup is crystal clear in comparison", he wrote) on Wednesday mornings and Saturday afternoons, prior to cleaning. Moreover, he could not understand why the outdoor pool should be forty yards long, when the maximum polo pitch was thirty yards. Meantime, the milk-bar Bogarts of the outdoor pool demonstrated their prowess in towel fights, on the springboards, or built a tan. It was ever thus.

Whatever the merits, or otherwise, of the Kettering public baths in the 'thirties, it is clear that boys had the opportunity to learn to swim, develop their strokes and water safety, gain survival skills, and enjoy water games, fifty years before the National Curriculum decreed their desirability.

The tireless Mr Woodward was still coaching life-saving in 1949, when Barnard, Hadden, Inns, Lorimer, McLester, Southwell, Vickers and P. Wilson gained the Bronze Medallion and Intermediate Certificate. The examiner described their standard as "excellent and very proficient." Such epithets are equally applicable to the unstinting efforts of A. W. H. Woodward, in fostering the School's well-being. Those of us who benefited from his

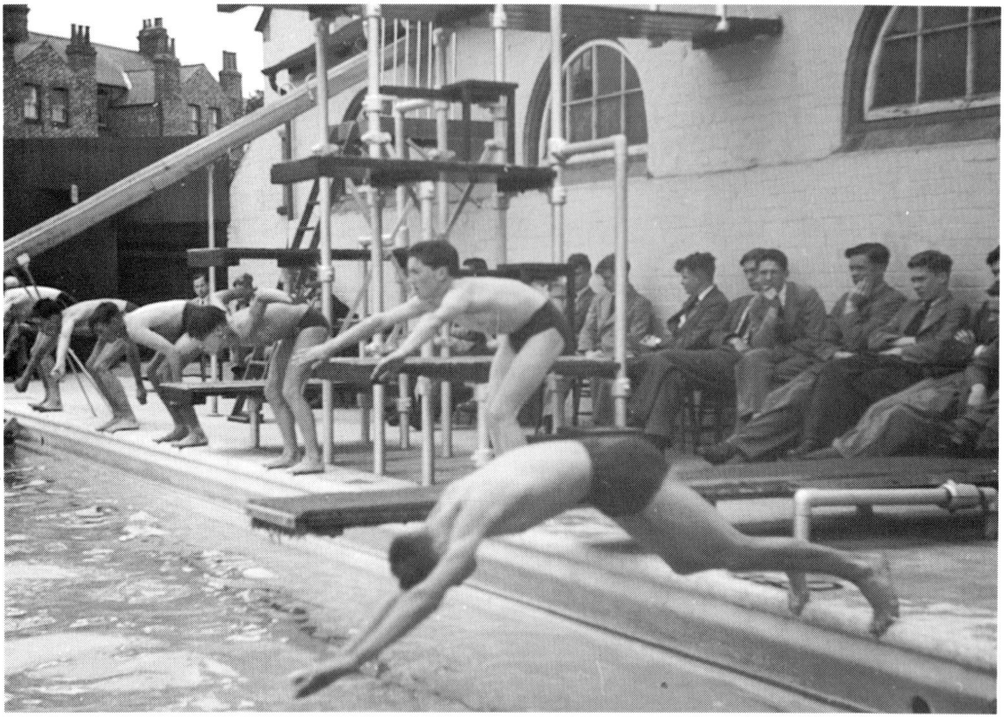

The Swimming Gala, 1952, at the Kettering Outdoor Pool in Baths Lane.

The soporific ''Long Plunge'' scrutinised by George Laywood, (centre judge).

scholarship in the classroom, were perhaps unaware of his broad contribution outside it, from Rugger Concerts to Railway Club.

By 1952 Vickers and Wilson, along with Earl, Kelly, Spence, Thompson and Vendy were talented swimmers who began to monopolise the prizes at the School's annual gala, now complete with races. The 1954 gala (watched by the entire School) included the popular, if bizarre, "Dressed Race" and the wearisome "Long Plunge". Neither event graced the Olympics, but received a delirious welcome at Butlin's. In 1956 came the first inter-school fixture when Northampton Grammar School were thrashed, in their own open-air pool, by a K.G.S. team containing five county representatives and champions. That same year the School's gala moved to the indoor pool.

By 1959, all members of the First Form were receiving swimming lessons from Miss Bonham, juniors entered the Fineshade Cup, the fixture with Northampton now included Water Polo, and the "Dressed Race" and "Long Plunge" had sunk, it might be said, from the annual gala. The times were becoming more serious, though the Plunge briefly resurfaced in 1962. Nick Brooks, who died tragically young while on the staff, R. Brown and R. Patrick were notable performers at the end of the decade. C. Sharpe was one of the few successes at county level during a mundane period in the early 'sixties, but 1966 was a better season, especially in the County Schools Gala (revived after fourteen years) where the School teams won the Under 13, 15, and 17 competitions. Alan Sherbourne and Duncan Emerton were accomplished swimmers in the eighties; Duncan also played county rugby.

John Clarke, at one time the Labour MP for Marghill, railed against boxing because it drew together "an army of bookies, touts, pimps, card-sharks, pickpockets and usually wound up in an orgy of drunkenness, assault and battery." That seems a slight exaggeration as far as K.G.S. was concerned, but not unexpectedly the rise and demise of school boxing reflected what was happening in the professional version of the sport. There were around a thousand registered professional fighters in the 1940s, but that number fell sharply in the 1950s, as boxing's dangers overwhelmed the notion of its being "the noble art of self-defence".

Boxing at School started in 1946, when Mr R. Coakes returned from the army. Known with *Beano* subtlety as 'Basher', he was reputed to have held some lightweight championship in the Armed Forces. Rex Moore recalls that initially there were few facilities: four benches formed a makeshift ring and the fourteen ounce gloves were somewhat dilapidated. Coakes insisted on essential coaching before any boy was allowed into the ring and he was meticulous in aiming to forestall physical damage. Moreover, it was easy to leave the "ring", by simply hopping over the benches. Rex also remembers an exhibition arranged with a local promoter (Fred Hefford) who brought two professional boxers into the School: 'Boy' Gavigan and 'Kid' Smith. They gave a demonstration bout and then provided coaching for the boys. Each year there were House matches (in the Drill Hall or the canteen in St Mary's

Road) and external fixtures with King's Peterborough, Bedford Modern, and the Uppingham-Corby Boys Club. Ian Doble, Nigel Howe and Phil Werblow were among several useful boxers in the early years.

Jack Young took over from Coakes in 1949 and Mr P. S. J. Adkins began to assist him in 1951. Set training was now initiated before matches and could take place in the newly purchased ring, "glorious in its bits and pieces." It was a floor ring, but capable of taking the strain of heavyweight contests. There were several sessions for novices and in the early 'fifties the sport flourished.

The Corby boys generally dominated the inter-House competitions and there was genuine talent among them: Jim Moodie, Jimmy Plenderleith, Alan Walton and Clive Hall are fixed in the memory. Clive Hall was later to be a force in local professional boxing. In a match against the Corby Sea Cadets in 1955, few of the participants had far to travel. Inter-school fixtures tended to be with the independent sector – Bedford featured regularly – as few other grammar schools encouraged the sport. Indeed, by 1957 interest was declining, outside a small band of enthusiasts. In the 1980s, several old boys of the School boxed professionally, notably Scott Markie.

House Boxing, 1951-52. John Cowell is one of the judges.

★ ★ ★

The arrival of 'Paddy' Adkins in the 'fifties probably accounted for the introduction of basketball, originally seen as American netball. Scepticism soon evaporated as the School entered the County Senior League and prospered in it. This was no mean achievement, considering that other teams were invariably older and more experienced. An influential figure in local

Winners of the County Basketball League for Men, 1957-58

Back Row (L. to R.): R. J. Coles, Mr G. S. Brown, K. J. Woolmer.
Front Row (L. to R.): J. Chapman, R. L. Hill, J. F. Newing.

basketball at that time was an Old Cytringanian who had competed in the 1948 Olympics, Mr Phillip Clarke. He donated the League's original shield. One of its early recipients, in 1958, was the K.G.S. team: R. Hill, J. Chapman, R. Coles, J. Newing, and K. Woolmer. This all-star cast excelled themselves, not only on the basketball courts but in most facets of school life and their distinguished careers thereafter. The School's first Globetrotter was Roger Toseland. The rapid emergence and popularity of the sport owed much to his enthusiastic coaching during his year as Head Boy. By 1956 the School entered two teams in the League, with occasional guest appearances by staff, such as Gordon Brown, Ken Mandale and David Allen.

In 1955 an American exchange teacher, John F. Joline Jnr., brought panache and innuendo about "imported professionals." Similar mutterings were heard in the Kettering and Corby Schools League in 1990, when K.B.S. teams were inspired by the skills of two visiting Spanish students. The Grammar School had withdrawn from the men's County League in 1962. Without that imposed momentum, in the mid-sixties there was a decline in the game's perceived significance, rekindled at the formation of the Schools League. David Drew was one of the area's leading players in the 1970s and remains so today. The School won the League on three occasions in the 'eighties, with a squad (as the jargon now required) of S. Allaway, P. Bainbridge, R. Barrett, C. Parris, W. Penfold, F. Theanne, and N. Garnett. Wesley Penfold, and his brother Tony, also gained national honours at judo.

Whereas the School had basketball teams until it closed, and continued to enter the inter-schools cross-country championships, its own annual racing extravaganza had finished, vomited, showered, and gone home long since. The sponsored walk became the fashionable substitute. The Grammar School's first formally organised run appears to have taken place in March 1926. The course was about three and a half miles and the seventy runners, except one, covered the distance in approximately thirty five minutes. Much of the course took in roads and allotments, which indicates the changed social scene; not many cross-country races will hurtle across London Road in 1996 and even the keenest gardener is hard pressed to find an allotment, alas. Contemporary accounts record the assiduity with which competitors indulged in pre-race training. Practice at six in the morning, or "night trots" (not that sort) were commonplace weeks beforehand, often prompted by House Captains. Whether they joined in is not known, but consensus management had not yet been invented. Entrants, who had to be over thirteen, were handicapped according to age. In 1928 A. J. Clarke, of 3A, was first home in the record time of 19 minutes and 6 seconds.

By 1933, the earlier idyllic tone of the race reports is tempered by humorous reality. Most of the competitors, such as the thoroughbred Clement, ran seriously, but others preferred friendly company on the journey. Cads like Barber and Hodges, for example, "ambled in fifteen minutes after the rest." Ah, the shame of it, yet they claimed their enduring moment of history and unknowingly endorsed Warhol's belief that we all have our fifteen minutes worth. In succeeding years the late returners, including the wonderfully named Cramp (yes, honestly) ended in the finest hiking style. The exception, in 1936, was when the onomatopoeically titled "scrim-shankers" finished in a lorry. If that shows initiative, real class belongs to a Burtonian friend of mine. He covered most of the course driving a milk-float.

The Mill course was introduced in 1933 and Gardner, designated "a legend", dominated races in 1935 and 1936, starting from scratch (or worse). In 1937 the winner was the aforementioned Phillip Clarke, another fine all-round athlete. There are countless anecdotes surrounding the course, mostly originating from "scrim-shankers" down the years. Their credo, of whatever decade, combined Byron's description of running as a "valorous kind of cunning" with *Proverbs,* whose author questions the point of running "when you are on the wrong road." Cunning was rife and often involved "the wrong road" or field, in spite of the investigations of the F.B.I., or course stewards. In the 1930s, for example, some participants recall a certain Mr T. Corke stationed in an advisory capacity at the infamous water jump, where he is reputed to have saved many lives. His inside information on the sinking of the Titanic doubtless proved invaluable. Several charlatans maintain they might have won the race, had they not stopped to enjoy Tom's stories. "He that runs, may not listen", as Tennyson almost said. More verifiable climatic evidence seems to confirm current fears about the effects of global warming.

Not a "scrim-shanker". Alan Godson (right) wins the House Cross Country Race in 1950. Note the background of the Mill Course: the Ise Village was still a twinkle in the planners' eyes.

The race was always run in March, nowadays a month of blossom, birds' eggs and Ambre Solaire. Pre-war accounts seem obsessed with the grim conditions; "thick, brown mud" seemed everywhere. For this reason, the event had to be postponed in 1938, until the Summer Term. You cannot escape that lightly.

It is fruitless to compare times between decades from 1926, for the simple reason that the official course was altered, in structure and length, on several occasions. In 1952 it was increased to 4½ miles, when the winner was Alec Tite in just over 21 minutes. Paul Lamont, another celebrated athlete, finished in 1957 in 17 minutes and 40 seconds. Competition was hot around this time (whatever the weather) from the likes of Eric Turner, David Denton and Jim Chapman. In 1962 D. J. Blount is listed as setting a new school record of 17 minutes and 7 seconds; the distance, however, was just under 3 miles. It was increased to 4 miles in 1965. Pay your money, take your choice. Comparisons, if not odious, can be meaningless.

In the 'fifties the School began to enter District championships. By the mid-sixties there were County and "All England" events, alongside inter-school matches. The Whymant brothers, B. Cumberpatch, P. Bradshaw, G. Sowler, D. Markham and K. Jones achieved various forms of representative honours.

One of the Grammar School's most meritorious sporting successes was that of the Tennis team in 1954, which received too few plaudits at the time. I am indebted to Michael Cotton for what follows and delighted to quote him verbatim:

"Tennis was, and remained, a minor sporting activity at K.G.S., with fluctuating fortunes and attachments. It was, of course, for girls: though this was not necessarily a deterrent, and may even have played some role in its persistence during the post-fifties. There are rumours also of earlier ventures onto the green lawns, though these, if true, remain to me shrouded in a misty past of long flannels and gentility. I apologise in advance for such gaps in my knowledge, ancient and modern, hoping only in what follows to stir at least a few memories.

My earliest recollections of K.G.S. sport were of rugby and cricket. I was dimly aware that a few Sixth-Formers dabbled in the curious art of lawn tennis – classified in my mind at that time alongside bowls and croquet. Strangely, most households had old raquets (that was the spelling then) lying around and eventually a few of we despicable juniors infiltrated the arcane precincts of the tennis court. Not that we saw it that way; our first experiences were on the public courts of Wicksteed Park with badly warped, wooden-framed, broken-stringed pre-war cast-offs. No respectable club would have us, even if we could have afforded the subscription. So we ran ourselves ragged over the generous scattering of molehills, grazing our disgustedly dirty knees on the grit of those unlevel playing fields.

From small beginnings our numbers grew. Eventually many of us did join tennis clubs (of which at that time there were more than a dozen in Wicksteed Park alone), most of them run by the various churches in the town – the Parish Church, St Andrews, the Congregational Church, Methodist etc. Most of us played other sports to which at first we were more committed. Keith Foreman, Roger Long, John Knibbs, David Buckby, Philip Brading and many others who took up tennis represented the School in other sports. Other names that come to mind are Norman Smith, Bob Barnard, John Lillyman, Roy Church, George Wood and Alan Walton.

I am thinking now chiefly of the years between '47 and '50. It was about this period that, as far as I can discover, a School club and tennis team were formed for the first time. Also, a number of things happened which gave the game's reputation something of a fillip. The British LTA had adopted a post-war policy of encouraging the game nationally. To promote this, Dan Maskell, the British Davis Cup coach and himself a former Davis Cup player, was engaged to tour the country with a "Focus on Tennis" roadshow, aimed especially at young players. Accompanying him was the greatest British player of all time, Fred Perry, who was three times Wimbledon champion in the 'thirties. Kettering was selected as a centre. What was particularly significant for us was that we all knew Fred Perry had lived near Kettering, that his father had been its Member of Parliament for a time and that, rumour had it, Fred Perry had even attended K.G.S. (though this I have never been able to confirm). Nevertheless, the connection was close and abundantly apparent to us aspiring tennis players.

The event was organised by Jimmy Renwick, a former Northants County player and K.G.S. was more than adequately represented. We all watched the great Fred Perry play three sets of singles against Dan Maskell (on a court from which the molehills had been scrupulously deleted) before going on to take part in the coaching and demonstrations of various strokes before an audience from all the surrounding clubs in the county.

Coverage in the local news was thorough, and after this things took off as far as tennis was concerned. Bob Barnard, who was then in the Lower Sixth was keen to approach A. F. Scott. He told him we had a School team ready and waiting to be unleashed on unsuspecting opponents. What else he said only he knows, but the outcome was the Head's blessing for the formation of an official School tennis team for the first time in its long history. Mrs Cousins, the then Head of P.E. at the High School, allowed us the occasional use of the few grass courts at her disposal. A generous offer under the circumstances of that time.

After the arrival of J. K. Dudley as headmaster in 1951-2, tennis became a recognised School sport. We hired our own courts in Wicksteed Park and played fixtures against the best local clubs – the Kettering Park and Stewarts and Lloyds. Thanks largely to the enthusiasm and support of the late and much liked 'Joe' Young, we became serious contenders on the national scene. 'Joe', a keen sportsman himself, organised practices, training and coaching sessions for the lower school during lunch hours, and generally power-housed the whole concept of tennis throughout the School.

At this time, K.G.S. pupils (P. Brading, D. Buckby, J. Cooper and M. Cotton) were cornering most of the junior tennis titles in this county, as well as a few in others. Out of four county representatives sent to compete in the Boys Junior Championships at Wimbledon in 1952, three were from K.G.S. We easily defeated Northampton Grammar by a 9-3 margin, in spite of the fact that their team contained two experienced county players – one of whom was Bill Knight, British Junior Singles and Doubles Champion, destined within the next two years to become British no. 1 in the Davis Cup.

1954 was the first year we entered the Glanvill Cup competition – the national schools' trophy for tennis. Most schools in the competition were much larger than ours; many were public schools with excellent facilities, even their own coaches, and we approached the matches with, to say the least, open minds. But having defeated King Edward VI Grammar School, Birmingham, in the first round, we went on to win a close-run three-cornered tie at the Leys School, Cambridge, eventually reaching the final at Queen's Club. We lost narrowly to Westminster School, but it was, to coin a phrase, no mean first effort."

The new all-weather hard courts provided a further boost to the game in 1963 and the pleasing match results from 1964 to 1966 reflect this. D. J. Robins and G. R. Smith were notably successful in 1965. In the 1980s Kim Davis enhanced facilities by introducing marked courts for "short tennis". A number of outstanding players emerged in this decade, not least the bands of brothers. Elliott and Jason Starmer, Roberto and Claudio Domizi, were later to coach the game professionally, as did Ian Bailey. Andrew Lingley, probably the School's best-ever table tennis player, should now have joined them.

A comparable batch of talents emerged in the late 'seventies in another racket sport, badminton. Chris Matcham, Nick Pettman and Jon Pulford continued the line of gifted players that stretched back to the likes of Brian Greasley, son of English international Ray, P. P. Marshall and the tennis team mentioned above. A Badminton Club had been formed in 1951. Few schools had a team at that time, but there were regular fixtures with local churches and the staff. 'Joey' Ashworth was the Club's first mentor (and still showing his playing expertise in 1959), succeeded by Cliff Brown. Limitations of space restricted participation to the Sixth Form before the move to Windmill Avenue, when a junior section was started in 1965. The game remained an attractive option in the Physical Education curriculum, until the nets were lowered for the last time. Its memory lingers with the dusty, irretrievable shuttlecocks on distant ledges and the faint odour of sweat.

The changing face of sport in schools is nowhere more apparent than in the reports about athletics between 1900 and 1993. It is arguable that they also identify wider, universal shifts within the sport itself, attitudes to it, and even education itself. If so, that is another story, for another time.

At the turn of the century the "Athletic Sports", as they were known, took place on the Kettering Town Cricket ground. They lasted all day and were a social occasion, well attended by parents, Old Boys, and other interested worthies. In 1904 the organising committee, somewhat disdainful of the cricket pavilion, arranged for a spacious marquee to be erected. There were lavish prizes (a watch for winning the hurdles, a cricket bat for the 100 yards, were not to be sneezed at). The presentation ceremonies were conducted by distinguished local citizens, generally female, and reminiscent of medieval romance films, starring Stewart Granger. In 1900 total expenditure on prizes, printing, labour, flags, refreshments, postage and sundries was £16. 11s. 11d., covered by subscriptions. That was a lot of money in those days, as my mother used to say. Wrestling, kicking the football, donkey and "consolation" races jostled alongside old favourites like the obstacle, sack, and three-legged contests. The egg and spoon race attracted 93 entries in 1917, and probably complaints from the hens. Some records take your breath away. It seems the spectators craved these pythonesque competitions in preference to the orthodox. Thus, in 1901 the "jumps" were castigated as "tedious" and the Old Boys' walking race as "appalling". Curt, perhaps, but the prospect hardly seems mouthwatering.

In the early years of the century, the reporting of times and distances was at best spasmodic and maybe deemed irrelevant. Handicapping was customary, indeed it was not abolished until 1931. Events were repeated should dead-heats occur. The Brideshead atmosphere can be sensed in an extract from the 1904 magazine that outschmaltzes David Coleman: "The afternoon was an ideal one for the occasion. There was just enough sunshine and a clear sky to give animation to the whole scene, from the white-flannelled competitors to the many shaded dresses of the visitors. It is true the wind blew across the field; in fact such a breeze was welcomed by many, and the runners were not heard to complain." Nor, apparently, did the unfortunate Mrs Adams, who had possibly nodded off, in spite of the breeze. "We very much regret the accident that happened in the cricket ball throwing," was the soothing apology.

This was a world far removed from lycra outfits, television, part-time jobs, and the insidious maw of examinations that beset today's students. Sixty years on, in instructive contrast, the Captain of Athletics (N. B. How) wrote this: "The 1966 season was depressing. The weather curtailed many after school practices and the encroachment of exams made the arrangement of school matches an impossibility. In 1967 it is expected that all school matches will take place before G.C.E. exams begin and this means a short season with frequent competitions." This stark, honest assessment is clear proof that sport, at least in state schools, was already responding to different demands and expectations.

It was around 1952 when the School's athletes began to approach life more earnestly by competing in a range of meetings: District, County, Midland Counties, and All England. That is not to imply that accomplished and serious competitors had not existed before that. Far from it. The Victor Ludorum lists, and recorded peformances (granted their accuracy) suggest otherwise. H. Fitzjohn, the Senior Victor Ludorum in 1928, cleared 18 feet 8 inches in

Roy Chapman: Cambridge University Athletics Blue in 1958.

the Long Jump. Forty years on, A. Lamont achieved 19 feet 3 inches. In 1922, the multi-talented P. E. Coles was certainly running faster over 440 yards than his Victor Ludorum counterparts in the 'seventies. That proves little in itself.

What is undeniable, however, is that the ubiquitous 'Phip' Coles was one of the many sportsmen who prospered within the grammar school ethos that fostered, because it expected, all-round excellence. 'Phip's' nephew, Richard, rivalled his uncle as a games player in the 1950s, played Othello, and eventually read Law at Cambridge. In 1931 J. E. Walden was Victor Ludorum and captain of rugby and cricket. C. N. Marlow was Victor Ludorum in 1939 and a highly-rated cricketer. J. F. Sykes and P. Sansom are two examples from the 'sixties: both Victor Ludorum, both highly capable bowlers. This selection is an arbitrary smattering; numerous other names could prove the point, headed for many by Ian Runciman.

Others would opt for Roy Chapman as the epitome of the Renaissance athlete. Victor Ludorum in 1955, he also competed with distinction at national level. In addition, he was inspirational on the rugby field and a 1st XI cricketer. In his final term he played Hamlet (as had H. Fitzjohn) and won a Scholarship to Cambridge, where he gained a "blue" for Athletics. If you think this eulogy overstated, try learning Hamlet's lines. The effort has destroyed the lives of many professional actors. By the way, do schools produce *Hamlet* these days? Did it cross Roy Chapman's mind that he should not run, play rugby, basketball, cricket, or Hamlet because of examinations? Rumour has it that he also led a full social life. It is difficult not to draw comparisons with 1974, when this comment appeared in the School magazine: "The athletics season was affected by courses and examinations: no senior athletes were able to compete owing to A-Levels." The hidden agenda in that, not least about what was happening to education in the 'seventies, is also too multi-faceted to explore in this context.

A pattern of fixtures for athletics was established in the late 'fifties: a triangular meeting with Northampton and Wellingborough Grammar Schools and the five schools encounter (Watford, Luton, Cedars and Dunstable) were added to various District and County competitions. Thus, the top athletes, particularly those who made the "All England" championships, were offered a genuine breadth of sporting experience.

There were many commendable performances from the élite (not forgetting that some were gained on grass tracks). D. J. Blount ran the mile in 4 minutes 34 seconds in the Five Schools meeting of 1962. Both he and T. D. Rigby had turned in encouraging performances in the "All England" championships the previous year, as did Matthew Bell and Craig Davis in 1992 and Tony Lallard in the 'seventies. Indeed, in 1971, Tony represented Northamptonshire, for the third consecutive year, at the national championships in the 400 metres Hurdles. John Thorpe, Victor Ludorum in 1956, is widely held as the pick of a crop of class athletes around the mid-fifties: M. Cwynarski, J. Panter and R. Newbold were others who excelled in different events. Mark Cwynarski also shone in another sphere; in 1956 he reached the finals of the East Midlands Fencing Championship.

Some old buffers believe that the increasingly professional approach to sport is responsible for inculcating the wrong values, not to mention blatant skulduggery. The athletics reports lend support to that theory, albeit in what is left unsaid, as well as in their preoccupations and manner of presentation. Pre-fifties, for instance, descriptions of the weather were often more concerned with its effect on female spectators than participants' times.

Recipients of the Victor Ludorum trophies, 1956.
Mr G. Brown, J. Panter, J. Thorpe, A. Roberts, Mr J. Ashworth.

The best illustration, however, is that for more than thirty years the principal source of interest on the big day was Mr Whitney's blunderbuss. It was 1921 before he first procured a starting pistol, "thus saving himself much labour and language." Perhaps that was just as well, as Lady de Capell Brooke presented the prizes that year, accompanied by "much cheering". The eternal 'Pop' was still stealing the show after the war. This was J. D. Dodge's (another admirable athlete) account of Sports Day, 1947:

"After the austerity sports-day of wartime, it was decided to make this year's occasion memorable. Accordingly, a loud-speaker van was installed to replace Mr Woodward's megaphone and the cup, tankards, medallions and certificates were presented on the field by Mr W. C. Cooke. However, Mr Whitney, together with service-rifle, was retained as starter, and the competitors, inspired no doubt by his efforts, made havoc of numerous records."

A year later and he remained the focus of attention, ahead of star athletes such as Dodge, P. A. Toseland, P. A. Oram and a frisky dog. "A much discussed feature of the afternoon was the decision, by Mr Whitney, to start the races by means of a flag instead of his usual apparatus. It must be noted that the races began promptly for the first time since we can remember."

Chariots of Fire bonhomie is less evident in 1961, as this report makes plain: "Owing to the lack of space in the Wellingborough Grammar School field, all the throwing events were omitted from the programme, thus making it necessary for some of our best performers to be left out of the School team." Surely, I hear you say, Wellingburians would never stoop to such dastardliness. There was certainly no base motive behind the School's 1963 decision to alter the finishing straight to downhill, or so I'm told.

Craven conduct seems far removed from the days of flannelled competitors, cream teas, a smoking blunderbuss and lashings of ginger beer. Yet Jamie Murphy, who represented Great Britain in the Discuss and Javelin in the 1990s, epitomised the philosophy that manners maketh man, in the athletics arena and outside it.

Nestling among the 1921-22 football team's string of convincing victories lies a juicy 12-0 defeat of Northampton County School (presumably the forerunner of the Grammar School). In the Christmas Term, eleven games out of twelve were won: the other result was a 1-1 draw against the Old Boys. It is ironic that the season's notes concluded with this comment from a spectator at one of the matches: "Your boys have played a game worthy of any school in the country; I didn't think it possible for such a perfectly balanced team to be got together." The speaker was certainly unaware of the implications in his remark, but no K.G.S. team was "got together" (at

Kim Davis, all-round sportsman (and bon viveur) controls the tug-of-war, 1988.

Sponsored walk refreshment point, Grafton Underwood, late 1980s. The organiser, Jim McGinn, is in the background.

least officially) for another forty three years. This time span might account for the ignorance of the 1965 correspondent, who wrote: ''The School appeared in the Corby Six-a-Side tournament at the end of June. Since September, matches have been played at Senior and Middle School level and considering that this is the first time the School has played any organised soccer, the results have been encouraging.''

Not only was ''organised soccer'' not played at the School after 1922, but there was total silence about it, as though it had never been. It was something the family did not talk about. In January 1924 the editorial in the Magazine was adamant that: ''Rugger . . . is now indisputably the School's winter game.'' Is there a subtext to this? It is true that the number of pupils, and available facilities, did not allow for the co-existence of both games, but the stink of snobbery is inescapable. Gentlemen played ''Rugger''; oiks played ''Soccer''. Inevitably, of course, snobbery makes an ass of itself; in 1922, what might be termed the ''most distinguished'' of our public schools played soccer. In 1995 rugby boasts of its universal appeal, if only to guarantee its share of Heritage money from the Lottery. ''Snobbery is but a point in time'', it is said, as mean and pathetic as fashion. Whatever the reasons for the School's rejection of soccer, they were not recorded. The impression, from the abrupt silence in the 1920s and the unbridled criticism of later years, is that the game was unclean, tolerated nasty habits and was best forgotten.

Those who believed this seventy years ago, or still do, could point to the Magazines between 1900 and 1922 in justification. The liturgy of moans and excuses rivals those of today's professionals, although it is unlikely that Manchester United would need to look for a substitute en route to play against Desborough Boys Brigade, or arrive with ten men. Some of the whines are instantly recognisable from *Match of the Day* manager-speak. The School lost 9-0, in 1900, to Excelsiors in what was described as a ''rough'' match. Worse, ''the referee, too, was several times at fault, especially in the matter of time, for time was up several minutes before he blew the whistle.''

Tirades against the opposition also followed a predictable pattern. The Co-operative Society marred an early fixture by their ''unsportsmanlike conduct''. Self regulation, of a kind that would delight the Football Association, ensured that co-operation improved for the re-match. ''The Society's captain was sportsmanlike in not allowing those men to play who were objectionable on the last occasion.'' Some opponents were accused of brash duplicity. For example, in 1902, Wellingborough (who else?) were strengthened by Old Boys: they also arrived late. The next year finds Northampton attacked for being a ''heavy lot'' and three years older. The most heartrending sob story occurred in 1904, when Geddington All Stars (seriously) were so powerful that they had ''four subs, all of them better players than the average of their team.'' For Blackburn Rovers 1994, read the Geddington All Stars 1904.

There is also a foretaste of the relegation zone in the vitriol against individuals or team inadequacies. Goalkeepers have always had their individual quirks. In 1903, one unfortunate, ''Held the ball for a long time, gaining no ground, but turning round and round.'' It is said of another in 1901, ''. . . the less said of him the better: we are utterly unable (and we believe he confesses himself to be in the same plight) to explain what was the matter with him.'' By the 1918-19 season, culprits were named. After the School had lost 8-2 to Brigstock and 7-0 to an Army XI, A. N. Patrick is castigated for, ''Having little idea of getting down to a ball.'' The note of utter despair in another report will find sympathy with all those who, throughout history, have found themselves in goal because they are too fat, spotty, or simply hopeless. ''There is a regrettable idea abroad that the position between the posts is not a place of honour and we can find no one to play in goal regularly.''

Tactically, there was no delight in the beautiful game; route one (then known as ''kick and rush'') was the preferred option. The 1913-14 side suffered through a mid-field ''whose work was good, even pretty, and perhaps for that reason, too often led to nothing. . . .'' It is no surprise they lost 13-1 to Pytchley. In 1902 the ''front rank'' are attacked for their disposition ''to play with the ball and make circles, instead of going straight ahead.''

The wheel of misfortunes rolled on. Sometimes it was the weather. A heavy shower soon after kick-off caused ''a stampede to the pavilion''. On another occasion, a foggy morning meant it was impossible to see the goal from a distance of twenty yards. Outbreaks of measles brought the cancellation of many matches, while in 1916-17 "farm-work prevented our having all the practices desired." Fog, farm-work, and the measles took their toll. "But when sorrows come, they come not single spies, but in battalions." The old Queen died. "Football matches were at a discount during the early part of term, owing to the death of our much-lamented Queen." In spite of it all, one correspondent still had the sauce to grouse about the mediocre attendances at matches. It is a marvel that anyone turned up, not least the goalkeepers.

What happened to the nineteenth century phlegm, encapsulated in Charles Kingsley's classic moral defence of sports? "Through sport, boys acquire virtues which no books can give them; not merely daring and endurance, but, better still, temper, self-restraint, fairness, honour, unenvious approbation of another's success, and all that give and take of life." Sport was supposed to be not just a source of bodily purification, but part of a general programme of rational recreation and practical Christianity.

Maybe this is part explanation of the School's fixture list. In the 'fifties, shoe factories had cricket teams; before 1922, churches had football teams. There were few inter-school games, but regular tussles with Burton St Mary's, Desborough Baptists, Finedon Wesleyans, Rushden St Mary's, Fuller Church

Soccer 1st XI – 1917-18, with Edgar Towell as captain.

Back Row (L. to R.): Mr R. Scott, J. W. Middleton, W. L. Goode, S. E. Smith, G. C. N. Fountain, J. E. Percival
Middle Row (L. to R.): J. T. Pettit, S. C. Hoyles, E. F. Towell, F. G. Yorke, M. T. Wilson
Front Row (seated): A. J. Caswell, J. K. Andrew.

Institute, Rothwell Congregationalists, Rothwell Church Athletic and Miss Dryland's Bible Class. Thus is the changing face of society reflected in its local football teams. Once it was the church and factory; now the Sunday Leagues are contested by pubs and hairdressing salons. Muscular Christianity replaced by lager and gel.

Never mind the early teeth gnashing, there was no shortage of individual talent. The forward line of 1915-16 – Panter, Butlin, Yorke, Tailby and Towell – was full of local names and goals to match. In 1904, V. P. Mobbs was designated the "second Johnny Hart". Other familiar Cytringanian names had their moments and were second to no-one. In 1918-19, Wilkes was described as "very fast with heaps of dash, never allowing opponents to rest." By 1920, however, it was felt that he often "rushed about to no purpose." Mind you, some critics said the same about the dribbling of Sir Stanley. In 1921, Bennie, praised as a "dashing raider", shone against the East End (of Kettering, not London). Brading, meantime, "could always be relied upon." Many theatrical producers would say amen to that.

A number of Old Boys have had their share of footballing kudos, some nationally, in the professional or semi-professional game. A. J. Caswell proved a capable left back with Queen's Park Rangers and E. G. Kirk played for Peterborough United. In 1902, the entire School went to see Kettering against Sheffield United, who included Old Cytringanian (Herbert Winterhalder) at outside left. In April 1901 Mr Hartley played for Kettering against Tottenham Hotspur, "who had just proved victorious in the English Cup Competition." Mr Hartley scored; the entire School cheered loud and long. After one fixture in Northampton, the School side watched Northampton play West Ham, before returning home, "trying to find excuses for our own inglorious display." The number of trips to watch sport, in days gone by, would cause apoplexy in today's world of attendance contracts and truancy

An "illicit" K.G.S. soccer team. Cup finalists on the Kettering Town ground in 1955.

league tables. Perhaps if there were more trips nowadays, it wouldn't be necessary to have such bureaucracy.

The black spot imposed after 1922 did not stop the illicit appearance of K.G.S. teams, in disguise, on Saturday afternoons after morning inter-School rugby matches. One or two, not surprisingly, enjoyed their moments of glory. After all, their skills were honed in playground conflicts, with a threadbare tennis ball, at best. This was ''total football'', long before Malcolm Allison introduced it at Manchester City.

There were also several noteworthy sides after the game was accepted back in the fold, in time for England to win the World Cup and K.G.S. the York Cup, coached by Messrs R. Rattley and N. Barker. There is a delightful tribute to Dick Rattley in the 1974 magazine, which is worth repeating for its wider implications. The 1st XI record their thanks to Mr Rattley ''who constantly struggled against 'work-to-rule' to gain fixtures and gave up his spare time to look after us.'' That kind of sentiment, repeated down the years, highlights the kind of staff who ensured the provision of School sport, even in the difficult times. Ironically, a potentially exciting team in 1979 (E. Wells, D. Peck and A. Redding played for the County) had a restricted season through fixture problems elsewhere.

In the 'sixties, Ian Addis flirted briefly with Leyton (or possibly Clapton) Orient before his lengthy wedded bliss with the United Counties League, as player and pundit. Other semi-professionals at this level included Steve Birch, Kim Davis, Gus Mabelson, Karl Peasnall, the Redding brothers (Andy, Paul and Neil), Mick Wildman and Andy Wyldes. In the 1980s Steve Roberts played for Kettering Town in the G.M. Conference, while still at School, and the gifted Nick Garnett should have done. Around the same time Luke Bettridge was a professional with Notts County, before injury intervened. In the 'seventies, another eminent football name, Ritchie (Bob), played full-time, most famously with the Arsenal and Gordon Livsey kept goal, and later managed, in the Football League. In 1992, Jimmy Simpson began a professional career with Norwich City. Some of these maestros still display their skills and torn hamstrings for an arthritic Sunday morning XI. Wisdom, wrote Plautus, is drinking old wine, seeing old plays, or the delight of the old at play.

In 1903, Mr Miller, Tom Stanley and John Goss had played rugby football for a town side and had doubtless been among those who went to St James End to see the 'Jimmies' play Blackheath. Rugby, however, was not played at the School until the end of the Easter Term 1922, although a reference to its possible introduction occurs in a letter in the Magazine of December 1921. The anonymous writer (RFB of VA) mentions correspondence in the local paper which ''informed us that Kettering Grammar School was hoping to take up Rugger as well as the Association form.'' RFB felt that the game should be given a try and dismissed the objection that the School would not be able to find matches. He suggested that for the first year, at least, matches could be among themselves, "to see whether the game was approved of on the whole."

With varying levels of "approval" it was played for the remaining seventy years of the School's life. Indeed, for much of that time it was the winter game most closely associated with grammar schools and projected a middle-class image. A ruffians' game, played by gentlemen, as the favoured cliché had it. Rugby had been frequently advocated in the "newer" public schools, largely because it was thought to require more courage: courage without cruelty, a civilised form of simulated war.

The pioneering spirit is inescapable in the language of the early accounts, as "Rugger" replaced "Soccer", whatever the truth behind the change. "Our only hope was to put up a good show", wrote the reporter of the initial encounters with club sides such as the Old Aylestonians. In 1923, the revered P. E. Coles was "to be congratulated upon the whole-hearted way he entered into the spirit of the game, in the interests of the School," and H. W. Lee and C. P. Tutt were "most enthusiastic in the cause of Rugger." These plaudits appeared in the first ever notes on the game, and the writer had more to say in a similar call-to-arms. He believed that the first difficulty was to "inculcate the right spirit and enthusiasm . . . the spirit which rules is the spirit of being willing to take the risk, understood only by those who play the game, and that principle applies more to Rugger than any other of our national games." That "spirit" was frequently underlined by comments about tactics and skills, which turned sections of the Magazines into coaching manuals, such as this extract from 1924: "The only possible method of checking a forward rush is to throw oneself on the ball. This appears an ugly duty to perform, but when boldly accomplished the desired effect is realised without the least trace of injury to the defending player." My own playing experience would suggest otherwise, confirmed by long hours in hospital casualty departments. That kind of rallying cry, however, remained characteristic of many annual reports, with reference to individuals or the entire team. Sometimes, the method is ironic understatement: "Smith would benefit in the loose if he looked where he was running," (1959). Elsewhere, the assault is full-frontal, as with the 1966 side, who displayed "the simple, yet brutally obvious fault of bad tackling."

Yet in spite of the surly broadsides, there were many highly successful seasons. The first was 1925, when the 1st XV won ten and drew their other fixture, scoring 202 points against their opponents' 36. Soon afterwards, however, physical activity was curtailed. This time it was not for measles, fog, or even a royal death. "The small pox epidemic in the town interfered considerably with our programme for the Easter Term and we were only able to play three matches." At the Speech Day ceremonies there was praise for Mr Rees, who was deemed largely responsible for "the fine record of the Rugger team." The prevailing euphoria probably accounted for the advent of caps for the fifteen; these were made of red velvet with white braiding and a white badge. The idea of a special tie was also mooted.

As with cricket and association football, the teams of the 'twenties and 'thirties were often bolstered by staff. One conspicuous example was Mr Hopkins. Greeted on arrival as a "Keen rugby player", he was soon heralded for his "invaluable help as coach and playing member of the team." Thirty years later, many of us were grateful for his "invaluable help" as a Mathematics coach. Even then, his imposing presence was a pointer to the prowess of his playing days, had we but known.

A School trip to watch Leicester v The Kiwis, January 31st, 1946.

The most successful period in the School's rugby history was from 1944 to 1948, certainly in terms of results. In 1947 the 1st XV was defeated for the first time in three years and the extraordinary record, of forty one consecutive matches won, came to an end. Even then the feeling remained that the standard of play had not deteriorated, "although it must be admitted that the team's musical taste had somewhat declined." 1947-48 was another highly creditable season: K.G.S. scored 291 points, the opposition a mere 20 and only two schools scored tries against them. In 1944-45, when all eleven matches were won, the tally was 230 points with 22 against. The next year brought the following statistic: played 14, won 14, 233 points for, 36 against. This was at a time when the School's matches were fully reported in the press and the justifiably euphoric headlines tell the tale: "Opponents outclassed", "Taste of Defeat is Unknown", "Another Big Win", "They Did it Again", were a few samples.

The sides involved contained many names that became familiar in local rugby circles, such as 'Bertie' Clews, Garth Drake, Ron Jacques, Alan

Jenkinson and Bob Scotney. Bob, captain in 1948-49, received rave notices for, ''His knack of swerving, side-stepping and sure kicking''. These qualities continued into his long and productive association with the Kettering Club and, for a time, with Northampton. His half-back partnership with Duncan Bennie, who also played for the Saints and Denstone College, was surely Kettering's best-ever.

Others from these fifteens achieved national recognition, principally David Bland and Victor Leadbetter. David was sufficiently prominent with Northampton to be selected for England trials. In 1947-48 Victor scored thirteen tries, as a forward, and was praised in the School Magazine for ''holding the scrum together (quite literally).'' He also gained a State Scholarship to Cambridge at a time when rugby forwards thought ''marmalade'' was a big word and eating it proof of sophistication. After Cambridge, Victor progressed to Edinburgh Wanderers and in 1954 was selected for England, against Scotland and France. His predecessor as a full international was Trevor Smith, who was at School from 1931 to 1936. Trevor, who was ''capped'' against Wales in 1951, finished his playing career with the Kettering Club, in those halcyon days at Northampton Road.

The School won ten of its twelve matches in 1951-52, sustaining a rare defeat in the long standing fixture against a particularly powerful County Police team. Alan Southwell and Roger Toseland, colleagues in a respected pack, both progressed to the first-class game. Alan was a popular stalwart with Northampton and the East Midlands, while Roger also represented the Saints and Oxford University. Ten years later another forward shone in a School XV with a comparable record (played 15, won 13) before advancing to the higher echelons. Dick Tilley, after gaining international honours at school level, played for Wakefield and Yorkshire. Dick has also coached the Saints, Kettering and Bedford, and been a selector for England Schools.

The 1969 side lost only one (to Loughborough Grammar School) of its sixteen matches and one of its members argues that they faced a stronger fixture list than teams in the 'forties, and were not bolstered by teaching staff. The 1978 team lost one out of ten (against an Uppingham XV). They provided nine of the County XV and six for the East Midlands: Tim Barker, Alex Burnett, Michael Green, Andy McClure, Graham Peck, and Edward Wells. Every age is golden for someone.

Other Old Boys have played their first-class rugby with Northampton, such as Les Berridge, Vince Cannon and Trevor Harden. In a lengthy career Vince also represented the Midlands, the Barbarians and was an England substitute. Informed opinion says that he was one of the best forwards not to win a full cap. Les played for Devon and Trevor for the East Midlands. Roy Brown, son of Gordon, had seasons with Jedforest. In 1993-94, Matthew Foster played a number of games in the centre for Northampton, shortly after leaving School, and in 1994 he captained the Midlands against the New Zealand tourists at under 21 level.

In 1993-94 Matthew Foster played for Northampton Saints soon after leaving School. In 1994 he captained the Midlands XV against the New Zealand tourists at Under-21 level.

All the above were also players at Kettering. This continued the traditional links between the School and Club which began to sprout seventy or so years earlier, with the likes of F. A. Cox, J. E. Mustin and A. O. Mason. This lifeblood for the Club can be illustrated by the following incoherent list of players, dictated by memory, and representative of the decades since the War: S. Horrocks, M. Miller, D. Panter, S. Dellett, R. McIntosh, J. Newing (when not mountaineering), D. Bale, A. Jervis, J. Hunt, Alan and Roy Godson, D. Croft, D. Lee, J. White, A. Parker, C. Taggar. The list, of course, could be increased many times over. Several staff, who played themselves (such as Ken Mandale or David Greenwood) were often instrumental in encouraging pupils to progress to the Club. The School has also provided numerous Kettering captains: Les Berridge, 'Dougie' Bridgeman, David Buckby, Tony Dee and Trevor Harden are among them.

It is not just homespun philosophy which says that in rugby, more than any other sport, clubs are rightly proud of the community spirit and values they foster. Any club's well-being cannot rest solely with its 1st XV, even in these days of a cut-throat league structure. The game needs its servants. Some Old Boys and former players have refereed at the highest level, such as John Chaplin. Equally important are those who give up their time to benefit the mysterious world of the Extra B. One such was Jim McGinn, whose humour was invaluable, as referee and friend. Clubs need their administrators, old farts, alickadoos, and someone to run the line when it's cold and wet in November. The School has produced them all. Continuity

Traditional links between the School and Kettering R.U.F.C.: pre-training 1957. 25 (or more?) were Old Cyts or taught at the Grammar School.

and tradition; take them away and hark what problems follow.

Those who believe in the wheel of fortune will find their tenet endorsed in the history of the School's cricket, the game that was the last to die. The first printed record, in 1914, of the "new school" in Bowling Green Road shows that the cricket team was a mixture of staff and boys, whose opposition included Kettering Iron Company and Saint Crispins. Some eighty years later, at the time of closure, the School side – now also a mix of boys, staff and Old Boys – faced similar opponents in the booming Midweek League. However, whereas the number of pupils in the School in 1914 and 1993 was identical, the style of cricket was not. For example, in 1914, before limited overs matches were the norm, the School drew with Kettering Thursday XI (213 for 4 in two hours) and twice defeated Kettering Wanderers, with Mr Jones taking five wickets for five runs in the first encounter in May. Some things did not change. In 1914 tributes were paid, not only to Mr Peet's "Patient displays" with the bat, but also to his "thorough and painstaking organisation of the game." His successors deserved comparable accolades, not least Kim Davis (batting patience apart).

Kim, who became Head of Physical Education after Gordon Brown's death, was spared Mr Peet's major organisational headache. Between 1914 and 1922 there are frequent references to the frustration of not owning a playing field. In 1914 the Magazine records it was necessary "to hunt all over Kettering before we could even get a field." There is more. A year later and ". . . we still labour under the disadvantage of having for our grounds only part of a field, and that sub-let to us."

It was 1921 before the Headmaster announced that a playing field had been bought by the Education Committe, with the rider that it would not be in use for some time. As is often the case, its eventual appearance was far from the universally anticipated panacea. The following comment was made in 1924, without a trace of irony. ''One of the disadvantages of the new sports field has been its distance from the School, which has resulted in a good deal of wasted time and some fatigue on the part of those boys who do not possess bicycles. Consequently, a special bus service has been arranged on games days, and for a small charge a quick and comfortable journey is made.'' Those generations educated in Bowling Green Road are now spitting blood. If so, prepare for more. What about this report of the new pavilion in 1925? ''The convenience it affords is greatly appreciated. There are dressing rooms for both the home and visiting teams, baths and hot water obtained from a gas-heated boiler.'' Laugh, as they say, I nearly bought the beers.

Mr H. Barrett

Mention the boiler and you had best tread softly. It is a truism of school life that non-teaching staff are often remembered more vividly than teachers. One such example was Mr H. Barrett, appointed permanent groundsman in 1926, accompanied by the following managerial forecast: ''We shall soon have a cricket pitch that will rouse pangs of jealousy in the heart of the groundsman at Lord's. The 'Blues' have played matches on our rugby pitch; when shall we see a County Match (or a Test Match) on our cricket ground?'' Whilst it is true that pitches at Lord's are sometimes of variable quality, the above prediction still seems a trifle optimistic.

Known affectionately as 'Harry' (but not in his earshot) Mr Barrett took pride in the spruce maintenance of his fields and their surrounds, closely followed by his forthright views on their use. The showers would grace any Hampstead bathroom and probably did. He also revealed a seventeenth century relish for the double or treble negative construction to achieve emphasis. This anecdote from Fraser Gold illustrates Harry's feel for language, not to mention his boiler.

''It was a fair walk from School to playing field, and there was no telephone linking the pavilion and the School. In very inclement weather if games were cancelled, we sat in one of the corrugated iron huts and did our homework, supervised by staff who otherwise would have been on games duty. All was fairly simple if the weather was dreadful all morning, and the ground was unfit. Sometimes it turned nasty at lunchtime or later, which was unfortunate, as the boiler for the showers would have been heated up ready.

One afternoon our homework studies were disturbed as the door was flung open by the irate Barrett. Addressing himself to the master, he exploded, 'Nobody didn't not never tell me there wasn't no games today.' The master suggested that it was fairly obvious that conditions were unfit for games. Barrett's rejoinder was loud and fierce: 'Well, what about my bloody boiler then?' ''

In appearance 'Harry' was distinguished by his watch chain, cap, rat-trapper trousers, and Gulliver boots. He would fit comfortably into a Tom Sharpe novel. Legend has it that the 'fifties advertising slogan, ''Walk the Barrett Way'', had our Mr B as its inspiration. His gruff voice was belied by his twinkling eyes and a kind heart. He gave K.G.S. a lifetime's loyal service, before retiring in 1959. His renown remains.

The cricket squares at School and at Lord's did share one common problem for a number of years: frequency of use. In 1917 only three matches took place – ''We found great difficulty in arranging matches owing to increased train fares.'' If it's not the fog, measles, small-pox, or a royal death, it's the trains. During the successful 1924 season, however, the 1st XI alone were playing eighteen matches. By 1929 the figure had risen to twenty-two (between April and July 30th) and, of course, they were not the sole users of the square. Two other busy and memorable seasons before the War were 1931 and 1933 (played 19, won 15, lost 1, drawn 3).

The tired adage about lies, damned lies, statistics, and cricket statistics still holds good when trying to compare performances between 1900 and 1993. The number of matches, whether they were governed by time or overs, and the quality of the opposition, are but three variables. Another has already been mentioned in other contexts; masters, and some Old Boys, played into the 'thirties, certainly against club sides. In 1900, Mr Gill is described as giving ''invaluable service'' (61 wickets at 4.45). Likewise, in 1922 much of the Eleven's success was due to Mr Rees whose ''Batting often turned the tide in our favour and his enthusiasm in the field has been an object lesson to all of us.'' Strangely, the averages show that Mr W. R. Rees scored a mere

78 runs in 7 innings (with a top score of 19). Irony perhaps, or tact? Messrs Ashworth, Godfrey, Hopkins, Smith, Tynan, Whitney, Wood and Woodward were among the staff who played. None of them suffered the fate of Mr Berry in 1902 who, "batting in a practice game without pads, received a blow on the shin which kept him in bed until the end of term." There are several sombre passages. Mr Jones, applauded for his "breezy hitting" and "deceptive slows" in 1914 was killed in action in 1917, shot by a sniper. His wicket-keeping pupil, G. Lansom, died in battle three months later.

As with other sports, the class performers would have sparkled in any era. E. F. Towell and R. Wooster played in the same first-class fixture for Northants against Dublin Unversity in 1925. Edgar Towell made 59 and Wooster took 5 for 55, including the hat-trick. *The Northampton Independent* prophesied a "brilliant future" for Reginald Wooster. He never played for the County again. The reason why is unknown. Suffice to say that quirky decisions are not unknown at the County Ground. Cricket quiz aficionados will know that a certain Nobel Prize winner played in the County's game with Dublin University a year later. Edgar Towell, unlike his schoolfellow, became an established figure in the County Club's history. On the field, he had 111 innings between 1923 and 1934. He also showed his affection for the School by returning to coach on many occasions; in 1994, he was designated "an old boy who has played for Kent", which might not have pleased him. Other visiting coaches from the County Club were a Mr Hawtin in 1930, Mr Bellamy in 1938-40 and Brian Reynolds from 1991-93.

Probably the best Northamptonshire-born batsman never to play in the County Championship is Stan Leadbetter. He joined the County staff after

Northants v Lancashire: County 2nd XI Championship, St. Helens, 1956.
Stan Leadbetter, an outstanding Northamptonshire cricketer for over 40 years, is on the front row, second right.

scoring heavily for the School in 1952 and 1953 and later represented the R.A.F. and the Combined Services when they had first-class fixtures with the Counties. Compulsory National Service ensured that the Armed Forces had strong sides. Stan was a power in club cricket after leaving the professional circuit and is still active in the game as captain of Northants over 50s.

It is hoped that his playing career will rival that of another distinguished cricketing Old Boy, Cyril Hollinshead. Cyril received the rare tribute of a full-page spread in an M.C.C. publication of April 1993. The previous season he had bowled 6 overs for 16 runs against the Gloucestershire Clergy. Steady, if unspectacular: except that he was ninety years of age. 'Holly' played for Lincolnshire in the 1920s, several "friendlies" for Derbyshire in 1934 and one game for Gloucestershire in 1946. He began his club career with Rushden Town (as did H. E. Bates) and in a game against Bozeat took five wickets in successive balls, all clean-bowled. He then went to the Higham Feast and captured twenty-nine coconuts. Cyril also played for the famous invitation side of Sir Julien Cahn, the Midlands millionaire industrialist and cricketing buff, as well as for the M.C.C.

The most dynamic cricketer of recent vintage is Ian Reynolds, who secured a place in a powerful Loughborough University side and a First-Class Honours Degree to go with it. He is currently one of the leading batsmen in the County League.

Statistics, match reports and oral history indicate numerous other talented individuals. In 1914, C. G. Bagshaw's "easy style was commented on very favourably by the critics on the town ground. . . ." (no mean achievement, I assure you) and in that same season took 9 wickets for 6 runs against Wellingborough. No one appears to have taken "all ten", but there are other nine wicket hauls. John Hawthorne (a quality slow left arm bowler) also achieved 9 for 6 against Bedford Modern in 1955, R. C. Shapiera took 9 for 12 against Kibworth in 1948 and B. D. Smith 9 for 24 against Market Harborough Grammar School in 1953.

It is fair to say that the greater number of matches, against lesser opposition, partially accounts for some remarkable bowling analyses in the 1920s. C. Wright 46 wickets at 7.0 (1920); R. Hardwicke 68 at 5.9 (1921); F. A. Cox 50 at 7.8 (1925); W. H. Burchell 61 at 6.8 (1927); and topping them all, A. L. Smith in 1929. His season's figures were 221 overs, 66 maidens, 503 runs, 83 wickets, at an average of 6.1.

Notable post-War bowlers include Edward Brew, Niven McMaster, Michael Parkinson, and Paul Coe, the leading wicket taker in 1954 with his leg breaks. The bowling of R. Pitts, G. Livsey, M. Perrott and P. Sansom was a major contribution to the successful teams in the mid-sixties.

A. L. Smith ranks highly among the foremost all-rounders. In 1930 he headed both the batting and bowling averages with 273 runs and 58 wickets. P. E. Coles, J. E. Mustin and H. F. Dawes in the 'twenties, G. W. Ashman and R. C. Shapiera in the 'forties and R. J. Coles in the 'fifties, were other considerable contributors with both bat and ball.

Known centurions were G. W. Ipgrave (100 against the G.P.O. in 1938), R. J. Coles in 1957, with 101 against Wellingborough Grammar School and R. C. Shapiera, whose 102 was against Wyggeston in 1950. In 1954, Ian Runciman had a prolific season with 420 runs, averaging over 50; in contrast, Michael Parkinson did not score at all (he did take 32 wickets). Terry, Tilley and P. Jackson each had effective seasons with the bat in the 1960s.

There were many successful First Elevens, not least those of 1931, 1933, 1962 and 1964. In 1931, 1933, 1948 and 1952 the only defeats were gainst the Old Boys. A pointer to the strength of the 1933 side is that four batsmen each scored more than 250 runs (R. S. Garnett 334, R. Arnold 274, N. A. Kilborn 269, A. E. Dainty 262). In 1953 and 1954 the only defeats were against club sides in the Limited Overs Knock-out Cup. Those apart, the School had an eight year sequence of unbeaten seasons during the 1950s. In addition to those already mentioned, many others provided strength in depth: L. Berridge, F. Crosier, J. Lack, P. Larcombe, C. Mellor, J. Newing, J. Sykes, J. Triggs, K. Woolmer, B. Ward, R. Watts, G. Willson and M. York were variously talented competitors.

The high quality of cricket throughout that period (and beyond) owed much to the positive influences of the staff, especially John Larcombe. He was a gifted coach, generously prepared to spend his own time in helping others to play better. He loved the game, was informed about it, and communicated well. Above all, he was concerned that cricket should be played with humour and grace. He was supported by colleagues such as Edgar Lindley, who spent most summer Saturdays umpiring, with the calm aplomb possessed by nature's gentlemen.

John Larcombe and his family came to Kettering in 1951. He has fond memories of that time when "that great enthusiast" Jess Ashworth was in charge of Physical Education. He is certain that those years were outstanding in Northamptonshire inter-school sport – "far superior to anything that exists today." He points especially to the remarkable quality of the fixtures among the grammar schools and the independent schools, and "regrets the passing of the old order."

John's selfless efforts on behalf of the game have also been evident in his long association with the Kettering Club. His son, Peter, himself a splendid cricketer, has continued the connection. Other Cytringanians are similarly associated with Northamptonshire clubs. Ray Dainty and John Wells at Rothwell, Neil Mobbs at Rushton, Alan Griffin at Burton, David Garton at Corby, the Kellands at Isham, Richard Watts at Desborough and Michael York at Great Oakley: a few examples from different generations.

John Larcombe's comment about post-War fixtures is a reminder that inter-school games were not always the norm. There was a time when every community, factory, or organisation had its own team. Without doubt, the most popular fixtures were the early encounters with Dr A. Stokes XI, played at Weldon. One match report described how Dr and Mrs Stokes entertained the team to tea and they all "felt it was no mere form which prompted the very hearty cheers on starting for home, after doing the Weldon Fair." A further insight on the fixture lies in the expression of relief "that the results of the collision of five cyclists was not more serious."

The annual reports offer many glimpses of a lost world. Games against the Rectory Bible Class, the introduction of First Eleven caps and blazers ("the colour scheme of red and cream is most effective"), and the courtesy, "Neville's work as scorer has, I am sure, been appreciated by all of us." Even the language of the reports themselves is neo-Cardus: "The wickets fell to the seductive, slow spin bowling of Cohen, who was to the opposing team rather as were the Syrens to unwary voyagers, than as the Romans to the Sabine women." It is also no surprise that there were frequent half holidays, not only to watch Mr Hartley play against the County on the Town ground, but for the annual match against the Post Office.

Various forms of cricket were played on the School field until the gates were finally closed in August 1993. Inter-school matches at junior level provided opportunities for any boy with the ability or desire to participate. The Midweek League offered biff-bang entertainment for an interesting mix of Cyts, under the engaging leadership of Kim Davis. Kim, who epitomised the School's capacity to produce all-round sportsmen, also assumed responsibility for maintaining the cricket "square" to a standard that would be welcomed by several clubs in the County League. In 1992 and 1993 the School hosted the Primary School Cricket competition, organised by Brian Reynolds and sponsored by the Old Grammar School Foundation. Both occasions were hugely enjoyable and helped to foster interest in the game at that level. Finally, the School's nets were a major source of pleasure, and not only during the day. In addition, they were occupied in the evenings, throughout the summer, by a mixture of pupils, staff, Old Boys, and assorted club cricketers, who recognised a proper net when they saw one. The enterprise was inspired by Fred Barker: coach and supreme enthusiast.

Similar plaudits applied to Ian Coleman, an old Cytringanian, who took over the teaching of "Outdoor Education" after the death of his mentor, Gordon Brown. Gordon had pioneered this area of the curriculum within the School, and across the county, and Ian developed it with zest and imagination. He enthused the likely, unlikely, and downright lethargic into enjoying physical activities, such as rock-climbing, surfing, canoeing, and skiing (on dry slopes and abroad). His final triumph was a camping expedition in the North of England for the entire School (staff and boys) immediately prior to closure.

Mention of those activities, which Ian pursued (not least at weekends), indicates that the School took an increasingly catholic approach to what is, or is not, "sport". It is difficult to separate "sport" and "physical recreation", even inappropriate to do so. Sport in schools was transformed between 1900 and 1993, but the half-hidden continuities between generations remained significant, especially at the Kettering Grammar/Boys School. Physical Education is not just physical, but inevitably cultural in the broadest sense. Economics impose limits of time and resources, but what schools choose to do within such limits is influenced by changing behaviour patterns, taste, and traditions, not governed or explained by material considerations alone. An editorial in *The Times* of May 1995, on the matter of reviving games in schools, argued that money was not the only requirement: commitment, enthusiasm, and concern for both the game and the child are more important. A simple truth, but it needs restating. The School never lacked staff who possessed those qualities nor the belief that sport is part of the British heritage, shared by all classes. It can generate equality, which deepens the irony of its perceived decline in many state schools.

The Government is now addressing this apparent lack of physical activity among eleven to sixteen year olds (a 1995 report claimed that two thirds of this age group have no more than the equivalent of a brisk, ten minute walk once a week). It is necessary to examine, certainly the team games beloved of John Major, David Mellor et al, but also the provision of opportunities for a wide range of activities – such as those introduced by Gordon Brown and Ian Coleman – not only to enrich health, but life.

Whatever is offered, some individuals will escape the ''dread of games'' by seeking refuge behind the pavilion, or vicarious exercise in front of a screen. So be it. Others will support the opinion of Sir Roger Bannister, expressed in 1994, to a group of independent school Headmasters: ''For every child who may be put off by compulsory sport, there will be nine others sufficiently well taught to delight in their skill and repay the benefit of this training over a lifetime.'' The figures might be arguable, but the history of this School's sport endorses the general sentiment. My golfing partner would be the first (among many) to stress my shortage of skills, but I am grateful for that chance to be one of the nine.

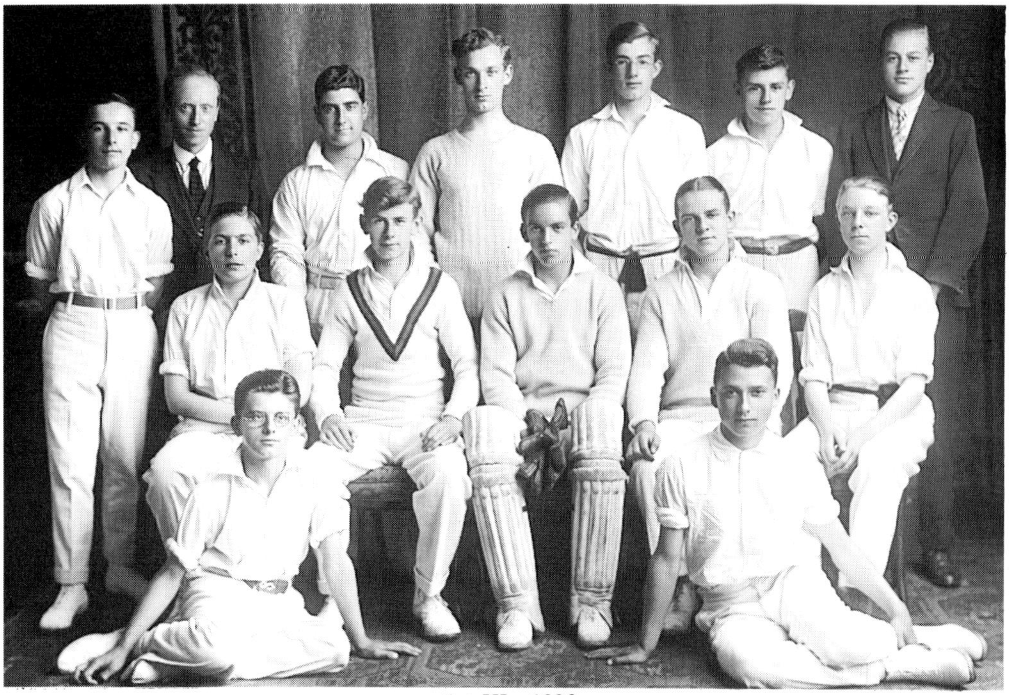

1st XI – 1928

Back Row (L. to R.): J. E. Ward, Mr Whitney, P. T. C. Jones, Mr Ashworth, J. E. Walden, S. N. Allen, C. F. G. Dimbleby
Middle Row (L. to R.): H. A. Clark, C. W. Elliott, A. W. E. Flood (Capt.), L. A. M. Brading, C. Church
Front Row (L. to R.): W. J. Allen, A. L. Smith

A. L. Smith must rank as one of the School's best-ever all-rounders.

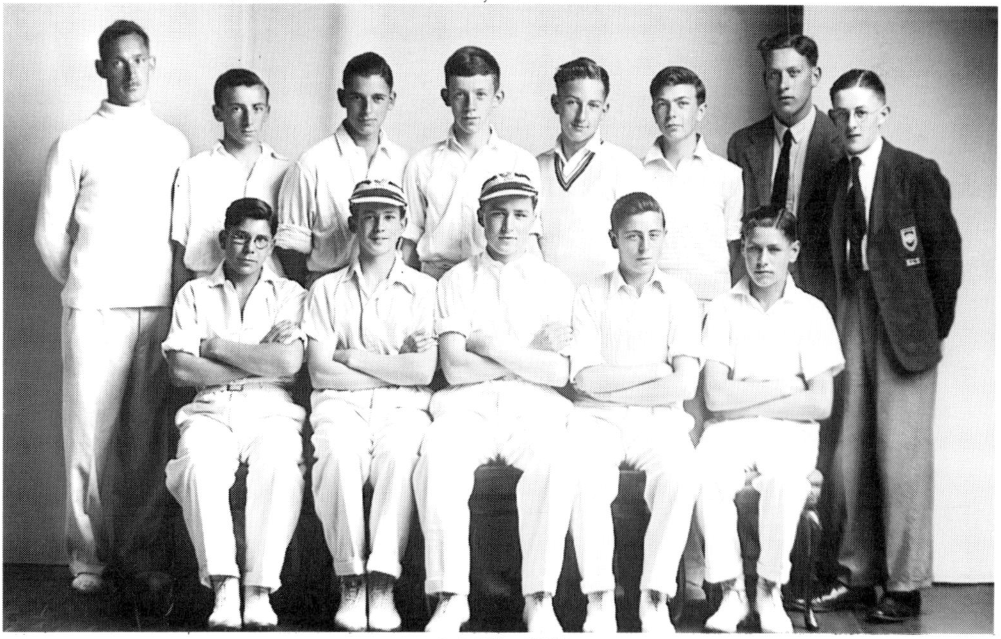

1st XI – 1942

Back Row (L. to R.): Mr J. Ashworth, C. J. S. Bumpus, F. W. Knight, R. P. Dyson, J. A. D. Maybury, E. J. Colville, J. E. Chaplin, P. J. Blackmore (Scorer); Front Row (L. to R.): G. R. Riches, A. J. Colvin, T. H. Holmes, J. Shapiera, J. L. Wells.

1st XI – 1953

Back Row (L. to R.): Mr Larcombe, J. Bates, E. Brew, R. Long, G. Cunnington, T. Harvey, J. Chambers
Middle Row (L. to R.): I. Runciman, B. Smith, T. Swales, R. Williams, S. Leadbetter
Front Row (L. to R.): J. Hawthorne, J. Triggs.

1st XI – 1957, the best ever? or just editorial bias?

Back Row (L. to R.): J. R. Larcombe, M. J. Guy, J. Lack, K. J. Woolmer, C. P. Mellor, R. M. Watts, R. J. Abbott (Scorer)
Middle Row (L. to R.): C. J. Sharman, N. McMaster, B. J. Slough (Captain), R. J. Coles, J. F. Newing
Front Row (L. to R.): D. J. Allbury, J. A. P. Larcombe

1st XV – 1923-24, shortly after Rugby Football was accepted as the major winter game. The team was captained by C. P. Tutt, with E. Corby on his right and J. E. Mustin on his left.

1st XV – 1935-36

Back Row (L. to R.): Mr Ashworth, J. C. Pollock, W. E. Cherry, H. H. E. Freeman, E. A. Cooke, B. A. Tait, E. H. Beaver
Middle Row (L. to R.): D. G. Fennell, F. J. Lawrence, D. M. Heeley, G. C. B. Bull, D. A. Panter
Front Row (L. to R.): T. H. Smith, L. S. Brace, N. D. Stebbings, D. Collins
Trevor Smith (front row) played for England in 1951.

1st XV – 1946-47

Back Row (L. to R.): M. A. Williamson, B. J. Loasby, P. Finney, V. Leadbetter, P. Werblow, J. B. Hammond, P. A. Toseland, R. S. Barton. Middle Row (L. to R.): P. Cohen, R. T. Scotney, J. D. Dodge, R. W. Harrison, G. N. Ashman, H. B. O'Connor, H. Clews. Front Row (L. to R.): G. C. Hulett, R. C. Shapiera

Victor Leadbetter (back row) played for England in 1954.

1st XV – 1949-50

Back Row (L. to R.): J. F. Lord, E. E. Sharpe, C. G. Coe, D. F. Inns, J. A. Bald, J. H. Lilley, A. L. Gunn. Middle Row (L. to R.): G. M. Hillyer, A. Godson, F. A. D. Bland (Vice-Captain), R. C. Shapiera (Captain), R. T. Smith, S. B. Horrocks, R. F. Smith. Front Row (L. to R.): R. Summerly, P. R. Mattocks.

David Bland (Middle row) had an England trial.

1st XV – 1951-52

Back Row (L. to R.): A. H. Gilbert, T. A. Tite, R. M. Long.
Middle Row (L. to R.): Mr Ashworth, R. C. Williams, K. Foreman, P. Wilson, J. P. Briggs, J. S. Moodie, G. S. Boulby
Front Row (L. to R.): D. Swingler, R. Toseland, C. Southwell (Captain), J. A. Bald, J. F. Lord
Seated: P. A. Croft, J. R. Knibbs.

Ist XV – 1958-59
L. G. Berridge (third left, middle row), played for Devon, Northampton Saints, and captained Kettering R.U.F.C.

1st XV 1969-70
Standing L. to R:—S. P. Eady, M. J. Mellors, D. J. Mason, D. A. Baggaley, M. Close, Mr G. S. Brown, R. P. White, A. Burton, A. P. G. Morgan, K. R. Samuel.
Seated L. to R.:—R. P. McIntosh, I. H. Jones, B. R. Mason, R. T. Winsor (Capt.), A. Mallard, C. J. Breslin, M. A. J. Boughton (Vice-Capt.)

1st XV 1972-73
Roy Brown, son of Gordon, later played for Jedforest. He is seated front left.

Jim McGinn's U-15 Rugby Team – 1985-86

Back Row (L. to R.): Mr J. D. McGinn, J. Shaw, S. Allaway, P. Bainbridge, S. Webb, G. Woods, R. Barratt, A. Bannell, L. Hawthorn, K. Terry, S. Whitmee.

Front Row (L. to R.): C. Parris, P. Gill, R. Stewart, A. Osborne, P. Steedman, M. Soi, D. Brooks.

The successful U-15 football team, 1985-86. Nick Garnett is fourth from the left on the back row. Steve May is the coach.

Winners of the Fineshade Cup 1947
J. Goldsworthy, B. Osborne, S. Fletcher, J. Smith, Mr J. Ashworth.

The Boxing Club – 1948-49
Mr R. Coakes, the coach, is next to Mr J. Ashworth.

CHAPTER 22

Mr J. M. Steane
Headmaster 1964-1976

By a Colleague: A. J. Cowell

In 1964 John Steane succeeded John Dudley as Headmaster of Kettering Grammar School. He stayed in the post for the same length of time as his predecessor, twelve years, and lived in the same house in the Headlands.

John Steane was 32 years old, then, younger than many of the staff. He was a graduate of Oxford University, and had been at Magdalen College. He had previously taught History at Southport Grammar School, but his new post required a wider discipline.

We had been used to the rather controlled care of Mr Dudley but John Steane was different. He was a tremendous enthusiast who, while appreciating the need to consolidate his position with staff and boys, was determined to be a ''doer'' outside the usual ambit of a Head. He was entranced by the past, and what we could learn from it by inspection and research. He was a devoted practising archaeologist, who liked nothing better than to be out and about exploring old buildings, fishponds, Roman sites, medieval tile making in England, old railway tracks in Wales. His energy and enthusiasm attracted a number of boys into the School Archaeological Society, and eventually at least two of them, 'Digger' Dix and Robert Carr, became professionals.

John Steane was an enthusiastic painter, encouraged no doubt by his wife Nina, a very accomplished artist, who worked as Nina Carroll. A professional household, with John contributing readily to learned periodicals.

As far as staff and boys were concerned, John ruled with a loose rein. He could be very genial, but had strong opinions and could make himself understood when the occasion demanded. He showed stoical qualities when removing an old unexploded land mine, brought to School by a well-meaning schoolboy, and burying it in the long jump pit.

He was a great believer in Grammar Schools, and when the first whispers of comprehensive education were heard, he decided that he did not feel justified in running a system in which he did not believe. He left Kettering Grammar School in 1976 and worked for the Oxford Museum department, a post which gave him great scope in a discipline in which he was at home.

John Steane left his mark on Kettering Grammar School. He had high educational standards, and showed innumerable boys what could be achieved, in his case, archaeological triumphs, if you have the will and energy to do it.

J. M. Steane unveils E. E. Kirby's portrait. The artist was Nina Carroll (Mrs Steane).

By a former pupil: Paul Stamper

In 1972 John Steane became a Fellow of the Society of Antiquaries of London, a signal honour for any archaeologist and a considerable achievement for one whose involvement at the time was as an amateur. His election recognised a twofold contribution to antiquarian studies: to the archaeology and history of Northamptonshire, and the introduction of archaeology and local history as a subject for serious study in schools. Those two interests came together, above all else, in Kettering Grammar School's Local History and Archaeological Society.

J. M. S.'s most substantial published work on the county has been *The Northamptonshire Landscape* (1974), in the major *Making of the English Landscape* series edited by W. G. Hoskins. In his typically generous Preface J. M. S. paid tribute to Hoskins, who almost single-handedly in the 1950s developed the analytical study of England's historic landscapes, both as friend and teacher. He also thanked the Society's successive boy Chairmen – Carr, Dix,

Walker, Crane and Croft (it was surnames only, and J. M. S. was always ''Sir'') – for their enthusiasm, librarians and archivists for their assistance, and farmers for allowing access. Finally, he paid tribute to his wife Nina, ''who has suffered the deluge of papers, books, boys, maps and mud with unfailing patience over the years.''

On winter Sundays the ''deluge'', six to eight strong, would arrive at the Steane household, a large, Victorian villa in the Headlands, to be shown into the front room by Nina or one of their daughters. For most of us it seemed an extraordinary place: both Steanes were poets and talented painters, and the place overflowed not only with paintings but also with books, pots and *objets trouves*. None of our parents had a mantelpiece decorated with a medieval cooking pot and a ploughshare and neither, we were sure, did any of our homes have carpets that were quite as threadbare or a sink of such museum vintage. It was all so different, it was difficult to make sense of.

Once assembled J. M. S. would appear, wearing olive cord trousers of an improbable thickness and carrying a bulging briefcase containing the essentials: maps, bags for collecting pottery, tapes, a vast flask of hot sweet tea or sweet black coffee, and Mars bars. Fresh loaves of bread, bought en route in Brigstock and ripped into hunks by J. M. S., were an occasional dietary supplement. The boys would then be crammed in to his car, in the late 60s and early 70s a battered black Morris Traveller, the smallest two (or three) knees up in the space behind the rear seat. For many years the focus of research, of field walking for pottery, earthwork survey and in the summer excavation, was the Lyveden valley between Brigstock and Oundle, and as we travelled out there J. M. S. would keep up a running commentary and question and answer session about the landscape we were passing through, the car swerving with predictable regularity as the landscape or the boys in the back were addressed rather than the line of the road.

Much of that fieldwork, both in the methods employed and the subjects studied, was remarkably precocious. Lost medieval villages and farms were discovered and surveyed, medieval deer parks and fishponds identified, and the terraces of long abandoned Renaissance gardens explored. Expeditions often yielded a rich haul of finds, especially pottery, brought back to School and washed in the Art Room sinks in lunchtimes and evenings over the following week before being bagged and marked. After a time the sheer volume of material recovered became something of a problem, and any spare cupboard or space – beneath the desk in the lecture theatre, Eric's boiler room – was commandeered for storage. By the early 1970s it seemed that pottery was leaking from half the cupboards in the School.

The amount of material found fieldwalking was dwarfed by that recovered by the Society's excavations, on Roman sites in Kettering at Mitchell Street (where to the reported fury of Gordon 'Jock' Brown, the games master, the First XV were worked to a standstill backfilling the site) and Kipling Road (where the site hut was, literally, a pig sty), and at the important deserted medieval village of Lyveden. Such excavations, and especially the last, run each August between 1965 and 1973 with J. M. S. as Assistant Director for the Ministry of Works, gave a rare opportunity for boy excavators to gain archaeological experience, several going on to become professional archaeologists.

It was not only storage requirements, or backfilling, that dragged others from the School into the Society's activities. Lyveden was home to medieval potters and the excavations found a number of kilns. Replicas of these were built near the cricket pavilion and fired overnight on open evenings, the pots made by the Art department and the temperature measured by a team from Physics. Damaged chairs and desks made excellent firewood, although Eric may have been ignorant of this. Later, finds of iron smelting hearths and furnaces at Lyveden led to attempts to smelt iron, relays of boys manning an air pump supplied by a local blacksmith.

J. M. S. was always at his most effective as a teacher, gown billowing as he scribbled furiously on the board in his distinctive handwriting, pausing only to seize coloured chalks to produce incredibly accomplished drawings. History in the Lower forms and General Studies for the older boys allowed him to expound on themes close to his heart, issuing Hoskins's *Making of the English Landscape* and Mortimer Wheeler's *Archaeology from the Earth,* texts well outside the usual rather arid grammar school compass. Participation would be ensured, not only because of the healthy respect in which J. M. S. was held, but also because of the constant stream of questions which he would fire out as well as instructions to participate: ''Come on boys'', he would say, ''let's have Saxons walking through the swamp noises'', with which he would wrap his gown around him and stride around in an exaggerated fashion making loud sucking noises. Then the only problem was the restoration of order after 2P followed suit. Once a year the boy archaeologists themselves would take centre stage at a lecture theatre open evening when the results of the year's excavations would be presented to the parents. Often the high spot was the ''social scene'' lecture at the end when a Pythonesque commentary would be provided by Bob Ellis on a succession of slides taken by Jim Norris showing equipment-laden boys losing their boots in the mud, falling in streams, or J. M. S. floridly blowing his nose. At other times the Society would pack into J. M. S.'s car (we never did learn) and go off to an archaeological lecture or ''day school'' at Brackley or Northampton. During the lecture J. M. S. would slouch in a chair, scratching furiously and audibly in a notebook with a Rotring pen, and at question time would often dig a boy in the ribs and prime him with a question. An unsatisfactory answer (for such it was sure to be) gave J. M. S. the chance to come in with a supplementary point, as he spoke his hand slowy twisting to and fro in mid air as if unscrewing a pickle jar lid.

As boys we surely did not appreciate enough the energy, vision and generosity of our extraordinary Headmaster. Thirty years on I think we do.

CHAPTER 23

The Moving Sixties

Dr. Peter Freeman

A search of the attic revealed little in the way of memorabilia, except for a copy of the programme for the Speech Day on the 18th March 1965. I was in form 5Q at the time and the address on that day was given by Mr Boase, President of Magdalen College, Oxford.

I attended the School between 1960 and 1967, following which I went to read Economics at the University of Southampton. Now, some 25 years or so down the line, I am a partner in a consulting firm in Pretoria, specialising in development and transport economics. I live in Johannesburg and have had the privilege of witnessing a political transformation in this country that few thought possible. My wife, Judy, is a former Kettering High School girl – proof yet again that the segregation between the Schools did not work!

When I joined the School it was about the time that the wearing of caps became optional. My mother, in her wisdom, insisted on sending me off to School on my first day with the regulation cap. I quickly observed on arrival though that nobody else was wearing one and stuffed it down my trousers. I never wore it again.

Classes in those days for the younger pupils were located in a series of prefabricated buildings clustered around the playground. They were surrounded by a drainage channel which was commonly referred to as ''the moat''. It even became a verb at times as in the cry, ''Let's moat him'', which was part of the initiation of new boys and consisted of merely pushing the victim into the ditch in the largest puddle available.

The old School building had lots of character. There was a feeling of pride in belonging to the School and a sense of history going back to the sixteenth century. The hall doubled as both hall and gymnasium. There was little room to seat all the boys, however, and it was not uncommon to see boys keel over and faint during morning prayers, as standing for long periods in the early morning seemed to be at conflict with their hormones. Gym, on the other hand, was great fun and especially enjoyable at the end of term when we played ''pirates''. This consisted of being chased over the apparatus and up the wall bars by two or three boys designated as buccaneers. You were not allowed to touch the floor during the chase or you were eliminated from the game.

Three years after joining Kettering Grammar School I experienced the excitement of moving to the new premises in Windmill Avenue. It was lovely to go to a brand new building, brand new desks (without 'Troll' engraved next to "Kilroy was here") and brand new facilities. Incidentally, in all the time I was there, I never discovered exactly why Mr Layward, the Maths teacher, was called 'Troll'.

Somehow the new building did not have the same character as the old building but it was certainly easier to study in. We were also very proud of the achievements of Mr Perry with his exploits in tracking Russian satellites and regarded his protégés as real boffins.

Curiously enough, the move away from Kettering High School came at a time when contact between the Schools was increasing. Judith Olney, now my wife, suggested to me that we form a joint Folk Dance Club. This did in due course materialise and boys and girls were formally permitted to touch each other on School premises!

The new building had another advantage in that it was adjacent to Wicksteed Park and so convenient for despatching boys on cross country runs. Sometimes we would be instructed to run around the lake, which was usually drained in the winter. There were far fewer amusements in the Park in those days, but the miniature railway was there and we would lark around in the tunnel if we had half a chance.

It was with great sadness that I learned that the School had closed, thereby ending 400 years of history. This would have seemed unthinkable when I was a scholar, as there was no shortage of pupils. We were the "bulge babies" born after the war. This was before Kettering was overlooked as an overspill town and before the population began to age. However, the demise of the boot and shoe industry was already beginning.

A Bow Tie, A Thermos Flask and Wheelbarrows

P. Joyce

I started at Kettering Grammar School in 1963 after the worst winter for many years. The School had recently moved from Bowling Green Road, so the buildings were new and still well kept. The School was, at that time, quite a prestige establishment (at least I thought so) and it was good to have passed the eleven plus! The Head was J. K. Dudley: as an eleven year old, I felt that he was a figure who had an air which commanded respect. I suppose he was a gentleman.

Each year was split into four forms P, Q, R and S. We were told that they were not streamed, but they obviously were. It soon became evident that P represented ''perfect'' and S ''stupid'', as popular mythology decreed.

The School buildings were considerably larger than any of us were used to, but we soon found our way around. The only question I had about the layout was why the architect put the Music Room in the balcony to the hall. A strange move, unless the room was an afterthought. Music never was a strength of the School. The Music teacher, Maurice Till, was the typical musician; the bow tie obviously part of the uniform.

As I was less than proficient at any sport, the weekly games session was somewhat of a drudge. The cross country runs, which substituted for rugby when the field was too wet, took place over the nearby fields. On reflecting, we ran around what is now the Ise Lodge estate, or around Wicksteed Park if it was really bad weather. We soon realised that you could walk the course and still be back in time to change and leave School at the normal time.

The games team was ruled with a rod of iron by 'Jock' Brown. One was either accepted or rejected by 'Jock' until a new teacher, Barry Batterham (I think that was his name), arrived. He seemed to believe that there was a way of delivering the message to anyone, whatever their inclination. I believe this teacher was also responsible for introducing hockey to the School.

My clearest memory of him was a cricket lesson. He was demonstrating keeping wicket, showing that if the ball approaches from the left, you catch it and swing your hands and the ball across the bails from left to right. If the ball approaches from the right, the same manoeuvre is undertaken from right to left. However, if the ball approaches from above, you catch the ball and knock the bails off with your knee.

The only other games/PE teacher I can remember was a tall chap with a wispy beard. He also taught Maths. There were many horrendous stories of the way the Fourth and Fifth years treated him. He was clearly very clever but found teaching difficult. I believe he left the School at the end of my second or third year and was reported to be emigrating to Australia. Our PE lessons were something of an ordeal for him.

Apart from the odd lesson from the new Headmaster, J. M. Steane, which was dreaded by all, the most memorable member of staff was a small, quiet chap whose name I've forgotten. Most lessons he would arrive in the classroom, tell us to read a particular chapter of a book, place his briefcase on his table and promptly sit down behind it. He would then remove a thermos flask from the case and drink coffee.

My years at the School coincided with the development of the Satellite Tracking Group by Geoff Perry and Derek Slater. This was a very successful enterprise which received acclaim and commendation from organisations ranging from NASA to the UK press and TV stations. During the 1960s there were regular appearances on television of Geoff Perry, or some of the pupils demonstrating the techniques used to detect the launch of the latest Russian COSMOS satellite, using very basic ex-WD radio equipment. The equipment was slowly improved by donations from Industry, such as a modern Racal receiver.

I recall the universal outrage within the School when the Satellite Group were given a reasonably large sum of money (I believe it was for a TV appearance or the like) which Steane, the Head, decided should be used for the purchase of wheelbarrows for his pet archaeology group. His popularity fell even further.

This was the time well before electronic calculators and Mr Perry's favourite toy was a mechanical calculator. Basically, to multiply using his machine, one would turn a large handle clockwise the appropriate number of times, shifting the carriage for each increment of ten. As with other staff, Perry had to supervise at Saturday morning detentions. He would set long multiplication sums on these occasions and take delight in demonstrating how quickly he could calculate the answer ''on my little machine here''.

It's probably because I got on well with Woodwork, Metalwork and Technical Drawing, but I found the staff in this area very approachable and interested, particularly Ken Mandale and Idwal Jones. There was some excellent work produced by the Fifth and Sixth forms. I particularly remember a superb wooden cross which was, I was told at the time, destined for Rothwell Church. It would be interesting to know whether it is still there.

CHAPTER 24

The Extra-Curricular Satellite Research Studies

Geoffrey E. Perry, MBE, C.Phys, F.Inst.P.

I am frequently asked, "How did you get started with the satellite work?" There were several milestones which I will list chronologically. In 1944, a V2 fell a few miles from my home in Braintree with a double bang. At the time we did not know what it was but as soon as it was revealed to have been a rocket I realised that "space travel" was no longer a wild dream. Then my late cousin gave me, for Christmas 1951, a copy of Arthur C. Clarke's *The Exploration of Space* setting out the principles based on fundamental physics. Thirdly, I anticipated that the Oxbridge Scholarship papers would include a question/essay on the International Geophysical Year and so I read up the topic which included plans for the USA and the USSR to launch small satellites. As it happened, there was nothing in the exams about the IGY but when Sputnik 1 was launched on October 4th, 1957, I was mentally prepared for it. Russell Gladden, the Senior Science Master, made several visual observations of its rocket, getting up before dawn to do so. I did not get up to see it but I did see and photograph Sputnik 2, which carried the dog, Laika, into orbit one month later. John Osborne, of Stowe School, played a recording of the signals from Sputnik 1 at the Annual Meeting of the Science Masters' Association in Leeds during the Christmas vacation of 1957. The whole-octave Doppler shift in pitch was remarkable and he promised me a copy for use as a teaching aid – it never came.

When radio amateur G3FOZ, Derek Slater, was appointed to the staff as Senior Chemistry Master, following the untimely death of Fred Lawson, I realised that here was somebody with the means to let me listen to the satellites that I had been observing visually and photographically for the past two years. Without Derek's expertise, equipment and cooperation this account would never have come to be written – but I will leave him to give his own version.

We achieved success at our first attempt to receive signals from the newly launched Sputnik 4, very early one Monday morning in May 1960. Tape recordings were made throughout the week and then a borrowed signal generator was returned to Cyril Dobson and Derek's CR-100 reverted to use

Numerous distinguished guests visited the School to see the work of the Satellite Research Studies Group. Here Sir Rhodes Boyson and Roger Freeman, M.P. for Kettering, meet with Geoffrey Perry, Derek Slater and James Bambridge, in March 1984.

by his Radio Club. I had my Doppler recording, and that was that. Actually, we missed the opportunity to share in a world news scoop. On the Friday, signals were received later than expected. When asked why, I responded that the satellite must have moved higher. It had – unintentionally! The Russians had tried to recover a spherical capsule containing a dummy cosmonaut but the spaceship had been pointing in the wrong direction when the rocket motor fired.

At a course for Physics teachers, held at University College, London, in the summer of 1961, I learnt that the Radio & Space Research Station at Slough supplied predictions to amateur observers and I applied to be added to their mailing list. Until then I had relied on predictions printed in the *Daily Telegraph*. Predictions during the autumn half term holiday indicated that the American Discoverer 32 was transmitting in the shortwave band and so the apparatus was reassembled and observations were made until it decayed. These were forwarded to Slough and were said to be "useful". It was suggested that we might monitor Discoverer 36 and we decided to wait until the Christmas holiday when it would be nearer to decay. Unfortunately its batteries failed after we had monitored it for a few weeks but, by adding our Discoverer 32 decay curve to the observations, I was able to predict the decay date with some accuracy.

The USSR inaugurated its Cosmos series of satellites in April 1962 and this has provided me with a source of objects to monitor to this day (as of July 6th, 1994 we have now reached Cosmos 2282). Concentration on a sub-set of Cosmos satellites which disappeared from orbit after flights lasting only eight days or less – long before they would have decayed naturally – was the key to unlocking many of the secrets of the Soviet military space programme carried out under the Cosmos label.

In that summer term two officers at RAF Henlow wrote to ask if they might visit the School. Wishing to establish a satellite monitoring project for their cadets, they had been to the Minitrack station at Winkfield. On expressing their dismay at the amount of expensive apparatus in use there, they had been told, "Why don't you see the folks at Kettering Grammar School? They are doing useful work with 'backyard equipment'." It was important to choose a satellite which would permit a "live" demonstration. The Russian Cosmos 5 filled the bill but, as soon as I heard it, it was obvious that its signals were of an unusual character. A periodic variation in pitch was superimposed on the normal Doppler shift. After his A-levels, Robert Jones made a study of the variation which indicated that it was due to a partly faulty solar battery.

During a trip to Wales in the autumn half-term holiday I called at the Physics Department at Aberystwyth, having read that they had also made observations of Cosmos 5. Ken Edwards, the chief technician, had a large collection of pen-recordings of the signals which showed that they ceased completely when the satellite was in the earth's shadow, confirming our hypothesis.

The development of our computational capability over the years has been quite extraordinary. Initially we employed slide rules and graphical techniques. In 1964 through the friendship of Ron Smith, we used Autocode with the Elliott 803 computer at the CWS corset factory at Desborough to analyse pupils' visual observations of the Echo 2 balloon satellite, moving on, with Ron, to Algol programming on SATRA's 4120. I purchased a hand-cranked mechanical calculator before electronic pocket calculators came on the scene and, in 1972, I was given a 30-step programmable desk-top calculator by the US Ambassador, Walter Annenberg. Within a week of taking delivery it had been used to identify a constellation of Soviet navsats. Brief use of the ICL 1900 at County Hall, necessitating trips to the Technical College in St Mary's Road to prepare the data, ended with the arrival of the Commodore 4032 which brought computing with programming in Basic into the laboratory. Today, members of the Group all have their own PCs with DOS or Windows. My daughter, remembering the excitement of the early days, dismisses the modern technological map displays and prediction print-outs with, ''I don't call that tracking!''

When Cosmos 112 was launched on March 17th, 1966, it quickly became apparent that there was something very different about it besides its departure from the standard 65° inclination to the Equator. Signal duration was shorter and it was being controlled from a more northerly station than usual. Examination of its initial ground track revealed that it could not have been launched from Baikonur. I wrote a letter to the editor of *FLIGHT International* claiming that the USSR was using a new launch site but it produced little or no reaction. There were more launches at similar inclinations but it was not possible to locate the origin precisely. When Cosmos 129 was launched in October 1966 I phoned my data to Ron Smith at SATRA. When I collected the output I saw that my orbit-count differed from US data, being three too many. This, together with the inclination of 64.6° instead of 65° led me to realise that Cosmos 129 had also been launched from the new site. The intersection of its initial ground track with that of Cosmos 112 lay some 200 miles south of Archangelsk. I announced the coordinates of the site at a meeting of the British Interplanetary Society in London and followed it up with a second letter to *FLIGHT.* Once again there was no initial reaction but the late Dr. Charles S. Sheldon II, of the Congressional Research Service of the US Library of Congress, wished to include details of the site in a report. His manuscript had been returned by the CIA with that section marked ''Classified''. His reaction was to alert the press to what I had written in *FLIGHT* and on the day after we broke up for the Christmas holiday, *The Times* ran the story under the by-line ''From our Washington correspondent''. My life changed from that point.

It rained on the morning of the Friday of the 1967 autumn half-term holiday. It started when I was on the fourth tee of Corby's municipal golf course and I got soaked to the skin. I went to the Labs in the afternoon and switched on the CR-100. It was not long before I heard a short burst of irregular pulses. I ran the tape recorder and recorded further 30-second bursts at two-minute intervals. In 1966 Ken Edwards had sent a pen record of some strange signals for me to identify. They, too, consisted of 30-second bursts of irregular pulses at two-minute intervals and proved to have been from Cosmos 140, a precursor of the ill-fated Soyuz 1. My signals were from the first test of a Soyuz since Komarov's tragic death.

On the following day I had a phone call from Peter Fairley, of the *London Evening Standard,* who was off to Cape Canaveral for the first launch of a Saturn V. As the fiftieth anniversary of the Russian revolution was imminent he wondered if anything of interest had happened. I said, "No – apart from an unmanned test of a Soyuz." The Soviet Union had yet to announce the launch and he broke the story with the banner headline, "Schoolboys Tune In To A Space Secret", in the midday edition. Two world scoops within twelve months! Clearly this was no accident. Old Cytringanian, Robin Turner, of the *Daily Express,* happened to be in Kettering for his brother's wedding and found me at the Labs on the Sunday, listening to the signals. The CR-100 was becoming temperamental, needing a smart tap with the hand from time to time, and Robin remarked that I "could do with something better". I told him that I knew of a second-hand RA17 which could be had for the cost of refurbishment – I had already applied unsuccessfully for a grant to purchase it. Next day he phoned my wife and told her that he had persuaded his editor to "go halves" with Racal and give me a new receiver. I was lecturing to the BIS at the City University on the Tuesday evening. Before the lecture I was presented with a brand new, state of the art, transistorised RA217 by the chairman of Racal, (now Sir) Ernest Harrison and John Young, assistant to the editor of the *Daily Express.* Their gift removed all the uncertainty whilst retaining all of the pleasure.

I am also often asked how the Kettering Group came into being. Like Topsy, in *Uncle Tom's Cabin* – it just grew. The first pupil to be entrusted with the key to the Labs in order to make an observation was my next door neighbour from Southgate Drive, David Sinnett, who helped me occasionally at weekends. The first pupils to make regular observations were the Sixth Form girls from Kettering High School who came to us for Physics, Chemistry and Mathematics and who sat in the empty Physics A during some of their free periods as there was nowhere else for them to go. One day, as I went off to teach in another room, I said to them, "If that thing starts to bleep, note the time for me on the blackboard." That was the real start of pupil involvement. It soon paid dividends. *FLIGHT* reported that Cosmos 32 had decayed on June 18th, 1964 at 1200 ± 12 hours – no better than saying that it had come down on Thursday! Barbara Jacques and Derek had logged it at 1129 BST that day and so I wrote a letter to the editor of *FLIGHT* narrowing down the time, signing it "Barbara M. Jacques, G. E. Perry & J. D. Slater". A letter came back addressed to Miss Jacques and her pupils. After we had clarified the position, Ken Owen from *FLIGHT* visited the School and published a two-page article, ''Kettering's Cosmos Scholars'', in their space special issue of July 22nd, 1965. That was the first international media exposure that we received.

In 1974 I began receiving regularly by airmail two line orbital element sets for all objects currently in orbit. These are produced in NORAD's Cheyenne Mountain complex by US Space Command and are distributed to *bona fide* researchers by NASA's Goddard Space Flight Center near Washington DC. The elsets enable one to compute a satellite's position, velocity and acceleration at a particular instant and to predict its subsequent motion. Although we were receiving signals from only a few satellites, I realised that these elsets were a valuable source of data from which deduction could be made about the purpose of various classes of Soviet satellites which we could not monitor. Individual pupils were allocated different sub-sets of satellites and by collecting the elsets, analysing plane-spacings, orbital periods, etc., they were able to infer the operational status of communications, navigation, missile early warning and electronic intelligence gathering constellations. The results were published from time to time, jointly in their and my names, in the technical press and US senate and Congressional Reports.

In January 1966, a Swedish student sent me a tape recording of signals which he believed to be from Cosmos 104, asking me for confirmation. Our association has continued to this day and Sven Grahn, the first overseas member of the Kettering Group, is now the General Manager, Science Systems Division, of the Swedish Space Corporation and has been responsible for their Viking and Freja satellites. Other adults in the UK and abroad, with interests, have worked closely with us over the years. They are professional people with expertise in electronic engineering, communications, meteorology, photographic interpretation, etc., but all share the excitement of participation in a hobby of amateur observation and analysis of space programmes, many of which are still considered to be secret.

As the number of adults from the UK and overseas, associated with the Group increased and the assured change of the School's name upon disorganisation along comprehensive lines loomed larger, I decided to drop the words ''Grammar School'' from the name and since the mid-'seventies published observations and results under the title of The Kettering Group. At my suggestion, John Marshall produced the logo of a satellite in orbit around the rose from the Grammar School blazer badge. The centre of the rose was at the focus of the orbit since the Group was frequently the focus of media attention and the orbit was elliptical to support the popular belief that I am eccentric!

I never claimed that no one else knew about the USSR's northern launch site – only that I was the first to publicly disclose its use and reveal its approximate location. Somebody looked up the coordinates and gave it the name Plesetsk. The USSR did not acknowledge its existence until more than

17 years later, in 1983 *Pravda* articles by V. Gubarev. Charles Sheldon called at the School in October 1967 when he was motoring around the UK with his wife. A friendship and cooperation developed which lasted until he died in 1980. He quoted my work in *Soviet Space Programs, 1971-1975.*

> ''Hence, with the passage of time, these Kettering techniques have given a highly professional, consistently positive identification to many aspects of the Soviet space program from completely unclassified, private sources, which are not matched by any public release of data by the Soviet, United States, or British governments. The general public interested in data on Soviet flights owes a debt to the Kettering Grammar School whose published findings in a few instances may have been factors towards influencing the official bureaucracies to ease up on the rigid suppression of what is essentially non-sensitive information about space flights.''

He invited me to contribute to the 1971-75 study and to collaborate with him on the 1976-1980 study. After he died, the Library asked me to complete the work in collaboration with Marcia Smith, one of his specialists, who is continuing his work. I count Marcia as a Kettering Group member and we worked together on the 1981-87 study.

I was appointed an Ordinary Member of the Order of the British Empire in the 1973 New Year Honours List for ''founding and leading the Satellite Tracking Group, Kettering Grammar School''. In 1974 I received the Royal Astronomical Society's Jackson-Gwilt Medal and Gift – the £50 was spent on an antenna and pre-amplifier. The Universities of Loughborough, Reading and Leicester and the Open University conferred Honorary Masters Degrees on me and I have accepted all of these with the realisation that it was the work of the Group that was being recognised. The Kettering Group was awarded the Royal Aero Club's Prince of Wales Cup for team effort during 1983 and a large number of members, including three from the USA and Sven from Sweden, attended the presentation at the Science Museum in December 1984. A personal honour which gave me great pleasure was one of the first Institute of Physics Teachers of Physics Awards in 1986 and I was very pleased to see that John Marshall, now at Beaconsfield High School, received one of those awards this year.

Relations with the media have blossomed over the years becoming a far cry from the days when I had to seek permission from JK ''when you've heard one, you've heard them all'' Dudley to give a story to the *Evening Telegraph.* As our work became more well-known and valued I adopted the policy of notifying Reuters of our ''discoveries'' and then waiting for the press and TV to contact me. The link with Peter Fairley continued when he moved to ITN and I was a member of their Studio Panel in 1971 for Apollo 15. In 1975, Frank Miles, then science editor at ITN, persuaded (now Sir) David Nicholas to invest his budget in using our Group for their coverage of the Apollo-Soyuz mission when American and Russians linked in space with Frank's "handshake over Bognor" – but that is another long story. The radio at the School, with Derek and the boys, was linked by direct line to the pen-recorder with me in the studio in London. When I retired from teaching in 1984, David asked me to work exclusively for ITN and our agreement has been regularly renewed. Although it is increasingly difficult to get space stories on news bulletins, I am still ITN's space consultant. Furthermore, the work of the Group continues – only the pupil segment no longer exists.

Derek Slater

I never intended to take the Kettering job.

It was 1958. I'd been in my first job for five years, and it was time for a move. I didn't care what part of the country Job Number 2 took me to. I intended to go back to civilisation, North of the Ribble, with Job Number 3. I had a few simple requirements, though.

No Saturday morning school. I was heartily sick of teaching five periods on a Saturday morning, when I knew most of the schools in the country managed perfectly well without.

Decent laboratories. It wasn't so much that the buildings dated from the turn of the century, but so did most of the equipment. It was like trying to teach Chemistry in the Museum of the History of Science.

Everything else was flexible. It would help to have a Headmaster who didn't regard Science teachers in the same class as gynaecologists and undertakers, quite useful chaps in their own way, but not to be mentioned in polite conversation, much less to be taken seriously by cultured people.

I scanned *The Times Ed.* and sent off a few applications. I'd come across Kettering before. It was a place one passed through on the way to Silverstone. When I was called for an interview, my wife and I decided to pay a visit, to have a look at both town and School.

So it was that a wet Saturday afternoon found us poking round a damp and deserted yard. The close proximity of the Cattle Market didn't bother me, but where were the labs? I spotted some burettes through a downstairs window and climbed on a window-sill for a better look. I gazed down into a Chemistry Lab. "That's it, let's go home." Phrases involving frying-pans and fires were invoked in the car on the way home. I knew what a good, modern, well-equipped school Science laboratory looked like. I'd been taught in one.

I decided to come to the interview. I had another one the following day, down in Wiltshire, and it would be good experience. However, I must, at all costs, avoid being offered the job; for, if I were, and turned it down, I should have to pay my own travelling expenses.

The day came. The candidates assembled, under the stern gaze of Miss

Richards. Mr Dudley said a few words of greeting, then said, ''Mr Gladden will take you up to the new Science Block and show you round.'' . . .

The rest is history. Well Chemistry, actually twenty-seven years of teaching it, together with Physics, Electronics, radio, satellites and the excitement and intellectual stimulus of doing original research. Job Number 3 slowly becomes less attractive, disappearing somewhere along the way, as I put down roots.

I never heard Sputnik One. The equipment I used in my Amateur Radio station was either home-built or converted Government Surplus. It didn't cover the right waveband. However, in the Summer holiday before I came to Kettering, I had the chance of buying a top-quality communications receiver. It was a tremendous bargain at £25, but that was almost half a month's take-home pay, even at the increased salary of my new job. I have a very understanding wife. The receiver came to Kettering with us.

I was intent on establishing an Amateur Radio station in the school. My previous Headmaster had been most discouraging when I asked permission to sling a hundred and thirty six feet of transmitting aerial across the sacred Quadrangle. I told myself that it was the wrong time to ask, he was still a bit peeved over the homemade television set. I had managed to convince him that the 4½" wide, bright green picture which appeared fleetingly in certain weather conditions counted as experiment and not entertainment, thereby not requiring a licence, but had been requested to remove the aerial concealed in the roof space.

I was convinced that a modern Science Department needed a radio station and a radio station needed an aerial. The syllogism was completed when I discovered that one of my pupils had a father in the building trade. A scaffold-pole appeared overnight. Radio G3FOZ was on the air. However, since I was more interested in building the equipment than using it, operation was sporadic.

Geoff Perry and I got on famously from the start. We had two things in common: a conviction that the understanding of Science is supremely important, in that it transforms and enhances our own enjoyment of the world, and secondly, that we were determined to build up the best school Science Department in the area, whatever it cost in effort. Apart from that, we had completely different personalities and temperaments. Still have. I tend to be casual, procrastinating, bored with fine detail and administration, excited by the next project before I've finished the first one. Geoff isn't.

Maybe this is why we managed so well to bounce ideas off each other, although, occasionally, we infuriated each other beyond measure.

I don't have a very clear memory of the very first time we picked up signals from a satellite. If I'd known how it was going to affect my life for the next twenty five years, I'd have taken more notice.

Staying up all night to listen to the mush and crackle of a radio receiver was nothing new. A bit nostalgic, really, as I'd spent much of my time in the RAF doing just that. One would be shattered the next morning, of course, but a lot less shattered than after a student all-night party. What I do remember, very clearly, is the excitement; the thrill of participating, in however small a degree, in the biggest technological advance of this century.

What came later and endured, was the realisation that we could extract useful information from the signals, that the superpowers could spend millions of dollars and roubles putting these things into orbit and we could sit there with what someone kindly described as "backyard equipment" and extract information, not only about the Russian space programme, but about the Earth's atmosphere and ionosphere.

Somehow, though, when it came to the actual process of hearing and recording the signals, the magic never failed. Even though the purpose was merely to confirm a prediction or check that a particular satellite was still in orbit, there was a real thrill in picking up the signal, whether it was a watery, tentative, fluttering sound of an object still below our horizon, the sudden switch-on of a reconaissance satellite or a calm and cheerful Russian voice from a spacecraft calling a tracking ship in the Caribbean. There were, of course, countless hours of listening to nothing but hiss and crackle, bored but alert – rather like fishing in some lonely pond for the monster carp which may not even exist.

Fairly soon, all Amateur radio activity ceased. I was always much more interested in building equipment than using it. It always seemed an anti-climax when, having spent many obsessive hours creating something, all it was good for was to exchange pleasantries with some boring idiot in Milan or Stockton-on-Tees. A contributory factor was that the new high-powered transmitter, which was to make the voice of Kettering heard across the USA, also blotted out all TV reception in Windmill Avenue.

I shall not attempt a chronological account of what followed, but merely pick out a few highlights from the next twenty five years. Don't forget that I was paid to teach Chemistry and that's what I did for most of the time, to the best of my ability and with great enjoyment. It has always been my belief that the processes of teaching and learning are interlinked. The day you stop learning, you may as well stop teaching. It is nothing to do with the rapidity with which the knowledge and understanding of Science progresses, the absolute necessity of keeping abreast of one's subject, the fact, particularly true in the 1970s, that a twenty-year-old Science degree is about as valid a qualification for teaching Sixth Forms as a swimming certificate. It's more a matter of not forgetting what the learning process is like, the elation, frustration and hard work involved. Keeping that part of the brain alive helps to keep open the channels of communication with one's pupils. It matters little what new knowledge or skills are gained, solid-state electronics, Greek, metalwork, computer programming.

Well, we certainly had our opportunities to learn, with the whole of Space at our fingertips. Blake would have understood: "To see the world in a grain of sand", – and the ionosphere in a whistling sound.

In 1966, the Americans had launched a series of weather satellites, transmitting pictures of cloud cover. I became obsessed with the idea of obtaining a picture of the British Isles. Let me stress here that at no time was a single penny of Education Committee money spent on Kettering Group equipment. Everything we used was our own property, either a gift or loan from some kindly person or organisation or, as a last resort, purchased by Geoff or myself. We needed a directional beam aerial, rather like a giant TV aerial. The late Vic Hartopp, of J-Beams, Northampton designed one for us and let us have it for the cost of the materials. We had a suitable receiver, on loan from the Radio and Space Research Station, Slough. I had just purchased a good-quality tape recorder. The decoder was built from the contents of the junk-box, plus some relatively inexpensive bits and pieces, a special valve being provided by a local Radio Amateur friend. The picture appeared, line by line, on the screen of a Physics Lab oscilloscope, to be photographed as a time exposure.

The only thing we lacked was an automatic aerial tracking system, which would keep the beam pointed at the satellite as it came over our horizon. We solved this one by putting the aerial on the roof of the Science block to be held by one of the tracking group. He was provided with a pair of headphones and instructed to point the aerial where the signal was loudest. The perfect servo-mechanism (Latin "servus", a slave). The first trial was on a drizzly afternoon after school. Complaints from the automatic tracking system that the rain was collecting on the aerial and running down his arms were ignored. Later, when a good signal had been recorded for a full six minutes or so, there were congratulations all round. We had completely forgotten the tracking system until there was a plaintive cry from the roof. "Can I come down yet? I think it's going to thunder."

Subsequently, a heavy equatorial mounting was made for us by Tom Welch, out of some scrap steel tubing. This was winched up to the roof of the main building one weekend. The roof of the main building in Windmill Avenue is an interesting place. It slopes down from the edges to the middle, so that rainwater can drain through the service shaft. Anyone keeping low down and close to the centre, particularly on the South, Wicksteed Park, side is completely invisible from the ground. A perfect site for the Mk II (non-complaining) aerial mount. I discovered, then, that it was also a perfect site for the assistant caretaker to do a spot of nude sunbathing. As far as I know, the tubular steel mount is still there.

Unfortunately, most of the early pictures consisted of boring old clouds. We had to wait until an absolutely cloudless day coincided with a suitable satellite pass which was not in lesson time. Eventually, we got a fuzzy but recognisable shot of the southern half of Britain. Faced with the alternatives of rebuilding the whole system to get better quality or doing something else, I decided to do something else. Nowadays, any school with £1,000 or so to spare can buy a complete system, giving good quality pictures at the press of a switch, but this was 1967, remember.

The activities of the Group took us to some interesting places, including a free dinner at the Savoy. The occasion was the Annual Dinner and Soirée of the Institute of Physics. Geoff and I and a couple of Sixth Formers were singing for our supper by staging a small demonstration of tracking techniques. I set off after School in my elderly estate-car, carrying the equipment and dinner-jacketed Sixth Formers. The car chose to break down in the centre lane in Whitehall. I had no option but to get out and fix it (ignition lead) while traffic bore down on us every time the lights changed in Trafalgar Square. I was glad I had opted to take my dinner-jacket etc. and change there. I got some funny looks from the cloakroom attendant. I don't suppose the Gents' washroom at the Savoy has Swarfega available these days. It certainly hadn't then. The dinner was memorable, too.

''To he that hath, it shall be given unto him. . . .'' As soon as the Group caught the public eye, we were showered with gifts from admirers of the ''Schoolboy Boffins''. Geoff has mentioned the wonderful Racal communications receiver, but other items ranged from the useful to the bizarre. We gratefully accepted the large box of fizzy sweets called ''Space Dust'', but regretfully declined the generous offer, from one of the TV companies, of a life-sized papier maché mock-up of the Soyuz spacecraft. The computer microwave transmitter and receiver (on two four-foot racks) which had once formed part of a communications link, was surprisingly easy to convert to a Doppler radar set which, for a few entertaining lunchtimes, picked up the movements of cars, cycles and pedestrians on Windmill Avenue. That was about the only illegal activity which went on behind the drawn blinds of Physics A.

Quite apart from the publicity we were getting, we were both expert scroungers, with a wide circle of friends. I certainly ended up with the best-equipped Chemistry Lab of any school in the Midlands, with equipment that included an infra-red spectrophotometer and gas-liquid chromatograph, both past their first youth, but repaired, running and able to tell Stork from butter, as our lunch-time research group proved.

It wasn't all satellites, of course, as my previous sentence indicates. Twenty seven years of Radio Club on Thursday afternoons after school, for one thing. Not wishing to sound like Mr (silicon) Chips of Kettering, it gives me a lot of pleasure to think of the large number of ex-members who are now working in the electronics and communication industries. Only one anecdote here, but made public for the first time.

A small group had been working on a design for a very small short-range radio transmitter, with a lot of discussion as to how to cram the components into as small a space as possible. One morning, shortly afterwards, a fresh-faced youth appeared at the staffroom door, asking for his Form-master. He handed over an expensive-looking portable radio: ''Please Sir, would you look after this for me till lunch time? I've brought it to hear the cricket scores.''

The radio was duly placed in the staffroom. Morning break found the youth and other Club members huddled round a VHF receiver, trying to make sense of the babble of staffroom conversation emanating from the ''bug'' concealed inside the radio set.

School plays, with Evan Roberts and Ted Ward, were a delight. I wasn't involved in my first year at Kettering, but went to the *Taming of the Shrew* out of duty. I laughed till I ached, at a high-speed slapstick production which included custard pies. Thereafter, I provided sound and ''special effects'', from battery-operated red-hot pokers to coloured smoke, for both School and Hygram productions.

Youth-hostelling round the continent with Geoff, Ted Ward and assorted pupils had its moments. Counting heads through railway station barriers. I always seemed to be the one who went last, which was fair enough, because Geoff was the one who knew where we were supposed to be going, he had the tickets and I could scour the compartments for packets of sandwiches, cameras and the like, left behind by our charges. I suppose this is what led me to be in the rear half of a Belgian trolley-bus and trailer with six boys, no tickets and a conductor who only spoke Flemish. Geoff was in the front half with six more boys and all the tickets. He doesn't speak Flemish either.

Trying to buy nineteen bananas in Switzerland without knowing the German for nineteen (or banana) was good character training for me, just as buying their own lunches was for our charges. No one came to harm, although I remember the pupil who developed chest pains at the top of the Jungfraujoch (indigestion) and the one who, in Amsterdam, ''. . . met a very funny man in a café. He kept trying to buy me drinks. I think he was a sailor.'' (innocence).

These are only a few of the highlights, of course. One tends to forget the frustration, tedium, exhaustion, worry and personality clashes. Apart from marking all those yellow exercise books, I enjoyed it all.

Dr. Andrew Sims

Looking back at the ''cold war'' years, it is easy to see why the satellite tracking project achieved such recognition. The image was an appealing one; a small group of school boys led by two enthusiastic Science teachers seemed to be a thorn in the side of the mysterious and secretive Soviet space programme. Furthermore, tools of the trade consisted of surplus or borrowed radio receivers, cardboard ''calculators'' and simple pen and paper. Despite this, the Group's efforts were not amateurish; first public announcement of a new Soviet launch site at Plesetsk in 1966 and accurate prediction of the orbital decay of Cosmos 1402 (with its radioactive power supply) in 1983 are well known testimonies to the quality of Science carried out within the group.

Perhaps the greatest achievement of the ''Kettering Group'' as it became known, was its role in educating those pupils who took part. Perry had hit upon a technique for teaching Science which was quite different from the traditional ones practised in class. By encouraging pupils to look after their own mini-projects (in my case analysing tracking radar observations of Soviet ''Molniya'' communications satellites) techniques and tools of scientific research were learned by trial and error rather than by rote. Experimentation was encouraged; ''What happens if we do this?'' often led to more exciting results than merely following a prescriptive approach. In addition, the desire to explain our observations provoked a thirst for more knowledge of facts; after spending a year or so in the Group, most pupils had learned the basic principles of orbit theory and satellite technology to a standard far beyond A-level.

Of course, pupils were not initially attracted to the Group by some high-minded ideal that they were helping to pioneer a new learning technique, but instead were drawn by the Group's involvement in ''space'' (we had all grown up with vivid pictures of the Apollo programme) and by the intellectual challenge. But in joining we had, in effect, become members of an informal but highly motivated research team. In my experience, it is this aspect which has proved to be of greatest benefit to life after the Kettering Group; we were learning how to do research and, perhaps for the first time in our lives, were part of an academic team. Certainly there was an element of friendly competition between team members and we all hoped that our ''own'' satellite system would start to behave in an interesting manner.

By the time I joined in 1979, the Kettering Group had become internationally recognised and frequently attracted visits from journalists and television film crews. Generally, these came from abroad (especially the USA, Japan and Germany) and it is noteworthy that the British media showed far less interest. Whilst enjoying the attention, we quickly realised that many of our media visitors were primarily interested in presenting us as rather eccentric amateurs using Heath-Robinson style equipment. It is rather ironic that many organisations involved in today's space business are bristling with hi-tech equipment but often show less intuition and enthusiasm than the Kettering Group.

The ''cold war'' is over and details of the Russian space programme are widely available in the open literature and at airshows and trade fairs where launch and design capabilities are being actively marketed to western organisations. But the Kettering Group has endured, and remains active in spite of the closure of Kettering Boys School. Today, its educational role may have diminished but there are many ex-members whose careers have been strongly influenced by their experiences in the Kettering Group.

Sven Grahn

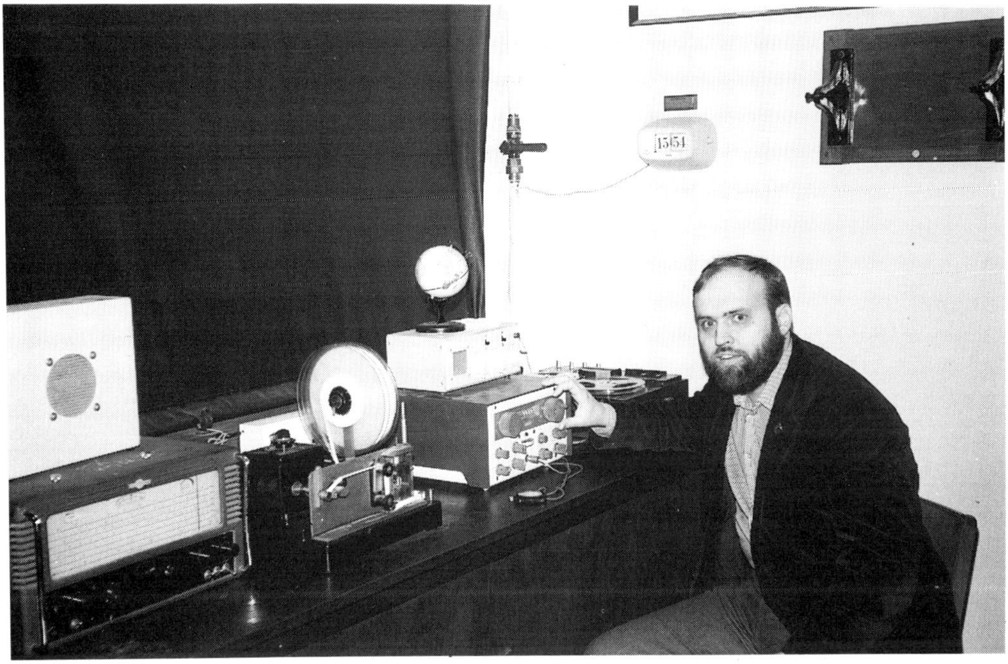

Sven Grahn with the tracking equipment. "Do more with less."

In November 1957, at the age of eleven, I caught the "space bug" when the Soviet Union launched "Lajka" into space. I then realised that human spaceflight and perhaps people travelling to the Moon would happen in my lifetime! My head spun with the thought: "I will live to see this happen." It may sound melodramatic, but from that day, I wanted to know all there is to know about Man's greatest adventure – breaking free from Earth and I wanted to participate in this great endeavour to whatever degree possible.

My first "hands-on" contact with space technology came in the summers of 1962-64 when I worked as a rocket assembly technician during the sounding rocket launchings from Northern Sweden in cooperation with NASA to investigate the so-called noctilucent clouds. This was a great experience for a teenager, but it ended when Sweden joined the European Space Research Organisation and the makeshift summer rocket base manned by grammar school and university students was abandoned in favour of professional operations at ESRO's new base in Kiruna in the northernmost corner of Sweden. I started studying for my Masters degree at the School of Engineering Physics at the Royal Institute of Technology in Stockholm. I was longing for a new "hands-on" connection with space technology.

During the early years of the space age there were often newspaper reports about radio amateurs picking up radio signals from Soviet space satellites – even hearing cosmonauts talk. If radio amateurs could pick up these shortwave signals (usually near 20 MHz) so could I! In October, 1964, the same month I started my courses at the Institute of Technology I bought a Lafayette HE-30 shortwave receiver paying, the (to me) astronomical sum of £30 at the local electronics shop. I was still living at home and I convinced my parents I needed to string copper wire antenna across to a concrete wall on the opposite side of our yard. The HE-30 lacked one crucial feature: an accurate tuning dial, and it lacked the standard remedy to this in the days before digitally tuned radios – the crystal calibrator. So, I really did not know exactly to which frequency the radio was tuned. I tried to find the exact frequency 20 000 kHz, but it was not until late 1965 that I was able to pick up the U.S. time-signal station WWV that transmits at exactly 10, 15 and 20 MHz. So, finally in late 1965, after a year of trying, I was able to set the dial to the most common Soviet satellite frequency on shortwaves, 19 995 kHz. I was quite busy studying, so I did not expend much systematic effort in trying to find signals from Soviet satellites. To be successful, I needed an element of luck.

On January 7th, 1966, I came home at 1.30 p.m. My father, uncharacteristically, was home from his work as purchasing manager of a newspaper. When I came through the door he said that the radio news an hour earlier had said that the radio observatory in Bochum in West Germany had announced that they had picked up signals from a newly-launched Soviet satellite. I switched on the HE-30, checked that it was tuned to slightly below 20 MHz and sat down at my desk with my textbooks. At 3 o' clock I heard something from the radio that I thought sounded just like a satellite ''beep-beep''. I recorded it, it faded out after 7 minutes, came back an hour and a half later and also the next day. I was pretty sure that this must be the Soviet satellite Kosmos 104 that the newspaper reported the next morning.

However, what good is it to finally hear signals from a satellite unless you can share the excitement with someone? I had read two articles in *FLIGHT International* about satellite tracking work done at the Kettering Grammar School. These people obviously would be able to positively identify my recordings as genuinely coming from the Kosmos satellite, I thought. So, I wrote to Geoff Perry at the address ''Kettering Grammar School, Kettering, England'', including a little tape reel with the recording of my signals. I got a prompt reply a week or so later recommending me to listen to Kosmos 105 that had just been launched into orbit and buying myself a good stop watch to get more accuracy into my reception reports. (I still have the old Omega stopwatch and I still use it while tracking satellites). The Spring of 1966 brought a long string of discoveries. Being a new enthusiastic tracker I was glued to the radio. I stumbled upon the beacon signals from the recovery capsule of the Kosmos satellites when they were landing on the steppes of Russia, while Geoff discovered Plesetsk. I was hooked – to satellite tracking and to the ''Kettering Group'' – and I still am 28½ years later.

Why is it so addictive to track satellites launched by a secretive society?

I think the attraction lies in the fact that you get a feeling of participating in great events, while being able to use scientific methods to deduce the characteristics of the satellites that we track and future twists and turns in the Soviet (nowadays a much less secretive Russian) space programme. Geoff was (and still is) very good at making it fun to use deductive logic and basic Physics and Maths. I also think that Geoff and Derek took a certain pride (which I share) in doing all these things with relatively simple means. Our radios and computing method were almost always at ''the trailing edge of technology'', but I think Geoff regarded this as yet another pedagogical advantage. The use of simple methods puts emphasis on the deductive and ''basic Physics'' part of it all. This was all the more evident to me after having visited Kettering in September of 1967 and the Physics Lab in (pardon me for spelling this out so explicitly) the awfully ugly edifice of the School. The few radios in the corner of the Lab really epitomised what I think should be the credo of every scientist or engineer: ''Do more with less''.

Dr. David R. Dean

Even before starting at Kettering Grammar School I knew that I wanted to participate in the exciting activities of the Satellite Tracking Group, which I had followed with interest for several years in the local press. I was enthusiastic about everything to do with space and space-travel and wanted desperately to become one of Geoff Perry's team. But once at the Grammar School I found out that one did not simply become a member of the Group, one had to wait to be asked, and whether this happened or not depended quite a lot on the results in the First Year Physics course, which Geoff taught. Fortunately, my performance was deemed satisfactory, and almost one year after joning K.G.S. I was asked to join the Group.

My first day, of what was to become five years of work with the Group, was June 30th, 1971. It was a dramatically exciting start as it was the day on which the three Soyuz 11 cosmonauts were killed while returning to earth after their successful mission. The telemetry signals received at Kettering Grammar School showed clearly the point at which they died and the activities of the Satellite Tracking Group again took a prominent place in the national and local press. This tragic event heralded a 27 month break in the Soviet manned space progamme and the beginning of a period in which the Group was only able to listen to unmanned satellites and try to decipher the telemetry signals we received.

I learned a tremendous amount in those five exciting years. Most significant was the scientific method: the structured, logical and methodological manner in which we patiently – sometimes for hours at a time – listened for the faint signals that would announce the satellite's arrival over the horizon. Meticulous timing and recording of the signals, measuring the lengths of the individual pieces of telemetry or decoding the Morse Code signals so often used by the Soviets at that time was often tedious, but was absolutely necessary to test our hypotheses on the meaning of the signals that we received. This was another aspect of scientific method that we learned. The insights were often quite amazing: we measured, for example, the rate at which film was being consumed and showed that this rate increased considerably during the Indian-Pakistan war of 1971. This experience was invaluable later when I pursued my Physics education at University.

Work in the Group had its excitement too, though. The Soviet manned flights resumed in September 1973 and enabled me to test my limited understanding of the Russian language, which I was studying for 'O' levels. We could clearly pick up discussions between cosmonauts and their earthbound colleagues. Once, on Soyuz 16, we heard the cosmonauts talking about stowing their equipment in preparation for re-entry. After a discussion within the Group – which included as a check the School's Russian teacher, Mr Brown, we decided to announce this unexpected end of the mission to the press. Sure enough, and to my relief and satisfaction, Soyuz 16 re-entered the atmosphere shortly afterwards.

The work had its responsibilities too: duty during the School holidays was common, and the older, more experienced members of the Group were responsible for teaching the younger members the tools of the trade. There was tremendous camaraderie in the Group, too. We regarded ourselves as something special – often to the annoyance of other pupils and sometimes teachers as well. Our work was an adventure with perks: meeting Neil Armstrong, appearing on TV and radio and in the press, participating in airshows and welcoming distinguished – and sometimes not so distinguished – visitors to the School, who wanted to meet Geoff and the Group and hear more about our exploits.

Twenty years on, I still look back on my time in the Satellite Tracking Group with immense pleasure: it was fun, hard work and a great learning experience. I respect and admire the efforts and achievements of Geoff Perry and Derek Slater in doing something that, to borrow an expression, led to Kettering Grammar School ''boldly going where no school had gone before.'' Through their efforts Kettering Grammar School achieved a reputation far beyond the county boundaries, and I am proud to have been part of that effort.

CHAPTER 25

Societies

"Pig Digs"

Sellick Norsworthy

One of John Steane's greatest contributions to the life of the Grammar School was his foundation of the Local History and Archaeology Society in 1964. Over a period of twelve years John's "Pig Digs", as they were affectionately called, gave many boys a fascinating insight into the world of archaeology. John maintained the enthusiasm throughout by engaging high quality speakers, including the legendary Sir Mortimer Wheeler, and arranging trips to important archaeological sites. So successful was his work, that no fewer than seven old boys, namely Brian Dix, Paul Stamper, Robert Croft, Bob Carr, Steve Dunmore, Roger Walker and Steve Maylin, all became professional archaeologists. Brian Dix is now the Head of Northamptonshire's Archaeological Unit. Another active member of the Society chose a slightly different path but has, nonetheless, achieved international recognition in his field. Peter Crane is now Professor in the Department of Geophysical Sciences at the University of Chicago and in 1993 was awarded the Charles Schuchert Prize of the Paleontological Society. In his response Peter acknowledged his debt to "two extraordinary teachers – John Steane, an archaeologist, and Tony Simmons, a forester."

The Society concentrated on research, rescue operations, recording the locations of archaeological sites threatened with destruction, excavating them and publishing its findings. Four Romano-British sites were excavated within Kettering. At North Park Drive Roman remains were found in trenches 2½-3 feet below the present surface. These included pottery of the first century from Gaul and pottery from Water Neston near Peterborough. Iron Age pottery was also discovered, the first evidence of this period ever to be found in Kettering. Also found were two fourth century bronze rings and four fourth century Roman coins. The excavation in Mitchell Street suggested that there had been an early Iron Age settlement in north Kettering and that the Roman occupation had begun in the second half of the second century and ended in the fourth century.

The deserted medieval village at Lyveden, discovered in 1965, was excavated over several seasons by senior boys acting as trowellers, barrowers,

John Steane at the Lyveden "dig."

surveyors, draughtsmen, pottery experts, photographers and site supervisors. The Lyveden excavations were published in the Journals of the Northamptonshire Museums and in the national journal, *Medieval Archaeology*. In the Spring of 1968 a potter's workshop was uncovered, only the second to be found in the Medieval English archaeology context. The excavations of 1972 produced the most extensive series of structural remains ever found in one season; they included a well preserved flue, a late fifteenth century tile kiln and a peasant longhouse from about 1400-1450.

One of the Society's most enterprising schemes was the building and firing of a replica medieval kiln in 1968-9. An article published in the *Cytringanian* Magazine of 1969 describes what took place:

EXPERIMENTAL KILN PROJECT 1969

Perhaps the most enterprising scheme in 1968 of the Society, was the firing of a kiln of medieval design. It began in March, when the foundations, in the form of a 3ft. square of depth 2ft. were sunk into the ground. This was to take the circular, double flued pottery kiln, much resembling an igloo; on either side of this pit were dug two shallower stoke holes. Under the expert guidance of Mr Tyrrell a successful brick mould was evolved, trapezium shaped. With clay dredged from the Ise Brook by the School Scout troop, about 80 bricks were manufactured. Construction went ahead rapidly, using a grey "grogged" body clay in a wet plastic state as a mortar. Two flue arches, of voussoir shaped bricks, were erected at each end to stoke up the fire, and a cylindrical pedestal was placed in the centre upon which to place the kiln bars, resembling the spokes of a wheel. The outer edges of the bars rested on a ledge set in the walls and a framework of supple willow branches bound together, for the dome, also rested on this ledge. The dome made from red potter's clay was only 4″ thick, whereas the walls were on average 7″ wide and the overall diameter of the structure was 3 ft. Meanwhile a quantity of yellow Lyveden clay had been left to soak for 7 days, was filtered, and left to dry to a plastic state. Several moulded and thrown pots were made from the ''ungrogged'' clay and placed on the kiln bars by one of the boys succumbing to the wishes of the majority, by crawling into the muddy interior. Also a number of Staffordshire cones, ranging from 700 to 1,000 degrees C. were placed on the bars to indicate the temperature, and were viewed through an asbestos pipe let into the dome. Firing began at 1.45 p.m. on Friday 24th May, using wood offcuts with fires going at each end. However, after a while, minor explosions were occurring due to pockets of air expanding. Also, firing was going too quickly but despite closing the N. flue, the roof of the firing chamber collapsed at midnight, and so, after making things safe, all retired to the base of the operation, the pavilion, for a well-earned rest. But despite all our misgivings 85% of the wares were on the whole quite well fired, and it is intended to attempt another firing in the future.

So successful was the kiln, and the later experiments in making charcoal and the firing of three replica medieval iron smelting plants, that they were reported in *Country Life* in December 1970. In an article entitled *Enlivening the Past for Young Minds*, John Steane's philosophy of education was shrewdly identified:

''Archaeology draws upon many different skills and disciplines and touches in some way upon nearly every subject in the school curriculum; this makes it an ideal basis for the 'integrated studies' approach.''

John's legacy continued for several years after his departure through the work of Douglas Clinton, another enthusiastic Oxford graduate in History and Archaeology. From the mid 1960s to the mid 1980s few schools in the country could boast such a professionally run society.

Society ''Squash''

T. R. Watson

When I arrived at Kettering Grammar School in 1973 to take up a teaching post in the Mathematics Department, there were already a large number of flourishing Societies within the School, catering for boys' interests and inclinations. Their existence was actively encouraged by the Headmaster, Mr John Steane, whose philosophy of education had so enormously influenced the direction of the School, and had reinforced its respected reputation.

It was clear that through its Societies, the School had accomplished something very special; a philosophy akin to university life pervaded the atmosphere of the buildings. Sound academic work, exemplified in the often outstanding examination results, was complemented by the research and investigations initiated by the Societies, and this, coupled with the opportunities available in sports and Outdoor Pursuits, presented the pupils of K.G.S. with a fulfilling and rewarding agenda, which was an example to all those engaged in the education of young people.

In the Foreword to the *Society Squash 75* catalogue, Headmaster Steane wrote:

''A school is more than a community for learning; it is also a society in which its members can find opportunities for developing social and intellectual interests outside the normal curriculum.''

This philosophy was put into practice by the Headmaster through his interest in Archaeology. The Local History and Archaeological Society, which he formed at the School, was regularly engaged at the weekends visiting Museums, sites, and conducting excavations. It was quite a common sight on a Sunday afternoon to see the Headmaster, clad in waterproof clothing, climbing boots and the unbiquitous woolly hat (in school colours, of course) leading a party of similarly-clad boys from his house in the Headlands to the School's Minibus, to set off for an afternoon's ''dig''. A recollection by one of the Society members:

''I only ever heard the Headmaster swear once, and that was when we'd driven into a farmyard to get permission to go into the fields, and suddenly a great big Alsatian dog rushed out of the house, snarling and barking, and leapt up at the driver's window, which Mr Steane had partly opened. He was very startled, and fell backwards from the window, exclaiming, 'Bloody Hell!' ''.

The Societies, in the main, operated in isolation from each other, going about their business unhindered by external diversions, quietly and unobtrusively conducting their affairs, (all hall-marks of academics?). Occasionally they would confer with another group if their proposed visits happened at the same time. Each Society was aware of the others in the School, but seemingly preferred to work independently. And, of course, there were some members of the School who, for one reason or another, did not belong to a Society at all.

It was to counteract these two facts that the idea of a ''Squash'' came into being. Initially, it was to give an opportunity to each Society to demonstrate to the rest of the School what were its aims, aspirations and achievements, and to offer to those pupils whose interest was aroused in these activities, the chance to become new members. The secretaries of all the Societies in the School were invited to lunch-time meetings in B10, and all the forthcoming suggestions and ideas were discussed at length.

Finally, it was decided that to avoid disruption (academic work at that time had priority over everything), the venue for the ''Squash'' would be under the balcony in the Hall – thus giving a literal meaning to the word! Each Society would have its own display area and would man its stall with two or three members, who would demonstrate the activities of the group, and enlist new recruits. The whole atmosphere was to be like a bazaar, with all the Societies vying with each other to attract new customers. Any legal method to achieve this was allowed, ranging from competitions and quizzes, to crosswords and discounts at local stores. A competition prize for the most eye-catching slogan was also offered, and was won in the 1974 ''Squash'' by the Railway Society – ''You're on the right lines with the Railway Club''.

Contrary to expectations, the enthusiasm generated by these ideas was enormous. For weeks prior to the date of the ''Squash'', it was the talking point of the School. Society members were threatened with dire consequences if they divulged to outsiders even the merest hint of what their group was planning, and spies were enlisted by some Societies in an attempt to discover what others were preparing. But it was all done in a spirit of keen and serious competition, which helped all the Societies prepare their exhibitions carefully, and finely-tune their demonstrations to the nth degree.

The first ''Squash'' was held in 1974 and was a great success. It achieved its aims of introducing the work of the Societies to the School in general, and also encouraged many boys to join in the activities of various groups. It was determined to repeat the exercise each year, so that new boys could see at first hand what was going on in the School. It was also decided that parents should be invited to attend the next ''Squash'', which took place in October 1975.

For this presentation, a catalogue was prepared, giving details of all the Societies who were exhibiting. An addition in 1975 was the Sailing Club, whose Mirror dinghy No. 12586 was fitted with great difficulty into the hall, after being transported from Cransley Reservoir on a trailer, courtesy of Jonathon Austin's father. Another proud exhibit was at the Angling Society's display. It was of a large pike, mounted in a glass case. After many attempts by members of the School to discover who from the Society had caught it, it was finally admitted that the specimen had been borrowed from a local fish and chip shop! Anglers!

The ''Squash'' was well attended by boys and parents alike, and it was most refreshing from an organiser's point of view to witness so many people crowded together in the Hall, craning their necks to listen to an exposition from, say a budding archaeologist, describing an excavation at Lyveden, where ''ample evidence remained for us to reconstruct life on the farmstead about 1450'', or to hear a member of the newly-formed Astronomical Society relating how members ''witnessed a nova in the constellation of Cygnus, a phenomenon which lasted only a few days, but it was possible to make magnitude comparisons with the surrounding stars''.

A most impressive feature of the two ''Squashes'' was the depth of knowledge exhibited by the boys themselves, in relation to their specialist fields. They could talk at length and in perceptive detail about their subject and its relation to other spheres of knowledge. The designers of today's National Curriculum could have modelled their ''Extended Coursework'' requirements on the work which was being done voluntarily by the staff and boys of Kettering Grammar School twenty years ago.;

SCHOOL SOCIETIES – 1975

Slot Car Racing Club
Power Model Club
Wargames Society
Music Society
Satellite Tracking Group
Sailing Club
Philatelic Society
Natural History Society
School Bookshop
Radio and Electronics Club
Camping Club
Games Society
Aeronautical Club
Local History and Archaeological Society
Railway Club
Table Tennis Club
Council for Education in World Citizenship
Debating Society
Govilon
Film Society
Motor Cycle Club
Badminton Club
Astronomical Society
Junior Chemistry Club
Angling Club
Meteorological Society

The Meteorological Society

T. R. Watson

It seemed that I had scarcely set foot inside Kettering Grammar School in 1973, as a new member of staff, when I was approached by a Sixth-Former, Guy Dix, who informed me that he was the secretary of the Meteorological Society, and that the group was looking for a new Master-in-Charge, and would I be interested in fulfilling that role, please sir?

I was honoured by this diffident invitation, for the reputation of the K.G.S. Met. Soc., under the one-time leadership of Mr Russell Gladden, was renowned locally, through its daily weather readings, which were published in the *Evening Telegraph.* Weather observations had been made by the School, certainly since the 1940s, and probably long before that (remember the screen in front of the Grammar/High School buildings in Bowling Green Road?) and the records were made available to anyone who had need of them. The rainfall figures were sent monthly to the Meteorological Office in Bracknell, to form part of the national observations, and a duplicate copy of all the readings taken by the Society were lodged in the Reference Section of Kettering's Public Library. Headmaster Steane, in the Society "Squash" catalogue for 1975, wrote:

"The School is rightly famed for the work of its Societies which have engaged in long-term research projects: in space, in weather, and in archaeology. The continuity of support for these research projects has resulted in a valuable contribution to knowledge in these three spheres."

When the School moved into new buildings in Windmill Avenue, the Meteorological Society built a new compound to house all its equipment and instruments. Its construction and siting had to conform strictly with the regulations laid down by the Met. Office for the establishment of an official compound, and these regulations were followed to the letter, as the Society was desirous of becoming a full climatological station, which meant that all the readings would be accepted by the Met. Office, not just the rainfall figures. The compound was given official approval by the Met. Office, and the members were further encouraged by the siting, just outside the compound, of a new anemometer on a 20ft steel pole, a gift, I understand, from Messrs. Stewarts & Lloyds of Corby. A large concrete base was laid by Messrs. T. E. Welch and D. J. I. Jones of the Handicraft Department of the School, who also made the support for the pole, which was hinged so that it could be lowered in case the anemometer should need servicing. The weather vane was also made in the Handicraft Department, and it is a tribute to the craftsmanship of all involved in the anemometer project that, even as I write, the pole and the vane are still in position, a sad and poignant reminder of a once flourishing Society, and of a once-renowned School.

Such was the esteem in which the School was held that, in September of 1973, it was visited by the Lord Bishop of Peterborough, the Right Reverend Douglas Feaver. The Meteorological Society was invited by the Headmaster to organise an exhibition of its work for the Lord Bishop, and this was done in the foyer. Members of the group were presented to His Lordship, who showed a keen and knowledgeable interest in the Society, and in his honour a special celebratory reading was taken, with the Lord Bishop accompanying the Headmaster and observers to the Compound to watch the measurements being taken. To mark the occasion, His Lordship was made an honorary member of the Society and received, as did all new members, a membership card duly signed, dated and stamped with the Society's official insignia.

Becoming a member of the Meteorological Society was a business not lightly undertaken. After an initial request from a new recruit, he would be taken by official members to the Compound, and trained in the use of the instruments and measures, shown how to take readings from the Barograph, and how to record all the details neatly and accurately in the Society's official Permanent Record Book. This training and observation of the new recruit took several weeks, until the officials responsible for his instruction were satisfied that he was competent and reliable. Then he had to face a written examination, which had been carefully devised by the Society, and designed to cover all aspects of climatological conditions. (It was rumoured that new recruits, about to take "the test" the following day, could recite in their sleep all the conditions set out in the Beaufort Scale!). . . . It is worthy of note that the training, setting of the written test and its marking, was undertaken by the members themselves, with only occasional reference to the Master-in-Charge. Mr Steane recognised the importance of this aspect of the Society's work:

"Many boys' membership of School Societies has generated interests which have lasted throughout their lives. The opportunities for senior boys to run such Societies is a valuable social education in itself".

The interest in the subject, which was encouraged by this enthusiastic training, resulted in an admirable commitment to the Society by the boys. Day in, day out, for every single day of the year, holidays and Christmas Day included, the duty members could be seen at 9.00 a.m. going to the Compound to make and meticulously record their observations of the local climatic conditions. I well remember visiting the Compound on Christmas mornings to exchange the Season's greetings with the intrepid observers, and to share mince pies with them as they carried out their duties.

The reputation of the K.G.S. Meteorological Society was held in high regard throughout the county, through the publication of the daily weather readings, and by articles written about the Society in the *Evening Telegraph*. Nonetheless, it came as somewhat of a surprise when we were asked by the local Cable Television Company to prepare a programme about the work of the Society, which could be televised and broadcast to the local community. Naturally, everyone was excited at the prospect of becoming a television celebrity, and much careful thought and preparation went into devising a script which would give as much coverage to as many members as possible. The event was recorded at the Compound, with boys answering questions about the Society, and demonstrating the use of the instruments. As with the visit of the Lord Bishop of Peterborough, the making of the programme was a most enjoyable experience, and gave to the group a rewarding sense of achievement and recognition.

The end of the Summer Term, 1976, was tinged with sadness for the School at the departure of Headmaster Steane. This was especially so for the members of the large number of School Societies which had received so much encouragement and inspiration from his leadership. The Meteorological Society felt that it had, through his departure, lost a strong supporter and worthy champion of its ideals. So, indeed, it was proved to be.

The end of the Society was quick and unexpected. One morning, the duty observers reported that some kind of building work was going on adjacent to the Compound. It transpired that a large greenhouse was being erected, and despite all protests and representations, that construction went ahead, and, at a stroke, invalidated future readings as an official weather station. This had a disastrous effect on the morale of the members, and was soon compounded by acts of vandalism to the site and the screen. Instruments were stolen and smashed, and the protective fencing of the Compound itself was irreparably damaged. As meteorologists, we might have observed that there was a wind blowing at that time, but from a previously unknown quarter; a "wind of change", that was not only to see the fall of the Meteorological Society, but to witness the demise of the School itself.

MEMBERS OF K.G.S. METEOROLOGICAL SOCIETY 1975

R. G. Dix
T. Clegg
P. Gormley
D. Peck
I. Coleman
R. Watson
G. Reeves-Smith
A. Johnson
E. Bottaci
A. Pawluk
M. Wright
S. Till
P. Sharman
P. Baynes
I. Andrews
I. Bailey
S. Smith

The Daily Round, 1950.
D. J. Roughton at the School's Stephenson Screen in Bowling Green Road.

CHAPTER 26

The Mural

The School buildings in Windmill Avenue are now owned by The Tresham Institute of Further and Higher Education. We include an explanation of the mural by the artist himself, for the benefit of future generations of students – or passers by. The poem was written by a K.B.S. student in the 1980s.

A Numbered Diagram by the Artist

WHAT'S IT ALL MEAN?

Maybe I can answer that question now, I heard it so often as I worked up aloft on the scaffolding with my two assistants.

Stated briefly, the Mural portrays the Coat-of-Arms and Industries of Kettering: but its most important function is to decorate the building, in the same way that a brooch decorates its wearer.

Accepting this you will then ask why have I designed it in this way. The answer is partly that this is my style of work, but mainly, by reason of the limitations and requirements of Mural design.

(a) It has to fit naturally into its setting and be in harmony with the building of which it is a part.

(b) By reason of this, it must appear as a balanced and even decoration, in order to preserve the Architectural Harmony.

(c) There are no ''Lazy'' spaces, each part has its purpose, fitting into the next and gaining its form, to a large extent, from the shapes that surround it, whilst retaining its own identity. This naturally results in some distortion of individual objects, so these have been deliberately simplified to avoid confusion.

The mural is composed of broken tiles: some glossy, some matt, some dimpled, some dappled, and also glass mosaic to supply the reds and brighter yellow and blues. We have tried to make each area exciting by mixing our surfaces and colours to create variety within the limits of individual forms.

Now let's look at the mural itself. On the top left:

We have a crown standing on its rim of ermine (1). The original Grammar School was founded during the reign of Elizabeth I, and this reminds us of that foundation. On the crown are crosses and this same cross you will find in the centre of the Coat-of-Arms of Kettering. Beneath the crown and moving across there is:

The Griffin (2) with his wings outstretched and straight from the Coat-of-Arms except that his upper wing suddenly changes into coat sleeves (3) illustrating the local tailoring industry, made clearer by the addition of the shears.

Underneath our Griffin's beak there are a pile of boxes (4) depicting the local carton manufacturers, and next across (5) the mouths and clappers of two bells, reminding us that Kettering once had a Bell Foundry.

Above the bells is the Hide from the Coat-of-Arms (6), and over this three wheels (7) for the Printing Industry, printing Braille (8) and Tickets (9). Between these we find Flames (10) from the Coat-of-Arms and indicating the Ironstone furnaces. Alongside, and still moving to the right, are two Martins on ''Fountain Ground'' (11) taken from the Coat-of-Arms, and brought together for company.

Underneath them, the open upper of a boot (12) which I certainly could not omit, and which echoes the wing shape of the birds. Whilst right at the bottom, the shapes of Chains (13) leading round to Negroes in their white gowns (14). Although only one Negro appears on the Coat-of-Arms, I have used five, to remind us that the Baptist Missionary Society founded in Kettering, was largely responsible for the release of slaves. Hence our slaves wear their Baptismal gowns. Three wear earrings, and two hats and if you look carefully, you will see that they are not without features.

And what about the little motif in the bottom right-hand corner? Well, that's simple . . . 62 for the year, and between the numbers – a bud!

Kenneth Budd

MURAL

Christopher Kidman

A myriad of colours, shapes and sizes,
Each one chiselled and crafted
To contribute to the whole
Which is clearly visible
And meaningful to few.

The fragments do make sense
From a distance; see
How each constituent piece,
Alone seems worthless,
Proves invaluable.

This kaleidoscope construction took its identity
From its makers; they themselves were shaped
By their efforts, the recipients likewise moulded.
Thus three compounds grew from one structure.

Now it crumbles, its image splintering into confusion,
And those once affected whisper regret
As they recall the blurred vision from their past.

CHAPTER 27

School Plays

Stuart Horrocks

For more than a century Kettering Grammar School presented regular theatrical entertainment for the benefit of pupils, parents, staff and local citizens. Precisely when it started is unknown, but a reference in 1901 mentions twenty years of performances in the ''Schoolroom'' before moving to the Victoria Hall. There, Headmaster J. H. Gill and Miss Gill presented a mixed entertainment with two one-act plays, three orchestral pieces and a conversation. In the cast lists appear the names of many pupils later to become well known in the town, for example T. N. Bird, T. H. Palmer, Alf Bailey and B. E. Pledger (a pupil at the turn of the century and a master until after the Second World War).

By the First World War, the School had moved from Gold Street to new buildings in Bowling Green Road. For the first time there was a stage on-site. In 1916 the English play being studied for examination was *Macbeth* and it was proposed that the Fifth and Sixth Forms should give a recital to the rest of the School. As this progressed, it was considered that the work might be turned into a public performance. It was the start of a long association with these productions by the Headmaster, J. I. Scott. It also heralded the start of a long tradition of Shakespeare's plays being enacted with pupils operating both on and off-stage, with staff support.

As the sequence continued, more familiar names appeared on the programme, amongst them Roland Barlow, Guy Wilkes and H. E. Bates. Photographs of the day demonstrate a high standard of costume and scenery, these becoming more elaborate and with even more involvement of pupils in construction, decoration and shifting. There were occasional complaints about indiscipline among off-stage actors and stagehands with noise, especially along the balcony. Mr Scott sealed off the balcony during performances. This was particularly unfortunate for the lighting operators who worked there and who therefore had to prepare for two and a half hours isolation!

As the years unfolded, ladies of the High School Old Girls Dramatic Society were invited to take on some of the more taxing female roles. This led in

1924 to an historic development with the production of *A Midsummer Night's Dream.* It became a joint venture between the Grammar and High Schools. Mr Gash's scenery became an even greater matter of pride. Mr Curtis's orchestral band was supplanted by Miss Baskerville Butcher's orchestra of past and present pupils from both schools. The High School also took responsibility for the costumes. It was all an acclaimed success. Several hearts were temporarily broken. It was an experiment not repeated until 1947!

1927 saw the first production in the hands of C. W. (George) Godfrey, taking over from Mr Whitmore, an association which was to last until his retirement in 1956. F. G. (Bill) Ashby also made his first appearance on that programme, not as lighting director but as stage carpenter.

Two items about the 1928 production of *Henry V* stand out: the first being a stage appearance of B. A. E. Brading, the second a series of sketches of "a quarrelsome lot" – maybe the forerunner of John Tynan's cartoons.

What actually happened to the High School involvement from 1926-1947? It is noticeable that nearly all female parts were taken by former High School pupils who, in 1931, joined with Old Cytringanians to found formally the Hygram Players. In fact, this group had commenced productions in 1927.

The next innovation was the first play in Kettering to use an apron stage, for *The Knight of the Burning Pestle.* Reports of the School Play are often tolerant if not full of praise, but that for the 1935 production of *King Henry IV Part I* pronounced, "the courtiers, travellers, messengers, earls and lords were like Falstaff's applejohns, dry and wizened. They received everything in an extremely competent silence and indifference".

Richard III – *1936*

Next, in 1936, came *Richard III,* greatly acclaimed. Would anyone now recognise from the photograph the youthful John Martin, beautifully dressed and made up. Not surprisingly there were no productions at the start of World War Two, but commenced again with *Macbeth* in 1942. By 1945, Mr Godfrey had been joined as co-producer by Mr Tynan.

After the long break, 1947 saw the production of *Twelfth Night,* involving the High School again and this time the cooperation continued until the final musical. The sequence of Shakespearean productions was ended for a year with the return of the apron stage for *The Knight of the Burning Pestle,* Curly Curtis being required to smoke his clay pipe, thus choking Rosemary Gillett, Stuart Horrocks, the audience and himself. This was the last of John Tynan's productions, as he sadly died when his next was in rehearsal – dramatic to the end. He is fondly remembered, perhaps mainly for his thumb-nail cartoons indicating to each member of the cast how they should look, act and think.

In 1952 David Bishop and Ted Ward had joined the staff and George Godfrey as assistanst. Their enthusiasm added an Elizabethan stage to a strong production of *Romeo and Juliet.* David Barlow, a former pupil, who was by then a university lecturer, wrote the music (recorded especially by Munn and Felton's Brass Band) for *Julius Caesar* in the following year.
The School was fortunate to recruit Evan Roberts in 1954, who joined Messrs. Godfrey, Ward and Whitehead for *Hamlet,* followed in 1955 by *Henry IV Part I.* This was a thrilling time, George Godfrey appearing brilliantly as Falstaff in his own, and final School production, leaving others to follow on after responsibility for twenty three productions.

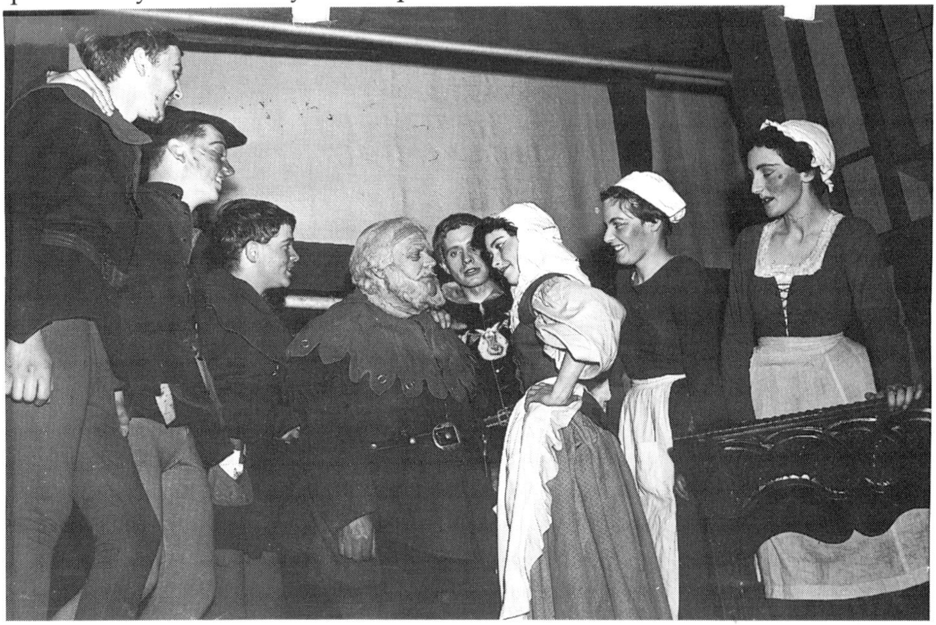

George Godfrey's farewell production, Henry IV, Part 1, *in which he appeared as Falstaff.*

For a school to transform Shakespeare in those days to the nineteenth century was a gigantic task, but in 1960 Messrs. Ward and Roberts did that with *Taming of the Shrew;* very enterprising. It also marked Bill Ashby's final production as lighting supremo, a stint going back to the 1930s.

The final play at Bowling Green Road was *King John* in 1961, followed by an ambitious *Troilus and Cressida* on a new stage, with ambitious sound and lighting effects at the new school in Windmill Avenue.

Although Shakespeare was selected for more years to come and Evan Roberts continued with his imaginative productions, there came changes and after *French Without Tears* and *The Ghost Train,* Evan bowed out as producer by appearing in his final production, *The Man Who Came to Dinner.*

73 Years of School Productions

1916 Macbeth
1918 The Tempest
1919 Twelfth Night
1920 Julius Caesar
1921 (Jan.) Richard II
(Dec.) The Merchant of Venice
1923 She Stoops to Conquer
1924 A Midsummer Night's Dream (with K.H.S.)
1926 The Rivals
1928 Henry V
1929 Hamlet
1930 The Taming of the Shrew
1931 The Knight of the Burning Pestle
1932 As You Like It
1933 King Henry IV (Part One)
1934 Twelfth Night
1937 King Richard III
1942 Macbeth
1943 Henry V
1944 The Merchant of Venice
1945 Hamlet
1946 Twelfth Night
1947 A Midsummer Night's Dream
1948 The Knight of the Burning Pestle
1949 The Tempest
1950 The Two Gentlemen of Verona and The Comedy of Errors
1951 Romeo and Juliet
1952 Much Ado About Nothing
1953 Julius Caesar
1954 Hamlet
1955 King Henry IV (Part One)
1956 King Henry VIII
1957 Coriolanus
1958 Othello
1959 Romeo and Juliet
1960 The Taming of the Shrew
1961 King John
1962 Troilus and Cressida
1963 Much Ado About Nothing
1964 Henry VI (Parts Two and Three)
1965 Love's Labours Lost
1966 A Midsummer Night's Dream
1967 The Rivals
1968 A Comedy of Errors
1969 An Italian Straw Hat
1970 The Beaux Stratagem
1971 The Importance of Being Earnest
1972 Arms and the Man
1973 Macbeth
1974 Hobson's Choice
1975 She Stoops to Conquer
1976 Charley's Aunt
1977 French Without Tears
1978 Arsenic and Old Lace
1979 The Ghost Train
1980 The Man Who Came to Dinner
1983 Oh What a lovely War
1984 Lark Rise to Candleford
1985 Godspell
1986 Bugsy Malone
1988 Oliver
1989 Wizard of Oz

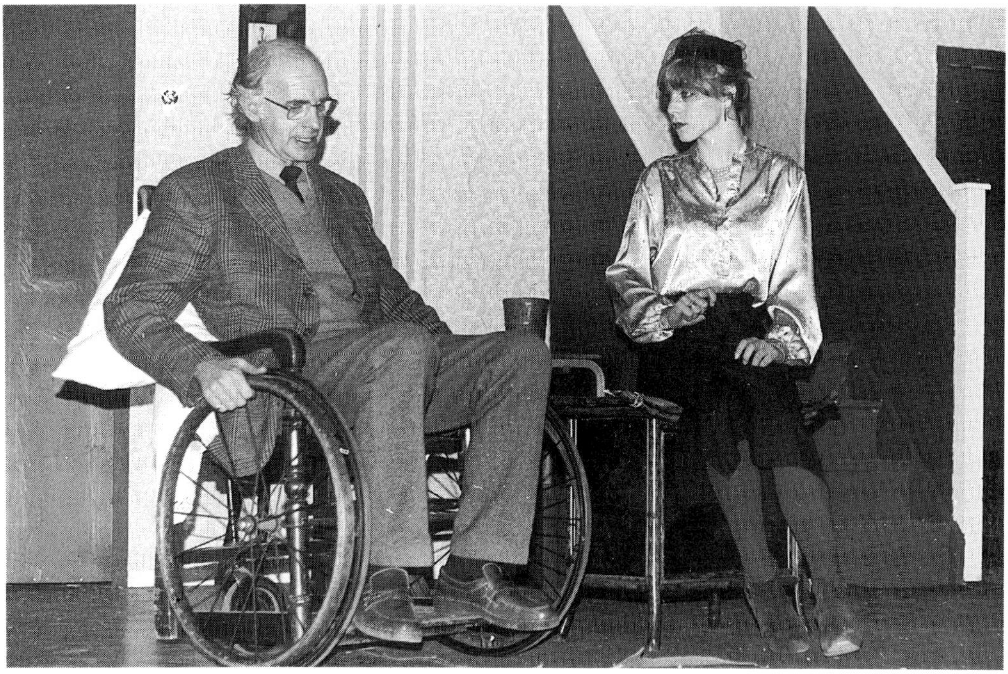

Evan Roberts appeared in his last production – The Man Who Came to Dinner – *in 1980. He had been involved with School drama for over 20 years.*

Godspell, *directed by David Hubery and Keith Tomlinson in 1985.*

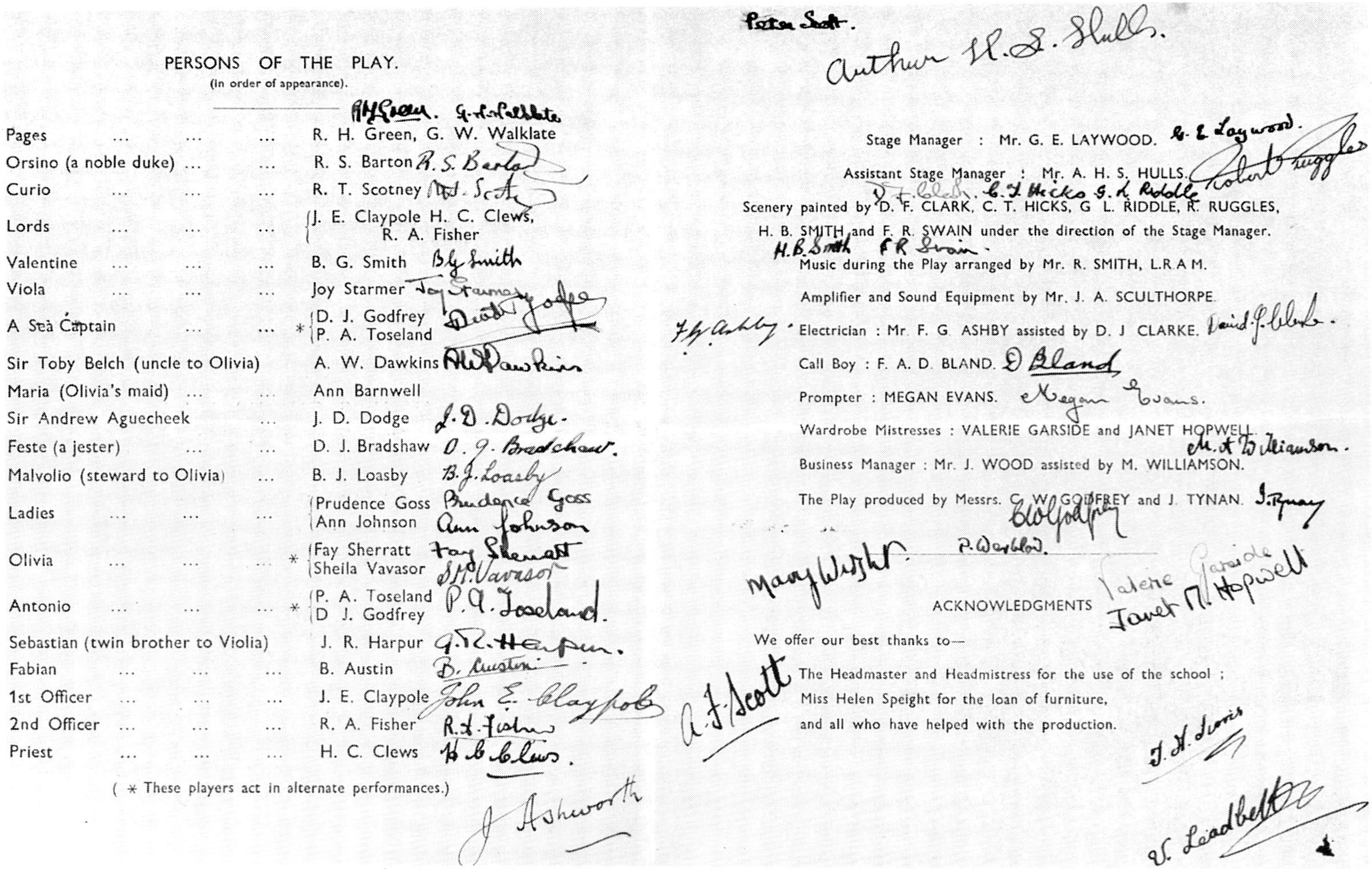

PERSONS OF THE PLAY.
(in order of appearance).

Pages	R. H. Green, G. W. Walklate
Orsino (a noble duke)	R. S. Barton
Curio	R. T. Scotney
Lords	J. E. Claypole H. C. Clews, R. A. Fisher
Valentine	B. G. Smith
Viola	Joy Starmer
A Sea Captain	* D. J. Godfrey / P. A. Toseland
Sir Toby Belch (uncle to Olivia)	A. W. Dawkins
Maria (Olivia's maid)	Ann Barnwell
Sir Andrew Aguecheek ...	J. D. Dodge
Feste (a jester)	D. J. Bradshaw
Malvolio (steward to Olivia) ...	B. J. Loasby
Ladies	Prudence Goss / Ann Johnson
Olivia	* Fay Sherratt / Sheila Vavasor
Antonio	* P. A. Toseland / D. J. Godfrey
Sebastian (twin brother to Violia)	J. R. Harpur
Fabian	B. Austin
1st Officer	J. E. Claypole
2nd Officer	R. A. Fisher
Priest	H. C. Clews

(* These players act in alternate performances.)

Stage Manager : Mr. G. E. LAYWOOD.

Assistant Stage Manager : Mr. A. H. S. HULLS.

Scenery painted by D. F. CLARK, C. T. HICKS, G. L. RIDDLE, R. RUGGLES, H. B. SMITH and F. R. SWAIN under the direction of the Stage Manager.

Music during the Play arranged by Mr. R. SMITH, L.R.A.M.

Amplifier and Sound Equipment by Mr. J. A. SCULTHORPE.

Electrician : Mr. F. G. ASHBY assisted by D. J. CLARKE.

Call Boy : F. A. D. BLAND.

Prompter : MEGAN EVANS.

Wardrobe Mistresses : VALERIE GARSIDE and JANET HOPWELL.

Business Manager : Mr. J. WOOD assisted by M. WILLIAMSON.

The Play produced by Messrs. C. W. GODFREY and J. TYNAN.

ACKNOWLEDGMENTS

We offer our best thanks to—

The Headmaster and Headmistress for the use of the school ;
Miss Helen Speight for the loan of furniture,
and all who have helped with the production.

The autographed programme for Twelfth Night – *1946*
"Methinks their very names shine still and bright." (Wordsworth).

Henry V *1928*

Twelfth Night *1946*
B. Loasby, A. Dawkins, A. Barnwell, D. Bradshaw, J. D. Dodge, B. Austin.

Hamlet *1945*
Messrs R. Smith and G. Laywood as Gravediggers.

The Boys of Godspell *1985*

Bugsy Malone *1986*

CHAPTER 28

Professional Retrospect

D. Bryn Williams

Upon the death of any man of reasonable distinction, there will gather together at his funeral a random assortment of people whose association with him arises from the various stages of his development as a person and from the various walks of the life he chose to live. There will be relatives, of course, both closely and more distantly connected; there will be friends from school and university with whom he has kept in touch; representatives from the profession or employment in which he last earned his living; members of the various clubs or societies where he spent his leisure hours; casual acquaintances met by chance on a train journey or in church or at a conference, and with whom Christmas cards have been exchanged ever since.

And at first, during the service, and at the graveside, they will remain together in those separate clusters, gaining comfort from the company of familiar faces and a shared sense of loss seen within a common context, and united only by the convention *Nil nisi bonum de mortuis* – say nothing save good of the dead.

Yet none of these groups will or can have known the whole man: the family, rightly, will be seen as the chief mourners, those whose loss is deepest and hardest to bear, but they will really have only such partial and subjective awareness of his working life as he has seen fit to relate to them, just as his friends and workmates will know of his pride in his children and his concern for his wife's health only at second hand.

It is only at the reception, as the various groups spread out and intermingle, and someone makes approaches to the odd singleton who seems to know no-one else there, that some more general awareness of the absent personality develops and it becomes possible to recall some anecdote which does not reflect entirely to the credit of the late lamented.

And so it is at the death of a school. There will be those at any gathering of its former members who have never met before, because there was no overlap in the dates of their attendance and perhaps nothing whatever in common in the course of their lives since, but who will find a shared memory in having been taught History (or, in the case of K.G.S., more probably Art) by the same man. There will be those whose chief memories are of the classroom, and academic success or failure; those whose memories lie more on the rugby field, or who glow with retrospective pride to remember that towering six over the pavilion, or that last final desperate sprint which captured the Cross-Country Cup; those who identify most closely with the School Play, or the Debating Society, or who can still close their eyes and repopulate the Bowling Green Road School hall with the Mock Trial of Napoleon Bonaparte. And, of course, those whose memories derive from the other side of the desk – the teachers who were the source of some of those legends still gleefully recounted by the taught. The chief mourners, by common consent, will be the Headmaster and staff at the time of the falling of the axe; the rest will group initially by age and mutual recognition, and subsequently by common cause.

And perhaps, at the end of the wake, they will between them, have arrived at some semblance of truth about their educational experience and will know more clearly whether they have been deluding themselves with a sentimental recreation of the comparative freedoms of childhood, or whether, as an institution, Kettering Grammar School has deserved to be mourned and held in remembrance. In his address to the Old Cytringanians annual dinner in January 1995, Hugh Moore began with the opening words of *A Tale of Two Cities:* "It was the best of times, it was the worst of times. . . ." and proceeded to apply this dichotomy to his memories of the School. In fact, he concluded, it was neither the best nor the worst of schools, but somewhere comfortably in between.

But just how good or bad was it? Whereabouts in the vast area of "in between" should we place the educational provision of K.G.S.? That is a question particularly relevant to my current interests. When I retire, at the end of 1995, from the Headship of a large grant maintained co-educational comprehensive school in Lincolnshire, I shall be free to devote myself full-time to what is now a hobby: research, conducted under the auspices of the Nottingham University School of Education, into the standards of state education between the Butler Education Act of 1944 and the Education Reform Act of 1988. Since this will take a minimum of two years, and since, like Hugh Moore, I joined the school in 1948, I shall have spent half a century in continuous association with the education service of this country and in a wide variety of roles and institutions.

I have taught in both primary and secondary sectors; and in Grammar, Bi-lateral, Secondary Modern and Comprehensive schools; I have attended or been otherwise associated with three universities; I am actively involved in the training of teachers for the PGCE qualification; and I am currently chairman of a committee which determines the proper positioning of 'A' level grade boundaries in English Literature for one of the examination boards.

I should, therefore, be as qualified as anybody to pronounce on the merits of K.G.S., and so, no doubt I am. The important thing, however, is that

I am no *more* qualified than anybody else. One of the things that has become obvious from my work on standards is that you cannot make legitimate observations on comparative performance unless you have verified that you are using the same system of measurement in each case. Now my personal experiences of K.G.S. were those of a boy, an adolescent, and a young man with a rather inflated valuation of his own intelligence; and however much I try to re-evaluate my memories in the light of subsequent experience and perhaps greater wisdom, I cannot actually change the eyes and emotions through which those memories were recorded. Those memories tell me that much of the teaching at K.G.S. was rather poor; dull, unimaginative, repetitive and boring, and occasionally downright incompetent: but punctuated by occasional flashes of insight, humour and sheer brilliance which remain in the mind as clearly today as at the moment they were stored there. English was always my own favourite subject, but I cannot remember any particular instance of being inspired or enlightened: rather of a constant sense of feeling that opportunities were being missed, that there was much more to be said, that my classmates were being deprived of the real joy of the subject, and, finally, not only that I could teach the subject better myself, but that I had a vocation to do so. It seems twisted, but because I have thoroughly enjoyed my life and my chosen career ever since, I have a debt to K.G.S. for pushing me in the right direction which should not go unacknowledged.

My second subject was History, largely because I was fortunate in encountering a genuine teacher in A. J. Cowell, some of whose classroom technique, those who remember it, might still recognise in my own. He seemed far more "laid-back" (though it was to be years before that word became available to describe him) than his colleagues, he could make and take a joke without worrying about his dignity, and simply because he never worried about it, without any way impairing his authority. Above all, he could convince his pupils that History was about real people in circumstances that he helped them to visualise – he made it come alive. His virtues as a teacher of History were emphasised for me by the man with whom he shared the teaching of my 'A' level classes in the subject – a man who, apart from his unquestionable knowledge of his subject, had perhaps the worst classroom method I have ever met. That knowledge he imparted by the unvarying technique of dictating notes, and not the content alone, but the way in which he required them to be set down. Can I be alone in recalling with a shudder that cold, harsh, flat voice saying "Three, B, Roman two, Underline twice"? But even from him I learned something – I can say, with absolute honesty, that I have never dictated a note to a class in my life! And to be fair, difficult though I find it, at least he praised and encouraged those who found material for his essays in sources other than his notes. He marked such essays with lengthy and helpful criticism, and on the one occasion on which he returned one of mine with a straight A grade and no comment at all, I found that circumstance as flattering as I have no doubt he meant it to be.

Latin I was always taught well, and have retained an enthusiasm for the subject ever since: there are few schools of any type in the state sector these days which continue to offer the subject, but the fact that one comprehensive in Lincolnshire still does so with some success is directly attributable to those who convinced me that it was an indispensable part of the true educational process: A. J. Cowell again, 'Gus' Phillips and 'Vici' Wood. French, on the other hand, I was taught appallingly badly, to the extent that I was totally illiterate in the language after four years. That I got an 'O' level pass a year later is a clear proof that E. J. Lindley, at least, could teach the subject, and deserves my lasting thanks. It wasn't a pass by much of a margin, but my place at Oxford depended on it; and as much of my happiness since has derived from the opportunities of my undergraduate days, I do well to remember that I did not get there by my own unaided efforts.

K.G.S., I suspect, did far more for some of its students than most of them will have realised at the time – which is not the same as saying that it did as much as it could or should have done.

In some respects, educational standards have improved out of all recognition since the Butler Education Act. For instance, K.G.S. results during my time there would make a very poor showing in the "League Tables" which parents are supposed to study so seriously today.

If we look at the results for the first few years after the introduction , in 1951, of the General Certificate of Education, Ordinary and Advanced levels, we find that the performance of Kettering Grammar School was remarkably consistent – indeed, in all aspects save one, the objective assessment has to be depressingly consistent. Every year, the School admitted around 90 boys and entered them five years later for the Ordinary level examination. And every year, about 55 of them obtained five or more passes, of whom no more than half stayed on into the Sixth Form to study 'A' levels. It is this kind of performance which illustrates more clearly than anything else could do the shortcomings of the selective system. Those 90 boys were the brightest pupils from the primary schools of a wide area, the successful competitors in a quite searching 11+ examination, identified as the most intelligent 20% of their age-group. Yet five years later, little more than half of them were achieving a standard of educational qualification now recognised as within the competence of some 45% of the entire age-range. Good comprehensive schools today, up and down the country, expect half their pupils to obtain the equivalent of 5 'O' levels, while those selective schools which survive have explanations to make if their results show less than a 95% success rate. And, indeed, the only explanation which they can make is that which probably explains the K.G.S. performance in the 'fifties; the depressing effect upon those who have been selected for being clever of finding that, *by comparison with their new peer-group,* they are in fact below average. It doesn't matter whether you call your classes A, B and C or disguise them as P, Q and R, or Science, Modern and General; those who are to all intents and purposes in "the bottom set" will be aware of their inferiority, conclude that the school's whole function was designed for someone else, and cease to cooperate with it, even where cooperation is well within their abilities. It is the great strength of the comprehensive system that it is comparatively easy to motivate the top half or even three-quarters of a year group, which is why a good comprehensive school will always, in terms of academic results, out-perform the combined schools of a selective area; and it is the great weakness of the traditional selective system that, having sifted out the considerable majority for whom its approach and methodology is unsuited, it then so often proceeds to "switch off" a substantial proportion of those for whom those qualities were actually designed, by an insensitive approach, an inflexibility of standards, and a positive rubbing-in of comparative inferiority of intellect.

This weakness is not inevitable, and awareness can do much to mitigate the danger, but that K.G.S. was guilty of this approach during my time there, is unhappily a truth which cannot and should not be suppressed. I do not mean invariably, of course, but sufficiently frequently for it to be improbable that any contemporary of mine would be unable to recall instances of classmates being treated with sarcasm and derision when they had been obliged to reveal their failure to grasp what was going on in the lesson. Small wonder that so very few voluntarily admitted that a point had escaped them and asked for repetition or assistance, even of those members of staff who would, in fact, most probably have responded positively to such an appeal. It could and did happen: there is, indeed, in the Form Notes section of the 1953 School Magazine a friendly joke at the expense of one member of 5R who was given to confessing that he was "confoozed": but I suspect, as is usually the case, with decreasing frequency as the need increased. After all, the butt of that particular joke went on to pass four 'A' levels, two with distinction, and win a State Scholarship to University College, London. It is those with confidence in themselves who tend to be prepared to ask for help, not those who have had that confidence jeered out of them. In this respect, K.G.S. unquestionably betrayed some of its pupils year after year, and this will be one of the factors to explain why some of those who attended the School will not buy this book, nor read it, nor care a damn what any of those who contributed to it have to say.

But if there was an underclass which the school neglected and whose departure at the age of sixteen was scarcely noticed, there was at the other end of the spectrum an area which it unquestionably handled extremely well. Even allowing for the enormous change in the expectations of and opportunities afforded by society over the period I am describing; and bearing in mind that, in the 'fifties, a school leaver at sixteen with a handful of 'O' levels had a range of employment opportunities that his equivalent today would find incredible; I suspect that fewer people stayed on into the Sixth Form than could or should have done. But very few of those who did take that opportunity can have serious grounds for complaint – for here is the one aspect of the School's performance that must be called impressively rather than depressingly consistent. The School Magazines issued for the years 1949 to 1957 list a total of 122 university places gained, and of those no fewer than 46 were at Oxford or Cambridge. There was not one single year during that period in which no such place was obtained, and only three in which the School had to content itself with one; while on four separate occasions it notched up five or six. For a little-known provincial grammar school this is a staggering success rate; and it may help to put it into perspective if I recall that when I arrived at Christ Church, Oxford in 1956, only six of the 124 freshmen had not been taught at public or direct grant schools, and two of us were from K.G.S.!

I think that part of the explanation for that success lay in the atmosphere of culture which seemed to be part of the Sixth Form ethos, and which spread downwards to those members of lower year groups who were likely to be the Sixth-formers of the future, through the agency of the various clubs and societies which featured as regular and attractive features in the extra-curricular life of the School. Foremost, of course, was the Debating Society – the Literary, Dramatic and Debating Society to give its full and somewhat grandiose title – and its offshoot the Junior Debating Society. There was the Music Society; there was the annual School Play and the prospect, for enthusiasts of amateur dramatics, of continuation into the Hygram Players; there was the special freemasonry of the School library for those who spent their free time there – the only place in the School where it was possible to engage in conversation with members of the opposite sex, a not inconsiderable element of culture in an otherwise exclusively male society; there was a general encouragement to read, to think, to argue and to discover, reinforced in each successive edition of the School Magazine by letters from the universities, written by members of the previous year's Upper Sixth who had clearly made the transition to higher education with ease and satisfaction. I am reliant on my emotionally charged memories again for details, but they tell that life in the Sixth Form offered a surprising degree of liberalism for the period, and a degree of toleration of the individual together with opportunity for personal development and self-education that, in some respects, could still not be taken for granted today. I have few memories other than happy ones once I had entered the Sixth Form, and if the first five years at K.G.S. might unkindly be described as a kind of obstacle course on an officers' training exercise, for those who survived and surmounted it, the benefits of membership of the mess were real and tangible. I remain convinced that the School should have been doing far more than it did to encourage a higher proportion of students to stay on and share in those benefits, but I suppose it has to be conceded that if the Sixth Form had been larger and less élitist, it might also have lost some of its sense of comradeship and shared endeavour, and some of the success that went with it.

So where do I place Kettering Grammar School in the vast tract of ''in between''? I am no nearer an objective assessment now than when I started this train of reminiscent thought, but I am conscious that twice in recent months, and within my own school, an awareness of my schooldays was brought suddenly back to me before I knew anything of the *Cytringanian Farewell* project or had been asked to write this contribution for it. On the first occasion, one of my Art staff was called away from his class to deal with a sudden emergency, and I stood in for him until he could clear it up. On each table was a random assortment of cardboard boxes, which the class was supposed to be drawing as an exercise in perspective. Most of them were making a fairly hopeless mess of it, and I was searching, having absolutely no artistic ability at all, for words that might explain where they were going wrong, when I suddenly heard myself saying ''All upright lines are upright on all occasions''. And as rubbers were produced to remove supposed verticals that had been initially supplied at every kind of inappropriate angle, and as they were replaced by genuine verticals and the drawings at last took on some semblance of accuracy, I realised that the biggest joke on the K.G.S. staff and certainly its most enduringly eccentric member, had contrived to engrave upon my brain a useful and permanent truth. What more can any teacher hope to do?

The second incident was at the grand opening of our new half-million pound Science building by the Lord Lieutenant of the County, complete with sword – a formal, full-dress and somewhat pompous affair which thrilled the Governors for weeks in advance and gave every prospect of boring me rigid – until a few days before the event the Chairman of the Governing Body decided that the Head Boy and Girl should be involved: perhaps I could find an appropriate passage for the one to read while the other might be invited to present a bouquet to the Lord Lieutenant's lady? Instead, the Head Girl offered to write and deliver a speech for the occasion – a suggestion which I eagerly accepted. And at an appropriate moment in the proceedings, the speech was duly made. It was urbane, witty, literary, intellectual, relevant, and delivered with genuine authority – with a real social message for scientists and just the tiniest hint of mockery for the formality of the proceedings.

In short, it was a very good speech indeed, and many of the audience were staggered that a seventeen-year-old was capable of that degree of sophistication. But I wasn't, because as she spoke I was suddenly conscious of other voices behind hers; voices of equal skill that I used to take for granted but had forgotten for years: of 'Taffy' Hebron, David Palmer, Stuart Horrocks, Michael Hurst, Brian Short, Don Dale-Jones, Michael Taylor, Fraser Gold and many others; and I realised how many years it had been since I had last heard a Sixth-former speak so eloquently, and effectively. In that respect, at least, education has gone backwards – and mine was privileged!

So, at the last, I will make no attempt at a final objective assessment. Instead, as Hugh Moore began his address with the opening words of Dickens' *A Tale of Two Cities,* I will end this retrospect with the final words from Hardy's *The Woodlanders* – the lament of Marty South over Giles Winterborne, and as fitting words as any for my farewell to K.G.S.:

". . .no, no, I never can forget 'ee, for you was a good man and did good things".

CHAPTER 29

Vox-Pop: 1973-1980

(Questions devised by E. H. Gormley)

Name: Martin Dawkins.

What is your life like now? I am a military test pilot, working for the Ministry of Defence. I am married and live in a small village in Dorset.

School Career: The School grey man. Prefect.

School nickname: 'Penguin' or 'Dawks'. There was another 'Dawkins' in the School. I was the soft one.

Your happiest moment: Receiving my A-Level results in the School office. They allowed me to go to university.

Your worst moment: I was close to a road traffic accident in which a pupil from the School died.

How would you describe your schooldays? Happy. I enjoyed the experiences and met people whom I will remember for life.

Have you anything to confess? Unfortunately, no.

How would you like to be remembered by classmates? To be remembered would be nice.

How do you think you are remembered? Martin who?

Which teacher made the biggest impression on you? Geoff Perry: a man larger than life, who had tremendous enthusiasms. He made the science world interesting, even if I always felt unintelligent as everything seemed so simple to him.

What do you think of your schooldays now? Great days of carefree fun (it's human nature to forget any bad times). I rate my years in the Sixth Form amongst the best in my life. Only after leaving do you realise how much you owe to the people who taught you. I am proud to have been a pupil at the School.

Name: Eddie Gormley.

What is your life like now? I am co-director in a Public Relations Agency that specialises in producing publications. I am married, own a dog and live in Coventry.

School career: Kirby House Captain. Occasional School team footballer. As a prefect I was given the feared bike shed run with Paul Collins.
School nicknames: The rebel without a hairdryer. Deadwood.
Your happiest moment: Ringing Mrs Perkins from a building site to get my A-Level results.
Your worst moment: My one detention in the third year. I was something of a swot, and news of my dishonour seemed to spread like wildfire.
How would you describe your schooldays? Generally happy. Two years in the Sixth Form were among the best in my life – parties, no major life worries, and we discovered that there were girls at the High School.
Have you anything to confess? I gave up football to play tennis in the Sixth Form. After 'Dixie' Dean took the register, I would bunk off to see my girlfriend who lived near to the courts.
How would you like to be remembered by classmates? I'm not worried about being remembered.
How do you think you are remembered by classmates? Scruffy bastard who had too much to say for himself.
Which teacher made the biggest impression on you? Brian Slough. He talked about Shakespeare's characters as though they were people you would meet in the pub. As a result of his enthusiasm, I studied English rather than modern languages at college and avoided becoming a faceless Euro-crat.
What do you think of your schooldays now? I attended one of the last Old Cyts dinners before the School closed. Geoff Perry reminded us that K.G.S. pupils had fought in every war since the Battle of Naseby. It was the first time I felt proud of my schooldays as well as happy about them.

Name: Andrew Mitchell.
What is your life like now? Quiet and that's how I like it. I teach History and Politics at Basingstoke College and write on historical topics. I will shortly be getting married to Kerry . . . another historian.
School Career: Member of Dene House. Member of the School cricket team in the second and third years. I was very surprised to be made Head Boy in the Sixth Form because I had no sporting prowess whatsoever and there were many others who had more impressive "leader of men" credentials.
School nicknames: 'Mitch'. Others I can't repeat in polite company.
Your happiest moment: Knowing, after A Levels, that I could pursue History at university. It also meant a lot that my friends at School all had the same option to go to college.
Your worst moment: Dropping the catch that would have ensured victory against Wellingborough School cricket team in my third year. No one

talked to me afterwards. Getting very, very drunk trying to match Bernie Goodman pint for pint after an end of term game of tennis.

How would you describe your schooldays? Happy and contented. I was a conscientious student and spent most of my time reading, fishing and making models. A complete anorak in fact!

Have you anything to confess? As a second year, I would regularly miss Technical Drawing with John 'General' Jackson because he always made us draw the same cylinder each week. I felt guilty about sagging off but I couldn't see the point of attending.

How would you like to be remembered? Posterity doesn't bother me.

How do you think you are remembered? As the boy who dropped that catch.

Which teacher made the biggest impression on you? I was taught by some of the worst and best teachers at K.G.S. and the difference between them was astounding. Sellick Norsworthy's enthusiasm and commitment to History teaching initially fired my interest in the subject and his advice and help thereafter has been invaluable.

What do you think of your schooldays now? Thanks to the efforts of Sellick, Brian Slough and Bob Evans, I left as an eighteen-year-old, mentally equipped to do something useful. My strongest friendships were forged at the School and survive to this day.

CHAPTER 30

Reflections on a Distant Prospect of Kettering Boys School

Chris Kidman

As my parents live quite close to the Boys School building, whenever I visit Kettering I invariably cast my glance at some point over the Barton Road gate towards the School field and that distinctive edifice, with its stopped clock and its rows of glass, an architectural testimony to the era in which it was built. The rooms behind the panes seem permanently grey now, but in my mind every one of them holds a cacophony of colours, images and memories which are the legacy of my secondary education.

With the passage of time, the precise details of events which seemed to be so crucial and interminable as they happened, flow inexorably into the depths of the long-term memory, stored for any occasion on which I might find myself in the company of my schoolday peers, reminiscing on the actions and characters of those times.

More easily recalled is a series of snapshot images, trickling steadily from the mind like droplets from a leaking tap: meeting up with friends from primary school on the first day; the whole class lined up to be slippered by the P.E. teacher, unable to get attention for more than a second and unwilling to wait any longer; the whole class in uproar as the Physics teacher steadfastly refuses to open any windows until he is convinced that the contents of a jar of hydrogen sulphide, festering unannounced at the back of the lab since break, have diffused to every part of the room; dodging the snowballs aimed at the Sixth-formers in the tuck shop as we head for the warmth of winter lessons; and the creak of the invigilator's shoes on the polished floor of the exam hall as we sweat our way through the paper. Thus seven years of schooling are swallowed in a few arbitrary gulps.

There are, of course, many other images, but I would rather not exhaust the supply in this piece at the risk of flooding the reader's attention with my own self-indulgence. After all, school memories are unique to the individual, and we could all, given the opportunity, pour out a stream of humorous, frightening or important incidents from our teenage years. What is worth noting, however, is that the staff, lessons and friendships of my years at Kettering Boys School played a great part in shaping my future, not

K.B.S./K.G.S. Sixth Forms, 1985-86.
A particularly talented group of young people.

only in terms of my academic success but also in the formation of my character; I would suggest that it is similar for every former pupil of the School.

As a teacher myself, I am aware that the same could be said of any school by its ex-pupils. One of the great frustrations of education, and yet paradoxically one of its rewards, is the realisation that students only really appreciate the benefits of their school retrospectively, long after they have left behind their complaints about the injustices of their teachers and of their workload.

And so I, too, now look back wistfully upon the buildings and fields of the Boys School, and feel that curious sense of satisfaction at having survived and, I dare now admit, enjoyed my years there. Its closure is, for me, another symptom of the changes which have swept Kettering since I headed off to university eight years ago. My attachments to the School and the town are now greatly weakened by time and distance; yet I shall always retain much affection for the town in which I grew up, and for the School in which my capacity to enjoy life and learning was nurtured.

CHAPTER 31

Kettering Boys School

Personal reflections by Tom Bowker, Headmaster 1976-1989

SPLIT SITE

1. Stamford Road School links with Kettering Grammar School.

In September 1976 Kettering Grammar School was replaced by Kettering Boys School in the official County Council list. The School was still made up of selected pupils apart from the first contingent of boys transferred from the former secondary modern school in Stamford Road. These boys transferred into the third year and so rejoined their peers from whom they had been separated by selection at "11 plus". At the same time the new first year of the comprehensive school started their secondary experience at Stamford Road.

This gave each school not only an unnatural profile but also an unusual mix of pupils. The psychological effect of boys being transferred to the institution from which they had been barred two years earlier gave us some concern. The numbers involved in the first transfer were about 120, thus doubling the size of the third year.

Those who had been interviewed for the Headship of this School in May 1976 were informed that there would in due course be six, six-form entry comprehensive schools in Kettering. By November 1976 the estimate had been reduced to five-form entry. This made it impossible to have the new Design block at Windmill Avenue completed as planned. When the new comprehensive third year boys were asked what they wished to study in the fourth year, thirty boys suggested Cookery, an option already eliminated by the reduction in the new facilities.

Because of similar uncertainties about the future the essential upgrading of Library, Office, Careers and Music rooms to serve the new situation had to wait six years until 1982, when the position had been clarified.

The challenge for the Headmaster and staff in the new situation was a complex one; they were committed to providing the full Grammar School curriculum for all those to whom it had been promised, but at the same time developing a comprehensive programme for the new first and third year boys.

T. A. Bowker presents retirement presents to R. A. Rattley and J. K. Mandale, 1987.

J. M. I. Scott presents the J. I. Scott Award to Andrew Corvesor, 1988.

This took a great deal of time, consultation and thought. Visits were made by departmental staff to other experienced comprehensive schools to see what might appropriately be adopted.

The Headmaster of the Lower School was in the complementary position, with his remaining older pupils, and the new mix of a comprehensive first year. The new Head at Windmill Avenue had responsibility for the curriculum at both schools, but was in partnership with the Head at Stamford Road. This itself could have been a complete disaster if it had not been for the willing cooperation of Alan Rosser.

The pressure on the staff soon began to tell. It had been decided that it would never be appropriate for pupils to move between the two sites, and that therefore teachers would commute, where necessary, the two miles for the next lesson. Problems of this arrangement could easily be imagined, especially when the growing realisation of pupils had its effect:

> ''Lesson 3, Mr X has to come down from Windmill Avenue, so we're free for another five minutes!'' For the teacher, the effect of this delay was hard to counter, and it became cumulatively more wearing as term progressed.

Nevertheless we achieved a great deal of continuity for both academic and non-academic pupils. The new Head still had to deal with sixty UCCA forms for university entry, and with many applications for apprenticeships. Then there were the celebrations of success as a very powerful wave of rugby players passed through the School. A number of these also represented the county. The School Play took place as usual each year, under Evan Roberts' experienced direction. Geoff Perry and his boys continued to track satellites until he retired from the School in the mid-'eighties. Gordon ('Jock') Brown unfailingly led the annual expedition to the Cairngorms, organised two expeditions to Canada, and was able to expand his programme of Outdoor Pursuits into the curriculum.

The two Deputy Heads John ('Tarzan') Cowell, and Ken ('Chippy') Mandale, with years of experience of Kettering boys, continued through thick and thin to organise and counsel the guinea pigs of the new system.

2. The new Montagu School starts.

In 1979 Alan Rosser and a number of staff went off to Weekley Glebe Road to inaugurate the new Montagu School. John Cowell had at first refused to believe that another school was necessary, or that it would be built! He was confounded, but in essence he was right to question; the need for more school spaces was temporary; an extra school was not needed.

By this time a number of new staff had been engaged at Windmill Avenue, but others knew that they were already appointed at a future date to join their colleagues at Montagu School. As time went on the number of pupils dropped as planned, at the Upper School, and the intakes were shared between the six schools now open in the Borough. One effect was the need to remove from Kettering Boys not only those staff already booked for Montagu School, but to demand of the School, a reduction of 11 or 12 teachers a year for three years. Inevitably, this involved those who were still able to look to other schools for their careers. The net result was to reduce the staff very largely to the older more senior staff whose experience had been mainly in the selective system. The History Department at one stage consisted entirely of the three former Heads of the History Department of the Central, Stamford Road, and Grammar Schools!

At this time the size of the School began to reduce, so that the six mobile classrooms which had been sited in the yard and on the edge of the playing field could be removed.

We had also reached the stage where most of those boys who had had to work through both systems of education had left. Inevitably the problems of discipline were greatest when the Fifth Year, with the usual proportion of disaffected sixteen year olds, was at its peak of 250 boys.

This was a size of group outside the experience of any of the Staff. The Year Heads especially had a heavy responsibility to keep their pupils on the right track. Obviously, too, among these boys were those whose criminal activities in the town brought them to the attention of the police. More visits from police, social workers and consequently more forms and references to be completed added to the bureaucratic load. This took time, not easily spared from the fundamental work of teaching and running the School.

The games of the School continued to change, as they did throughout the country. Cricket enthusiasts kept the game alive when other schools were beginning to waver. Both styles of football were also maintained, but there was a growing number of boys for whom the team game was less appropriate. Many of these were quite willing to match their muscles against a set of weights, or an exercise bicycle, in the pursuit of improved physical development.

3. Kettering Boys School: All in one place at last!

In 1983, when all the tedious development building work had been completed, and Stamford Road School had finally closed, Kettering Boys School was at last on one site. The staff, who had had a few years experience of what was now required, were at last in place. This was the stage for which we had been waiting and working. There should then have been a settled period in which all the inefficiencies and many of the hindrances would have disappeared.

Unfortunately, two unrelated developments made this another difficult time for Kettering schools. The first was that the government and the teacher unions decided to proceed on a collision course. Teacher cooperation, essential to the running of any school, was reduced and redefined. All extramural activities were under threat. All school meetings out of teaching time were

The programme cover for The Wizard of Oz, *drawn by Paul Holland (1988).* The Wizard *was one of a series of musicals produced in the 1980s.*

cancelled for over one year. Where staff at the Boys School were willing to continue to run school matches, other schools were not willing to provide the opposition. Nevertheless, the School had embarked on a series of Musical Plays, *O What a Lovely War, Lark Rise, Godspell,* etc. and they continued, in spite of various limits imposed by the unions. Cover for staff who were absent or ill was in some cases not available, and finally, walk-outs of staff for different periods on different days were arranged by the unions.

This period was not one of progress and development, but more a time of battening down the hatches and waiting for the storm to subside. It is a tribute to the staff who belonged to one of four different unions or to none, that personal relations did not deteriorate. Many features of school life were to disappear for ever in most schools. Duties at lunch time could no longer be required, and other arrangements had to be made. The cohesion of the school community was never the same again.

The second threatening development was the progressive reduction in the size of Primary School year groups.

4. Falling rolls and the "Alternative Approach"

What John Cowell had believed was now to come to pass, and the Area Education Officer began to hold meetings to consider the effect of the falling pupil numbers in the borough, which made the future of the six schools problematical. We had only just finished dealing with expansion when the next challenge was how to deal with falling rolls. Inevitably, in the changing climate, the suggestion from others was that the Boys and Girls Schools should merge. This was not the view of either of those Schools, and at that time their numbers were still being maintained. The question was: what would happen when the smaller year groups fed through from the Primary Schools?

With Mr Henley, the County Education Officer in the chair, many weary meetings were held, in which schemes were proposed, and rejected by those who would have been affected. At last, as he himself admitted, Mr Henley was provoked by Eileen Lake of Southfield School to "do something constructive". He proposed a novel and imaginative plan for the secondary schools of Kettering to work together in a consortium under a coordinator, who would be of equal status with the Headteachers. In order to operate this plan it was necessary for the County Council to vote for Kettering an extra budget of £100,000 per year. This was agreed for a period of three years in the first instance. Then the experience was to be evaluated and further decisions made.

The schools agreed to join in the plan, with varying degrees of enthusiasm. It required a good deal of extra committee work for all Departmental Heads, but it gave the opportunity to develop many new approaches to the curriculum. In particular it was a means of cross-fertilising the schools with the best ideas available in the area. A great deal of excellent development took place, and the final external evaluation of the plan was very approving of the work that the schools had done. It strongly disapproved of the withdrawal of the funds by the County Council at the end of the three years. The title of the scheme was "The Alternative Approach" and Tim Bartlett, who was appointed as coordinator, had many visitors from other areas. They were impressed by the idea and by the way in which it was being implemented.

With the end of this device to help schools to survive as comprehensives with smaller intakes (which would otherwise have caused closures), the writing was on the wall for the schools of Kettering. Another exhausting round of meetings was held, and further schemes of closure or amalgamation were discussed. The implementation of a merger of three schools: Henry Gotch, Southfield, and Kettering Boys, was finally stopped in its tracks by the successful application by Southfield to become one of the first batch of Grant Maintained Schools. It was then absolved from taking part in any further local discussions, and so the merger was stymied. As the County Education Officer declared, planning for the reduction of the schools of an area became impossible.

This was equally true of Corby.

A year before this final development had taken place I had told the Governors of the Boys School that I intended to implement my longstanding conviction that a Headmaster should not remain in post beyond the age of sixty. I therefore retired in April 1989.

In my first year in Kettering I had to preside over the celebrations for the Quatercentenary of the Grammar School. We had a type of pageant and were able to quote the original charter to the effect that Kettering, having many boys and youths, should be provided with a school for them. I believed that we could still offer what Queen Elizabeth had in mind. The national trend has seen to it that boys and girls should in most cases learn together. From Primary school to University, and not excluding the Public Schools, the choice is for coeducation. Most boys' schools have now closed or merged, but we know that many pupils both enjoyed and benefited from them.

Mr N. C. Barker and the Sixth Form, 1981-82.

CHAPTER 32

Closure

Michael Dean

''A change many of my generation regret is the loss of Kettering Boys School, successor to Kettering Grammar School which dated from Elizabethan times. Why it closed puzzles me, when by contrast the former High School carries on and flourishes as Southfield. A plucky rearguard action to save the school was taken to the High Court by father and son Alan and Stephen Kingsbury, but they lost. The school, which had declined from 800 boys to 120 because of uncertainty about its future, closed without ceremony at the end of the summer term 1993.''

So wrote the authoritative and indefatigable chronicler of twentieth-century Kettering, Tony Ireson, in the introduction to Book 4 of his *Old Kettering – A View from the 1930s* series.

The necessity for closure puzzled many people, yet the basic answer is included in Mr Ireson's quote; the School closed because it did not have enough pupils. Why it did not have enough pupils is a complex question that will never be answered satisfactorily. There will continue to be a variety of opinions on whom is to blame and there will continue to be argument about whether the High Court action could really be termed ''plucky''.

Schools need to be viable both educationally and financially. There is a strong correlation between the two but a school becomes educationally unviable before it is financially unviable. It is possible to run a poor school (with, for example, large classes and a lack of specialist teaching) on a small budget. Schools need to be larger now than in Mr Ireson's day, principally to support the amount of specialist teaching that is required today. This is particularly important at post-16. Although the school leaving age remains at 16, there has been a de facto raising of the education or training leaving age. A myriad of post-16 courses have evolved and it requires a large base of students to produce sufficient numbers to pay for a wide range of courses. Small schools simply cannot offer the variety of a large tertiary college, yet schools, partly due to generous funding and partly due to a desire to attract well qualified staff, want a share of the post-16 market. Kettering Boys School became too small to be educationally viable and its closure came as it approached financial non-viability.

Any analysis of the closure of Kettering Boys School needs to begin by looking at the overall situation in the town. The organisation and provision of secondary education within the Borough of Kettering has undergone several changes in the last twenty years.

In 1972 Kettering Grammar School was a four form entry (120 boys each year) selective school taking eleven-plus successes from what is basically today's Borough of Kettering. By then its catchment area had been considerably reduced; the Corby boys were long gone and the last Welford pupil left in 1972 and the last from Tansor went a year later. The area surrounding Kettering was served by a number of new comprehensive schools: Welford children went to Guilsborough; Walgrave boys to Moulton, though the brainiest youngsters of Weston by Welland still trekked to Windmill Avenue or Lewis Road.

Eleven-plus failures at that time had three choices: the mixed Church school, Bishop Stopford in its new building in the Headlands; the mixed secondary modern Henry Gotch; or one of the Secondary Schools – the Boys in Stamford Road and the Girls in Rockingham Road.

In the 'seventies selective schools were rapidly disappearing and it was no surprise when it was announced that Kettering, the last area of Northamptonshire to retain selection, would lose that distinction. In hindsight, it appears remarkable how little fuss was made. These days a furore is caused by something as trivial as a change in the entrance door at a library, yet the passing of the Grammar and High Schools passed with little mention.

The 1976 reorganisation involved the Grammar School merging with the Secondary Boys School as a split-site comprehensive school with nine form intake (270 boys each year). The first two years were taught at Stamford Road, whilst years 3 to 5 (this was just after ROSLA, the raising of the school leaving age to 16) and the Sixth Form were resident at Windmill Avenue. Teachers commuted, some more than others, at break times.

The High School and the Secondary Girls School were involved in a similar merger whilst Henry Gotch and Bishop Stopford were nominally unaffected. The new Latimer School was opened at this time and a school in the north of the town (Montagu) was promised. Indeed the Boys School Head, Alan Rosser, was to be the founding Head of Montagu and a number of teachers in the reorganised schools were promised posts when the School opened.

The building of Montagu would enable the Rockingham Road and Stamford Road sites to be closed and, according to the plans of the Education Committee, sold off as lucrative commercial sites, thus financing the construction of the north end school.

There was, prior to the reorganisation, a process of consultation which seemed to consist of an LEA employee visiting the Grammar School to tell the staff what was going to happen. A number of questions were asked; some may have been answered. A linguist asked why the Grammar School was not being amalgamated with the Secondary Girls School (and the High School with Stamford Road) in order to make a mixed comprehensive. The answer was straightforward: girls' toilets would have to be provided (and girls' craft rooms) and there was no money available for this – not even, presumably, from the sale of the Secondary School sites.

There was no opposition from the staff of the Grammar School. A couple, including John Steane, left whilst the majority stayed to meet the new challenge. The French department became the first commuters, travelling to Stamford Road the year before the merger, because there were no foreign language teachers at that school.

It would be untrue to say that the ensuing years were trouble-free. The Boys School was over-crowded and difficult to manage, since it was over-large and on two sites. The staff were too busy meeting the demands of integration to give any thought to the School's long-term future, though, we all believed, it would all be much better when we were on one site.

That would not happen until the north end school was built, though, even as it was being constructed, serious doubts were being cast on the necessity for the town to have an extra school. A political commitment had been made to build a school in that part of Kettering, but it would mean that the town would have too many secondary school places.

By 1983 the Northampton mandarins had cottoned on to this fact. They arranged a series of meetings in Kettering, putting over the message that there were too many schools and asking the people of Kettering what they would like done about it. No school volunteered to be closed. The thriving Church school was clearly not a candidate; Latimer and Montagu were too modern. One obvious candidate was the small and unpopular Henry Gotch, but the merger of the Boys and Girls Schools was another likely option. Some argued that the town needed just four schools and the two to go would certainly have been the single-sex ones.

With no volunteer and a difficult political choice – there had been much more outcry about the possible abolition of the single sex schools than there had been about the abolition of the selective schools a few years earlier – the decision was one of the all-time great fudges. No school would be closed, but they would all work together. A Curriculum Development Unit would be set up, based in the Headlands and headed by a Headteacher (though with no school). The Unit would coordinate work to enhance curriculum development in the six schools, much of it being done by staff seconded from the schools.

There is no doubt that this was a superb educational initiative and indubitably much good work was done. But it did not solve the problem of spare capacity. It also added considerably to the education budget and its acceptance was variable in the participating schools. One of its main aims was to ensure the continued provision of minority subjects, such as Russian. Such a subject would be taught at one school and pupils from other schools would travel for lessons. Whilst this got off the ground at 'A' Level with what was known as KESP (Kettering Education at Sixteen Plus), no progress was made in the lower years because schools could not, or would not, agree to a common timetable.

The next reorganisation attempt was made in 1988. The Curriculum Development Unit was finished. Not only was it too expensive, but also changes in education legislation hastened its demise. On the horizon was the National Curriculum which would reduce the time available for minority subjects. Also not far away was LMS (Local Management of Schools), the main feature of which was the allocation of a budget to individual schools based largely on their pupil numbers.

This innovation would make it difficult for schools with spare places. A school of 1,000 places but only 750 pupils would have the fixed costs of 1,000 places but would receive revenue for just 750. The variable costs are largely labour costs, particularly teacher wages which typically account for over 70% of a school's budget. It did not take much reasoning to come up with the conclusion that such a school would have to employ fewer teachers. That would make the class sizes larger, make it less attractive for parents (who, now that catchment areas had been effectively abolished, were entitled to express a preference for the school they wished their child to attend), reduce the number of pupils in the school still further, and so on, until closure came as a result of market forces.

That crudely, is what happened to Kettering Boys. It is what some people predicted in 1988. But it certainly did not happen in the way which anyone envisaged when, in 1988, the LEA consulted, again. This time their plan for Kettering involved the enhancement of four secondary schools and the closure of two. Bishop Stopford, Montagu, Latimer and Henry Gotch would become four schools of roughly equal size and with ''parity of esteem''. The single sex schools were to be closed, or to be amalgamated with Henry Gotch, the difference being academic.

The smart point of this plan was that four schools would be expanded whilst two closed so, inevitably, the democratic discussion would conclude with at least two-thirds of those interested voting in favour. The less than smart point of this plan was that it ignored many of the current trends in education thought.

Although Kettering had the same six schools in 1988 as it had in 1983, there had been significant changes in some of them. Bishop Stopford continued to flourish and Montagu was bursting at its inadequate seams. Latimer remained strong yet was not entirely immune to the decline in pupil numbers, whilst Henry Gotch had made considerable educational improvements, even if it was not always easy to convince the public of such. The single-sex schools had declined in numbers; the Boys School much more rapidly than Southfield. In 1983 the Boys School had a larger roll than Southfield, but by 1988 the position had been reversed.

There were two other players on the scene. In Rothwell the former Rothwell

& Desborough Secondary School had become the well-respected and over-crowded Montsaye School: sometimes it was treated as part of Kettering and sometimes it wasn't. In Corby the City Technological College was soon to open. Taking many of its students from the Kettering area, this would increase the number of places available and make the recruitment battle even more difficult.

The consultation process consisted mainly of a series of meetings at which the LEA put forward its "Preferred option" of the four enhanced mixed comprehensives, an arrangement which, had it been proposed fifteen years earlier might have been painful at the time but which would have eliminated all the subsequent trauma. The preferred option naturally drew overwhelming support from those connected with the four, whilst the single sex-schools were obviously now in mortal danger.

The meetings produced little more than expressions of self-interest and virtually no debate about education. At the meeting for the Boys School staff, some of the educational issues were raised, but the Chair of the Education Committee was unwilling to listen to much of what the staff wished to say.

Prior to this attempted reorganisation in Kettering, Daventry and Wellingborough had been dealt with. In both towns the proposals were for 11 to 16 Secondary schools (i.e. no Sixth Forms) and a tertiary college for post-16 education. There are very strong reasons why such an arrangement is desirable in the current education and training climate. But schools without Sixth Forms are electorally unpopular; it is difficult to convince parents that schools with Sixth Forms cannot provide the range and depth of courses that a tertiary college can.

Daventry, after a struggle, had its scheme approved and the attention turned to Wellingborough. There, spirited opposition defeated the tertiary college option and retained the status quo. In Kettering there was no tertiary option offered because, the LEA argued, different local situations demanded different solutions. It had nothing whatsoever to do with electoral expediency.

There was also no debate on the "Parity of esteem" point. At the time Bishop Stopford had as many 'A' Level students as the other five schools combined. Some argued that the Church school was too dominant, some even dared to suggest that it had evolved into an academically selective school. But the truth was, that of the four schools to be retained and enhanced, some would have much greater esteem than others.

One issue that was discussed and which generated some heat was the location of Rothwell. Part of the Borough of Kettering, but apparently not part of the Kettering educational area, there were protests from some parents who thought that the LEA was not explicit enough about options available to children transferring to the secondary sector.

The future for the single-sex schools was bleak, but a new piece of government legislation offered them hope. Grant-maintained status had been created. Schools which had previously been subject to LEA control would now be able to ''opt out'' of that control, receive their funding from central government and be independent though still within the public (i.e. free) sector.

The two single-sex schools soon decided to pursue this avenue. That immediately put the LEA's plan on hold; the law forbade them to do anything whilst the GM applications were being considered. After the parents had been balloted (and voted in favour) the submissions were prepared in May 1989 and the outcome awaited. Rumours abounded but the smart money was always on Southfield being accepted and the Boys School being rejected.

Such an outcome had been strongly hinted at by the representative of the Grant Maintained Trust at a meeting held in the Boys School. Some thought that equal opportunities legislation would prevent such a decision but that was not his opinion. It was an opinion that proved correct, the announcement reaching the Schools in November 1989.

No reasons were given for the decision, but by 1989, the Boys School annual intake had fallen below 50. Southfield's was less than adequate, but it was significantly larger. There had been a general decline in the demand for single-sex education, a decline much more marked for Boys Schools. The figures in Kettering reflected that trend and the Department for Education's decision perhaps accepted it.

The decision left the Boys School in limbo – which was no new experience. Whilst decisions had to be made about transfer to secondary schools in September 1989, nobody knew whether the Boys School would close or whether it would stay open. And the November decision did little to clarify the position. The LEA had no contigency plan: Southfield was safe for the foreseeable future and whilst the immediate threat of closure of the Boys School had been lifted, there was still a vast number of surplus places in the town, many of them at Windmill Avenue.

Legislation which gave full delegation to secondary schools came into effect under the LMS proposals in April 1990. This reduced considerably the powers of the LEA. It was now up to the Governors of a school to make decisions about its viability, or, to be a little less obtuse, the closure of a school now had to be initiated by the Governors.

It had been clear to those close enough to the situation to see that, with its current intake, the Boys School could not survive much longer. But there was unbridled optimism about the School's ability to attract more students. Unfortunately, there was no evidence to support such enthusiasm. The School was operating in a market with a decreasing number of potential customers and an increase in the number of competing suppliers (the Corby CTC). It was operating with its potential customers fully aware of the recent closure proposals and it was operating with a continually reducing staff as large groups of sixteen year olds were replaced by small groups of eleven year olds. And it was operating in a national climate of diminishing support for boys-only schools.

By now closure was inevitable. It fell to the School's senior management to persuade the Governors that they needed to take action to ensure a programmed closure with the minimum of disruption to the education of the boys then on roll. It was a far from easy task for the senior management to take this step; they were effectively signing their own redundancy notices as well as those of their colleagues and friends. Many of the staff at closure were unable to find any sort of job, those that did manage to obtain employment generally doing so under inferior conditions.

The job of managing the closure was also a harrowing one. It was helped by the professionalism of the staff who, despite knowing their careers were irreparably blighted, continued to give their best right until the last day. It was not helped by the shortage of support from the LEA who had been put into a position where sensible and reasonable involvement was often precluded by legislation. And the futile attempt to keep the School open did nothing to help either the educational development of the boys of the School (and the other children of the town) or the employment prospects of its staff.

The reasons for closure were complex; blame can be laid at the feet of many. Mr Ireson's question cannot be completely answered, though I suspect the consensus will be that the 1975 comprehensive reorganisation should have been done differently. There was no ceremony at the end, none of us had the desire for any. The penultimate week was marked with the entire School spending three days in the Peak District, whilst some staff "celebrated" amongst themselves on the last lunchtime with fish and chips and a bottle of Stella Artois. The last afternoon was spent on the playing field. The last pupils to leave were those who caught the bus to Burton Latimer. On the following Monday all equipment of any value was removed by representatives of other schools.

Eheu fugaces labuntur anni!

CHAPTER 33

The History of the Kettering Old Grammar School Foundation

J. N. R. Harker

Over four hundred years ago, on the fifteenth day of June, in the year 1577, Queen Elizabeth I ''granted lands and properties for the establishment of a school in Kettering. In consideration that Kettering was a large town, and great in number of boys and replete of youths, and that the said town might be adorned with a learned suitable, and lettered man and schoolmaster and youths there might be instructed and educated in good learning and the fear of God.''

So became established the first system of organised education in the town, and the seeds of the Kettering Old Grammar School Foundation were sown. Over the following four centuries the fortunes of the Grammar School and its Foundaton were to ebb and flow, as circumstances in Kettering changed, but it gradually grew in importance and prosperity until it is, today, one of the largest and wealthiest educational charities in the County, with substantial assets in property and investments, and a considerable income which is administered for the educational benefit of thousands of young people in the Kettering Borough area.

Having started with a flourish, the School continued successfully to educate the young men of Kettering in various locations in the town. It generally taught around fifty scholars, but on occasions numbers dwindled, and by the mid-nineteenth century only a few young men were on its roll, and they were required to walk to Burton Latimer for some of their lessons, as the Schoolmaster was also Curate there.

This situation was rectified on the appointment of a new Schoolmaster when the number rapidly grew, and in 1856 on the 13th June, an appeal was made to the public for funds to build a new ''Master House and School.'' The appeal was so successful that building was started immediately, and in December 1856, a dinner was held at ''The Three Cocks'' to commemorate the completion of the new buildings. These buildings were situated in Gold Street and were demolished in 1964 to make way for the new shopping centre.

The School was well thought of in the town, and, over the years it had received a number of endowments of land and property. According to Bull's

History of Kettering in 1887, it was realised that the property and land which they owned had greatly increased in value, and so a new scheme was proposed for the administration of the School and its property. Under this scheme, the Foundation would in future be administered by a governing body, and this governing body was known as *Kettering Grammar School Foundation.* This scheme was approved by Her Majesty in Council in 1888, and it would appear that this body continued with its responsibilities of administration of the School, and its properties, until 1911, when the scheme of 1888 was repealed, and a new one was drawn up by the Board of Education under the Endowed Schools Act 1869, 1873 and 1874 for the Amendment of the Scheme regulating Kettering Grammar School.

This scheme was approved by Her Majesty in Council on 4th May 1911, and in this scheme it is stated: ''The Foundation and its endowment (including the particulars specified in the Schedule to this scheme) shall be administered under the name of the *Kettering Old Grammar School Foundation.*''

Thus, on 4th May 1911, the Kettering Old Grammar School Foundation, as we know it today, was born.

The scheme also states the words ''New School'', which refers to the new Secondary School for boys and girls to be provided at Kettering by the County Council. That, of course, was the School in Bowling Green Road, now the offices of Kettering Borough Council. When this new School was opened in 1913, the Governors ceased to be responsible for the administration of the old Grammar School, but they continued to be responsible for administration of the property. A schedule of that property is in the scheme.

So, from the opening of the new School, the Governors of the old Grammar School Foundation were responsible only for the property and lands in accordance with the 1911 scheme, and after the payment of all expenses of management, the net income was paid to the County Council.

This money had to be used by the County Council to provide ''Out of net income of the Foundation, and so far as that income will permit, maintain in the new School, not less than 12 total exemptions from payment of tuition fees and entrance fees to be awarded on admisson to the School to pupils who have for the preceding two years attended Public Elementary Schools in the Urban District of Kettering with as near as possible equal divisions between boys and girls.''

Any residue of funds could be used for the making of Maintenance Allowances for a yearly sum of £10 to pupils in need of financial help.

This scheme of 1911 remained in operation until 1944, but the 1944 Education Act made great changes and the Boys Grammar School, and Girls High School, along with other Schools came under the direct control of the County Council, and with it came the end of fee paying Grammar Schools.

The School buildings and any assets automatically became the property of the Local Authority, but the Northants County Education Authority also claimed the endowments of Kettering Old Grammar School Foundation. So began a long hard fought battle lasting several years, until 1955.

In May 1946, Mr Reg Tailby was appointed by Kettering Borough Council to be a Governor of Kettering Old Grammar School Foundation, and in the Minutes of the meeting held on the 21st August 1946 it is recorded – "Mr Tailby and Mr Potter called to the attention of the meeting, as to the administration by the Education Authority of the money paid over by the Governors from time to time in accordance with the scheme governing the Foundation, and were desirous of obtaining further information as to how the money was applied, more especially how they were affected by the Education Act of 1944".

It was resolved that Messrs Tailby, Potter and Hodge be appointed a deputation to go into the matter with the Education Authority.

At the next meeting of the Governors on February 13th, "Mr Tailby stated that the committee appointed at the last meeting, to consider the effect of the Education Act 1944 on the Foundation, had not met, and requested that it be called within the next week or so, and that it should especially consider the question of whether the effect of the Act was to abolish any particular benefit to Kettering, from the Endowment of the Foundation, in view of the fact that all Secondary Education was now free."

Although the Minute Book contains no records of the meetings of this appointed committee, it is very evident that they got down to business very quickly and became most concerned as to how the Education Authority were using the income of the Foundation. According to the Minutes, a letter was sent on 14th May 1946 by the Foundation to the legal branch of the Ministry of Education, pointing out the desirability of amending the present Foundation scheme.

The Minister replied on 13th June 1946, saying that the present scheme dated 4th May 1911 clearly states that the residue of the net income of the Foundation shall be used for the maintenance of the County Schools. He therefore considered a new scheme was not necessary, and he doubted very much whether there were sufficient grounds for amending the present scheme.

The Foundation replied the next day, pointing out that the income from the endowments had greatly increased since 1911, and as none of the income was now used to provide free places in the School, the Governors felt very strongly that part of this, at least, should be used for the benefit of Kettering pupils in some other way, and in particular for the purposes of Higher Education. It also asked if the Minister would be prepared to enquire of the Education Authority just how the income from the Foundation was used.

The Minister replied to the effect that the Governors of the Foundation should make their own enquiries of the Education Authority, which they immediately did, enquiring how in fact had the monies received from the Foundation since 1st April 1945 been used and in what special manner did the pupils of Kettering benefit, and was a separate account kept.

No reply was received to this letter, so at a Governors' meeting, held on 19th November 1948, it was decided to hold over any future payments to the Education Authority until further considerations of the present and future position of the Foundation had been established.

From 1947 and during the next few years, the specially appointed committee of Tailby, Potter and Hodge, fought a tremendous battle to protect the Foundation.

The Education Authority maintained that the income of the Foundation belonged to them, and the Kettering Governors argued that the 1911 scheme transferred the endowments from the School to the Foundation, and a new scheme should be introduced to protect the original interests, and that this income should be used for the benefit of Kettering Grammar School and the Girls High School.

They had many meetings with the County Council, and a number of trips to London to meet the Minister for Education.

The Foundation's Solicitor, Mr Holmes of Lamb & Holmes, was instructed to enquire of Foundations up and down the country, to see how the 1944 Act had affected them, and Mr Tailby and Mr Potter were prepared to meet anybody, and go anywhere to gather information that might help in their fight.

The Education Authority refused to change their mind, and remained adamant that the endowments rightly belonged to them, and refused to support the Foundation's application for a new scheme. Mr Holmes had been unsuccessful in obtaining any information that might help.

The Minister refused to agree to a new scheme, and informed them that no Foundation was being allowed to retain its endowments under the 1944 Education Act.

Still the legal battle continued, still Potter and Tailby refused to give in. Eventually, the Governors were threatened with a High Court Writ, but still they refused to hand over the endowments. Things were beginning to look bleak, but the battle was still not lost.

Reg Tailby was also Chairman of the Borough Libraries Committee, and he used to go into the Library once a week to look through all the educational publications to see if he could find anything to help. Then one day he found featured in one of those publications, two schools in the London area where the Foundation had been allowed to retain the assets.

With great glee and hopefulness, off they went again armed with this information to the County Council, and to the Minister to state their case again. Eventually, after a very heated meeting with the Education Authority, this time led by the Chairman of the Governors, Mr Harry Johnson, and accompanied by Mr Tailby and Mr Potter, the County Council did agree to support the Foundation in their new scheme.

The Minister could not but agree to the application.

This scheme, which is an amendment to the principal scheme of 1911, was approved by Her Majesty in Council on 24th February 1955.

At the next meeting of the Governors, the Chairman, Mr G. H. Johnson, tendered his resignation and Mr Reg Tailby was elected to fill the vacancy. A fitting tribute to the work he had done to bring into being this 1955 scheme, which has been a tremendous benefit to education in Kettering throughout the years.

This new 1955 scheme provided for the income to be used as below, after the payment of all expenses:

(a) One third of the net income to be used by the Governors in making grants to any County, Voluntary or Special School in the Borough of Kettering, and grants to pupils in need of assistance, etc.

(b) Two thirds to be paid to the County Council for the maintenance and benefit of Kettering Grammar School and Kettering High School.

The affairs of the Foundation then went smoothly for the next few years, and the monies were dispersed in accordance with the new scheme. Then in 1962, Mr J. K. Dudley (Headmaster of the Grammar School and a Governor of the Foundation), asked how this two thirds of the income was used for the benefit of the Grammar and High Schools. There began another encounter with the Education Authority. It transpired that this money was being absorbed in the General Education Account, and there were no specific benefits going to either school.

After rather prolonged discussions, it was eventually agreed that this money should be put into a separate account by the County Council, and used by the Foundation, with the agreement of the County Council, for the direct benefit of Kettering Grammar School, and Kettering High School.

That agreement has enabled the Foundation to carry out many projects for these schools, some of which are listed below.

1968	Grammar School	Sixth Form Common Room	£2,000
1967	Grammar School	Landscaping and tree planting scheme	£400
1969	High School	Junior Centre and Library	£2,000
1970	High School	Landscaping	£200
1971	Grammar School	Purchase of boat	£100
1971	High School	Windows and ventilation to Junior Centre	£110
1973	High School	Careers Room	£300
1974	High School	Mobile Cloaks Unit	£70
1974	Grammar School	Visual Aids Room	£1,500
1974	Grammar School	Arts Departments	£200
1975	High School	Junior Library Careers Room	£800
1976	Kettering Girls	New Office Accommodation	£500
1976	Kettering Boys	Rehabilitation of Staff Room	£500
1978	Kettering Boys	Garage and Maintenance Bay for Minibus	£750
1978	Kettering Girls	Sixth Form Common Room Improvements	£500
1985	Kettering Girls	Storage Building	£15,000
1986	Kettering Boys	Refurbishment of Balcony to Main Hall	£13,000
1989	Bishop Stopford	Stage Extensions and Store	£32,000

In 1970 the Foundation took the lease of a Village School with Master's Cottage attached at Govilon in Wales, for the establishment of a Field Centre. A small plot of land at the rear was also purchased and a Portakabin-type building was erected for a classroom. This has proved to be of very great benefit to Kettering Schools. It has progressed well and is occupied most weeks of the year, with nearly 1,000 Kettering children benefiting annually from the facility.

There is a qualified resident tutor/warden, and a variety of subjects and activities are catered for.

Throughout the years, it has been necessary to make further amendments to the scheme for the administration of the Foundation.

In 1971, slight amendments were made:

(a) To allow the Governors to pay from the Benefits Fund, £200 per annum to Kettering Grammar School and Kettering High School instead of £100.
(b) Applicants for benefits must not only reside in Kettering but also to have attended a school in Kettering for not less than two years.
(c) To allow the Governors to pay into the Building Fund such sums as may be approved by the Secretary of State for Education and Science, instead of a ''sum not exceeding £500''.

1974 was the year of Local Government Reorganisation, and the boundaries of Kettering Borough were extended to take in neighbouring towns and villages. Our schemes when drawn up, were for Kettering Borough, which then consisted of Kettering Town only. As many pupils from all parts of the new Borough were attending Kettering Grammar School, and the Girls High School, it was agreed by the Governors that we accept applications for benefit from any schools, individuals, or organisations who qualify for benefit under the rules of the scheme, within the boundaries of the new Borough.

The introduction of Comprehensive Education in 1976 caused another problem, as it meant the end of Kettering Grammar School and Kettering High School for Girls, and the majority of the income was for the benefit of these two schools. However, this was resolved by the addition in the scheme after the words ''Kettering G.S. and Kettering G.H.S.'' the words ''and their successor schools''. In 1976 there was also a further alteration to the 1955 scheme. This scheme changed the constitution of the Board of Governors. The number of Borough Councillors was reduced from four to three. County Councillors from three to two and increased the number of co-optative Governors from two to four. This was done to enable the Governors to co-opt people with a special expertise, and to guarantee more continuity.

The scheme also contains an up-to-date schedule of assets, and instruction, as to the vesting of property in the Official Custodian of Charities and the investment of cash.

The next really big change came in 1988, when further, and far reaching alterations were made. Previously, two thirds of the net income was held by the County Council for special benefits for the Boys School and the Girls High School, and one third was retained by the Foundation for the Benefits Fund to be used at the discretion of the Governors, for making grants to schools and individuals etc.

After rather prolonged negotiations, it was agreed by the Charities Commission, the Board of Education, the Northants County Council and the Old Grammar School Foundation, that the total income should be administered by the Foundation in accordance with the terms of a new scheme to be agreed by all parties. That new scheme was sealed on the 20th May 1988.

The effect of this scheme is that it gives the Kettering Old Grammar School Foundation complete control of all its assets, and to receive and disperse the entire income in accordance with the scheme.

The income of the Foundation is dispersed in the following ways:

1. The first charges are the expenses of management affairs, insurances and all other charges and outgoings.
2. £3,500 must then be paid into the Building Fund to ensure a reserve fund for extraordinary repairs, alterations, improvements or rebuilding of property belonging to the Foundation.
3. The Foundation shall apply the remainder of the income in the following ways:
   (a) In or towards making such special benefits of any kind, not normally provided by the Local Education Authority for any County, Voluntary or Special School within the Borough of Kettering, preference shall be given to Kettering Boys School and Southfield School for Girls or any substituted school, of £1,000 each per annum.
   (b) In promoting the education, including social and physical training of persons who are resident in the Borough of Kettering, and who are attending, or who have attended, an educational establishment within the Borough for at least two years.
   (c) In awarding to such persons scholarships, exhibitions, maintenance allowances, or grants tenable at any School, University or College or other Institute of Further (including progressional and technical) Education.
   (d) In providing financial assistance, outfits, clothing, tools, instruments or books to assist such persons to pursue their education (including music and other arts), to undertake travel in furtherance thereof, or to prepare for or enter a profession, trade, occupation or service on leaving School, University, or other educational establishment.

The first complete year of operating under this new scheme was most rewarding to the Governors of the Foundation, because in this financial year of 1989-1990 they were able to:

(a) Give a new minibus, licensed for one year, to each of the seven Secondary Schools within the Borough.
(b) Give a grant towards travel to all Junior Schools on a basis of £2 per capita with a maximum of £1,000 and a minimum of £200.
(c) Give grants of £1,000 to all Special Schools.
(d) Provide stage extensions and a new equipment store at Bishop Stopford School.
(e) Give a grant of £2,000 to Avondale School for the setting up of a special unit within the School.
(f) Give a grant of £5,000 towards a new minibus at Wren Spinney School.
(g) Give grants amounting to several thousand pounds to individual applicants going on to Further Education.

In 1945 the net income was £1,509. 7s. 9d. and it has now grown to such proportions that the Charity Commissioners have agreed that a firm of Financial Managers be appointed to manage the Foundation's investments. The present disposable income amounts to over £150,000 and this tremendous growth over the years is due entirely to good estate management. The schools, pupils and indeed all the people of the Borough of Kettering owe a tremendous debt of gratitude to those Governors of Kettering Old Grammar School Foundation, who fought hard and bravely from 1944 to 1955, to retain the endowments of the Foundation for future education in Kettering. It was a tremendous pleasure to the present Governors, that at the ceremony held to present the minibuses to the various schools on 27th January 1990, Mr Reg Tailby, the only surviving member of those early Governors, was able to be present and tell something of that early struggle.

In writing this history of Kettering Old Grammar School Foundation, one name has not been mentioned, and that is the name of the late Colonel R. C. Jeffery. He came to Kettering in 1948 to join the firm of Messrs. Gotch, Saunders & Surridge. Mr Ralph Surridge was then Clerk to the Foundation, but he handed most of the work the office entailed to Bob Jeffery, and when Mr Surridge died in 1952, Bob was appointed Clerk and Surveyor in his stead.

Right up to his untimely death in January 1989, he was the guiding light to the Governors of the Foundation, and did much of the negotiating between the Northants County Council, Charity Commissioners, Ministry of Education and the Foundation. He was instrumental in the buying, selling and redevelopment of the property and his vision and expertise is manifested in the terrific growth of the Foundation and in the numerous projects that have been undertaken.

He is remembered with affection and admiration, and with tremendous gratitude for this devoted work and achievements on behalf of Kettering Old Grammar School Foundation, and the Governors have recently re-named their Field Centre in Wales "The Robert Jeffery Centre", in memory of his outstanding service to the Foundation.

The Kettering Old Grammar School Foundation, being in such a healthy and wealthy condition, the Governors look forward to the future with confidence and anticipation in being able to carry out some exciting projects for education in Kettering. This is largely due to the vision and dedication of the Chairman of the Foundation over this time, Robert L. Denney, M.B.E., who has served as a Governor for 32 years, and has been Chairman since 1971. Working as a team over a quarter of a century, the two Bobs – Bob Jeffery and Bob Denney – have built on the valiant efforts made in the 'fifties to save the Foundation, and have so cultivated its assets and activities over the years to make it, now, one of the most important, and wealthiest, Charities in the County. A few years ago, Bob Denney wrote a history of the Foundation, and it is his account that has provided the majority of this chapter. We are very grateful to him for his permission to use large sections of his work which, in itself, stands as a testimonial to his interest in and devotion to the Kettering Old Grammar School Foundation.

Clerk to the Governors, County Councillor J. N. R. Harker in his schooldays. Troilus and Cressida, *1962. Jim is second left.*

CHAPTER 34

Old Cyts and Local Government

Barrie Chambers

Barrie Chambers, under "political pressure", in Shakespeare's Henry VIII, *in 1957.*

The link between Kettering Grammar School and Kettering Borough Council may be seen by some merely in terms of the fact that the Council now occupies the former School building in Bowling Green Road. Others now see it primarily in terms of the fact that the Council demolished the old School building in Gold Street. Although both of these are in their way significant, the part played by Old Boys of the School in shaping the town is of far greater importance.

Perhaps C. W. (George) Godfrey typifies this connection between town and gown most vividly. As Second Master and, for a brief period, Acting Head, George was a major figure in the life of K.G.S. after the Second World War. Apart from his work at the School, he devoted much time and incredible energy to the service of the community. He was a producer for the Hygrams, president of the Argyll Working Men's Club, an official of the Horticultural Society and much else besides. For most people this would have been service enough, but not for George. He was a prominent Borough Councillor as well.

Serving as Labour councillor, George comfortably bridged the political divide, gaining the respect and affection of all parties. Even so, he was always highly combative in the chamber. In 1964 he became mayor, but sadly died during his year of office.

The only other member of the K.G.S. teaching staff to take to political life appears to have been Russell Gladden. It is hard to imagine two men more different than Gladden and Godfrey. Whilst George was essentially a man of the people, Russell was of a more patrician disposition. Strangely, they both occupied similar positions in the School; Godfrey as Second Master and Gladden in charge of the new Science campus in Windmill Avenue before also becoming Deputy Head. He briefly represented the Conservatives, not on the Borough Council, but in the more rarified atmosphere of County Hall.

At roughly the same time Bill Asbrey sat as a County Councillor for the Conservatives. His time on the council was brief but, not surprisingly, colourful. Jim Harker Jnr. remains the School's most notable County Councillor.

One ought to mention one other member of staff in connection with local

Ken Woolmer converts. K.G.S. v The County Police XV, 1957-58.
Ken became an M.P. and Economics Lecturer at Leeds University. The referee is Ian Bidgood.

government. In the days when the local evening paper reported local council meetings in detail, they frequently published news of what went on at parish councils. In the 'fifties, one such council frequently made the pages of the *Evening Telegraph* and almost invariably due to the eccentric utterances of one Thomas Corke.

Turning to former pupils, there was one particular form at K.G.S. which contained a number of boys who later had careers in various forms of public service. One, Ken Woolmer, became a Member of Parliament. Another, John Newing, became a Chief Constable. Two, Chris Groome and Barrie Chambers became mayors of the town, and Brian Slough became Headmaster of the School.

Barrie Chambers was elected to the council in 1964 and remained a councillor for nineteen years. He became a leading figure in the controversies over the redevelopment of the town centre, the reorganisation of the Borough in 1973/4 and in the campaign for the construction of the A14 road. He became the Borough's youngest mayor in 1973.

Chris Groome entered Borough politics after the merging of the old Borough with the surrounding rural and urban districts in 1974. Representing his native Burton Latimer as an Independent, as was the way with Burtonians, he soon rose to prominence, bringing his keen mind to bear on the problems of the Borough with particular reference to housing matters. In 1993 he became the latest in the line of Old Cyt. mayors.

The present Council contains other Grammar School Old Boys. Peter Bradley, son of Old Centralian ex-MP Tom Bradley, John Richardson and Terry Freeman. All three represent the Liberal Democrats, harking back to Kettering's old Liberal traditions.

Looking back over the years, there are numerous names on the list of councillors and mayors which have also been on the registers of Kettering Grammar School. Terry Wright, who was mayor in the late 'seventies, followed in the distinguished footsteps of former K.G.S. Chairman of Governors. Ald. Mrs Clarke, in serving as Chairman of the Library Committee. Another Chairman of the School's Governors who served as mayor is T. J. Freer.

The reorganisation of local government in 1974 brought a number of Old Cyts into the council chamber. Ray Dainty of Rothwell was briefly a Borough Councillor, after years of distinguished service in Rothwell; Len Axe of Loddington and Jim Harker Sen. joined the new Borough from the Rural District. Whilst not having Tom Corke's loquacious and irrascible streaks, Jim Harker did have a lovably idiosyncratic side, which contrasted sharply with Len Axe's droll manner.

Old Cyts have served as councillors wearing a variety of party labels. In the 'sixties the Ratepayers Association was a force in local affairs and among the handful of councillors elected in their cause was Jim Andrew. Despite his deserved reputation as a leading actor with the Hygrams, Jim eschewed

In 1983, during his year as Mayor, Councillor T. J. Freer invited Staff and Sixth-formers to a nostalgic gathering in the Bowling Green Road School.

theatricals in the Council Chamber. Instead, his quiet, self-effacing manner won him much respect on all sides. He became an alderman and served as a committee chairman for a number of years.

Post-war local government was a more powerful force than it is today. Besides George Godfrey, two other K.G.S. Old Boys made their mark during this period. One was Edgar Newman, who sat as a Conservative for many years and became committee chairman, alderman and mayor. He also became president of the National Federation of Cremation Authorities.

Perhaps the most distinguished Old Boy councillor of this period was another Conservative alderman, Reg Tailby. Industrialist, financier, supporter of sport and the arts, Reg was devoted to Kettering. He had led the right to save the funds of the Old Grammar School Foundation from the clutches of the 1944 Education Act and was a prominent figure in the council throughout the post-war period. He was always proud to have been mayor at the time of the Queen's Accession.

Even in the days of the Kettering Local Board, Old Cyts figured among the leaders of the town. In the last two decades of the nineteenth century ex-Grammar School boys John Wallis, J. T. Stockburn and J. T. Iliffe occupied the chair of the Board for all but one year. These were the days when the sons of prosperous local families saw it as their duty to serve the town.

One such family were the Gotches. D. F. Gotch was chairman of the School

Board from 1890 until 1902, a period which saw numerous important developments in education in the town. Henry Gotch was Chairman of the Urban District Council in 1906/7 and also a county alderman. Architect Alfred Gotch became Charter Mayor in 1938.

A number of K.G.S. Old Boys have had distinguished careers in local government as officers. Len Ingyon was Borough Treasurer for many years after the Second World War and Paul Bailey was Acting Town Clerk in the early 'seventies. Bert Stafford, John Althorpe and Phil Margetts are among many Old Boys who have served as council officers. Perhaps few people know that probably the School's most eminent academic, Professor Albert Halsey, was briefly employed by the Council in its Cleansing Department before he moved on to academe.

The diminution of the power of local government, and with it the respect in which the Council is held, may have reduced the number of people willing to participate in its work. In years gone by, councillors were prominent public figures and the Council had enormous impact on the life of the community. It was vital that the town was served by men of vision if it was to survive. It is fortunate that over the years Old Boys of Kettering Grammar School gave of their time and talents for the public good and continue to do so.

CHAPTER 35

The Old Cytringanians

(Formerly The Kettering Grammar School Old Boys' Association)

Rex Moore

"The Call of Their School. Memorable Re-Union of Kettering Old Boys". So runs *The Evening Telegraph* headlines for Monday 10th January, 1938, for the Jubilee Reunion Dinner held on the previous Saturday. Over three hundred ex-pupils had gathered in the School hall for this celebration. To cope with this number (never surpassed) even the balcony and other rooms were utilised.

Gone were the wishful thinkings of a bigger venue, voiced by various speakers in earlier years, when the dinners had been served in the dining room at the top of the School by Mrs Warren, the wife of the then School caretaker. This was a truly grand occasion!

The Evening Telegraph gave three page-long columns to this event, plus a photograph, recorded in this book. The attendance far exceeded the actual membership of the Association at the time.

In fact, the words of the late J. I. Scott, Headmaster since 1914, reported that more than one quarter of all the boys who had attended the School were present. He also directed a tribute to the chief organiser of this event, Mr R. W. (Reg) Tailby, who was by now establishing himself as a stalwart of the Association, a position he was to keep, in one way or another, for the next forty or so years.

To hear this, and other speeches made by P. E. Coles, Howard Smith, Peter Wilson and Mr Kirby, all the guests crowded into the hall – which explains the number standing around the walls in the photograph. One wonders what the fire officer would have to say today?

Various entertainments were offered, including "vocal items" by Bert Brading and C. W. Godfrey. An excellent hot dinner was served by the K.I.C.S. catering. In those days the Co-operative movement was very strong in all fields of retailing in Kettering; a shop on nearly every corner, together with the Newland Street shopping complex with its glorious arcade, and the Central Hall.

The whole proceedings were overseen by Mr Leslie Smith, using "the ringing tones of the old school bell" to keep order.

The Jubilee Dinner 1938. Reg Tailby can be seen standing, second right.

It will always be difficult to decide who is the most famous Old Boy. However, at this time there was no doubt in the mind of J. L. Holland Esq. the County Secretary for Education. He names in his speech, Mr J. A. Gotch: a member of the famous Kettering family, he was responsible for designing the Bowling Green Road School. The tribute also extended to Mr H. G. Gotch, his brother, who was Chairman of the Governors at the time of the building.

In his reply, Mr Gotch recalled his own schooldays, some seventy years previously, at the Gold Street establishment. In his day, he reported, the one room that was supposed to be devoted to the purpose of the School was too small. Consequently, the boys had to pass through the small front playground and the Master's garden to a building that was previously a barn, but which had been made comfortable for the use of the School.

Tribute was paid by Mr J. L. C. Loake on behalf of the Old Boys Association to the then President, J. I. Scott. An extract from the report says:

''To imagine the Association without Mr Scott would be like playing *Hamlet* without the Prince of Denmark. . . . He was a friend, often a candid friend, but none the less a friend for that!''

In 1993, at the 75th annual dinner, the Association invited several lady ex-members of staff. Breaking new ground? Certainly not. J. I. Scott mentions, in his 1938 reply to the Old Boys' tribute and presentation of an ''Illuminated Address'', two former lady members of staff. They were Miss E. Chattle and Miss M. J. Chalmers, from the 1914-1918 period. The latter is the same lady so fondly remembered by Harold Tailby in his contribution elsewhere in this book.

Indeed they were not the only ladies present. Among those named are Miss J. White, Headmistress of the High School, and her predecessor, Miss A. E. Bristol. Mrs C. W. Clarke, JP., Mrs T. N. Bird and Mrs Kirby.

For further details and personnel of this dinner, it is necessary for the reader to consult the archives. However, in the obvious air of celebration and happiness, one sombre note makes its appearance. Mr Holland, reporting the hopes of a separate school for the girls says:

''Whether that can be granted lies on the knees of the gods, and depends to some extent on Adolf Hitler''.

The noise for the residents of Bowling Green Road that night must have been considerable as ''Round the large hall and through the long lines on the balcony above voices rose in the swelling chorus of *Auld Lang Syne*''. If that was not enough to disturb the local tranquillity, the Secretary's report for the same year tells us that at 11.15 p.m., one hundred and fifty cars had their engines revved up as the guests departed. That must say something for the status of many Old Boys, when one considers car ownership in 1938!

The recorder of the last item was a Maurice Chamberlain who, in 1995, sent a kind letter welcoming the writer to the secretaryship of the Old Cytringanians.

The Association had been born in the Spring of 1919 at a reunion of Old

Boys returning from the First World War. This reunion is graphically described in the 1920 edition of the School Magazine.

''The laughing eyes, the happy light of recognition of slightly forgotten face, the shaking of hands, the hubbub of chatter, the exciting experience, the marvellous escapes, all tended to make one feel he had just broken from the harsh and exacting shackles of service and was indeed glad to be alive. Some hands alas we could not shake . . . some we would see no longer at the School.''

These words were written by T. W. Hill, the first Secretary, and would seem to describe well the aftermath of the events of 1914-1918. Sixty names are listed, together with J. I. Scott as President. Indeed, throughout the next twenty years, names of Life and Annual members are recorded in the School Magazine for any reader wishing to consult them – certainly too many to print in this publication. Subscription charges were set at a guinea for life or 2s. 6d. (12½p) annually.

BALANCE SHEET

RECEIPTS	£ s. d.	EXPENDITURE	£ s. d.
Balance from April Dinner	0 2 6	Per Beaty Hart (Printing)	2 5 0
Members' Subscriptions	8 2 6	,, Chamberlain	0 6 0
Whist Drive	1 12 0	Envelopes and Post Cards	0 11 6
		Stamps	1 5 6
		Whist Drive and Prizes	1 15 9
		Balance in Hand	3 13 3
Total	9 17 0	Total	9 17 0

Signed,

J. I. SCOTT, M.A., Pres.
T. W. HILL, Sec.

F. G. YORKE, Sec.
C. BAGSHAW, Treasurer.

The balance sheet for 1920 makes interesting reading. Steady growth financially is shown by the annual report of 1928. It tells of ''a very satisfactory balance sheet.'' Good enough, indeed, to invest spare funds in a Conversion Loan, the interest to be devoted to an annual Old Boys Prize. This was the forerunner of the J. I. Scott prize of later years.

In 1927, Messrs Godfrey and Kirby are attending the Annual Dinner and the School rugby team playing the Old Boys' side was strengthened by three members of staff: Hopkins, Tynan and Hum.

An Old Boys' tie was introduced in the same year, costing 3s. 6d. (17½p). Paradoxically, at the AGM of 1995, a proposal was made to renew this emblem of membership. The inordinate cost today will probably prohibit this.

The era of the reported Dinner saw an explosion in the activities of the movement. The birth of the rugby section in 1930 is recorded by L. S. (Len) Axe, who himself became a playing member and captain in subsequent years. It is interesting to record the ''line up'' of the Association from the Magazine for 1932. This was the year that the title ''Old Cytringanians'' was officially adopted. Previously the somewhat cumbersome name had been that of the sub-title of this Chapter.

USEFUL INFORMATION

OLD CYTRINGANIANS:

The President: J. I. Scott, Esq., M.A.
Vice-Presidents: E. E. Kirby, Esq., C. W. Godfrey, Esq.
Hon Secretaries: L. Smith, 5 Garfield Street, Kettering,
C. S. Harvey, Braybrooke, near Market Harborough.
Hon. Treasurer: L. F. Hales, Church Walk, Kettering.
Magazine Secretary: L. S. Axe, ''Hillcrest,'' Queensberry Road, Kettering.
Annual Subscription: Two Shillings and Sixpence.
Life Member's Subscription: One Guinea.

OLD CYTRINGANIANS' RUGBY FOOTBALL CLUB

The President: J. I. Scott, Esq., M.A.
Hon. Secretary: L. S. Axe, ''Hillcrest'', Queensberry Road, Kettering.
Hon. Treasurer: B. Smith, 40, Blandford Avenue, Kettering.
Hon. Team Secretary: L. J. Newman, 49, Newman Street, Kettering.
Captain: A. O. Mason; Vice-Captain: M. J. Miller.
Member's Annual Subscription: Five Shillings. Due 1st Sept.
Club Colours: jerseys and socks black, red, and white, with blue knickers.
Training: Held at the School Gym, every Tuesday evening at 7.30 p.m.

In the same year B. A. (Bert) Brading became the Secretary of the newly formed Hygram Players.

It should be said here, to keep historical records straight, that a joint Old Boys', Old High School Girls' production *Of Mice and Men* had been given in the School Hall in January 1927.

The comment of the Senior Prefect at the dinner gives us not only a few names but also the feeling of the time. The writer might well be S. P. House, who has contributed elsewhere in this book.

THE OLD BOYS' DINNER

(As seen by a present boy.)

I entered the ''Royal'' for this annual re-union with a feeling of trepidation. However, I found I had fallen among friends – George Dickins, across the way, 'Tubby' Hague on one side as we sat at table and 'Beefy' Panter on the other.

The dinner was excellent, served with admirable speed, and so good that I dared not attempt the last course at all. When 'Dump' Smith got up and shot out epigrams, and another speaker contested the gold standard with 'Phip' Coles, I began really to feel at home.

Two fellows, just opposite, were discussing the climate of Alexandria: further up, 'Bomus' Bird held forth on the perils of Air Force life. In the distance Mr Secretary Smith played little tunes with a fork on a row of glasses collected from his neighbours. His cheery atmosphere grew jollier still when the tables defeated each other with song, and when 'Flop' Marlow chanted good-humoured jests about "cub" and "tub". Eleven o'clock found me almost looking forward to the time when I, too, will be an Old Boy.

1934 saw the introduction of Old Boys' blazers. These were in black, red and white stripes and could be obtained from Messrs. Webb Bros. Ltd., High Street, upon the production of a certificate of authorization, presumably from the Secretary, for 37s. 6d. inclusive of badge. For a provincial Grammar School Old Boys Association, these were somewhat ostentatious affairs by today's standard. A first-hand memory of Harry Fifield wearing one after the Second World War is very clear.

The sentiment expressed earlier concerning Adolf Hitler is reflected in the 1940 Magazine, where we find eighty pupils and one member of staff called up for active service. The first of many fatalities of the Second World War is reported – F. J. Coulson, killed on 8th November, 1939. Eventually over three hundred Old Boys served in the Forces.

As a result of the outbreak of World War II there is, in fact, no report of the Association activities at all for 1940. Oddly enough, the pessimistic references to the gradual demise of rugby football, written into the 1939 Magazine, were confounded in the war years.

Due to young leavers and servicemen coming home on leave, it would seem that it was possible to field a team through most of the war years, at least on a casual basis. There are no reports as to whom the opposition was, but one speculates on possibly police, and Services' sides, and of course the School. Trevor Holmes remembers games against Stewarts & Lloyds.

The Reunion Dinner continued throughout the war years, organised by R. W. Tailby, who was also responsible for keeping the whole of the Home Front Association Activities going in those years. Interestingly, several of the reports of the Dinner were written by the various Senior Prefects of the time.

Whoever it was in 1941 probably got quite a shock when, judging by his report, he heard 'George' (C. W. Godfrey) sing several songs of questionable taste. He admits that, surprisingly, he enjoyed them! This Senior Prefect was Alan Baker – a fact deduced and confirmed in a conversation with him.

Dances were held in the School for Old Boys on home leave, in conjunction with the Old Girls of the High School. They are reported as being well attended. According to R. W. Tailby, there were nine of these functions in 1943 alone.

The writer's embryonic memory of the Old Cytringanians is of going to see a game of rugby on the School field, probably in the early part of the autumn of 1945 or 1946. Of the game, nothing survives, but an indelible memory of three people on the right hand side of the sports pavilion remains. Johnny Chaplin nonchalantly seated on the rail, Trevor Holmes standing by him and a few feet away, the late Roy Dunkley. Roy was arguing. When didn't Roy argue?

The report of the first post-war dinner in January, 1946, as written by Maurice Chamberlain, is transcribed here to set the tone of the time.

THE RE-UNION

February 23rd, 1946

Owing to difficulties of catering, one hundred and fifty was the most the committee could invite and the fact that instructions had to be given to ''book early and avoid disappointment'' was an encouraging sign of the strength and enthusiasm of the Association.

The list of diners was divided, unlike Gaul, into four parts: the Ancient, the Semi-Ancient, the Semi-Modern and the Modern. The Ancients, who have formed the backbone of the war-time Old Cytringanian functions, were strongly re-inforced by those, who, despite their comparative senility(?) have been doing great deeds in the Services. The Modern and Semi-Modern contingents have also been well represented at our war-time dinners. The great pleasure of this dinner, however, was the return of the lost legion, the Semi-Ancient, whose faces have been missing for so long. That pathetic figure, the man who could find no-one he knew, has, I hope, vanished for ever.

The meal itself was so good as to prompt 'Scriv' Harvey, in a speech which showed what fluency can be gained from natural aptitude and long practice, to suggest that it must have been provided from the President's household points. ''The beer,'' to quote the Headmaster, ''flowed freely, if somewhat unevenly, around the tables.''

The speeches were of a high quality, but I believe it will be detrimental to no-one to say that the high-spot of the evening was Geoff Ipgrave's toast of ''The School,'' and the Headmaster's reply. Ipgrave was quiet and dignified, giving a moving and sincere account not of the horrors of his imprisonment but the simple things he had missed and remembered. Mr Scott's reply succeeded, as one Old Boy said, in ''knocking 'em into the aisles.'' My own opinion is that his only peer is Mr Gillie Potter.

A fitting conclusion to this account is perhaps his most noble remark ''Intactis opulentior,'' which rendered into Basic English means, ''if the meat's too tough you can always stick your fork in the gravy.''

Probably many were disappointed in the rationing of numbers! In spite of the austerity existing at the time, hopes were high.

Suggestions were made for the formation of swimming, rambling, badminton and photographic clubs. These, however, did not come to fruition.

As befits the times, appeals for subscriptions to a war memorial were made to remember those killed in the two wars. Webb's advertised sufficient material to make up six blazers with badges and six without badge. Ten coupons were required for these and delivery was ten weeks.

The Dinner was once again held in the School, with nostalgic references made to the lockers and familiar faces. Mr Kirby and Mr Pledger were among those who made speeches. The latter was, of course, on the staff but was also an Old Boy. His photo appears in the 1904 School Cricket Team published in this volume.

The Old Cytringanians Dinner, 1946. A. F. Scott, flanked by E. E. Kirby and Reg Tailby, on the top table. Messrs Hulls, Pledger and Laywood in foreground left.

It is with cricket that we begin our look at the post war activities of the Old Cytringanians. Here again personal memories play a part. As a young teenager, the writer spent many summer Saturday afternoons, either watching or scoring for the Kettering Wanderers on the Town ground. The Old Cytringanians shared this ground, using the smaller white pavilion as their changing room.

Childhood innocence remembers a considerable camaraderie between the two teams. Names that come to mind from those days are Jack Miller, Trevor Holmes, Dennis Smith, John Chaplin, Leslie Smith, Eric Corby, and Dick Wooster. Childhood innocence did not fail to notice a certain mild haughtiness from some of the players, or was it the deference then expected of the young by their elders?

The public image of the team was heightened in 1948, when it won the Kettering Knock Out Cup, an annual event, with the finals held on the North Park ground. The team beaten in the final was indeed the Kettering Cricket Club XI.

This year saw the institution of the Holmes Cup, given by Trevor Holmes' father for the best seasonal all round performances. The winner the first year? By secret ballot – Trevor Holmes.

There is a sad note in the compilation of this section of the Association's history.

The writer, in search of information, called Dennis Smith's home number, in Burton Latimer, to be told that Dennis had died two days before. Dennis was the Honorary Cricket Section Secretary from 1947-1957 and, in recognition of this, was presented with a writing case at the 1957 Club supper.

A fast bowler at school, where he played for – and captained – the Ist XI, he became a useful leg beak bowler as an Old Boy. His wife Brenda was very understanding and later talked about those happy, far-off cricketing days, and donated several photos to the Association.

Mention must be made here of the most famous "honorary" Old Cytringanian, David Green. A fast bowler, he was also a somewhat extrovert character. Tales on and off the field are legion: too numerous, or perhaps too outrageous to record here. He recently recounted how he became involved with the Old Cytringanians. Coming to Kettering in 1942, he worked in a bank alongside an Old Boy, Peter Rudkin, who inveigled him into some of the wartime rugby games already reported. From there, due to his prowess as a bowler, he became involved in the cricket side.

Trevor Holmes, who became captain in 1949 and played through to the end of the Club's activities, described the team and times as being very happy. Some of the atmosphere can be gathered from the photograph of players and their wives taken at Rockingham around 1950. He also mentions the annual trip to play Clacton on the Essex County Ground: very enjoyable, but a game they never won.

In 1954 the Club was given notice by Kettering Town Cricket Club that the leased pitch in Northampton Road was no longer available.

This made it necessary to play away fixtures for much of the season, but permitted use of the School ground from the end of the summer term.

With more pupils achieving university entrance, some difficulty arose in fielding a truly Old Boys' team. Good relations between the cricket team and the Kettering Rugby Club enabled the team to keep going into the 'sixties. Ron Heels, Duncan Bennie and Wally Kelland were some of the "guest"

Old Cytringanians 1950. Winners of the Kettering Town Knock-Out Cup.

Back Row (L. to R.): Eric Smith, Dick Wooster, John Braybrooke, Eric Corby, Jack Miller, David Green.
Front Row (L. to R.): Jack Mobbs, Dennis Smith, Trevor Holmes, John Chaplin, Peter Jackson.

Some of the Old Cytringanians cricket team and supporters at Rockingham in 1950.

Back row: Jack Miller, Ron Shapiera, Jack Mobbs. Seated: Trevor and Thelma Holmes, Leslie Smith, David and Mary Green, Harry Fifield, Reg Tailby.

players. Indeed, in 1955, the last named headed the batting averages and so won the Holmes Cup.

As a mark of appreciation, for use of the School field, the Club presented a new scoreboard and some cricket books to the School.

The Rugby XV was reformed after the war, the secretary being the same Peter Rudkin who had introduced David Green to the Old Cytringanians.

Sadly, it was disbanded in 1948, due to the problem of finding a ground and the fact that the Kettering Rugby Club was attracting players and expanding. Many Old Boys played for the latter side and some are mentioned elsewhere in this publication. Again, Trevor Holmes was a full time member of the post war team and, with others, felt quite bitter about the closure of the Club.

The demise of the *Cytringanian* magazine in the 1970s requires the writer to use the various minutes to continue the story of the Association. The copious and detailed nature of these says something for the Committee and its officers of the time.

Problems were encountered, not least of which was one that has dogged the Association throughout its existence: that of the best venue for the Annual Reunion Dinner.

The George Hotel, the Strathclyde in Corby and the Windmill Avenue Hall were subsequently used. Many other suggestions were made and either found to be unavailable or unsatisfactory. Dinner numbers were a perpetual problem, Tony Ireson even offering to pay personally for an advert in the *Evening Telegraph* to boost numbers. An all time low was reached in 1972, when only thirty seven attended, including three ladies, one of whom was an *Evening Telegraph* reporter.

The brighter side of the Association was, however, reflected in the very successful New Year's Eve dances held generally at Wicksteed Park and usually attended by well over 250 people. These were both profitable and enjoyable.

An exhibition was promoted in 1970 with photographs and various artefacts connected with the School on show.

The reunion for 1974 was also solace to the organisers. Back in the Bowling Green Road hall, the Diamond Jubilee Year was celebrated by over 130 ex-pupils. This was as a result of the Council granting special permission for a return to familiar territory. Many of the true "Old Guard" turned out. A group of these, an *Evening Telegraph* photograph shows us, were Messrs. A. Linnett, E. A. Timson, E. W. Stopps, J. Bailey and L. F. (Les) Hales. The latter, as guest speaker, addressed the gathering "with a series of witty reminiscences of times past".

The Tennis Club came and went. The annual cricket match with the School continued and changing times brought about a soccer confrontation as well as the annual rugby match. In 1973, 700 spectators saw the School beat the Old Boys by three goals to two. No doubt "the gate" was a captive audience!

The new Year's Eve dances, which ended in 1986, were replaced for a few years by Barn Dances organised by Ken Mandale.

The Hygram Players were almost certainly the best known face of the Association as far as the public were concerned. This section ran from 1927, as already mentioned, until its final report in 1979.

Derek Gray, performer and Secretary for many years, remembers the activities as very happy times, with great co-operation between the participating members of staff of the High and Grammar Schools, and the ex-pupils. From the staff he mentions, among others, Miss Wilkinson and Miss McGhie, John Tynan and "Mr Hygram" himself, C. W. Godfrey. They were the foundation of the movement for many years. Jealousy, as far as casting was concerned, was never apparent. David Bishop said that if he had told the cast he was going to produce *Bradshaw's Railway Guide* they would have accepted it; except to ask if there was a good part for Bert Brading.

Leading Hygram player, 'Bert' Brading, performs one of his duties as President of the Old Cyts in 1956. The Junior Victor Ludorum is A. Roberts.

Twelfth Night – *1957*
St. Peter's School gardens.

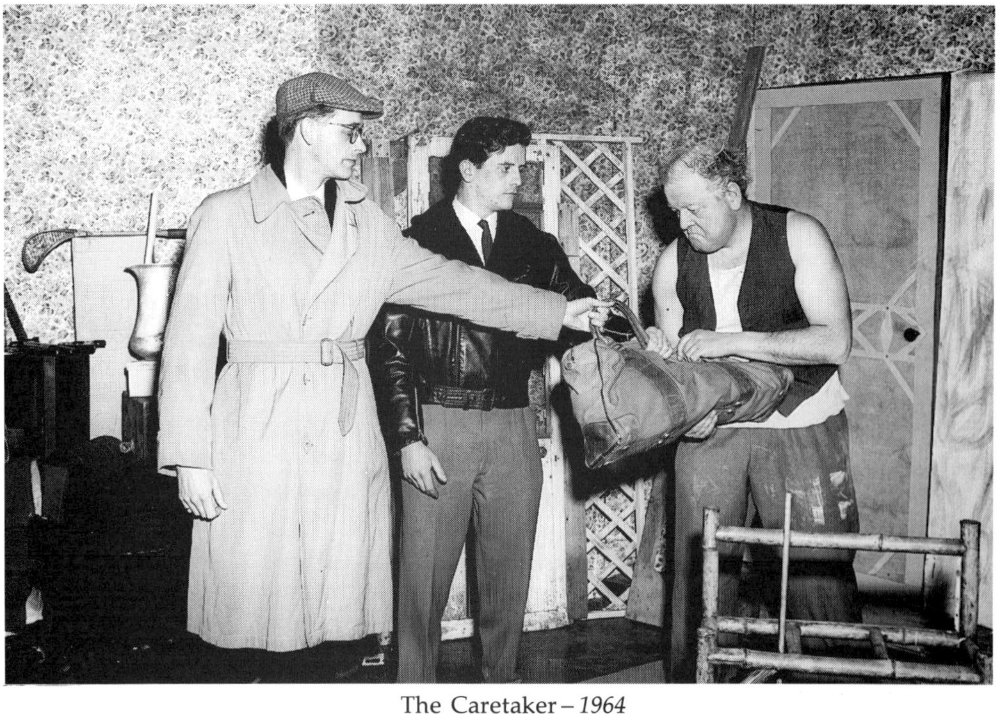

The Caretaker – *1964*
Evan Roberts, Richard Brading, Ken Collins.

Performances took place, not only in the School Halls of Bowling Green Road and Windmill Avenue, but also in the now defunct Central Hall. Productions were entered in Drama League Festivals. Enactments of Shakespeare took place in the 1950s in the open air environment of St Peter's School gardens. In 1958, a pioneering production of *Ring Round the Moon* was performed "in the round".

What of today? Barring some completely unknown and unlikely happening, the life of the Association is finite. In the short term, however, that situation may well strengthen the movement.

This book, and the exhibition planned for 1996, are certainly creating a great deal of interest amongst members, and those Old Boys who are not members. In the writer's position of Secretary, this is very plain to see.

The 1995 reunion saw over eighty ex-pupils, of variable vintage, sitting down to an excellent dinner in the Kettering Masonic Hall: yet another venue to add to the very varied list over the seventy odd years. The speeches were excellent, a sentiment expressed by all, with the guest speaker, Rev. Hugh Moore, talking appropriately, on "The Best of Times, the Worst of Times".

Perhaps the most remarkable event of the evening was the attendance of George Dickins. Why? Because his last dinner, as a retiring Secretary, had been in 1935. Yes, sixty years ago! And what a marvellously alert and active octogenarian he is. Not only has he contributed to this book, but also he promises to be at the 1996 event.

Another important development is the acquisition of a headquarters, and resource centre, for the Association in the Tresham Institute in the Windmill Avenue building. This stroke of good fortune is entirely down to the good offices of Jim Harker.

Jim and his father, Jim senior, were very much a part of the Old Cytringanians' scene for three decades. They served on the Committee (at the same time) and both were Presidents of the Old Cytringanians.

Like many others, they were very sad to see the end of the Grammar School era. They continued, however, on the Committee until Jim senior died in 1984 and Jim himself resigned in 1989.

Today, Jim is Clerk to the Governors of the Old Grammar School Foundation and it is he who has negotiated the lease of a room for the aforementioned purpose, in return for providing the Tresham Institute with certain joint facilities. Eventually he would like to see the extension of its use, if required, to the High School Old Girls and the Old Centralians.

Equally important are his persuasive powers in getting the Governors to sponsor this book. Without him, it would have been very difficult, if not impossible, to produce.

In recent years, some of the remaining activities of the Association have ceased. Even before the School closed, the annual football and cricket games against the School had become casualties. The practice instituted in 1975, of the Old Cytringanians' Lecture, continued until the close. The first of these

Lectures was given by Dr. Dickie Dyson, whose face appears in many school sports photos in the late 'thirties and early 'forties, and is a regular visitor to the Annual Dinner. Other speakers included the late John Dodge, John Newing, Professor Halsey, the late Jim McGinn and Jeff Kyte.

Over the last few years of the School, several sponsored walks were organised by Ken Mandale, the proceeds of which were devoted to the Special Schools in the area.

A fund was set up in honour of Jim McGinn, who died in 1992, to enable grants to be given to pupils of practical potential. Jim was an Old Boy, popular member of staff and President of the Association. When the School closed, this fund was passed to his wife, Lyn, to be used by KEEP (Kettering Employer Education Partnership) to encourage links between education and commerce.

The brightest note, apart from the innovations already mentioned, has been the annual Reunion Dinner attendance. The last six or seven years have seen over eighty Old Boys together every January, and in 1993 one hundred and seventy attended the 75th anniversary in the Windmill Avenue School Hall.

Tribute must be paid here to the various members of staff, some of whom were not Old Boys, who helped keep the Association going through very difficult times. Sellick Norsworthy and Keith Tomlinson filled the onerous and somewhat thankless job as Secretary between 1985 and 1995. John Cowell, Les Berridge and Ken Mandale have served on the Committee for many years.

In presenting the other members of the current Committee, one feels like a band leader introducing the various players. Simon Thornton, son of Pat Thornton of musical fame and a long standing member of the Association. Jim Andrew, rambler, Hygram player, and Toastmaster. Brian Jackson, one of a trio of brothers who have served in various capacities for many years. 'Bert' Stafford and Ray Fullilove "our Scoutmasters".The present President, Harry Pope, "the prodigal come home". Phil Margetts, our liaison legacy with the Central School. Bill Asbrey and Keith Traynar with over twenty years service each. Jeff Kyte, Tony Hadden and the writer give some background support with Derek Slater, of satellite fame, providing the hospitality for the Committee's newest venture, the annual barbecue. Michael Bosworth represents our younger members and finally last, but far from least, Phillip Clarke looks after our financial affairs as Honorary Treasurer.

What are the writer's credentials for putting this section together? Very few in fact. Originally a "lapsed" Old Cytringanian, one of those who was a bane of Secretaries. Never attending the New Year dances. Too young for the rugger club, not a cricket lover and never, by the wildest stretch of the imagination, eligible for the Hygram Players. For thirty years an attender at every seventh dinner.

Two incidents come to mind from those dinners. When I had a fruit and greengrocery business in Kettering in the 1960s, John Wood and 'Joey'

Ashworth came round after the speeches to shake Old Boys by the hand. The former's utterance, in his characteristic bass voice of many a Latin lesson will remain a memory for ever. ''They tell me that you can't get up Market Street these days for cabbages and cauliflowers''. On another occasion, in the Windmill Avenue School, John Cowell became the first teacher to buy me a drink, albeit with a token, as there was no bar licence.

In writing this section I have tried to present an interesting, yet historically correct account of some part of the Old Cytringanians. To cover the complete story would need far greater space than that available. For the reader, or historian of the future, there exists a wealth of information in the School Magazines and Secretaries' annual reports.

Sixty Years of ''Manners Maketh Man''

J. E. Andrew

Shortly after my tenth birthday, on June 7th, 1931, I was taken to the School in Bowling Green Road for an interview. After a brief test, I was accepted for the Autumn Term, at the princely sum of £3. 15s. 0d. per term.

The first year at School was devoted to meeting new poeple and making new friends. In those days many of the boys came from out of town: a bus load from Corby and Geddington; others from Rothwell, Desborough, Broughton and even one from Rushden. The majority of the staff and boys walked or cycled to school; two noteworthy exceptions were 'Dodger' Whitney chugging in in his Jowett, and Atkinson-Blaxland in his open-topped MG Sports.

The second year was spent in ''the Hut'', rather like being on a desert island, splendid in Autumn and Summer, with the sound of music from Rufus Smith's singing class at the opposite end, but cold in Winter, in spite of the coke stove in the middle of the classroom. As the fire died down in Winter, top coats could be worn.

To get to ''the Hut'' we had to cross that wonderful area of activity – the playground. My most vivid memories are of cold, snow-covered winter days with long slides enjoyed by boys and staff. Messrs. Ashworth, Hopkins, Wood and Woodward escaped from the smoke-filled Staff Room to join us.

Form outings stand out in my memory for the Third and Fourth years: to Hendon to see the Aircraft Museum, and watch the unforgettable flying displays. The highlight entailed animal-shaped balloons being shot down by airmen in biplanes, using twelve bore shotguns. To London by train, down the Thames by boat to Dagenham Ford Works, and the thrill and pride of having holes burned in school blazer and cap by sparks from the blast furnace. The cars came off the production line so fast that a man had just enough time to walk round each one with a paintbrush decorating a raised ridge in the bodywork.

Our main sports were cricket in the Summer, and rugby in the Autumn and Winter, with opportunities for playing against other schools as far afield as Daventry and Bedford. Two other annual events were the Cross Country run wich included jumping or wading through the Ise Brook, and the School Sports Day.

A ''one-off'' event was staged in 1937, with a production by C. W. Godfrey of *Richard III.* Tommy Corke was responsible for the set and parents and staff for the costumes. At that stage there was no fraternising with the High School next door, and ladies' parts were played by either boys in drag or ladies from the Hygram players.

After taking the School Certificate in June 1937, it was time to find a job. They were in short supply but I was selected as an apprentice Dental Technician, wage 5s. 0d. a week, less 1s. 3d. for the Insurance stamp, taking home 3s. 9d. Having acted in the School production of *Richard III,* it seemed a natural step to join the Hygram players after leaving school. Their most memorable production pre-war was André Obé's *Noah,* produced by John Tynan, who also made some outstanding papier maché masks of bear, monkey, tiger and lion. C. W. Godfrey played the part of Noah; Bert Brading, Cyril Dickerson and Jim Andrew appeared as Ham, Shem and Japheth.

In 1940, the older members having gone to war, I became the Hygram representative on the Old Boys' Committee. During the war, if you were lucky enough to be on leave at the right time, you could attend a dance in the School Hall under the watchful eye of J. I. Scott. After the war, we had marvellous New Year's Eve dances, filled to capacity, arranged by Malcolm Jackson, and latterly by Phil Margetts – everyone in formal evening dress, music provided by Cissie Richardson and her band, or the Arden Players. These dances provided most of the funds used by the Old Boys' Association. At this time, the Hygrams were engaged not only in twice yearly, Three-Act productions, but also One-Act plays for the British Drama League Festival, and we toured with various concert parties. Our major triumph was a full length production of *The School for Scandal,* produced by Miss W. E. Wilkinson. This play was entered for the British Drama League Festival and we were chosen to appear at Toynbee Hall, London, where we came first in the Eastern area finals, and went on to the all-England final at Harrogate, where we were placed third.

Not having been allowed to mix with the High School girls during our school days (except for brief moments when retrieving the ball from their playground when playing cricket, and provocative glimpses of red tops and black pants seen from the balcony on our way to 'Reggie' Gladden in the Science Lab) we made up for it afterwards. Numerous weddings followed: June and myself; Dickie and Audrey; Derek and Elizabeth; Geoff and Anthea – to name but a few.

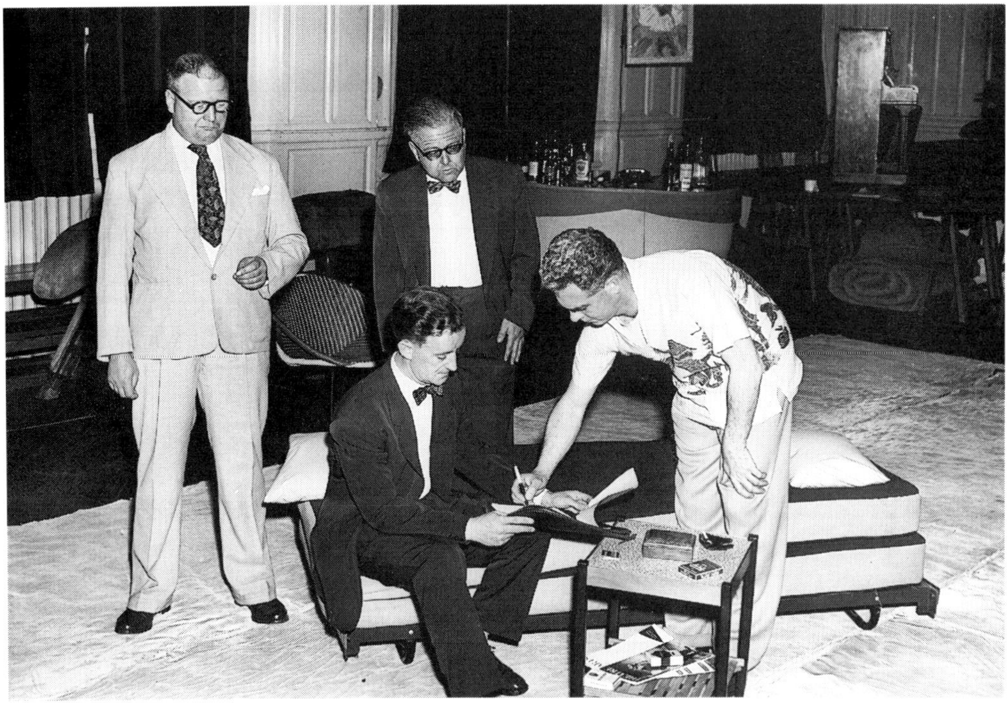

The Big Knife – *1959*
Ken Collins, Derek Gray, Ted Ward, Jim Andrew.

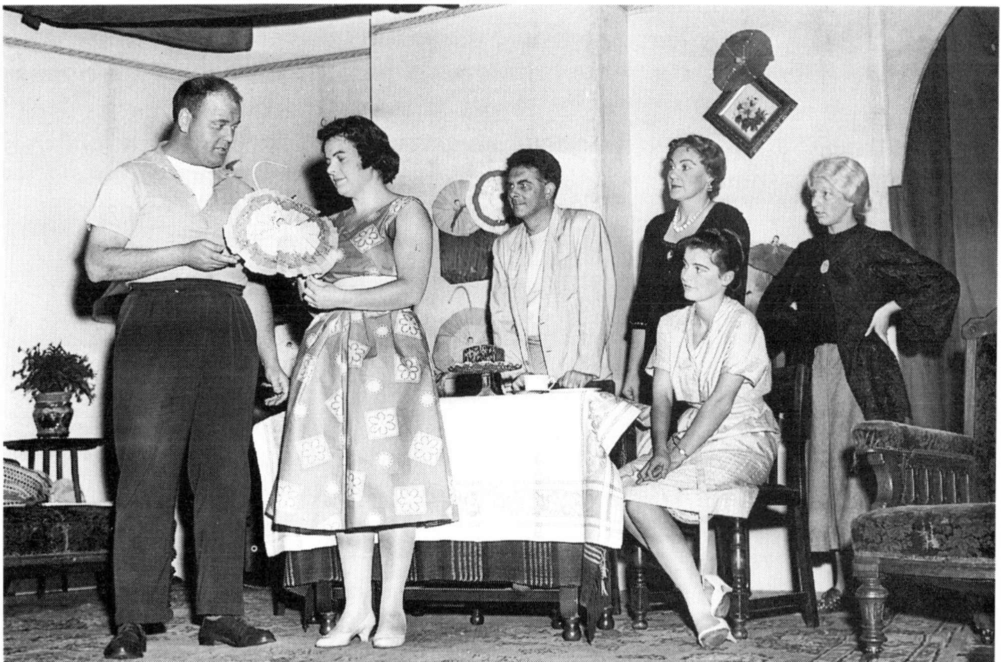

Summer of the Seventeenth Doll – *1959*
Ken Collins, Prudence Goss, Jim Andrew, Margaret Fonville, Eileen Gerard, Barbara Shorley (seated).

In 1963, I was elected to Kettering Borough Council as a Ratepayer representative and finished acting with the Hygrams after 25 years. In the 1960s I became a Governor of the School. After C. W. Godfrey died, I was asked to be Toastmaster at the Annual Old Boys' Dinner, a position I have now filled for over 25 years. So after 6 years at the school, 50 years associated with the Old Boys' Committee, 25 years with the Hygrams and 25 years as Toastmaster, perhaps I will be a suitable candidate for the *Guinness Book of Records*!

Another Secretary's Report

A. H. Buksh

I arrived as Secretary of the Old Cytringanians via several years in the Hygram Players, coupled with work on the Old Cyts' committee. This was followed by Presidency of the Association in 1971, much of the whole period alongside David Leverett, who gave many years of hard work as Secretary to the Cyts.

Presumably my own secretaryship resulted from lack of candidates, since I had no special abilities that might prove of benefit or use to the role. My greatest asset, perhaps some might say, the only asset, was enthusiasm for the comradeship of old School friends and the wish to continue support for the work of former post holders.

It was not easy to undertake the work, despite its not being overly time consuming, but I was already working long hours, seven days a week, in a busy office environment.

Nonetheless, it was a challenge and an extension of my interest in the Cyts activities which then still included Hygram Players, Hygram Tennis Club, annual cricket match, The Dinner, New Year's Eve dance, Annual debate with the School and provision of the occasional speaker for Assembly.

Regular committee meetings required precise minutes to record the earth-shattering decisions and transactions that controlled our yearly cycle of happenings.

Perhaps one amusing feature of our gatherings, both general and in committee, was the year-in, year-out reference to the accounts of the nearly defunct Tennis Club. I believe the amount was about £37. Yet, like some hoary old chestnut, it was dredged out to be considered, chewed over, then sent back for "consideration at a later date"!

Eventually it was accepted the Club would probably never again field a team of racquet bearing enthusiasts and the funds were absorbed into the general balance.

The New Year's Eve dance was still a thriving social and financial success that provided an annual injection into funds.

Always over-subscribed and anticipated with unfailing enthusiasm, it was an event when everyone looked forward to reunions and meetings with old friends and School colleagues not seen since the previous dance.

Why this ceased I have never quite understood, but presume it was due to change of fashion or social ideas, or more likely the advent and restriction of the feared breathalyser tests.

Whatever the reason it was the sad loss of a happy occasion, bursting with optimism for the coming year.

My special achievement was in 1974 when, for our 55th Annual Dinner we were able to use the hall of our former home in Bowling Green Road. I cannot recall the total number attending, but we completely filled the hall space, and I remember the long line, as former Presidents filed in to take their seats. It was truly memorable, especially with the thought that we would never meet there again.

Special memories include the decision to welcome ladies to attend the Dinner, not with the approval of all members, an idea that seems to have lapsed. And the one time prior to that change when, as we were standing for Grace, one member arrived with his wife, unaware of the ''Men only'' rule. They stopped only long enough to enjoy the meal, then tactfully departed.

If asked to single out my greatest pleasure during the secretaryship, I would choose the opportunity I had to read through the entire collection of wartime *Reveilles,* the Old Cytringanians' magazine sent to all members serving in the armed forces.

They were busy, bustling days, involving a lot of work, but providing a splendid chance to meet, to contact a wide range of age groups, those whom I had known at School, those who preceded me and the younger generations that followed my own time.

If for those reasons alone, I would consider my time as ''Hon. Sec.'' more than justified and worthwhile.

The Hygram Players

A. H. Buksh

I came into the Hygrams around 1963, encouraged by the indefatigable Ken Collins, already by then a Hygram of long standing.

Ken guided me into the producing hands of Stuart Horrocks, another veteran member, engaged in mustering a cast for his One-Act Play Festival entry, *The Form,* by N. F. Simpson.

The following year Stuart again produced a Hygram entry for the Festival, *Box and Cox,* in which I played opposite Richard Brading, son of another veteran Hygram, Bert Brading.

A mishap causing me a back problem and conseqent use of a stick, Stuart was obliged to take the stage reading my part from the script; not a happy experience.

Previously I had little time to spare for the world of Amateur Dramatics. Now, with free time available, I found the environment of producers, props, prompters and rehearsals very much to my taste and took the first steps towards 25 years of involvement with Hygrams: acting, producing and even writing my own plays.

In retrospect it seems somewhat unbelievable that we were presenting plays, both full length and One-Act, with casts varying from two to fifteen in number, yet the entire cost for sets, nails, paint etc. was quite often less than £5 for a play.

At the time of my joining the Hygrams, many of the well known names had retired from active participation. People like C. W. Godfrey, Evan Roberts, and others whose names have become lost in the sands of time, found other demanding interests.

A new generation arrived to fill the vacuum, bringing with them new ideas on play selection, often of a controversial nature.

Thus it was I took part in *The Hole* at a time of upheaval in professional theatre. The modernist Theatre of the Absurd pushed forward, prompting productions of *Next time I'll Sing to You, Thistle in Donkey Field,* and *The Thwarting of Baron Bolligrew.* All of them in a modern style were challenging; an adventure for players and audience alike.

We never did get round to Ken Collins' fervent wish to stage *Pantaglaize,* though I half remember one play by Ugo Betti, rehearsed for nearly three months, then abandoned when the leading lady was stricken with a serious illness.

There were many hectic and chaotic moments, such as when it was required for a shotgun to be fired at overhead magpies, and our effects man, a true ''boffin'', made appropriate arrangements. On the First Night the trigger was duly pulled twice resulting in two neat round holes appearing in the ceiling of the hall in Windmill Avenue!

On another occasion, in a sword fighting scene, one of the blades snapped off and flew out into the front row of the audience: Theatre of Reality, fortunately without injury.

One play was scheduled for staging in a week when there was a phased power strike, there being no power before 9.00 p.m. So the interval was held before the performance!

Staged excerpts from Dylan Thomas's *Under Milk Wood* are remembered for our having more in the cast than in the audience, yet we remained cheerful! On one occasion, a heavy iron bar fell from above the curtains, narrowly missing our leading lady. The same lady was less fortunate in having a car accident on the opening day of one play, courageously appearing on stage with surgical stitches protruding uncomfortably from face, neck and arms.

Producers came and went with near indecent haste, as they discovered they were expected to include set making in their task of producing a play. There was a general dislike of set making and painting, since most of the work had to be undertaken in the open, often on cold, wet Autumn days, usually on Saturday and Sunday afternoons. The same "flats" were used over and over again, until the arrival of another modern advance: plays without sets.

One of the first such was Becket's One-Act play *Krapps Last Tape,* in which the sole character simply sat at a table on an otherwise empty stage, slowly putting on his boots, while unpeeling a banana, most of the time drearily intoning into a tape recorder. This resulted in considerable harsh critical correspondence in the local paper, though whether that sort of publicity was good or bad, is debatable.

So the Hygrams marched forward with theatre that was the opposite end of the spectrum from those Shakespearean plays, in which most of us had cut our dramatic teeth at School.

Good solid, conventional "respectable" plays such as *A Man For All Seasons,* by Robert Bolt, were sandwiched between other more bizarre productions like *Lunchtime in Borage,* when further criticism was directed at Hygrams for the use of so called "bad language" on the public stage. It was all merely part of the radical changes that were taking place in theatre nationwide.

One full length play brought the mayor as traditional opening night guest, accompanied by our Society President, the late and greatly revered Guy Wilkes, a man who gave freely of his time, constantly working for Hygrams and Amateur Dramatics generally.

It was in those days the custom to play the National Anthem before the opening of a play. When a drum roll was heard, the mayor, Guy Wilkes, and the audience rose in anticipation, only to be greeted by the strains of *Yellow Submarine,* the Beatles musical hit of the 60s.

There was an uncomfortable atmosphere at the coffee interval, Guy Wilkes later revealing his difficulty in restraining the mayor from leaving the hall.

We were fortunate in having tremendous support from Eric Corby, one time Headmaster of Henry Gotch Senior School. Invariably, upon the announcement of a production, Eric would generously offer use of practically anything from his lovely home: the radio, settee, chairs or table. I never discovered how he coped with meals and visitors during our productions.

Another stalwart was Bill Ashby, who master-minded lighting and sound systems, and was regularly seen aloft a shaky ladder or edging his way round a narrow ledge, cables round his shoulders or dangling from fingers already in use for hand holds.

Sadly, the Hygrams have now vanished into history, as gradually it became increasingly difficult to find people prepared to give the necessary time for rehearsing and staging plays.

So many former Grammar School boys and High School girls who took part in the plays retain happy memories of their enjoyment, from the chilling moments of forgetfulness on stage, desperately trying to hear the prompter, to the fizzy effervescence of last night parties.

Many of the latter took place in a grandiose garden hut, by the kindness and generosity of Leonard Axe, himself a former Hygram, his mantle later worn by his daughter Margaret. I never did discover who posted back my shirt after one memorable wild party in Loddington.

Two inscribed boards on the School walls once featured the names of academically successful students. The boards of the School stages will long echo the voices of Hygram ghosts, as a phantom line of former thespians moves silently up right, or down left, to exit through invisible doors into the wings of yesterday.

Presidents of the Old Cytringanians

J. I. Scott 1919-43
C. W. Godfrey...........1944
E. E. Kirby 1945
R. W. Tailby 1946
J. L. C. Loake 1947
A. F. Scott 1948
L. Smith 1949
P. A. Thornton 1950
E. D. Knight.............1951
B. L. G. Wilkes..........1952
E. R. Corby 1953
F. G. Ashby 1954
J. K. Dudley 1955
B. A. E. Brading.........1956
H. J. Miller................1957
M. F. Jackson 1958
J. P. T. Eady.............1959
J. M. I. Scott.............1960
J. Wood 1961
D. Gray 1962
M. J. Harker 1963
C. W. Elmore 1964
S. B. Horrocks 1965
R. T. Smith 1966
J. M. Steane 1967
S. S. King 1968
J. Ashworth...............1969
J. E. Andrew 1970
A. H. Buksh 1971
J. N. R. Harker 1972
A. J. Cowell 1973
R. F. Smith 1974
W. P. Asbrey.............1975
G. E. Perry................1976
D. M. Leverett 1977
J. D. Slater 1978
H. K. Traynar 1979
T. A. Bowker.............1980
P. Margetts................1981
L. G. Berridge 1982
R. C. Dix 1983
P. C. Spence 1984
P. G. Mann 1985
J. K. Mandale 1986
S. J. Thornton............1987
P. C. Clarke 1988
J. D. McGinn.............1989
R. D. Moore 1990
S. C. Norsworthy.......1991
J. S. Kyte 1992
H. G. Stafford.........1992/3
H. Pope 1994

Teachers 1913-1993

G. Watson .... Sept. 1913-Aug. 1914
F. J. Eldridge .... Sept. 1913-Aug 1917
F. F. Peet .... Sept. 1913-Feb. 1917
W. N. Thomas .... Sept. 1913-Aug. 1915
W. B. Gash .... Sept. 1913-Aug. 1928
A. H. Essam .... Sept. 1913-Aug. 1925
R. N. Jones .... Nov. 1913-July 1917 *(killed in action)*
C. G. Clarke .... Jan. 1914-June 1914
O. C. Ellington .... July 1914-Oct. 1914
H. W. Grimes .... Sept. 1914-Aug. 1917
R. Scott .... Sept. 1914-July 1919
W. H. Sutton .... Oct. 1914-Oct. 1918 *(died of wounds)*
W. Humphrey .... May 1915-Aug. 1915
S. P. Moutrie .... May 1915-Aug. 1929
A. J. Ensor .... June 1915-April 1919
Gertrude Fletcher ... Sept. 1915-Aug. 1918
T. Williams .... Sept. 1915-Aug. 1916
G. R. Whitney .... Sept. 1915-Aug. 1954
A. Upward .... Jan. 1916-April 1916
H. P. Green .... May 1916-Aug. 1917
G. Mason .... May 1916-Dec. 1916
E. D. Hart .... June 1916-Dec. 1917
Violet Prideaux .... Sept. 1916-Aug. 1917
Muriel Chalmers ..... Sept. 1916-Aug. 1917
J. H. Marshall .... Feb. 1917-Aug. 1917
Frances Archer .... Sept. 1917-Nov. 1918
Edith Chettle .... Sept. 1917-Aug. 1919
V. W. F. Parker ...... Sept. 1917-Dec. 1923
A. de Lacy Mann ..... Oct. 1917-Aug. 1918
Dorothy Ridley .... Nov. 1917-Dec. 1917
Marjorie Wright .... Jan. 1918-Dec. 1919
W. O'Kane .... Jan. 1918-March 1920
Kate McGlashan ..... Sept. 1918-Aug. 1919
S. R. Rea .... Sept. 1918-Aug. 1919
Elizabeth Pedlow .... Sept. 1918-April 1919
Marie Sowden .... Sept. 1918-Aug. 1919
E. T. Evans .... Jan. 1919-Aug. 1921
F. J. S. Whitmore .... Sept. 1919-Dec. 1924
E. E. Kirby .... Sept. 1919-Aug. 1950
C. W. Godfrey .... Sept. 1919-Aug. 1956
F. L. Gaul .... Sept. 1919-Aug. 1922
Alice Owen .... Sept. 1919-Aug. 1920
Margaret Murray .... Sept. 1919-Aug. 1921
Doris Plowman .... Jan. 1920-Dec. 1920
Marjorie Wilson .... Jan. 1920-Aug. 1920
D. G. Bishop .... May 1920-Oct. 1920
Doris Platt .... Sept. 1920-Aug. 1936
T. W. Hill .... Nov. 1920-Dec. 1921
Ethel Miller .... Jan. 1921-Aug. 1923
W. R. Rees .... Sept. 1921-Dec. 1927
E. J. Harries .... Sept. 1921-Aug. 1924
A. W. Hare .... Sept. 1921-Aug. 1925
W. V. Amos .... Jan. 1922-Aug. 1923
F. H. McKay .... Sept. 1923-Aug. 1927
A. F. Robertson .... Sept. 1924-May 1927
G. Hopkins .... Sept. 1924-Aug. 1959
S. G. Chapman .... Oct. 1924-Dec. 1924
J. Tynan .... Jan. 1925-March 1949 *(died)*
F. G. C. Goddard ...... Jan. 1925-Feb. 1925
L. V. Ottaway .... March 1925 *(unknown)*
R. Hum .... Sept. 1925-Aug. 1929
R. W. Palmer .... Sept. 1925-Aug. 1928
A. W. H. Woodward Sept. 1927-Aug. 1959
J. Wood .... Sept. 1927-Aug. 1966
J. Ashworth .... Jan. 1928-Aug. 1963
R. Smith .... Sept. 1928-Aug. 1963
W. R. Cooper .... Sept. 1928-Aug. 1929
T. Corke .... Sept. 1929-Dec. 1965
W. Richards .... Sept. 1929-Aug. 1932
J. G. Graham .... Sept. 1929-Dec. 1929
N. F. Parbury .... Jan. 1930-Aug. 1931
K. C. Duncan .... Sept. 1930-April 1935
H. F. Onley .... Sept. 1931-Feb. 1932
R. J. Gladden .... Sept. 1932-Aug. 1969
R. B. Atkinson-Blaxland .... May 1935-Dec. 1942
Edith Hutchinson ... Sept. 1936-April 1944
R. Coakes Sept. 1936-Aug. 1949
G. F. Phillips .... Nov. 1939-41, May 1946-April, 1973
W. T. Adams .... Sept. 1940-April 1942
B. E. Pledger .... Jan 1941-Aug. 1952
Eillen Pierotte .... Sept. 1942-April 1943
G. E. Laywood .... May 1942-Aug. 1967
A. H. S. Hulls .... Jan. 1943-Dec. 1948
Daphne Nicholson ..... Jan. 1943-July 1943
R. Barnwell .... July 1943-Dec. 1943
D. H. I. Morgan. May 1943 *(killed in action)*
Lillian Jagger .... Jan 1944-Aug. 1947
F. Lawson .... Jan. 1944-Nov. 1957
Nora Cottrell .... May 1944-Aug. 1947
J. P. Watson .... Sept. 1944-Dec. 1948
J. W. Luxton .... Sept. 1947-Aug. 1951
A. J. Cowell .... Nov. 1947-Aug. 1981
M. Crabtree .... May 1948-Aug. 1955
J. W. Young .... April 1949-Aug. 1974

P. A. Garrett .... Jan. 1949-April 1949
J. V. Sherliker .... Jan. 1949-Aug. 1955
J. Mulhen .... April 1949-Dec. 1949
C. N. C. Carryer .... Sept. 1949-April 1951
E. Lindley .... Sept. 1949-Aug. 1974
T. F. Gibbs .... Sept. 1950-April 1952
M. Berry .... Jan 1950-April 1951
P. S. J. Adkins .... Sept. 1950-Dec. 1955
J. R. Larcombe .... April 1951-Aug. 1976
E. D. M. Bishop ..... April 1951-April 1958
E. J. Ward .... Sept. 1951-April 1964
H. Gifford .... April 1952-Aug. 1952
T. F. Thompson ..... Sept. 1952-Aug. 1977
K. C. Horton .... Sept. 1952-April 1961
C. C. F. Bowden Jan 1953-Nov 1953 *(died)*
I. R. Bidgood .... Sept. 1953-Aug. 1957
D. Whitehead .... Sept. 1954-Aug. 1955
G. E. Perry .... Sept. 1954-Aug. 1983
E. L. Roberts .... Sept. 1954-Aug. 1984
P. Wilson .... Sept. 1955-Dec. 1961
J. K. Mandale .... Sept. 1955-Aug. 1987
B. Perrett .... Sept. 1955-April 1969
M. R. Bar .... Jan 1956-Aug. 1957
G. S. Brown ..... Jan 1956-Aug. 1985 *(died)*
D. H. Greenwood ... Sept. 1956-Aug. 1959
J. E. Mules .... Sept. 1957-Dec. 1962
P. McClusky .... Sept. 1957-Aug. 1962
J. D. Slater .... Sept. 1958-Aug. 1989
D. C. Allen .... Sept. 1958-Aug. 1960
J. H. McKay .... Sept. 1958-April 1959
R. Armstrong .... Sept. 1959-April 1964
J. A. Gibson .... Sept. 1959-Dec. 1968
M. E. Marsh .... Sept. 1959-Dec. 1961
M. H. Hyndman .... Sept. 1959-Aug. 1962
R. Long .... Sept. 1960-Aug. 1965
R. L. Perry .... Jan. 1961-*(unknown)*
J. A. Jackson .... Sept. 1961-Aug. 1976
P. F. A. Sharpling .. Sept. 1961-Aug. 1979
R. E. H. Bucknell ...... Jan. 1962-*(unknown)*
N. P. Holland .... Sept. 1962-*(unknown)*
F. Whiteman .... Sept. 1962-Aug. 1965
S. J. Harris .... Sept. 1962-Aug. 1981
R. A. Rattley .... Sept. 1962-Aug. 1987
C. G. Brown .... Sept. 1962-Aug. 1993
K. Elliott .... Sept. 1962-Aug. 1965
W. D. Watts .... Sept. 1962-Aug. 1967
J. L. Beales .... Sept. 1962-*(unknown)*
D. J. I. Jones .... Sept. 1962-Aug. 1990
N. H. C. Barker ..... Sept. 1962-Aug. 1985
J. W. Hannant .... Sept. 1962-Aug. 1967
I. T. R. Welch .... Sept. 1962-*(unknown)*
T. E. Welch .... Sept. 1962-*(unknown)*

D. H. Hamilton .... Jan. 1963-Aug. 1966
B. Hodgson .... April 1963-Aug. 1965
H. O. Davies .... Sept. 1963-Aug. 1965
M. L. Till .... Sept. 1963-Dec. 1976
J. N. Everett .... Sept. 1963-Aug. 1965
B. Batterham .... Sept. 1963-Aug. 1965
H. F. Deakin .... April 1964-*(unknown)*
R. A. Jones .... Sept. 1964-Dec. 1970
T. W. Woodward .... Sept. 1964-Aug. 1967
D. H. Bone .... Sept. 1965-Aug. 1967
J. Marshall .... Sept. 1965-Aug. 1991
G. A. Ball .... Sept. 1965-Aug. 1966
E. G. Parry .... Sept. 1965-Aug. 1967
P. R. Morris .... Sept. 1965-March 1971
L. G. Berridge .... Jan. 1966-Aug. 1993
I. Layton-Matthews .... Jan. 1966-July 1975
R. Perryman .... Sept. 1966-Aug. 1969
B. H. Wright .... Sept. 1966-Aug. 1970
J. D. E. Stephens ... Sept. 1966-Dec. 1973,
.... Sept. 1982-Aug. 1993
T. C. Simmons .... Sept. 1966-Aug. 1979
D. A. Wade .... April 1967-Dec. 1969
N. L. Jones .... Sept. 1967-Aug. 1970
D. W. Fox .... Sept. 1967-Dec. 1971
R. V. Lambert .... Sept. 1967-Aug. 1970
B. Barker .... Sept. 1967-Aug. 1988
R. C. Adkins .... Sept. 1967-Dec. 1967
D. R. Jackson .... Sept. 1967-Aug. 1968
R. C. Butcher .... Sept. 1968-Dec. 1972
R. T. Allen .... Sept. 1968-Aug. 1972
A. A. G. Marshall .. Sept. 1969-Aug. 1976
M. J. Smith .... Sept. 1969-Aug. 1970
C. I'Anson .... Sept. 1969-Aug. 1973
A. Jackson-Robbins . Sept. 1970-Aug. 1972
R. W. Pope .... Sept. 1970-Dec. 1975
S. Jones .... Sept. 1970-March 1973
R. Tarleton .... Sept. 1970-Aug. 1975
M. D. Eaton .... Sept. 1970-Aug. 1974
J. C. F. Ward .... Sept. 1970-Aug. 1973
J. A. Halliday .... Sept. 1971-Aug. 1972
M. J. Dean .... Jan. 1972-Dec. 1993
J. Martinez .... Sept. 1972-Aug. 1973
M. D. Burgess .... Sept. 1972-Aug. 1974
A. L. Smith .... Sept. 1972-*(unknown)*
R. C. Goodwin .... Jan. 1973-Aug. 1973
S. P. Rowe .... Sept. 1973-Dec. 1973
Cecilia Hughes .... Sept. 1973-Aug. 1976
M. R. Evans .... Sept. 1973-Dec. 1979
T. R. Watson .... Sept. 1973-Dec. 1975,
.... Sept. 1976-Dec. 1985
G. Finn .... Sept. 1973-*(unknown)*
S. C. Norsworthy ...... Jan. 1974-Dec. 1993

G. W. Needle........... Jan. 1974-July 1988
Diane West-Robinson . Jan. 1974-Mar. 1977
J. Parkinson.......... Sept. 1974-Aug. 1978
J. Noel.................. Sept. 1974-*(unknown)*
R. B. Goodman...... Sept. 1974-Aug. 1979
D. P. Eames.......... Sept. 1974-Aug. 1976
C. Burdon............ Sept. 1974-Aug. 1980
Gesa Beales........... Sept. 1974-Dec. 1983
June Wright.......... Sept. 1974-*(unknown)*
W. Mangan........... Sept. 1975-Aug. 1978
P. Riddington........ Sept. 1975-Aug. 1978
K. E. L. Tomlinson . Sept. 1975-Aug. 1988
J. D. McGinn. Sept. 1975-Aug. 1990 *(died)*
M. Leybourn........... Jan. 1976-Aug. 1978
Elizabeth Kemp....... Sept. 1976-Dec. 1981
I. G. W. Tailby....... Sept. 1976-Dec. 1980
D. J. Clinton.......... Sept. 1976-Aug. 1982
D. A. Graham........ Sept. 1976-*(unknown)*
S. M. Rees............ Sept. 1976-Aug. 1978
A. C. Hulson......... Sept. 1976-Aug. 1980
D. H. Hubery......... Sept. 1976-Dec. 1992
Patricia Wright........ Sept. 1976-Dec. 1976
Gail Corby............ Sept. 1976-Aug. 1978
P. K. Atkinson....... Sept. 1976-Aug. 1993
S. M. Bowyer......... Sept. 1976-Aug. 1991
M. A. Cartwright.... Sept. 1976-Aug. 1993
E. Clarke.............. Sept. 1976-Aug. 1990
P. G. Coleman....... Sept. 1976-Aug. 1993
K. Davis............... Sept. 1976-Aug. 1993
G. W. Goding........ Sept. 1976-Aug. 1993
A. C. Hounsome.... Sept. 1976-Aug. 1992
K. D. Hunter......... Sept. 1976-Aug. 1993
Sylvia Kelly.......... Sept. 1976-Aug. 1992
H. S. Payne.......... Sept. 1976-Aug. 1986
B. M. Short........... Sept. 1976-*(unknown)*
Amanda Stacey...... Sept. 1977-Aug. 1986
C. C. Summerfield... Sept. 1977*(unknown)*
B. J. Slough.......... Sept. 1977-Aug. 1993
P. Douglas............ Sept. 1977-*(unknown)*
P. J. Buck............. Sept. 1977-Aug. 1979
P. A Knox............. Sept. 1978-Aug. 1989
I. H. Lancaster....... Sept. 1978-Aug. 1981
P. Hope................ Sept. 1978-Aug. 1979
C. R. Ramsden....... Sept. 1978-Aug. 1979
J. Nietrzebka......... Sept. 1979-*(unknown)*
M. A. Stephen......... Sept. 1979-Jan. 1980
Anne Browne......... April 1979-Aug. 1982
N. George............. April 1979-Dec. 1980
S. Heyward.......... Sept. 1979-Aug. 1981
N. B. H. Lingley.... Sept. 1979-Aug. 1993
S. C. Salsbury........ Sept. 1979-Aug. 1980
M. R. Abram.......... Jan. 1980-Aug. 1984
G. J. Davies............ Jan. 1980-Aug. 1981
Patricia White.......... Jan. 1980-Aug. 1981
R. A. Peacock.......... Apr. 1980-*(unknown)*
Marie Réné............ April 1980-*(unknown)*
Claudine Mauduit... Sept. 1980-*(unknown)*
I. Smith................ Sept. 1980-Aug. 1982
R. C. Farmer.......... Jan. 1981-March 1982
L. Hill..................... Jan. 1981-Aug. 1991
H. Gomes.............. Jan. 1981-Aug. 1981
M. A. Poole............ Jan. 1982-Aug. 1982
G. S. Ubhi.............. Jan. 1982-*(unknown)*
T. Rudkin............. April 1982-Aug. 1992
S. May................. Sept. 1982-Aug. 1986
Ann Crick............... Jan. 1983-Dec. 1985
C. P. Seaver........... Jan. 1984-Aug. 1990
Anne Kemp........... April 1984-*(unknown)*
A. C. Hall............ Sept. 1984-Sept. 1989
Christine Elliott...... Sept. 1984-Aug. 1993
J. Bishop............... April 1985-*(unknown)*
R. C. Woodcock..... Sept. 1985-Aug. 1993
I. L. Coleman.......... Jan. 1986-Aug. 1993
Dianne Tebbutt...... Sept. 1985-Aug. 1993
Leah Stirrat............ Jan. 1986-April 1988
A. P. Chambers...... Sept. 1986-Aug. 1993
A. R. Clark........... Sept. 1986-Aug. 1991
Sioned Exley.......... Sept. 1985-Aug. 1993
P. Tomkins........... Sept. 1989-Aug. 1991
P. G. Cooke.......... *(unknown)*-Aug. 1993
M. Phillips............ Sept. 1990-Aug. 1993
R. C. Gray............. Jan. 1991-Aug. 1993
Shona St Claire Rodd Sept. 1991-Aug. 1993

Linked School Appointments 1976-1979/80

Jean Andrews
T. E. Beattie
N. Brooks
F. J. Clipstone
R. S. Coe
J. Fitzgerald
P. N. Handley
Winifred Hopkins
C. W. Kelly
B. Linfoot
P. Marriage
A. P. Rosser
R. W. Tomalin
R. P. Trengrove
B. Underwood
P. R. Wright
R. Clay
B. Hoggarth
N. Woolnough
R. McKnight

Headmasters

Reverend Seaton	c.1635
Mr Howett	c.1653
Reverend William Fowler	c.1674
Reverend Samuel Sherwin	1680-84
Reverend Francis Sawyer	1684-1709
Reverend Richard Jones	1709-22
Reverend Thomas Allen	1722-55
John Warner	1755-99
John Warner, Junior	1800-01
Reverend James Hogg	1801-45
Reverend Richard Morton	1845-54
Reverend Frederick Tearle	1854-64
Reverend Thomas Widdowson	1864-96
James Gill	1896-1913
J. I. Scott	1913-42
A. F. Scott	1943-51
J. K. Dudley	1952-64
J. M. Steane	1964-76
T. A. Bowker	1976-89
K. A. Rainger	1989-91
B. J. Slough	1991-93

The Old Cytringanians wish to thank the following subscribers.

B. H. Abbott 1924-31
R. J. Abbott 1950-57
N. K. Adams 1960-65
I. D. Addis 1953-58
P. S. J. Adkins .... Staff
A. Aldaya 1946-51
G. Aldridge 1980-87
G. Allen 1952-57
J. Althorpe 1952-57
J. E. Andrew 1931-37
A. Androsiuk 1962-67
J. E. Antill 1942-47
N. E. Antill 1947-52
N. Armstrong 1969-77
R. Arnold 1946-51
J. P. Arthur 1975-82
W. P. Asbrey 1936-47
N. P. Askew 1976-81
A. R. Atkins 1944-49
P. K. Atkinson .... Staff
B. Austin 1940-47
R. G. Auty 1970-78
J. A. Aveling 1954-61
L. C. Aveling 1920-22

C. Bailey 1948-53
T. J. W. Bailey 1952-57
T. M. Bailey ....
A. E. Baker 1935-41
D. Bale 1957-62
N. H. C. Barker .... Staff
P. Barker 1965-70
M. Barratt 1946-51
B. W. Barringer 1935-39
D. W. Barritt 1932-39
N. P. Basford 1960-67
M. G. Bass 1971-79
J. L. and G. Beales .... Staff
R. M. Beaumont 1960-68
M. H. Beeby 1946-51
N. Bell 1947-54
D. Bellamy 1977-84
E. G. Bellamy 1943-50
M. Bellamy 1954-59
L. G. Berridge .... 1953-60. Staff
Revd. M. Berry .... Staff
A. S. Bickerstaff 1971-79
I. Bidgood .... Staff
S. V. Billings 1944-50
G. Binley 1972-79
G. R. Bird 1942-47
S. Bird 1920s
E. D. M. Bishop .... Staff
P. A. Blackburn 1957-64
T. Blackwell 1971-79

F. A. D. Bland 1942-49
J. Blewett ....
D. Blount 1955-77
M. Blundell daughter of the late
C. W. Godfrey ....
C. Bosworth 1946-51
K. Bosworth 1975-82
T. A. Bowker .... Staff
R. E. Brading 1953-60
P. Bradshaw 1962-69
T. Braines 1947.52
Dr. W. A. Bramford ....
D. Breckon 1947-54
D. G. Bridge 1948-56
P. Brown 1964-70
A. M. Brooks 1961-68
R. P. Brooks 1965-69
P. G. Brooks 1939-44
R. Bryan 1954-61
D. G. Buckby 1944-52
J. W. Buckby 1952-58
A. H. Buksh 1941-46
L. W. Buksh 1962-69
M. K. Buksh 1974-81
G. E. Burdett 1954-59
K. H. Burdett 1945-50
M. Burdett ....
R. P. Burdett 1958-63
A. T. V. Burnham 1941-46
I. Burns 1966-71
J. R. Burt 1954-61
E. M. Burwell 1947-54
R. Bury 1961-67
G. L. Butler 1936-41
Dr. G. Butlin 1953-60
T. J. Byrne 1951-56

R. B. Campen 1945-50
D. S. Canham 1972-79
P. J. Cannell 1939-45
A. R. Carter 1949-54
M. A. Cartwright .... Staff
J. Casey 1948-53
M. Chamberlain 1975-82
M. E. Chamberlain 1930-35
F. (John) Chambers 1947-54
J. E. Chaplin 1937-42
C. J. Chapman 1966-73
R. J. Chapman 1948-55
D. Chatwin 1948-53
A. C. J. Cheney 1947-52
Prof. R. A. Church 1946-54
B. Clark 1957-64
P. C. Clarke 1931-38
S. J. Clarke 1965-72

T. Clegg 1972-79
J. Cobley 1944-52
J. Cochrane 1952-59
C. G. Coe 1942-51
G. B. D. Cole 1948-52
M. A. Coleman 1953-58
M. E. Coles 1956-63
Revd. N. Coles 1969-76
R. A. Coles 1947-52
R. J. Coles 1951-59
M. J. Comber 1946-51
E. A. Cook ....
P. Cook 1940-45
D. J. Cooke 1971-78
P. Cooksey 1961-68
W. A. Collyer 1950-58
K. D. Cooper 1951-58
A. J. Cope 1968-75
M. Cotton 1944-55
J. Coulson 1975-82
John and Joan Cowell .... Staff
D. Cox 1950-57
R. W. Cox 1930-33
Mrs M. Craddock, sister of the late
M. G. Thurlow 1947-51
W. Creasey 1960-65
D. Croft 1973-80
G. Croft 1964-71
P. Croft 1947-52
R. J. Cullup 1955-60
I. D. Currie 1953-60
D. Dale-Jones 1946-54
C. R. Davenport 1958-65
S. Davenport 1940-46
Capt. D. L. Davidson, M.B.E. 1950-55
G. Davis 1950-55
K. Davis 1965-72
Dr. D. R. Dean 1969-76
M. Dean .... Staff
A. B. C. Dee 1956-61
A. Denley 1938-43
D. De Santis 1966-73
K. N. Devine 1957-62
G. R. Dexter 1945-50
C. F. Dickerson 1929-34
G. P. Dickins 1924-30
D. A. Dillon 1955-61
F. Dix 1936-41
R. Dix 1967-73
J. S. Dodge 1939-46
P. Dodson ....
R. J. Downing 1952-57
G. D. Drake 1939-45
A. Ducker 1971-74
S. L. Dunmore 1959-66
Dr. R. P. Dyson 1939-46

K. Eady 1968-74
S. P. Eady 1963-69
F. W. C. East 1932-40
J. East 1947-52
K. T. Edmond 1964-66
B. Ellerby, M.B.E. 1946-50
J. M. Ellerby 1975-82
R. A. Etheridge 1946-51
S. Exley .... Staff

H. Farr 1967-74
Mrs A. M. Farrer .... Staff: Governor
B. J. Ferris 1959-64
J. Filsak 1965-71
E. B. Finney 1936-40
R. A. Fisher 1941-47
K. Foreman, O.B.E. 1946-53
J. F. Foster 1937-41
R. W. Foster 1958-65
A. A. Foulds 1973-80
J. F. Foulds 1950-57
T. J. Freer .... Chairman of Govs. 1983-93
M. J. Freeman 1970-77
P. N. W. Freeman 1959-66
J. A. Freestone 1946-52
A. J. Frost 1949-56
R. E. Fullilove 1950-55

N. M. Garnett 1982-89
W. A. Gilmour 1936-45
R. Glithero 1937-43
Dr D. J. Godfrey 1940-49
M. Godfrey 1933-40
A. Godson 1943-50
E. H. Gormley 1973-80
Prof. M. J. Goss 1955-62
A. Gold 1950-55
G. F. Gold 1943-53
J. Goldsworthy 1945-50
T. H. Goode 1933-38
A. Goodman ....
C. Goodman ....
Mrs D. Goodman ....
K. J. Goodman 1965-73
M. Goodman 1963-68
R. Graham 1954-61
D. Gray 1933-37
T. Gray 1953-58
M. Gredzuik 1951-56
D. Green ....
R. H. Green 1943-48
R. J. Green 1972-79
A. J. Griffin 1950-55

C. J. Groome 1952-59
E. C. Groom 1941-44
P. Grove 1970-75
T. Grove 1946-51
C. J. Gunn 1955-59

A. L. Hadden 1946-51
A. M. Hadden 1969-76
Dr. P. E. Hadden 1949-51
P. G. Hague 1933-39
J. C. Hakewill 1965-73
P. J. Hale 1953-60
A. C. Hall .... Staff
A. G. Hall 1946-51
D. Hall 1959-64
Prof. A. H. Halsey 1933-39
J. Hammond 1942-47
J. B. Hanger 1929-34
N. Hanger 1965-72
P. J. Hanger 1938-42
R. Hanson 1942-49
T. Harden 1959-64
J. N. R. Harker 1956-62
The Late M. J. Harker 1928-37
S. Harris 1965-71
S. J. Harris .... Staff
T. Harris 1969-76
V. J. Harris 1950-57
A. Harrison 1969-75
M. H. Harvey 1945-52
J. F. Hawkins 1961-68
J. S. Hawkins 1951-58
A. R. Heath 1963-70
J. P. Heath 1967-74
Group-Capt. P. J. Hector 1946-51
K. Herbert 1947-55
A. C. Hewitt 1961-67
C. T. Hicks 1940-46
J. A. Higgins 1934-41
L. Hill .... Staff
M. T. Hill 1974-81
F. G. Holland 1922-28
C. Hollinshead 1915-17
T. H. Holmes 1938-42
A. J. Holt 1956-63
W. J. Hornsby 1959-66
V. J. Hopkins 1957-60
S. B. Horrocks 1942-51
T. Houghton 1953-58
T. Hounsome 1972-78
C. Howard 1948-52
Dr. G. F. Howard 1936-43
D. Hubery .... Staff
B. Hudson 1949-53
B. Hughes 1945-50

W. H. Hulme 1941-49
C. A. Humphrey 1967-73
R. B. Humphrey 1960-65
J. Hunt 1956-61
Mrs M. A. Hunt, wife of the late
J. E. Hunt 1919-23

G. W. Ipgrave 1935-39
T. Ireson 1921-29
D. Isherwood 1958-62
J. Isherwood 1951-58
S. Isherwood 1963-68
D. Issitt 1946-51

B. R. Jackson 1936-40
E. J. M. Jackson 1942-49
M. F. Jackson 1937-44
R. T. Jacques 1940-46
A. Jenkinson 1940-45
G. M. Jewers 1966-72
B. Johnson 1966-71
M. E. Johnson 1941-47
T. H. Johnson 1946-50
W. Jolley 1966-73
A. Jones 1950-53
D. Jones 1981-88
D. J. I. Jones .... Staff
L. and W. Jones 1988-93
R. M. T. Jones 1966-73
S. J. G. Jones 1961-68
P. Joyce 1959-64
P. Joyce 1963-68
M. A. Judge 1968-73

H. E. Keech 1941-46
Dr. J. P. Keech 1966-72
S. A. Keech 1970-75
J. R. Kemp 1950-57
E. Kendrick 1950-55
C. Kidman 1979-86
H. A. Kilborn 1927-34
D. C. Kilsby 1955-63
R. E. Kilsby 1935-38
S. King 1947-52
C. Kirk 1972-78
Prof. J. R. Knibbs 1945-52
K. Knibbs 1950-55
H. M. Knight 1955-60
P. J. Knight 1948-53
Revd. J. W. Knights 1945-50
P. A. Knox .... Staff
A. J. Kyte 1977-84
J. L. Kyte 1982-87
J. S. Kyte 1956-61

G. Langham 1938-43
R. Langley 1947-52
J. R. Larcombe .... Staff
Mrs J. Larratt ....
B. Lauff 1971-76
P. R. Lauff 1962-67
M. Law 1942-48
F. J. Lawrence 1931-38
G. A. Lawrence 1935-45
J. Lay 1946-51
D. J. Leach 1937-42
V. H. Leadbetter 1940-48
Rabbi M. Leigh 1939-47
A. H. Leslie 1971-77
D. M. Leverett 1958-65
M. J. Lewin 1958-63
J. Lillyman 1947-52
E. Lindley .... Staff
S. Ling ....
J. Loach 1990-93
I. D. Loasby 1975-82
R. G. Long 1946-53
M. Lovell 1960-68
J. A. Lusher 1945-50
T. W. Lusher 1946-51
P. B. Lutener 1961-68
H. C. Lutener 1957-64
E. C. Lyles 1933-38

G. Mableson 1967-74
J. K. Mandale .... Staff
G. E. Mandeville 1940-45
J. Mandeville 1941-47
P. Mann 1967-73
N. R. Manthorpe 1942-48
B. Manton 1948-54
N. P. Margetts 1971-78
C. N. Marlow 1932-39
C. T. Marlow 1932-38
D. Marlow 1935-40
The Late N. Marlow 1925-32
P. E. Marlow 1937-44
S. Marlow ....
J. Marshall .... 1955-61. Staff
B. R. Martin 1955-60
J. Martin 1935-40
N. C. Mason 1963-68
B. Matthews 1977-83
A. McClure 1971-79
L. McGinn, wife of the late
J. D. McGinn ....
G. McKenna 1980-86
Mrs N. McKeon (née Rowbotham)
K.H.S. 1950s
N. McKnight 1964-72

J. W. P. McMillan 1949-54
J. Meachem 1944-49
R. P. Mease 1932-37
J. Medley 1960-65
M. Messinger 1958-65
H. J. Miller 1928-33
M. Miller 1943-51
R. C. Miller 1956-61
T. D. Miller 1975-82
A. M. Mitchell 1973-80
K. R. Mitchell 1947-52
T. Mitchell 1944-48
J. F. Mobbs 1932-39
K. W. Mobbs 1937-43
T. Mobbs 1962-69
G. Moore 1937-42
Revd.Preb. H. D. Moore 1948-55
R. F. Moore 1944-55
R. D. Moore 1943-51
P. R. Morris 1965-71
A. Morrison 1948-55
A. Morrison 1944-52
J. R. Morrison 1945-50
G. F. Moule 1923-27
D. C. Murkitt 1945-50
N. J. Murkitt 1948-54
J. E. Mustin 1920-24
B. Mutlow 1955-58
Mrs J. Mutton, daughter of the late
J. Wood ....

G. W. Needle .... Staff
J. F. Newing 1951-58
D. Newton 1946-51
S. W. Nichols 1937-43
C. S. Norsworthy 1978-84
P. A. Norsworthy 1981-88
S. C. Norsworthy .... Staff
Northamptonshire Libraries ....
C. J. Norton 1963-70

N. O'Hara 1980-85

M. J. Pack 1958-65
M. J. Page 1942-47
R. G. Page 1957-64
B. Paling 1947-52
S. Paling 1983-88
Revd. Canon D. H. Palmer 1942-50
Revd. G. Palmer 1942-50
R. J. Palmer 1945-54
J. H. Panther 1959-66
M. J. Parker 1966-73
J. B. J. Parrott 1938-42
J. Partridge 1959-63

Mrs B. Payne ....
J. Peberdy 1979-86
G. Pentelow 1965-72
M. Pentelow 1962-69
G. Percival 1972-79
M. Perminas 1970-75
B. Perrett .... Staff
Mr and Mrs G. E. Perry .... Staff
R. Phelan 1978-80
Mrs C. Phillips .... Staff
H. O. Phillips 1936-40
Mrs I. Phillips ....
P. E. Phillips 1958-63
R. B. Phillips 1935-38
S. Phillips 1966-73
W. J. Phillips 1929-31
G. A. Pick 1947-51
H. Pope 1960-66
Mrs J. Pope ....
W. G. Pope 1966-73
R. C. Portwood 1939-47
E. G. H. Potter 1927-34
R. H. Potter 1926-29
Dr. I. C. Prescott 1962-69
N. Pugh 1948-51
T. Pulford 1947-53
M. R. Pycroft 1973-80

P. Quincey 1951-56

L. J. W. Reeves 1936-40
B. Reynolds 1924-28
K. M. Reynolds 1934-36
Dr. A. L. Rice 1949-56
Mrs B. Rice ....
B. E. Rice 1954-59
J. A. Richardson 1944-50
T. Richardson 1946-51
H. M. Rigby 1938-42
W. Robertson 1957-64
W. L. Robertson 1957-64
J. M. Robinson 1942-50
N. S. Robinson 1960-67
Miss D. Roughton ....
D. Roughton 1944-51
M. A. Roughton 1936-41
N. A. Roughton 1963-68
P. J. Roughton 1957-62
Dr. V. L. Rowe 1964-70
T. W. Rudkin .... Staff

R. H. Sanders 1947-52
M. E. Saunby 1946-53
P. J. R. Sawfoot 1951-56
R. T. Scotney 1942-48
J. M. I. Scott 1928-33
J. Seddon 1933-41
D. Shanks 1951-55
J. W. Sharman 1974-81
R. L. Sharman 1953-58
P. F. A. Sharpling .... Staff
Dr. C. M. J. Shorley 1959-66
G. H. Shorley ....
Revd. B. M. Short .... Staff
B. R. Short 1945-52
D. J. Short 1946-47
N. Short 1968-75
S. Shrive 1938-41
E. Shrub 1948-55
A. Simms 1969-76
J. Simms 1941-44
The Late M. Simms 1972-79
R. Simms 1919-25
T. C. Simmons .... Staff
R. Sindall 1930-35
Balbinder Singh 1980-85
The Late R. Sismey 1943-48
J. D. Slater .... Staff
B. J. Slough .... 1951-59. Staff
Ms M. L. Slough ....
Dr. M. A. Smart 1973-80
P. Smedley 1951-55
A. N. Smith 1967-74
B. D. Smith 1946-53
D. J. Smith 1956-61
H. B. Smith 1940-49
J. Smith 1946-51
M. C. Smith 1950-53
M. D. Smith 1963-70
P. Smith 1971-77
Wing Cdr. R. Smith O.B.E. 1948-53
Dr. R. Smith 1956-61
R. F. Smith 1942-51
R. T. Smith 1943-49
S. F. Smith 1935-39
R. Smyton ....
A. Southwell 1945-52
H. G. Stafford 1936-40
M. Staley 1957-62
J. R. Stanley 1936-40
N. D. Stebbings 1930-37
J. D. E. Stephens .... Staff
J. Stirling 1946-51
E. C. R. Stonehouse 1940-46
L. W. Streather 1930s
R. Stretton 1944-51
D. C. Styman ....
D. W. Swingler 1943-52
J. Sykes 1954-62

H. W. Tailby 1915-20
I. G. W. Tailby 1943-53
J. D. Tailby 1945-50
M. D. Tailby 1938-44
Mrs A. Taylor ....
The Late E. A. Taverner 1927-31
The Late F. Taverner 1930-35
A. S. Thompson 1959-66
C. T. Thompson 1926-31
I. G. Thompson 1961-64
N. J. Thompson 1959-64
R. Thompson 1952-57
S. J. Thornton 1945-48
R. C. Thorp 1943-47
M. Till .... Staff
R. J. Tilley 1956-63
Dr. W. L. Timmins 1937-43
P. Tiney 1945-55
R. J. Tomkins 1958-63
K. E. L. Tomlinson .... Staff
V. Tompkins 1947-52
I. C. Toseland 1964-71
M. F. Toseland 1938-44
R. Toseland 1945-53
S. G. Toseland 1960-67
C. P. Traynar 1969-71
D. I. Traynar 1967-69
H. K. Traynar 1936-40
M. J. Traynar 1968-74
D. P. J. Trelawny 1980-87
G. N. Trelawny 1975-82
Tresham Institute ....
J. Triggs 1949-56
J. A. Tyldesley 1932-40
W. R. Tyldesley 1932-40
O. Tynan, son of the Late J. Tynan ....

U.S.A.A.F 801/492 Bomb Group "The Carpetbaggers" Harrington 1944-45

R. N. Vandrill, J.P. 1951-58

A. P. Vanni 1967-72
R. Varley 1951-56
M. Vaughan 1967-74

W. H. Wagstaff ....
M. J. Walden 1944-49
S. G. Walklate 1959-66
B. F. C. Wallis 1948-51
A. Walton 1951-57
A. Ward 1974-81
E. J. Ward .... Staff
M. Ward 1949-54
N. Ward 1972-79

B. H. Waring 1943-48
R. Watts 1952-57
P. Weeds 1948-53
E. J. J. Wells 1973-80
J. L. Wells 1938-43
R. F. Whitwell 1934-39
S. Wildman 1967-74
R. Williams 1946-54
D. (Bryn) Williams 1948-56
C. Willis 1967-73
Revd. P. Wilson 1944-52
M. L. Wolf 1943-46
T. Wood 1967-74
G. J. Woolley 1938-42
P. Woolley 1960-67
A. T. Wright 1946-51
T. Wright 1931-35

B. York 1952-59
Mrs D. M. York, wife of the Late R. A. York 1930-35
G. York 1957-64
M. York 1953-58

W. Zarins 1976-80